ATLAS
of
OREGON
WILDERNESS

Moonrise over the Three Sisters at Scott Lake Campground (Area 11).

Published by the Navillus Press
1958 Onyx Street, Eugene, OR 97403
www.oregonhiking.com

Cover: Three-Fingered Jack in winter, Tombstone Lake, and Inga Mikkelsen. Spine: Borax Hot Springs. Back: Golden Lake. Frontispiece: Fourmile Lake. Opposite: Ramona Falls.

SAFETY CONSIDERATIONS: The areas described in this book include Wilderness and remote country where visitors are exposed to unavoidable risks. On any trip, the weather may change suddenly. The fact that a hike, backpack, climb, whitewater trip, snow excursion, or other adventure is included in this book, or that it may described as easy, does not necessarily mean it will be safe or easy for you. Prepare yourself with proper equipment, maps,and outdoor skills before entering Wilderness or remote country.

Every effort has been made to assure the accuracy of the information in this book. Nonetheless, storms, road construction, logging, and vandalism may cause changes. Corrections and updates are welcome, and often rewarded. They may be sent in care of the publisher, or to *sullivan@efn.org.*

ATLAS
of
OREGON
WILDERNESS

William L. Sullivan

Navillus Press

KEY TO MAP SYMBOLS

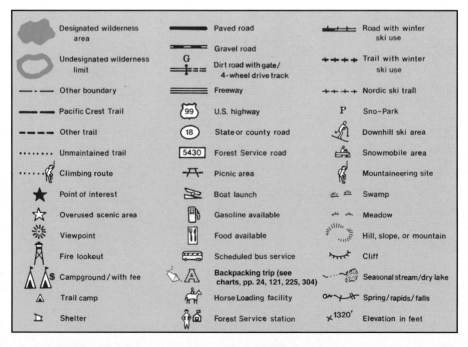

▭ Designated wilderness area	▬▬ Paved road	▬╪╪╪ Road with winter ski use
▭ Undesignated wilderness limit	▭ Gravel road	＋＋＋＋ Trail with winter ski use
—·— Other boundary	G ═╪═══ Dirt road with gate/ 4-wheel drive track	＋＋ ＋＋ Nordic ski trail
━━ Pacific Crest Trail	══ Freeway	P Sno-Park
━━━ Other trail	99 U.S. highway	Downhill ski area
••••• Unmaintained trail	18 State or county road	Snowmobile area
••••(Climbing route	5430 Forest Service road	Mountaineering site
★ Point of interest	🖃 Picnic area	↯↯ Swamp
☆ Overused scenic area	⛵ Boat launch	↯↯ Meadow
☀ Viewpoint	⛽ Gasoline available	Hill, slope, or mountain
🗼 Fire lookout	🍴 Food available	⌢⌣ Cliff
🏕$ Campground/with fee	🚌 Scheduled bus service	Seasonal stream/dry lake
△ Trail camp	Backpacking trip (see charts, pp. 24, 121, 225, 304)	⌒⌒ Spring/rapids/falls
🏠 Shelter	🐴 Horse Loading facility	✕1320′ Elevation in feet
	👥🏠 Forest Service station	

CONTENTS

Mt. Hood from Barrett Spur.

Crater Lake's Phantom Ship from Kerr Notch in winter.

INTRODUCTION

When Congress designated an additional 316 square miles of Oregon wilderness in 2009, many people grew curious about new areas with strange and unfamiliar names. The Badlands? Sisi Butte? Big Bottom?

This book includes guides and maps to help you visit each of the new areas. At the same time, the atlas is a celebration of favorite getaways in the state's other protected wilderness lands, from Mt. Hood and the Three Sisters to Hells Canyon and Steens Mountain.

Let this book also be an invitation to explore 27 of the state's most beautiful unprotected areas, such as the Devils Staircase in the coastal rainforest, Hardesty Mountain just outside Eugene, and the Zane Grey area along the famous Rogue River Trail. Some of these endangered lands include entire mountain ranges that the world seems to have forgotten.

So get out and get started! If you like to hike, you'll find more than 500 trails described here, with the easiest walks in each area listed first. If you're

Fog on Hardesty Mountain.

a backpacker, this is your ultimate trip-planning guide, with text, charts, and maps describing the state's top 146 adventures. Included too are Oregon's best places for snowshoeing, cross-country skiing, kayaking, whitewater rafting, and mountaineering.

Oregon is a magic cabinet of curious escapes, seemingly collected from all the continents of the planet. Only in Oregon can you trek through a fog-bound oceanshore rainforest, snowshoe up an Arctic volcano, raft a lonely desert river, discover a trailless forest lake, and then relax in a silent hot spring pool beneath the stars.

Wilderness is not just about protecting places. It's about preserving the magic.

HOW TO USE THIS BOOK

As a guidebook author, I am often asked the seemingly simple question, "What is the best trip in Oregon?"

The answer depends on where you are, what you like to do, and what season it is. This book is designed to help you discover the trip that's best for you.

Start by leafing through the possibilities, getting a feel for the type of terrain you'd like to visit. Pay attention to the "Climate" entries. These let you know when areas are free of snowdrifts or mosquitoes. Notice that some destinations are marked by a star on the maps. Starred attractions are favorites that can be crowded, especially if the star is hollow. If you're heading for a popular area, tread lightly and consider camping elsewhere.

After you've picked an area, it's best to take along a topographic map. This book covers the entire state, and although my goal is to get you safely to the trailhead and on your way, I don't have room to provide the level of detail you need for serious wilderness exploration. Fortunately, excellent topographic maps can now be downloaded for free from a variety of Internet sites. The descriptions and maps in this book are what you'll need to plan your trip.

The Maps

Get your bearings with the statewide wilderness locator map on page 4. Like the rest of the book, this map divides Oregon into four quadrants. Turn to the appropriate quadrant map (pages 22, 122, 226, or 302) to find the best highway approach to an area.

Individual area maps use symbols identified in a key on page 4. Note that solid gray areas denote wilderness designated by Congress. Undesignated wilderness—managed under quite different rules—is shown only by thin gray borders. Beyond the gray borders lies land generally unsuitable as wilderness because of clearcuts, roads, private ownership, development, or insufficient size.

Climber on the summit of Aneroid Mountain.

The maps' north arrows always point to true north. Magnetic north lies approximately 16° east of true north in Oregon—although this number is slowly falling as the magnetic pole wanders. In the few instances where north is not at the top of the map, a square of gray shading helps draw attention to the north arrow.

Dirt roads are shown with dashed lines. These "ways" are unimproved tracks that are probably not drivable for passenger cars. The maps do not show all the ways and roads. Particularly in southeast Oregon's desert country, backroad drivers may find the proliferation of unmarked ways confusing. Detailed topographic maps are good insurance here.

The Information Blocks

Each entry begins with a synopsis of area facts. The **location** tells the highway mileage and direction from major cities to the closest portion of a roadless area. The **size** reflects the approximate extent (in square miles) of all the roadless lands in each featured area. An area's **status** tells how many square miles have been Congressionally designated as wilderness so far, and the dates of those additions to the National Wilderness System. Other, less protective designations are also noted.

Next, each entry notes the roadless area's dominant types of **terrain**, as well as the highest and lowest **elevation** in feet. The **management** listing advises whether a National Forest (NF), a district of the Bureau of Land Management (BLM), or some other agency administers the area. These agencies can answer specific questions about road conditions, regulations, and permits. Contact information for these agencies is at the back of the book.

The topographic maps listed are printed by private publishers or government agencies, but it's often easier to download topographic maps for free from the Internet. Visit *www.digital-topo-map.com* or a similar site for this service.

An area's **climate** information generally includes average snow levels, temperature ranges, and likeliest seasons to find mosquitoes, wildflowers, or huckleberries. Average annual precipitation reflects the total of rain and melted snow. All of these figures vary substantially from year to year. Wilderness visitors should always prepare for inclement weather.

A FEW WILDERNESS RULES

The 1964 Wilderness Act defines wilderness as "an area where the earth and its community of life are untrammeled by man, where man himself is a visitor who does not remain." That law established strict rules, including:

- No mechanical transport. This bans off-highway vehicles (OHVs), motorcycles, bicycles, strollers, wheelbarrows, airplane drops, hang gliders, and helicopter landings — except rarely for rescue or fire fighting.
- No new mining claims. Mining on a few pre-1984 claims, however, continues.
- No commercial enterprises. An exception currently allows some cattle grazing. Guides and outfitters may operate only under permit.
- No motorized equipment (such as generators or chainsaws).
- Fishing and hunting are permitted with a state license. Check with the Oregon Department of Fish and Wildlife for regulations.

Many designated wilderness areas have other restrictions as well. The most common "No's" are:

- Cutting, chopping, or clipping live trees or dead snags.
- Grazing, picketing, or tying saddle stock within 200 feet of a lake or stream.

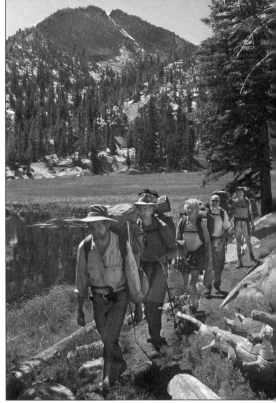

Backpackers in the Elkhorn Range.

- Discharging firearms within 150 yards of a campsite, or across any trail or body of water.
- Smoking while traveling.
- Traveling in groups larger than twelve.

In addition, some rules extend to all federal lands, wilderness or not:

- Collecting arrowheads or other cultural artifacts is a federal crime.
- Disturbing archeological sites or petroglyphs is likewise a criminal offense. Even making tracings or rubbings of petroglyphs can damage them.
- National Forests limit campers to fourteen days' stay at the same campsite in any calendar year.
- Permits are required to dig up plants on federal land.
- Rare plants and animals are sometimes protected by both federal and state law. Picking wildflowers may in fact be illegal.

HAZARDS IN THE WILDS

The Wilderness Act of 1964 insists that a wilderness should offer outstanding opportunities for solitude. Once I met a backwoods hiker who paraphrased this, suggesting a wilderness should offer outstanding opportunities for death.

In fact, the dangers of the wilderness have been vastly overrated. No one has been killed by bear, wolf, or cougar in the history of Oregon.

Grizzly bears have been extinct in the state since 1891, so there is no need to decorate backpacks with bear-warning bells. Oregon's black bears huff and scramble out of a hiker's way as fast as their little legs will take them—generally even when the hiker has accidentally passed a mother bear's cubs.

In a very few areas (notably the Wild Rogue Wilderness), bears have been trained over the years by careless campers to rip open packs and coolers at night for bacon, tuna, and sweets. Here a standard wilderness precaution will suffice: hang all food from a tree limb, at least 10 feet high and 5 feet away from the trunk. This will also keep food safe from the real scoundrels, chipmunks.

Populations of mountain lions (cougars) are recovering from years of being hunted with dogs, but because the lions are nocturnal, they have almost no interaction with humans.

Wolves were hunted to extinction in Oregon long ago, and although some now have migrated from Idaho to establish packs, particularly in Northeastern Oregon, they are focused on weak deer, elk, and moose, and have virtually no interaction with people.

Likewise, rattlesnakes will disappoint the danger seeker. These reptiles are rare enough that most people will not see one in 1000 miles of wilderness hiking. What's more, the aggressive diamond-back species is not found in the state at all. Oregon's subspecies, *Crotalus viridis oreganus*, is a retiring sort, absolutely incapable of such spuriously attributed feats of daring as crawling into a sleeping bag for warmth.

These days, the most threatening beast in the woods is a microscopic protozoan by the name of *Giardia*. This water-borne pest has forever changed the tradition of casually dipping a drink from cold, clear mountain streams. Those who ingest *Giardia* can expect debilitating diarrhea and nausea to appear in six to fifteen days, symptoms that abate only after medical treatment.

Many hikers and nearly all backpackers now carry a commercial filter, attached to a bottle lid or hand pump. Make sure the filter has been approved to remove *Giardia*. Some water purification tablets are also effective, but they tend to make the water unpalatable. Boiling water for ten minutes is a reliably safe treatment, but it requires both

Backpacker at Three Creek Lake.

fuel and time.

A few daring souls prefer to second guess the little paramecium. *Giardia* is spread only by mammals (often beaver, deer, cattle, or mice), enters the water by defecation, and only moves downstream. Thus, water from a spring or a high mountain watershed unfrequented by mammals has a lower risk of contamination.

Hikers in dry, grassy areas should check occasionally for ticks under their collars and cuffs, especially in May or June. If you find that a tick has attached itself to your skin, do not attempt to pull it off. Instead, twist its body like a screw for several complete rotations and it will let go.

In Oregon, only a handful of cases have been reported of Lyme disease, an ailment carried by tiny deer ticks. Lyme disease progressively affects the joints and nerves. Keep an eye on the site of any tick bite to make sure it doesn't develop the disease's characteristic bullseye-shaped sore (red with a white ring), followed within a month by a rash.

Of course, those who enter the wilderness without basic survival gears and skills are bringing hazard with them. Hypothermia is the number one killer in the wilds. It results from being wet and cold too long, and can be prevented by bringing proper clothing and shelter. Useful books and classes abound on preparation for hiking, backpacking, and climbing—with far more detail than this introduction can possibly include. Be prepared for the worst, and you will be able to enjoy the wilderness confidently at its best.

Finally, errors in mileage, trail location, and the like are inevitable in any guidebook—especially when new roads and logging are constantly adding confusion. Despite all my efforts to the contrary, I cannot guarantee the accuracy of the information included here, nor that the trips described are safe for everyone.

Poison oak is found only below 1000 feet of elevation on dry, sunny slopes.

Without at least a small element of danger, wilderness would not be wild. Visitors in these areas must understand that they are on their own.

TIPS FOR HIKERS

Choosing a Trip

The easiest trips in each area are generally described first. Those who rarely hike should look for the nature trails, lakeshore paths, and short riverside hikes listed near the beginning of an area's hiking section.

Remember that most mileages reflect the one-way length of a trail. Thus, a "1.4-mile trail to Twin Lakes" means a 2.8-mile round-trip hike. Also, the term "easy" is used only in relation to other hikes. Someone who puffs climbing a few flights of stairs will not find a 2.8-mile walk easy at all.

And speaking of climbing, pay attention to the elevation gains—they warn of steep uphill trails. Many of the hike descriptions mention the elevation gain in feet, but even when they do not, the elevations shown on the maps make gains for most hikes calculable. A 1000-foot gain is an arduous uphill trudge for out-of-shape walkers, particularly if the climb is packed into less than 2 miles. A 2000-foot gain requires frequent rest

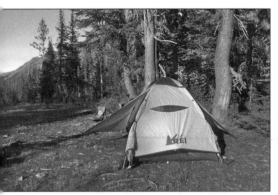

Choose a tent site on a bare spot in the woods, and never on fragile meadow plants.

stops even when hikers are in good condition. Hikers must be in very good shape—strong hearts and strong knees—to handle a 3000-foot elevation gain in a day. And only those in prime condition should tackle the 5000-foot climbs required by trails up Hat Point or South Sister.

Trail mileages given in this book are approximate, and may not agree with trail sign mileages, which are often incorrect. Likewise, official signs and maps often offer a confusion of names and numbers for the same trail. This guide generally avoids the debate by identifying trails according to their destination and starting point.

Road directions to trailheads are provided only when the map does not clearly show the route. When several obscure trailheads cluster together, complete car directions may be given to only one of them, with the understanding that drivers can then use the map to find the others.

A car shuttle allows a group with two cars to end their hike at a different trailhead. Drive both cars to the trip's endpoint, leave one there, and then drive in the other to the hike's starting point.

A key-swap hike requires less driving, but more careful planning. For this arrangement to work, two carloads of hikers must walk the same trail, starting at opposite trailheads. When the two groups meet at a specified time at the trail's midpoint, they swap car keys for the drive home. Better yet, swap duplicate keys before leaving for the hike.

Advanced hikers may be interested in the cross-country hiking routes suggested for many areas. Bushwhacking can be immensely rewarding. It's also the only way to hike in Oregon's trailless desert country. Although off-trail travel is more difficult in the dense forests of western Oregon's wildernesses, you don't need to bushwhack very far in such terrain before finding true isolation—even in an area billed as crowded. Perhaps the best way to walk lightly on the land is to walk where no one else has.

Cross-country hikers in particular should keep a topographic map and compass at hand, and have experience using them. All hikers should inform someone of their route before leaving, so that a 911 center can be called to alert the county sheriff's office to organize a search, if necessary.

Emergency Gear

Even on the tamest hike a surprise storm or a wrong turn can suddenly make the gear you carry very important. If you are lost, stay put and keep warm. The biggest killer in the woods is hypothermia—being cold and wet too long.

For safety's sake, your backpack should always contain the ten essentials:

1. Warm, water-repellent coat (or parka and extra shirt)
2. Drinking water
3. Extra food
4. Knife
5. Matches in waterproof container
6. Fire starter (butane lighter or candle)
7. First aid kit
8. Flashlight
9. Topographic map
10. Compass

Global Positioning System (GPS)

A global positioning system device can be very helpful in certain situations. By tracking signals from satellites, these handheld, battery-operated instruments are able to display the latitude and longitude of their location with a precision that varies by only a few feet. If you mark your location with a GPS device it will be easy to return later to the exact same place. However, a GPS device is no substitute for a map and compass. If you are lost, a GPS device will not point out north, nor will it show you your location on most maps. The devices are useless if their batteries fail. And some do not work in forested areas where trees block satellite signals.

On the other hand, a GPS device can be the simplest way to locate a poorly marked desert trailhead or to find a high-country ski shelter in a blizzard whiteout. This book occasionally gives a destination's coordinates using standard latitude-longitude notation (for example, GPS location N43°37.931' W122°00.202'). To locate the destination, use your GPS device's on-screen menu to mark a new "waypoint," edit the waypoint's latitude and longitude to match those of the given destination, and then select the device's "Go To" feature to show the direction and distance you'll need to travel to reach that destination.

Trailhead and Wilderness Permits

Northwest Forest Pass permits are required to park within a quarter mile of many trailheads in National Forests. These permits cost $5 per car per day or $30 per year, and can be purchased at ranger stations or outdoor stores. Note, however, that some areas are not included in this program. Northwest Forest Passes are not needed in the Umpqua, Winema, Ochoco, Malheur, Fremont, and Umatilla National Forests. Even in participating National Forests, some trailheads are free—for example, at Tim-berline Lodge and Multnomah Falls.

A wilderness permit is sometimes required to enter a wilderness area, but these are free and can generally be filled out at the trailhead. For Mount Jefferson's Pamelia Lake trailhead and the Three Sisters' Obsidian trailhead, however, entry permits are strictly limited and must be picked up in advance at a ranger station.

Trail Courtesies

Finally, remember a few "rules of the trail:"

● Step off the trail on the downhill side to let horses pass. Talking quietly to the horses can help prevent them from spooking.

● Pick no flowers.

● Leave no litter. Trailside orange peels and eggshells last for decades.

● Do not shortcut switchbacks.

● Divide large groups into independent hiking parties of twelve or fewer.

● Do not bring pets into the wilderness. A dog can dangerously anger bears, porcupines, and other wilderness users.

● Respect private land. This guide makes an effort to steer hikers clear of private property, but even designated wilderness includes some private inholdings.

Snowshoer at Odell Lake.

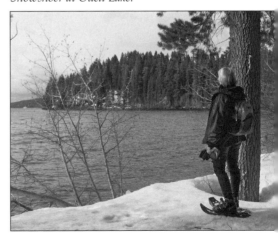

TIPS FOR BACKPACKERS

Choosing the Right Gear

People who shy away from backpacking are often surprised how fun and easy it can be with the right equipment. No, your pack doesn't have to weigh a ton, and yes, you can weather a rainstorm in comfort.

Balance lightweight gear against the need for safety. The "ultralight" backpacking systems touted in some guidebooks are designed primarily for California, where the weather is mild. In Oregon, a backpack that weighs a mere 4 pounds is almost certainly omitting lifesaving gear for wet, cold weather. If you are backpacking in Oregon, do not leave your raingear, tent, or warm sleeping bag behind!

On well-maintained trails, walking shoes suffice, but on rocky, wilderness trails you'll want serious boots. Especially if you're facing scree or loose rock, choose sturdy boots that extend above your ankle.

Do not believe the temperature ratings of sleeping bags. In most of Oregon, temperatures rarely dip very far below freezing. But a "20-degree" bag may well seem chilly at 30 degrees.

It is possible to buy a backpacking tent at a sporting goods store for $30. You are unlikely to use it more than once. Spend a little more for a tent with zippers that do not break, flies that cover the entrance, and floors that do not leak.

A debate rages over the virtues of internal frame versus external frame backpacks. Internal frame packs, with a cloth covering over a metal splint, offer better flexibility, so they work well for mountaineering, ski touring, and bushwhacking. External frame packs weigh less and hold more, so they excel for conventional backpacking on trails where you need not twist.

Menus a la Backpack

Plan your backpacking meals so that you need nothing more than hot water. Then you can cook quickly on with a small backpacking stove and not be tempted to light a campfire. Campfires blacken rocks, burn scenic wilderness wood, and in general are suited to car campgrounds rather than fragile wilderness sites.

The easiest backpacking breakfasts rely on packets of instant oatmeal and hot cocoa, spiced perhaps with raisins or brown sugar. Lunches should require no cooking at all. Standard lunch fare is gorp (an acronym for Granola, Oatmeal, Raisins, and Peanuts).

For dinner, a low-budget option is a pack of ramen noodles with a package of dried soup and possibly a clove of garlic. Many commercial freeze-dried

Camping near Crater Lake's rim is allowed only when the Rim Road is closed for winter.

entrees are tastier and likewise require nothing but hot water.

Leaving No Trace

Wilderness campers face a serious challenge—to leave no trace of their camp. Choosing the right campsite is critical. Savvy campers will not pitch a tent over the wildflower meadow they came to see, but instead will choose a spot on bare sand or the bare pine needle duff of the forest. Never tent in a hollow where rainwater will gather, making trenching a temptation. Likewise, never camp in a fragile alpine area, on a streambank, or within 100 feet of a lake. Best of all, bring a gallon's worth of water bottles per camper and pitch a dry camp, away from the water sources that attract camping overuse.

When an emergency requires a campfire, don't build a rock campfire ring—this needlessly blackens stones. Clear a circle of ground to mineral soil. Gather only small pieces of wood that can be broken off by hand. Never hack limbs with a hatchet. After use, drown the fire, scatter the cold ashes, and restore the site.

Do not bury or burn garbage. Limit the trash that must be packed out by bringing no canned or bottled foods, and by repackaging bulky foods into compact, lightweight plastic bags or containers.

Never wash dishes or bathe with soap directly in a lake or stream. Carry water at least 100 feet away from the shore and wash there.

Bury human waste in a small hole dug at least 100 feet from water. Choose a site where no one would ever camp. Fill the hole with dirt and cover the spot with a natural-looking arrangement of rocks or sticks. Do not bury toilet paper, because animals will dig it up. If you must use toilet paper (instead of leaves), seal the used paper in a plastic bag and pack it out.

When camping at an established

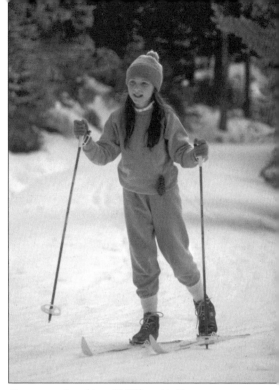

Cross-country skier at Willamette Pass.

site in the wilderness, try to restore it a little. Remove nails and clotheslines from trees. Dismantle racks, benches, or lean-to frames. Pick aluminum foil and trash from campfire rings and scatter the ashes. Remember, campers in the wilderness are visitors who should leave no trace of their stay. "Developed" campsites belong only at automobile campgrounds.

TIPS FOR CLIMBERS

This guide identifies mountaineering sites in the most scenic areas across the state—including Mount Hood, the world's second most climbed snowpeak, and Smith Rock, a mecca for technical climbers with 281 named routes. Routes in gravel pits and roadside cliffs are not featured.

Because other guidebooks discuss specific technical climbs in detail, this book provides an overview, noting the chief attractions of each climbing area and the range of difficulty of the most important routes. The rating system

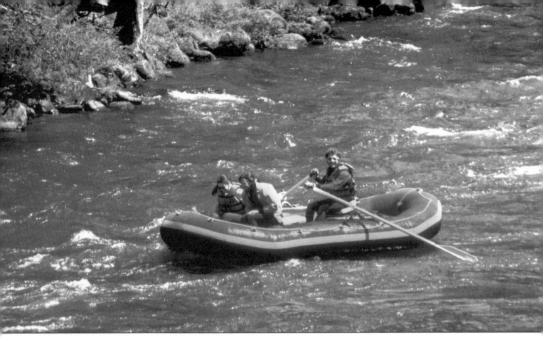

Whitewater rafting on the North Umpqua River.

used here, known as the Yosemite Decimal System, expresses the climb's overall difficulty first by a Roman numeral, then the climb's athletic difficulty by a number from 1 to 5.15, and finally (when appropriate) the difficulty of available artificial aid by symbols from A1 to A5, as follows:

Overall Difficulty (length of climb, degree of commitment)
I - up to 2 hours
II - up to a half day
III - a full day
IV - possibly requires a bivouac
Oregon has no grade V or VI climbs

Athletic Difficulty (class of technical skill needed)
1 - hiking
2 - scrambling over talus or through brush
3 - steep slopes or exposed ridges
4 - rope required
5 - rope and protection required

Class 5 climbs are broken down from 5.1 to 5.15 to indicate increasingly difficult pitches requiring rope and protection. Climbs above 5.7 are demanding even for experienced climbers.

Artificial Aid Difficulty
A1 - solid placements
A2 - strenuous placements
A3 - several marginal placements
A4 - many marginal placements
A5 - marginal protection throughout

Thus, the east face of Smith Rock's Monkey Face, rated II-5.7-A3, requires most of a day with advanced free-climbing skills and has several marginally secure aids.

Climbers should not add new bolts to established routes, both to decrease clutter and to preserve a route's challenge.

A WORD TO SNOWSHOERS & SKIERS

This guide covers most of Oregon's popular snowshoeing and cross-country ski touring areas, and many little-known spots as well. In the area maps, hatch marks along trails and unplowed roads indicate feasible winter routes for Nordic skiers. Snowmobile-shaped symbols designate winter OHV staging areas. These have been included on the maps because other winter users may wish to avoid such areas.

"P" symbols along highways represent plowed sno-park lots. From November 15 to April 30, cars parked in or near sno-park lots must display a valid permit or face a fine. The permit costs only $3 per day or $15 per season, so it pays to stop by a sporting goods store, ski shop, or Department of Motor Vehicles office to pick one up.

The Forest Service generally identifies non-wildermess ski and snowshoe trails with blue plastic markers nailed to trees. Snowmobile routes are signed with orange diamonds. Within wilderness areas, winter trails are identified only with unobtrusive oak diamonds, if they are marked at all. Travelers on wilderness routes need advanced route-finding skills.

Oregon's extremely variable snow conditions can produce delightful powder, heavy mush, and clattery ice all within a day's time. Waxless skis are usually the boards of choice.

Nordic skiers and snowshoers in Oregon need rain gear, plenty of warm clothing (wool is best), a rucksack with the ten essentials (see page 14), a repair kit, and an insulated seating pad for rests. Never set out without a topographic map and compass. Wilderness exploration can be great fun in winter, but the need for caution and survival training is likewise great.

Avalanches are extremely rare in the Oregon Cascades, but are relatively common in the Wallowas, and may occur anywhere after a snowstorm or high wind. Avoid slopes of more than 25 percent steepness—especially treeless slopes, since these may have a history as "avalanche chutes." Also beware of frozen lakes. Particularly in the Cascades, heavy snows can insulate the water, preventing it from forming solid ice. Even when skiers succeed in crossing the snow-covered slush, those on foot may fall through.

Finally, a few winter manners:

- Yield right of way to downhill skiers.
- Don't stop to rest in a ski track; step aside.
- Don't walk or snowshoe in a ski track; this ruins the smooth grooves.
- Leave pets at home.

A WORD TO BOATERS

This guide describes nine of Oregon's wildest whitewater river runs and numerous quiet spots for canoeing, sailing, or sailboarding.

The descriptions use a six-point scale to rate a rapids' difficulty for rafters, kayakers, and drift boaters:

Class 1: Easy
Class 2: Moderate
Class 3: Dangerous. Novices should consider lining or portaging boats.
Class 4: Very dangerous. Novices should line or portage.
Class 5: Extremely dangerous. Even experts should consider portaging.
Class 6: Unrunnable. Portage boats.

Those in decked canoes should add one point to the difficulty of each rapids. For open canoes, add two points.

Note that most of the featured rivers can be run only when water is high—but not too high. Suitable months for running rivers vary dramatically from year to year. Check at *http://or.water.usgs.gov/* for daily updates of river gauge levels.

Because floatboating concentrates visitor impact on the fragile camping beaches of wilderness rivers, it is important to follow the strictest no-trace

Kayaking on the Rogue River.

camping guidelines:

- Cook on campstoves. Those who insist on using campfires must bring all of their own firewood, build the fire in a firepan they have brought, and then pack up both pan and ashes without a trace.
- Use toilets when provided. When they are not, do not bury toilet paper. Buried human waste decomposes within a few weeks, but paper remains for a year or more in riverbank soils, and can be exposed by wind or water. Pack out the used paper in a sealed plastic bag.

Proper boating skills and safety are essential on wilderness runs because escape or rescue after an accident can be extremely difficult.

TIPS FOR EQUESTRIANS

The role of horses in the wilderness is in transition. A few new routes have been added for horses, but many trails bear the sign, "Hiker Only." The National Park Service at Crater Lake bans horses everywhere except on the Pacific Crest Trail, and allows no grazing.

As the no-trace ethic spreads, so have

Sunset at the South Steens Campground.

restrictions on saddle stock. Here's a list of guidelines that have grown into iron-clad rules in most wilderness areas:

- Keep saddle stock at least 200 feet from streams or lakes except for loading, unloading, watering, or traveling on a trail.
- Carry all the feed an animal will need. This cuts down on grazing.
- Bring no hay. It spreads weed seeds.
- Feed oats or hay pellets morning and evening from a nose bag, and not from piles on the ground.
- Never tie stock to a tree, even temporarily. Tethers can girdle trees and hooves can dig circular pits.
- Hobble, don't picket stock. This disperses grazing damage.
- Do not build corrals or hitching racks.
- When breaking camp, fill in paw holes and scatter manure.

Gone are the days of campfires, big coffee pots, beans and bacon, and canvas tents. As equestrians limit their loads and their pack strings, their gear increasingly resembles that of the no-trace backpacker: lightweight nylon tents, lightweight campstoves, and freeze-dried food.

A FINAL WORD

Once Oregon was entirely wilderness, from the Pacific to the Snake River. Now, only scattered islands of that great wilderness survive. Dozens of Oregon outdoor clubs and environmental groups are working to win wilderness status for the areas that still lack protection. If you'd like to help, a good place to start is to contact Oregon Wild at *www.oregonwild.org* or the Oregon Natural Desert Association at *www.onda.org*.

Use this guide to discover the beautiful but fragile heritage that remains to show Oregon as it once was. For the areas in this book, there is still time.

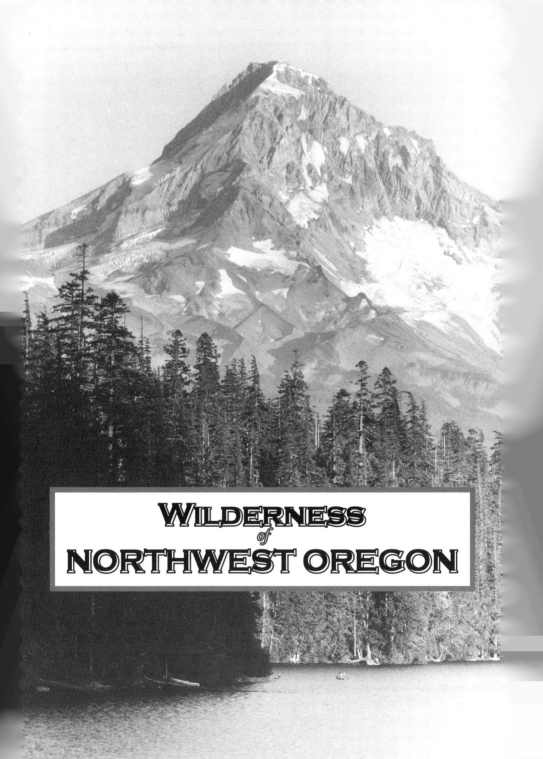

WILDERNESS
of
NORTHWEST OREGON

Mt. Hood from Lost Lake.

NORTHWEST OREGON

0 5 10 15 20 25mi
0 5 10 15 20 25 30 35km

N

◼ Designated wilderness
◼ Undesignated wilderness
◼ Designated wilderness islands

Washington

Vancouver
Portland
Gresham
Sandy
Oregon City
Estacada
Molalla
Mehama
Lacomb
Detroit
Sweet Home
McKenzie Bridge

Hood River
The Dalles
Tygh Valley
Maupin
Camp Sherman
Sisters
Terrebonne
Redmond
Prineville
Madras
Bend

Cascade Locks
Dee
Zigzag

COLUMBIA GORGE
MT HOOD
SALMON-HUCKLEBERRY
ROARING RIVER
CLACKAMAS
TABLE ROCK
OPAL CREEK
BULL OF THE WOODS
OLALLIE LAKE
BADGER CREEK
LOWER WHITE RIVER
LOWER DESCHUTES RIVER
METOLIUS RIVER
MIDDLE SANTIAM
MT JEFFERSON
DESCHUTES CANYON
OLD CASCADES
MT WASHINGTON
SMITH ROCK

Range
Cascade

1 2 3 4 5 6 7 8 9 10 11 12 13 17 18 19 20

5
84
35
26
84
216
97
197
213
211
224
214
22
20
26
126
97
242
126
20

Map Key	Destination	Total miles	Easy-M-Diff.	Days	Est. Mos Open	Uncrowded	Page
A	Eagle Creek Trail (Gorge)	7	M	2	•		37
B	Eagle-Wahtum-Benson Loop	27	D	3	VI-XI½		38
C	Dublin Lake	14	D	2	IV-XI	•	38
D	Ramona Falls	7	M	2	IV¾-X		44
E	Timberline Trail	39	D	5	VII½-X		44
F	Cairn Basin	8	D	3	VII½-X		45
G	Paradise Park	8	D	2	VII½-X		45
H	Elk Cove	8	M	3	VII½-X		45
I	Burnt Lake	7	M	2	VI-X		45
J	Elk Meadows	6	M	2	VI¾-X		46
K	Mirror Lake	3	E	2	V½-XI¼		49
L	Salmon River - Rolling Riffle	4	E	2	•		49
M	Rock Lakes Basin Loop	8	M	2	VI½-XI¼	•	52
N	Shining Lake	9	E	2	VI½-XI¼	•	52
O	Eagle Creek (Salmon-Huck.)	9	M	2	•		53
P	Twin Lakes (Mt. Hood)	4	E	3	VI-XI¼		55
Q	Badger Lake	8	D	3	V-X	•	56
R	Clackamas River (The Narrows)	8	E	2	•		58
S	Memaloose Lake	3	E	2	VI½-XI¼		58
T	Opal Creek (Merten Mill)	4	E	3	•		63
U	Pansy Lake	2	E	3	VI-X		63
V	Welcome Lakes	10	D	3	VI½-X	•	66
W	Big Slide Lake	11	D	3	VI½-X	•	66
X	Silver King Lake	13	D	2	VI½-X	•	66
Y	Twin Lakes (Bull of Woods)	16	D	3	VI½-X	•	66
Z	Red Lake Trail	6	E	3	VI½-XI¼	•	68
AA	Pamelia Lake	4	E	3	V-XI		74
BB	Marion Lake	5	E	3	V½-XI½		75
CC	Canyon Creek Meadows	5	E	3	VI½-X		75
DD	Jefferson Park (Whitewater)	10	M	3	VII½-X½		77
EE	Santiam Lake	9	M	3	VII-X		77
FF	Carl Lake	9	M	3	VII½-X	•	78
GG	Around Three Fingered Jack	20	D	3	VII½-X		78
HH	PCT: Breitenbush to Santiam Pass	36	D	5	VII½-XI½		78
II	Tenas Lakes (Benson Lake)	5	E	3	VII-X		84
JJ	Matthieu Lakes Loop	6	E	2	VII½-X		84
KK	Shedd Camp Shelter	2	E	2	IV-XI	•	92
LL	Donaca Lake	13	D	2	IV-XI	•	92
MM	Drift Creek S. (Harris Ranch)	6	M	2	•	•	96
NN	Drift Creek N. (Horse Creek)	7	M	2	•	•	97
OO	Alder Springs	3	E	2	IV-X		106

Memaloose Lake.

THE COLUMBIA GORGE

Wilderness drapes the waterfall canyons of the Columbia River's colossal gorge. Clockwise from above: Indian Point on Eaton Ridge, Elowah Falls, Crown Point, Punchbowl Falls, and Oneonta Gorge.

AROUND MOUNT HOOD

The Timberline Trail circles Oregon's tallest peak. Clockwise from upper right: sunrise at Timberline Lodge, Zigzag Canyon, Paradise Park, the McNeil Point shelter, Barrett Spur, the Eliot Glacier from Cooper Spur, and the Elk Meadows shelter.

BETWEEN HOOD & JEFFERSON

A bill in 2009 added and expanded many Wilderness areas, especially between Mt. Hood and Mt. Jefferson. Clockwise from upper left: Mt. Hood from Lookout Mountain, the Eagle Creek Trail in the Salmon-Huckleberry Wilderness, Opal Creek, Olallie Lake sunset, Timber Lake, Breitenbush Lake bogs, Bagby Hot Springs, Serene Lake, and Mt. Hood from Wildcat Mountain. Above: Sawmill Falls, on the trail to Opal Creek.

MOUNT JEFFERSON

Oregon's second tallest mountain shares a Wilderness with Three Fingered Jack. Clockwise from upper left: Mt. Jefferson from Scout Lake, Three Fingered Jack from Canyon Creek Meadows, Three Fingered Jack from a Santiam Pass ski trail, and Mt. Jefferson from The Table.

Tamolitch Pool on the McKenzie River.

Central Oregon

The dry side of the Cascade Range has become a center for outdoor recreation. Above: a daredevil jumps into the Deschutes River at Steelhead Falls. Left: hiking along the Crooked River at Smith Rock State Park. Below: the mouth of the Deschutes River, where whitewater raft trips end.

1
COLUMBIA GORGE

Several worlds collide in the Columbia Gorge. In the west, moss-covered rain forests cling to misty green cliffs. A few miles east, only scrub oaks dot a semi-arid scabland. And in between, a colonnade of more than 20 major waterfalls separates the alpine meadows of the Cascade Range from the mudflats of the Columbia River, nearly at sea level.

In the midst of these colliding ecosystems is the remarkable Hatfield Wilderness. Although it lies a mere half-hour freeway drive from Portland and overlooks a busy transportation corridor along the Columbia, it remains delightfully wild, protected by a ribbon of breathtaking 3000-foot cliffs.

Climate

The annual rainfall varies from a soggy 150 inches in the Bull Run Watershed to 75 inches at Cascade Locks, and just 29 inches at Hood River on the eastern end of the Gorge. Summers, however, are dry throughout. Snow covers trails over 3600 feet from December to May, but lower trails may be clear for hiking even in midwinter. Occasionally, winter ice storms drape the cliffs with icicles and coat trees and highways with silvery freezing rain—a result of warm Pacific clouds dropping rain through a layer of freezing air blown in from east of the mountains.

Ponytail Falls on Horsetail Creek.

Plants and Wildlife

Between the dense Douglas fir and sword fern rain forests of the west and the open oak grasslands of the east, the Columbia Gorge hosts twelve plant species found nowhere else in the world—including six strictly confined to the wilderness lands. Look for rare plants and flowers on the rock walls of the Gorge's cool, north-facing canyons, where even alpine wildflowers are often tricked into growing nearly at sea level.

The California condors that Lewis and Clark reported here in 1805, attracted by the Columbia's salmon runs, are now gone, although bald eagles may yet be sighted.

The darling of the gorge's many waterfalls is the water ouzel, a chubby little

Location: 24 mi E of Portland

Size: 107 sq mi

Status: 102 sq mi designated wilderness (1984, 2009)

Terrain: cliffs, densely forested canyons

Elevation: 100'-4960'

Management: Columbia Gorge National Scenic Area

Map: Forest Trails of the Columbia Gorge (Geo-Graphics)

COLUMBIA GORGE

0   1   2mi   N

0   1   2   3km

Table Mtn

Gillette

Hardy Ridge

Hamilton Mtn

Bonneville Hot Sp.

Bonneville Dam

Beacon Rock

Beacon Rock

Archer Mtn

Skamania

68

Elowah Falls

Vancouver 26mi

14

Ainsworth

Oneonta Gorge

Multnomah Falls

St. Peters Dome

Yeon Mtn

Nesmith Pt 3880'

1200'

3300'

Wahkeena Falls

Portland 24mi

Horsetail

Little Cougar

Triple Falls

Palmer Pk

Mt Talapus

Angels Rest 1600'

2200' Devils Rest

1520

Bridal Veil Falls

2800'

Oneonta

Troutdale 13

Larch Mtn 4056'

Bull   Run

Watershed

(Closed to public)

Carson

Columbia

Dog Mtn

Wind Mtn

WASH.
OREGON

84

Wyeth

River

Hood River 8mi

Stevenson

G

Indian Pt

Starvation Cr. Falls

Herman Creek

Cascade Locks

Nick Eaton Ridge

Lindsey Cr.

Warren Lk

PCT

X 3600'

Herman Cr.

4000' X

3900' X

G

Mt Defiance 4960'

Eagle Creek

Benson Plateau

East Fk

Bear

North Lk

2820

Ruckel Cr.

Green Point Mtn

Rainy Lake 4100'

Eagle

X 300

4100'

Punch Bowl Falls

Hatfield

2800' X

Tomlike Mtn 4547'

G

Creek

Dublin

A

C

800' X

PCT

Chinidere Mtn

Mud L

Tunnel Falls

East Fk

Wahtum L 3732'

G

Wilderness

Wahtum Lake

B

Tanner Butte 4500'

Indian Springs

Trail

G

X 3620'

X 1640'

4900' Indian Mtn

1310

13

Eagle Butte

Crest

Hood River 15

13

Pacific

18

Buck Pk

Lost Lake Butte

16

Lost Lk

Lost Lake

(See Area 2 Map)

Lolo Pass 8mi

slate-gray bird that builds its mossy nests behind waterfalls. Ouzels spend their days walking along the bottom of rushing mountain streams, poking about for insect larvae with their deft little bills. When this robin-sized bird is not marching around underwater it can be seen doing bobbing knee-bend exercises on creek rocks or whirring along just above the water with rapid, constant little wingbeats. Though common throughout western North America, this dipper can live only where water runs wild and white.

Geology

The many layers of columnar basalt exposed in the cliffs of the gorge are all part of the massive lava outpourings

Multnomah Falls.

which inundated 50,000 square miles of eastern Washington, eastern Oregon, and Idaho to a depth of up to a mile 10 to 17 million years ago. These rock floods—a result of the North American continent overriding the Pacific Ocean floor—surged down the ancient Columbia to the sea, pushing the river north to its present location. When the crest of the Cascade Range then gradually warped upward, making those mountains ever higher, the Columbia kept pace by cutting its gorge deeper. The original surface of the lava flows is now a tilted and well-eroded upland, evident in the 2000-foot plateau above Multnomah Falls and the 4000-foot Benson Plateau. More recent volcanoes—Larch Mountain, Tanner Butte, and Mount Defiance—protrude above this general silhouette.

During the Ice Age 20 small glaciers formed on the gorge's southern rim, carving the hanging amphitheaters that lie above many of the waterfalls. Much of the scenery of the gorge, however, can be attributed to a series of monumental Ice Age floods of the Columbia River. These "Missoula" or "Bretz" floods occurred every 30 to 70 years between 12,700 and 15,300 years ago when the continental ice sheet then covering Canada temporarily dammed the Clark Fork River in Western Montana. When the ensuing reservoir became deep enough to float the ice, the dam would burst, suddenly releasing a body of water half the volume of Lake Michigan across eastern Washington and through the narrow Columbia Gorge. The floods denuded the Gorge to an elevation of 800 feet and undercut the cliffs, leaving the graceful waterfalls visible today.

HIKING & BACKPACKING

The thorough trail network is very heavily used on weekends, particularly in the vicinity of Multnomah Falls and along Eagle Creek. The dramatic eleva-

Wahtum Lake.

tion gains on many trails (as much as 4000 feet) should be taken into consideration when planning trips.

Oregon's tallest waterfall, Multnomah Falls, has inspired a cluster of trails well-suited to day hikes. Paths within roughly half a mile of this 542-foot double cascade are paved due to frequent foot traffic. A good way to beat the crowds is to park at nearby Wahkeena Falls and make a 5-mile loop up the Wahkeena Trail to Multnomah Falls' top, passing half a dozen falls on the way.

Long, slot-like Oneonta Gorge is less well known than neighboring Multnomah Falls, but has equal charm. A 2.7-mile loop trail starts at Horsetail Falls, ducks behind Ponytail Falls, and peers down into Oneonta Gorge's mossy chasm from its rim. A worthwhile 0.9-mile side trail visits Triple Falls.

Oneonta Gorge can be more directly experienced by wading up the narrow creekbed 0.5 mile from the old Columbia River Highway bridge to an otherwise hidden 100-foot falls. Expect icy, hip-deep water in winter and cool, knee-deep pools in summer.

The historic Columbia River Highway was built 1913-1915 as a winding pleasure drive through the scenic Columbia Gorge. Several long-abandoned sections have been reopened as trails for hikers, equestrians, and bicyclists, including a 4-mile stretch paralleling Interstate 84 from Bonneville Dam exit 40 to Cascade Locks exit 44. This section includes the bridge-like, cliff-edge Tooth Rock Viaduct just west of Eagle Creek.

Half a dozen exhilarating day hikes switchback up to viewpoints of the Gorge. The spectacular rock bluff at Angels Rest is a 1500-foot climb in 2.2 miles from the old Columbia River Highway at the Bridal Veil exit of Interstate 84. Nesmith Point, just west of elegant Elowah Falls, is an ambitious 3800-foot climb in 4.9 miles to a stunning view. Two other viewpoint hikes climb through natural wildflower rock gardens: the extremely rugged 4.8-mile Ruckel Creek Trail from the Eagle Creek Campground, and the steep 3.3-mile path up Nick Eaton Ridge from the Herman Creek Campground. Both have loop options.

The spectacular Eagle Creek Trail features seven waterfalls, a high bridge, and one tunnel (which actually goes behind Tunnel Falls). Blasted out of the sheer cliffs in the 1910s, this trail is now very popular. A day trip can hardly do the trail justice; it is better seen on a two-day backpack, perhaps returning via the beautiful Benson Plateau, or the quiet Tanner Creek or Herman Creek trails. Camping along the Eagle Creek Trail is restricted to designated sites. On summer weekends space can be tight. Also note that cars at the Eagle Creek Trailhead seem unusually susceptible to break-ins.

The area's largest lake, Wahtum Lake, shimmers in a forested bowl at the headwaters of Eagle Creek. It's a popular campsite for backpackers on the Eagle Creek-to-Benson Plateau loop. Tenters at the lake are restricted to designated sites. Because the lake can also be accessed by a mere 0.2-mile walk from paved Road 1310, use has been so heavy that the Forest Service has discussed plans to require permits for day hikers and backpackers alike.

Three long-distance trail routes traverse the Oregon side of the Columbia Gorge. The 35.5-mile low-elevation Gorge Trail, between Bridal Veil and

Falls on the trail above Multnomah Falls.

Wyeth, avoids the steep climbs found on many other trails and is snow-free year round. It is used primarily to connect other trails, but it makes good hiking from end to end. And because of the Gorge Trail's many trailheads along the Columbia River Highway, sections of the path are easily accessible for relatively undemanding day hikes.

A higher elevation trail route winds 38 miles from 4056-foot Larch Mountain to 4960-foot Mount Defiance. Together with the low-elevation Gorge Trail, this route makes it possible to convert any of the area's 15 north-south trails into scenic loop hikes. Hiking the length of this high-elevation Gorge route is a challenging four-day backpack, zigzagging across several steep canyons in the most remote part of the wilderness. For a reasonable sample of this rough route, take an overnight trip to small, woodsy Dublin Lake. The 14.3-mile loop gains 4250 feet and begins at the Tooth Rock Trailhead at Bonneville exit 40 of Interstate 84.

The third long-distance trail in the Gorge is the Pacific Crest Trail (PCT), which passes Wahtum Lake and crosses the 2-square-mile, forested Benson Plateau. Those who just can't wait to see the summer display of alpine wildflowers will find them blooming as early as June along the Benson Plateau's northeast rim. Huckleberry aficionados can

Wahclella Falls on Tanner Creek is an easy 1-mile hike from the Bonneville Dam exit.

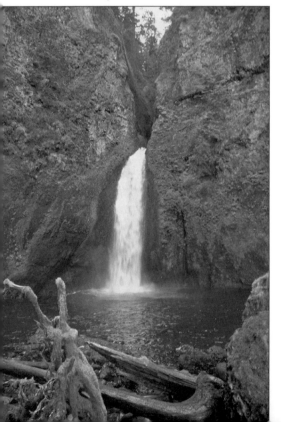

profitably prowl about Wahtum Lake in late August.

For those able to arrange a car shuttle between trailheads, Larch Mountain and Mount Defiance can be the starting points of dramatic, downhill day hikes. The Larch Mountain Trail drops 4000 feet in 6.7 miles to Multnomah Falls Lodge. The Mount Defiance Trail loses fully 4800 feet elevation to Starvation Creek Falls in just 5.8 miles. Both mountains offer dramatic views of Mount Hood, Mount Adams, and Mount St. Helens.

Throughout the Columbia Gorge, hikers should remember that poison oak is common below 800 feet, that trailside cliffs make some paths inappropriate for unsupervised children, and that underbrush and steep slopes virtually prohibit cross-country travel. Only the wider, well-graded Herman Creek and Pacific Crest trails are recommended for horses or pack stock. The Bull Run Watershed to the south, the source of Portland's water supply, is closed to the public except specifically for travel on the PCT.

CLIMBING

The Columbia Gorge is a center for testing technical climbing skills. For starters, good conditioning hikes include the nearly 5000-foot climb from Starvation Creek Falls to Mount Defiance and the numerous trails up to the 4000-foot Benson Plateau. Then head 3 miles west of Bridal Veil Falls to Rooster Rock (a 200-foot pinnacle with routes varying in difficulty from level I-4 to II-5.6-A3) and Crown Point (a 700-foot bluff with routes of difficulty II-5.4 and III-5.6). The Pillars of Hercules, a group of 100-foot basalt towers immediately west of Bridal Veil, rate difficulty levels from I-5.2 to II-5.8.

Little Cougar, a small thumb of rotten rock at 1300-foot elevation one mile east of Multnomah Falls, is a level I-4 or I-5.4 climb, depending on the route taken. St. Peters Dome, 1 mile east of Ainsworth State Park, consists of similarly poor rock but requires level II-5.6 or III-5.6-A3 skills. It is a 200-foot thumb at 1525 feet and was unclimbed until 1940.

By far the most popular and most extensive climbing challenges in the area, however, are on Beacon Rock, just across the Columbia River in Washington. This impressive 848-foot andesite monolith requires about five rope lengths of skilled climbing. Difficulty levels of II-5.6 to IV-5.11 are encountered on a total of 45 named routes and variations.

Mount Hood from Larch Mountain's Sherrard Point.

2
MOUNT HOOD

Oregon's tallest peak dominates this popular wilderness. Hikers can meet alpine vistas of Hood from every path of the area's well-developed trail network. The dormant volcano's summit, ringed with eleven active glaciers, is the goal of 10,000 climbers a year.

But the peak is not the area's only attraction. The 39-mile Timberline Trail circles the mountain through a succession of stunning alpine meadows filled with flowers. Ramona, Tamanawas, and a dozen other waterfalls grace heavily forested river valleys. Zigzag Canyon is an impressive 1000-foot-deep gorge on the mountain's flank. And 5000-foot Zigzag Mountain, an 8-mile-long western spur of Hood, offers lakes and ridges of its own.

Climate

The area's 150 inches of annual precipitation come largely as snow between October and April. Skiers and snowshoers will find the snow drier, and the skies often bluer, on Hood's east and southeast slopes. Snow melts off lower trails (up to 4000 feet) by about June 1, and off higher trails (up to 7000 feet) by mid-July. July and August yield warm days and cold nights. Sudden storms

Location: 34 mi E of Portland
Size: 115 sq mi
Status: 106 sq mi designated wilderness (1964, 1978, 2009)
Terrain: glaciated peak, alpine meadows, forested slopes
Elevation: 1800'-11,240'
Management: Mount Hood NF
Map: Mount Hood (Geo-Graphics)

Mount Hood from Barrett Spur.

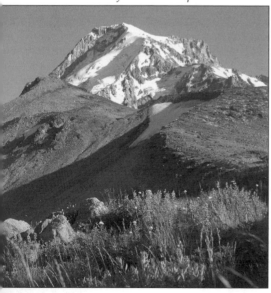

can bring snowfall in any month—a fact that has led to climbing tragedies.

Plants and Wildlife

Dense Douglas fir forests blanket the wilderness' lower areas, with an understory of Oregon grape, huckleberry (ripe late August), salal, and rhododendron (blooms late May). Higher forests are of mountain hemlock, noble fir, and subalpine fir. Near timberline (6500 feet), gnarled whitebark pines frame meadows of blue lupine, red paintbrush, beargrass plumes, penstemon, purple Cascade aster, and western Pasque flower ("old-man-of-the-mountain"). Profuse displays of white avalanche lilies decorate Paradise Park in July and Cairn Basin in August.

A bird checklist for Hood's south slope notes 132 species, from humming-

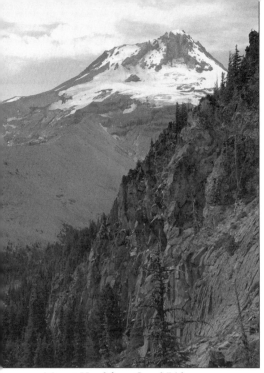

Mount Hood from Gnarl Ridge.

birds to bald eagles. Forty species of mammals live on the mountain's slopes, including black bear, mountain lion, and elk.

The whistling, squirrel-like animals often met on Hood's rocky timberline slopes are pikas. Pikas (also known as rock rabbits) are round-eared, apparently tailless animals the size of guinea pigs. Colonies of pikas live at higher elevations than any other North American mammal, cutting and sun-drying bushels of grass to last them through nine snow-bound months without hibernation.

Geology

Mount Hood is the most recently active of all Oregon volcanoes. In the 1800's, four minor eruptions of steam, ash, and magma alarmed observers as far away as Portland. In 1907 glowing rock near the summit melted part of the White River Glacier, causing floods. Even today, climbers encounter hot rock, scalding steam vents, and a powerful sulfur smell in the depression south of the summit, between Steel Cliff and Crater Rock.

The volcano itself had its beginnings after the surrounding hills and rivers were in nearly their present form. Lava flows filled nearby river canyons, forcing the rivers aside. When the rivers eroded the softer rock around the hard lava, the original valleys were left as lava-topped ridges—an example of "reverse topography."

Mount Hood reached its greatest height, about 12,000 feet, just prior to the Ice Age. Then, glaciers removed the crater and much of the north slope. Barrett Spur and Cooper Spur remain to show the mountain's earlier dimensions, indicating the ancient crater was north of the present summit. Crater Rock, south of the summit, was long thought to be a remnant of the volcano's central plug. In fact it is a recent side vent's lava dome, the creation of which smothered the Timberline Lodge area with cinder-and-mud avalanches just 2000 years ago.

History

Spotted in 1792 by a Lieutenant Broughton under explorer Vancouver's command, Mount Hood was named for British admiral Lord Hood. In 1845 Sam Barlow laid out Oregon's first toll road around the south base of Mount Hood, leading Oregon Trail wagons from The Dalles to Sandy over Barlow Pass. The route spared settlers the dangers of a raft trip down the Columbia River's rapids, but subjected them to the miseries of Laurel Hill, 3 miles west of Government Camp, a slope so steep wagons had to be skidded down with wheels removed.

A 4-mile section of the Barlow Road over Laurel Hill was rebuilt as a hiking and equestrian trail by the CCC in 1935. Other Depression-era work projects include the artistically designed Timberline Lodge and the Timberline Trail with its scenic stone shelters.

HIKING & BACKPACKING

The marvels of Mount Hood are so close to Portland that overuse is a real

(See Area 1 Map)
Red Hill
Kinnikinnick ▲$
Laurance Lk
2810
Parkdale 5 mi
Hood River 16 mi

35

2940
× 3250'
× 3950'

Branch
Branch
Branch

1650
× 4520'

Mazama Trail
The Pinnacle

Coe
Eliot
Wallalute Falls

3512
Cooper Spur
P
Polallie
A

Clear Cr
Ladd Cr
Vista Ridge
Barrett Spur
Elk Cove
★
F
H
Cairn Basin 5690'
Cloud Cap Saddle
A
× 4000'
3000' ×
Cr

Tamanawas Falls
★
Sherwood
▲$

Cathedral Cr
Ridge
McNeil Pt 6050'
★
Bridge out
6000'
A
Tilly Jane
A
Pollalie

Mt
Hood
Wilderness
Coe Gl

★ 6200'
Ridge
Sandy Glacier
Coe Gl
Eliot Gl
Cooper Spur
★
8514'
× 1
Newton Clark Gl

North
Fork
Cold Spring Cr

Nottingham ▲$

Reid Gl
11,240'

G
Illumination Rock 9543'
Mt Hood ★
Newton Clark Gl
Gnarl Ridge
6800' ×

Bluegrass Ridge

Paradise Park ★
5600'
Palmer Glacier
Clark Cr
Newton Cr
Trail

J ★
Elk Meadows
A

Canyon
Little Zigzag Canyon
Silcox Hut
Timberline Lodge 6000'
★
E
Timberline
Mt Hood Meadows
Umbrella Falls
5200'
5200' ×
Elk Mtn 5600'

Robin Hood
P

Summit
▲$
Alpine
PCT
Salmon R
35

P
P
5200'
P
Teacup L
× 4300'
East Fork
Pocket Cr

Badger Creek Wilderness
(See Area 4 Map)

Still Cr
▲$
Snow Bunny
P
P
4157' Barlow Pass
Bennett Pass 4674'

White River
48

3550

Badger Lk
A

Camp Windy
A

26
▲$
Trillium Lk
Maupin 43 mi
A Devils Half Acre

concern. The many meadows, with their wildflower displays and mountain views, have had to be protected by a complete ban on camping. Backpackers must seek out less fragile sites in forested areas—and even the forested "islands" in Elk Meadows and Elk Cove have been placed off-limits to tents or

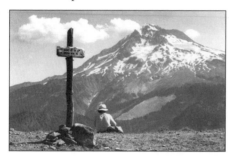

Mt. Hood from East Zigzag's trail junction.

fires. The small lakes of Zigzag Mountain, popular for their reflections of Mount Hood, are included in a general ban on camping within 200 feet of any lake's or stream's shoreline. Camping is not allowed within 500 feet of popular Ramona Falls, and fires are forbidden within 500 feet of McNeil Point—to save the gnarled dead wood at timberline for its own beauty.

This list of relatively crowded areas, however, also reads as a list of the wilderness area's top attractions, worth visiting

for day hikers or careful backpackers.

Start with Ramona Falls, a moderate, 7.1-mile loop hike from Road 1825 through the sparse forest along the Sandy River to a mossy, 100-foot falls on a stairstepped cliff of columnar basalt. If you're backpacking, head for a designated camping area just south of the falls.

A comparable, but less well known day hike on the east side of Mount Hood leads an easy 1.9 miles from the East Fork Trailhead by Sherwood Campground to 100-foot Tamanawas Falls.

The prime backpacking trip through Hood's alpine meadows is the 39.3-mile Timberline Trail, a three- to five-day trek usually begun at Timberline Lodge and undertaken clockwise around the mountain, so as to finish up at the showers and swimming pool (suit rentals available) at the classic old lodge. Five unbridged creek crossings on the route can be hazardous in the high water of June and July snowmelt: Zigzag River, Sandy River, Muddy Fork, Eliot Branch, and White River. Water is lower in August and during the mornings. Until a washed out bridge is rebuilt over the Eliot Branch, perhaps by 2014, that crossing is closed, with a 20-mile detour.

No fewer than 21 trails lead up the flanks of Mount Hood to the Timberline Trail, making all manner of loop hikes and day trips possible. Many of these

Mount Hood from the private Cloud Cap Inn on Cooper Spur.

Cooper Spur and the Eliot Glacier from the air (photo by Paul Scurlock for the Mazamas).

tributary trails ascend ridges that are scenic in their own right—notably Gnarl Ridge on Hood's east slope, the Zigzag Canyon Trail on the mountain's southwest slope, and the Pacific Crest Trail, Mazama Trail, and Vista Ridge Trail on Hood's north flank. This latter accesses Cairn Basin, a backpacking destination with an overused shelter and lots of quieter, off-trail places where you can hide a tent. All of these routes make excellent day trips for the fit hiker; distances average 3-5 miles one way with 2000-foot elevation gains.

Hikers who shy from such climbs can still sample the Timberline Trail's charms from two high-elevation trailheads. Timberline Lodge, set among wildflowers itself, is a good starting point for an easy 2.2-mile traverse to Zigzag Canyon, an impressive 1000-foot-deep erosional gash into Hood's volcanic scree. Continue another 1.8 miles west to spectacular Paradise Park, where open slopes of wildflowers are so fragile that backpackers are encouraged to seek out tent sites on sand or pine needles.

On the mountain's northeast flank, Cloud Cap Saddle Campground touches the Timberline Trail amidst 6000-foot-elevation meadows.

The adventurous hiker can climb well above timberline to view Hood's glaciers close-up at several points. By far the highest trail is 8514 feet up Coo-per Spur, overlooking Eliot Glacier, 3.9 miles from Cloud Cap Saddle.

A trail up from Timberline Lodge passes the Silcox Hut (a European-style hut with cafe and bunks) before petering out at the 8000-foot level. Yocum Ridge and the McNeil Point shelter are atop other very scenic, high trails. Barrett Spur's viewpoint is a cross-country scramble above the Timberline Trail on the less visited north side of Mt. Hood near Elk Cove. The high terrain near Elk Cove is a particularly nice backpacking destination. Although Elk Cove is so crowded it has designated campsites, there are plenty of sandy ridges nearby to hide a tent. Climbing beyond these points is technical, requiring special gear and climber registration.

West of Mount Hood, Zigzag Mountain is another popular hiking center, with four lakes, two lookout tower sites (West and East Zigzag), and six trailheads. The Devils Canyon trailhead provides the gentlest grades up to the area's best viewpoints—2.5 miles to West Zigzag and 4 miles to East Zigzag—but the access road is pretty rough.

A popular 3.4-mile trail up Lost Creek climbs to Burnt Lake, with a ridgetop view 1.2 miles beyond. Use is heavy here, so backpackers are limited to designated sites and space is tight on weekends.

East of Hood, Elk Meadows is another

popular destination, with its fine mountain view. From Highway 35, reach the meadow's three-sided shelter either up the 3-mile trail from the Mount Hood Meadows ski area or along the heavily forested 6.2-mile Cold Spring Creek Trail from the Polallie Picnic Area. If you're backpacking, camp in the woods away from the meadows and do not build a campfire. One of the best hikes for a foggy, viewless day is the 4.1-mile East Fork Hood River Trail, a level forest walk between the washed-out Robin Hood Campground and the bridge at Sherwood Campground.

Most equestrian use in the wilderness begins at the horse-loading facilities at Riley Campground, west of Mount Hood. Signs mark the fragile or hazardous trails closed to pack and saddle stock, including the non-PCT portion of the Timberline Trail, Mazama Trail, Vista Ridge, Pinnacle Ridge, Elk Cove, Paradise Park Loop, Castle Canyon, Yocum Ridge, Burnt Lake, and the north half of the Ramona Falls loop.

CLIMBING

First climbed in 1857, Mount Hood has become the second most climbed snow peak in the world—after Japan's sacred Mount Fuji. Portland's outdoor club, the Mazamas, was organized in 1894 by 193 climbers who convened on the summit in inclement weather. Hood has been scaled by a woman in high heels, a man with no legs, and a gibbon named Kandy. In 2004, speed climber Dan Howitt raced from Timberline to the summit in one hour, 56 minutes, and 39 seconds.

But Hood is still a technical climb, over crevassed glaciers and loose, rotten rock. Lack of caution, and the area's volatile weather, have given Hood one of the highest accident rates of any peak in the country. An ice ax, crampons, and rope are essential; helmets are recommended. All climbers must register either at Timberline Lodge or Cloud Cap Inn.

The easiest and most popular route to the top, the "South Side" route, proceeds at a true 5° compass bearing from the Silcox Hut to the Hot Rocks, a geothermal area between Crater Rock and Steel Cliff. A snow hogback north of Crater Rock leads to the summit wall, where a large crevasse must be circumvented before continuing to the summit. The climb takes 4 to 10 hours, and is begun in the pre-dawn dark to avoid the afternoon's slushy snow. A descent in poor visibility must be undertaken by compass. The tendency to return "straight down" often leads climbers southwest toward the dangerous chasm of Zigzag Canyon.

The second most common summit route, also rated level I-2, ascends the 45° snow slope above the Cooper Spur viewpoint on the mountain's east face. Avalanches can be a hazard here. There are twelve additional ascent routes varying in difficulty from I-3 to III-5.6.

Illumination Rock, a 9543-foot crag between the Reid and Zigzag Glaciers southwest of Hood's summit, offers some interesting climbing topography. Five level I routes, of classes 4 to 5.4, explore the rock's pinnacles and a summit "skylight" hole.

SNOWSHOEING & SKIING

Mount Hood offers the largest selection of snowshoe and Nordic ski routes in the state. Highways 26 and 35 are plowed in winter, providing access to five developed downhill ski areas and thirteen plowed sno-park lots. All of the downhill areas except Timberline Lodge rent cross-country skis.

From Timberline Lodge, snowshoers and Nordic skiers can traverse 2.6 miles to the brink of Zigzag Canyon on the PCT, or choose one of three heavily used routes for the 4-mile glide down to Government Camp. From Government Camp, numerous short trails lace the

Cliffs near West Zigzag's lookout site.

level area between Multorpor Meadows and the snowed-under Still Creek Campground. More advanced skiers can tackle the 6.3-mile Yellowjacket Trail, traversing from the junction of Highway 26 and the Timberline Lodge Road to the White River sno-park on Highway 35.

The site of former Snow Bunny Lodge, now a snow play center, is the starting point for the many Nordic routes on snowed-under roads around scenic Trillium Lake. The easiest trip is to Summit Meadows, north of Trillium Lake, where the graves of Barlow Road pioneers are marked by white crosses.

The winding, 2.4-mile section of old highway at Barlow Pass makes a pleasant ski route. The Giant Trees loop trail between the old and new highways explores an old-growth grove. Trailless exploration of the scenic White River Canyon is relatively easy from the White River sno-park on Highway 35.

Nordic ski routes from Bennett Pass head southeast along roads toward the Badger Creek Wilderness, crossing a steep slope known as the Terrible Traverse. From the parking lots of the nearby Mount Hood Meadows ski area, Elk Meadows makes a spectacular winter goal, but bring map and compass for safety on the 2.4-mile trail. The Robin Hood sno-park offers level, lower elevation skiing along the East Fork Hood River Trail, as well as on roads to the west, through Horsethief Meadows toward Bluegrass Ridge.

The Teacup Lake Nordic ski area just east of Bennett Pass (and across the road from the Hood River Meadows loop entrance) offers 20 kilometers of easy groomed Nordic ski trails for a suggested donation of $7 a day or $55 a year.

From the Cooper Spur Ski Area's sno-park, the challenging Cooper Spur Ski Trail climbs 1800 feet in 3 miles to the snowed-under Tilly Jane Campground. A more difficult return loop is possible on the Polallie Creek Trail.

Although there are no sno-parks on the west side of Mount Hood, the lower portion of Road 18 is typically snow-free, allowing access to good ski-touring country. Drive to the snow gate at McNeil Campground, then ski 5.7 miles east to beautiful Ramona Falls. Another trip from the snow gate tours 4 miles south up Road 382 into Horseshoe Canyon. In spring, when higher snow levels open Road 18 farther, drive to the snowline and continue on skis along Road 18 to Lolo Pass, where views open up in all directions. For a genuine challenge, ski the 9.2 miles back to McNeil Campground on Road 1828, around Last Chance Mountain.

Tamanawas Falls.

3

SALMON-HUCKLEBERRY & ROARING RIVER

Less than an hour's drive from Portland, this spacious wilderness remains relatively undiscovered. Hidden here are the delightful subalpine lakes of the Rock Lakes Basin and the spectacular Salmon River canyon. Yet the area's greatest charms are subtler: fog-draped ridgecrests of ripe huckleberries and lonely whitewater canyons lined with mossy maples.

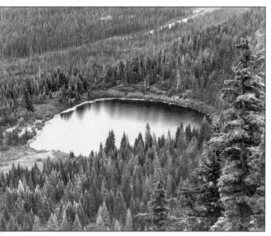

Mirror Lake from Tom Dick & Harry Mountain.

Climate

Trails below 2000 feet are usually snow-free in winter. Ridge trails and the PCT remain under snow from November to May. Spring and fall rains account for a share of the area's 80-inch annual precipitation. Summers are generally clear and dry.

Plants and Wildlife

Major runs of steelhead, Chinook, and coho salmon return annually to the aptly named Salmon River. The Roaring River's thunderous torrent is home to hardy anadromous fish as well, while every stream and lake of size in the area supports brook trout and rainbow trout.

Black bear and mule deer rely on the area's extremely rugged, snowless lower canyons for winter range. The large, trailless upper Roaring River valley shelters several shy wildlife species, including cougar, badger, fisher, and marten. Listen for the flute-like call of the hermit thrush in June and July. Water ouzels whir along streams year round.

The dense western hemlock and Douglas fir forests of the canyon bottoms are interspersed with droopy-branched western red cedar and red alder. Creekside vine maple adds brilliant scarlet foliage in fall. Rare Alaska cedar can be found on the fringes of Salmon River Meadows.

Ridgetops are mostly open, decorated in June with the white plumes of beargrass. The area's famed huckleberries, once the goal of annual harvest treks by Indians and pioneers

Location: 32 mi SE of Portland

Size: 164 sq mi

Status: 96 sq mi designated wilderness (1984, 2009)

Terrain: densely forested river canyons, ridges, lake basins

Elevation: 980'-5159'

Management: Mount Hood NF

Maps: Salmon-Huckleberry Wilderness (USFS); Mt. Hood Wilderness (Geo-Graphics)

alike, ripen in late August. The blue fruit is most abundant around Veda Lake, and on Indian Ridge, Huckleberry Mountain, Old Baldy, and Devils Peak.

Geology

The ridges of this area belong to the Old Cascades, a broad volcanic mountain range that erupted 10 million years before the High Cascades, and which now forms the rugged western foothills for those taller, snow-capped peaks. Devils Peak and Salmon Butte are probably remnants of once-tall volcanoes, but the erosive power of water and ice have reduced them to ridges. Broad, U-shaped glacial valleys, now filled with meadows and lakes, are recognizable at Rock Lakes, Squaw Lakes, Plaza Lake, and Serene Lake.

HIKING & BACKPACKING

Two very easy day hikes with views of Mount Hood are the 1.2-mile Veda Lake Trail (8 miles south of Government Camp on Road 2613) and the 1.4-mile trail that climbs 700 feet to Mirror Lake (1 mile west of Government Camp on Highway 26). Mirror Lake makes such a convenient backpacking goal that only 6 campsites are designated, and they fill quickly on weekends. An additional 1.8-mile climb gains the panoramic view atop Tom Dick & Harry Mountain.

The lower Salmon River Trail, paralleling Road 2618 for 2.6 miles, makes another pleasant warm-up trip, and is one of the closest places to Portland to see the big trees of an ancient forest. With lots of trailheads on Road 2618 you can choose your trip length. It's also fun to car camp by the trail at Green Canyon Campground.

The Salmon River Trail upriver of Green Canyon Campground traces a wilder canyon. The trail ambles amidst massive old-growth trees for the first 2 miles to Rolling Riffle's 10 designated backpacking campsites (where space is tight on weekends). Then the path climbs several hundred feet above the river, traversing steep slopes with viewpoints. The roar audible from the second viewpoint (3.8 miles in) is caused by a series of hidden waterfalls, but avoid the dangerous 0.2-mile scramble trail descending toward a slippery

Eagle Creek's valley in the Salmon-Huckleberry Wilderness.

SALMON–HUCKLEBERRY
ROARING RIVER

0   1   2mi
0   1   2   3km
N

Portland 32 mi
Road Closed   ×2920'
Wildwood
Wemme 1337'
Zigzag
Boulder Ridge
Camp Arrah Wanna
Welches
2518
Hunchback
Boulder Cr
McIntyre Ridge
1420' ×
Salmon R
36
2150' ×
×1600'
Douglas Trail
105
×3560'
Huckleberry Trail
Salmon–
Mtn
4200'
Bonanza Mine
Cheeney
Cr
Eagle
Eagle Creek
Wildcat Mtn 4480'
Green Canyon
1600' ×
Old Baldy 4209'
Coffman
Huckleberry
2380'
Salmon
Cr
Mtn
3400'
South
Fork
Plaza
Salmon
Salmon
Cr
Bighorn Cr
4614
Fork
4000' ×
G
Sheepshead Rock
Wilderness
River
Twin Spr
4219'
Salmon Butte 4877'
Squaw Mtn 4771'
Squaw Lakes
Plaza L
Mack Hall Cr
Dry
4610
G
Plaza Cr
Salmon L
G
×4290
Lookout Springs 3981'
River
Cr
Roaring
Cougar Cr
Huxley Lk 2552'
N
Shining Lk 3893'
Splinter
River
Signal Buttes
4611
1520'
South
Indian
Wilderness
5159 ×
Estacada 18 mi
Roaring River
×1020'
×4040'
Fork
Ridge
240
Roaring
Grouse Pt 4554'
Serene
Lower Rock L
G
Frazier 4666'
Sunstrip
M
Pup Creek Falls
224
Rock Lakes Basin
Pyramid Lk
The Narrows
Clackamas R
5830
Three Lynx
4635
Cache Mdw 4386'
Shellrock Lk
(See Area 6 Map)
×4267'
Cripple Cr Lk
Hideaway Lk

viewpoint where a fatal accident occurred. Ambitious backpackers can hike onward and upward to other trailheads. (Kinzel Lake is another 4.3 miles; Linney Creek, 5; Fir Tree, 10.7; and Mud Creek Road 309, 10.6).

The 7.7-mile Rock Lakes Basin loop trail offers the attractions of a High Cascades hike without the crowds. The loop passes three lakes (all good backpacking goals), a clifftop viewpoint, and the ruin of Cache Meadow's log shelter. Side trails plunge toward the Roaring River.

To reach the trailhead at Frazier Turnaround, take Highway 224 southeast of Estacada 26 miles, turn left just after the bridge at Ripplebrook onto Road 57, turn left again after 7.4 miles onto Road 58, head left after another 6.9 miles onto paved Abbott Road 4610 for 1.3 miles, and then go straight on rough, dirt Road 240 for 4.4 slow miles to its end.

From the same trailhead, try the 1.3-mile jaunt down to Shellrock Lake. Or you could drive back 0.2 mile to the primitive Frazier Fork Campground and hike an ancient roadbed 4.3 miles out a relatively ridge to Shining Lake, another good backpacking goal.

The Salmon-Huckleberry Wilderness has no fewer than five panoramic ridges with trails. Most of these hikes begin with long climbs. The closest to Portland is Wildcat Mountain, a 2.2-mile trip on the Douglas Trail gaining just 800 feet. Wildcat Mountain's summit is some-

what overgrown, but excellent viewpoints are about a mile north or south along the ridgecrest trail.

Although the drive to this trailhead is mostly paved, it can be confusing. From exit 12 of Interstate 205, take Highway 224 toward Estacada 14 miles, turn left on SE Wildcat Mountain Road for 3.8 miles, ignore a turnoff for Eagle Fern Park to the right, and in another 2.7 miles go straight at an X-shaped junction. Continue straight 9.5 miles to a fork. Veer right 200 yards, fork left for 0.7 mile, and then fork right on gravel 0.3 mile to the far end of a gravel pit (GPS location N45°18.045' W122°03.914').

Two good routes ascend Huckleberry Mountain—the Boulder Ridge Trail from the parking area at the BLM's Wildwood Recreation Site, and the Bonanza Trail, which starts along Cheeney Creek and climbs past an old mine's tunnel. Park along paved Welches Road and walk across a Salmon River bridge 0.2 mile to the "trailhead," where parking is forbidden.

The panorama from the historic, unstaffed lookout tower on Devils Peak is another worthy hiking goal. It can be reached either by the grueling 4.1-mile Cool Creek Trail from Road 2612, the 5.7-mile Green Canyon Trail from Road 2618, or the 8.1-mile Hunchback Ridge Trail from the Zigzag Ranger Station. Since all these routes gain over 3000 feet in elevation, it's tempting to take the easy 1.2-mile trail from near Kinzel Lake instead, even though this requires a bone-jarring 10-mile drive to the end of rutted dirt Road 2613.

The views from the open, rocky summit of Salmon Butte are reached by a woodsy 4.4-mile trail climbing 2800 feet from a trailhead near the end of Salmon River Road 2618. The path passes glorious displays of pink rhododendron blooms in June.

Another ridgetop trail center is at primitive Twin Springs Campground;

The Salmon River near Green Canyon.

Mt. Hood from Trillium Lake, popular both with summer campers and with winter skiers.

drive 6.5 miles southeast of Estacada on Highway 224, then turn left on Road 4610 for 18.4 miles. Twin Springs is atop "The Plaza," a 1-mile-square plateau. Follow the Plaza Trail 1.4 miles north to the Sheepshead Rock viewpoint at the tip of The Plaza, then hike another 3.6 increasingly rugged miles northeast for the view on Salmon Mountain.

Roaring River is one of the wildest and most remote streams in northwest Oregon. Quiet trails switchback down from Twin Springs Campground (2.3 miles) and the end of Road 4611 (1.2 miles). No trails or easy bushwhacking routes follow the river itself through its rugged canyon.

The Eagle Creek Trail follows a rushing stream through a towering old-growth rainforest. A small meadow at 4.7 miles makes a logical stopping point for day hikers or backpackers. The drive to the trailhead is unsigned and extremely confusing. Drive Highway 224 to milepost 19 (west of Estacada 4 miles), take Wildcat Mountain Road 2 miles, continue straight on Eagle Fern Park Road 2.4 miles, veer right for 1.7 miles, go straight on George Road 6.3 miles, turn right onto SE Harvey Road 0.6 mile, turn left for 1.3 miles, fork right for 0.1 mile, fork right again for 0.6 miles, and hike an overgrown road down to the right.

SNOWSHOEING & SKIING

Three excellent snow recreation centers border the area. Most popular is the Snow Bunny sno-park on Highway 26, from which a wide variety of tours are possible into the Trillium Lake Basin. Several short trips are described in the Mount Hood entry. Longer tours follow Road 2613 for 5.5 miles to a view on the Veda Lake Trail, or prowl the roads and clearcuts along Mud Creek and Mud Creek Ridge. Numerous loop routes are possible by cross-countrying between roads — remember a compass and topographic map.

The second major Nordic area focuses on four sno-parks, located 0.5, 1.5, 2.7, and 4.4 miles south of Wapinitia Pass on Highway 26. The area features road tours around Frog Lake (see map on page 54) and Clear Lake. A short, often overlooked trip is the half-mile jaunt to spacious Salmon River Meadows, 1.6 miles north of Wapinitia Pass on Highway 26, but hidden from the road by trees.

The high country southeast of Roaring River offers solitude for snowshoers and cross-country skiers. Head for the Ripplebrook Ranger Station 26 miles southeast of Estacada on Highway 224. Winter plowing extends as far as the Silvertip Work Center (not on map; 3 miles up Road 4630 from Ripplebrook) so after heavy snows, tours start there.

4

BADGER CREEK & BONNEY BUTTE

Draped across the eastern foothills of Mount Hood, the Badger Creek canyonlands form the remarkable transition zone between High Cascade forest and Columbia Plateau steppe. To the west lie Boulder Lake, Bonney Butte, and a patch of the Mt. Hood Wilderness that includes the lovely Twin Lakes.

Climate

East of the Cascade crest, Badger Creek is often sunny when western Oregon suffers from drizzle. Though the area measures just 14 miles end to end, the annual precipitation ranges from 80 inches on the windy western ridges to 20 inches in the dry eastern lowlands. Snows close the lower trails from December to March. The ridges' relatively light winter snowpack melts from the highest trails by mid-June. Afternoon thunderstorms occasionally interrupt hot summer days.

Plants and Wildlife

The higher elevations share the alpine rock gardens and Hudsonian forests of Mount Hood, but the eastern lowlands are part of a pine-oak biologic zone unique in Oregon wilderness. This

Location: 65 mi E of Portland, 44 mi SE of The Dalles

Size: 67 sq mi

Status: 48 sq mi designated wilderness (1984, 2009)

Terrain: forested canyons

Elevation: 2100'-6525'

Management: Mount Hood NF

Maps: Badger Creek Wilderness (USFS); Mount Hood, Flag Point (Green Trails)

Badger Lake.

open, park-like ecosystem of ponderosa pine and Oregon white oak extends only a short distance north and south of the Columbia River between Hood River and The Dalles.

Nowhere is the pine-oak zone's spring wildflower display as spectacular as on the School Canyon Trail, west from road 27 over Ball Point. Tall, purple larkspur bloom in mid-April, with pink shooting star in damp areas. By late May, great fields of lupine turn the hillsides blue, splashed yellow in places by balsamroot. By July, white death camas and purple onion remain among yellow, withered grass.

By late July the wildflowers of the pine-oak zone are gone, but the rock gardens of the alpine zone are at their peak. Amble along the Divide and Gunsight Butte Trails for penstemon, paintbrush, avalanche lilies, and stonecrop.

Geology

Volcanism from Mount Hood provided the raw material for this landscape. An Ice Age glacier scoured a curving, 2500-foot-deep, U-shaped valley from its cirque at Badger Lake down Badger Creek, leaving the dramatic cliffs below the Divide Trail. A second glacier cut the valley of Boulder Creek and left a cirque lake that has since filled in to become Crane Prairie.

HIKING & BACKPACKING

For an easy day trip on the Pacific Crest Trail (or a great backpacking trip with kids), hike 2.1 miles from the Frog Lake sno-park on Highway 26 to Twin Lakes. Ringed by forest with glimpses of Mt. Hood's peak, the two shallow, swimmable lakes are connected by a 0.7-mile trail and have shoreline loop paths.

The steep 2.4-mile route up to Gumjuwac

Saddle from a bridge on Highway 35 (between mileposts 68 and 69) offers good views of Mount Hood during its 1700-foot climb—and brings the hiker to the intersection of four Badger Creek trails suitable for longer treks.

Southeast of Gumjuwac Saddle, the Gunsight Trail parallels Road 3550 for 1.7 miles to the spectacular viewpoint on Gunsight Butte, passing ridgetop rock formations and rock gardens along the way. Due south of Gumjuwac Saddle is the 2.5-mile trail down to Badger Lake, a good backpacking goal.

A trail heading east from Gumjuwac Saddle drops 1300 feet in 2.2 miles to the Badger Creek Trail; from there, Bonney Crossing Campground is an enchanting 9.9-mile backpack downstream, past old-growth Douglas fir, green-pooled cascades, and finally, oak-fringed cliffs. Yet another trail from Gumjuwac Saddle climbs 2.2 miles northeast to 6525-foot Lookout Mountain's unmatched view.

An easier 1.3-mile route to Lookout Mountain starts off of Road 4410. To find this trailhead, drive Highway 44 between mileposts 70 and 71, turn east on paved Dufur Mill Road 44 for 3.8 miles, turn right on gravel High Prairie Road 4410 for 4.7 uphill miles, and turn left on High Prairie Road 200 yards.

Once you're atop Lookout Mountain, you can ramble east on a dramatic 3.9-mile portion of the Divide Trail to Flag Point's staffed fire lookout. The path is a

Flag Point's lookout can be rented in winter.

series of cliff-edge viewpoints, rock formations, and wildflower gardens.

To find the trailhead to Crane Prairie, in the lovely valley of Boulder Creek, take Highway 35 to Bennett Pass, drive 4 horribly rough miles on Road 3550, and veer right on Road 4891 for 0.3 mile. Another mile down Road 4891 is Bonney Meadows Campground, which offers several trails, including the pleasant 1.7-mile day hike to Boulder Lake.

On the eastern edge of the wilderness, four trails set out through the pine-oak forest. The 11.9-mile Badger Creek Trail to Badger Lake is more than a day hike, but worth it. The Little Badger Creek Trail fords its creek four times in the first 3 miles of its rugged canyon; crossings are easy except in early spring. Other trails climb to views at Ball Point and Pen Point. Access to the eastern Badger Creek trailheads is via Highway 197. At milepost 33, near Tygh Valley, turn west on Shadybrook Road for 1 mile. Then turn left on Fairgrounds Road for 1.1 mile and turn right on Badger Creek Road, which becomes Road 27.

SNOWSHOEING & SKIING

Popular snowshoeing and Nordic routes begin at a string of sno-parks along Highway 35, described in Area 2. If you're trekking into the Badger Creek Wilderness itself, start at Bennett Pass and follow Road 3550, but be warned that the route crosses a frightening slope known as the Terrible Traverse.

A fun trip from the Frog Lake sno-park on Highway 26 follows the PCT to Lower Twin Lake. A tougher loop continues to Frog Lake Buttes' viewpoint.

For an adventure, trek 6 miles from snowline on Road 2730 to the Flag Point Lookout, rentable in winter for $39 at *www.recreation.gov.*

Three private huts are available for winter rental south of the Barlow Pass sno-park 2 to 5 miles. The small, heatable cabins have 8 bunks and run about $150 a night (*www.cascadehuts.com*).

5
LOWER WHITE RIVER

The White River rages through a narrow rimrock canyon from the forests of Mt. Hood to the sagebrush savannah of Central Oregon.

Location: 65 mi SE of Portland

Size: 4 sq mi

Status: designated wilderness (2009)

Terrain: forested rimrock canyon

Elevation: 1680'-3250'

Management: Mt. Hood NF, Prineville District BLM

Map: Post Point (USGS)

Climate

Summers are hot and winters bring little snow in this canyon, with 30 inches of annual precipitation in the west and just 20 in the east.

Plants and Wildlife

The area provides critical winter habitat for deer and elk when Mt. Hood is under snow. Ponderosa pine forests in the west yield to grasslands in the east.

Geology

Mt. Hood's volcanism shaped this landscape, blanketing the terrain with lava flows and then pulsing glacial floodwaters through it to carve a steep, winding canyon. Lahars (hot mudflows) strip the canyon every few centuries, notably in 1781 and about 500 AD. The river looks milky because it carries glacial silt, rock ground by ice on Mt. Hood.

History

Sam Barlow scouted an Oregon Trail shortcut in 1845 that passed 2 miles north of here. The route became an important toll road to Oregon City.

HIKING & BACKPACKING

Rimrock and talus slopes block access to most of the canyon, but an unofficial trail explores the first mile of the canyon's upper end from Keeps Mill, a primitive, free, 5-site campground.

White River Falls, 13 miles downstream.

6
CLACKAMAS

The Clackamas Wilderness protects five widely separated patches of ancient forest, from the Clackamas River's headwaters almost to Estacada. Riverside trails and woodsy hideaways here are less than two hours from Portland.

The Narrows of the Clackamas River.

Climate

Summers are dry, but spring and fall are wet in this mossy rainforest, with 60 inches of annual precipitation in the Clackamas River's inner canyon and 120 inches in the hills, much of it as winter snow. Trails above 4000 feet are under snow from mid-November to mid-June.

Plants and Wildlife

Three-foot-long salmon struggle up

Location: 18 mi SE of Estacada, 42 mi SE of Portland

Size: 38 sq mi

Status: 15 sq mi designated wilderness (2009)

Terrain: river canyon, forested ridges

Elevation: 1000'-5618'

Management: Mt Hood NF

Maps: Bedford Pt, Fish Cr Mtn, Pinhead Buttes, and others

---

the Clackamas each October to spawn in pebbly river bars. The entire Fish Creek drainage—once heavily roaded and logged—has been set aside as fish habitat. Forest is reclaiming the abandoned logging roads there.

Geology

Most of the hills are heavily eroded remnants of the Old Cascades (16 to 25 million years old), but Sisi Butte is a much fresher, strikingly pyramidal volcano of the High Cascades.

HIKING & BACKPACKING

Start with a couple of hikes along the Clackamas River. The Clackamas River Trail traces the shore for 7.8 miles from Fish Creek Road 54 to Indian Henry Campground. Midway along the route (GPS location N45°08.93' W122°06.22') look for a 0.2-mile side trail to 3-tiered, 100-foot Pup Creek Falls. If you're backpacking, head 1.3 miles upriver to a campable beach at The Narrows.

The 4-mile Riverside Trail is farther from Portland but more heavily used because it follows the river between two popular campgrounds, Rainbow and Riverside. The easiest parking for day hikers is at a marked trailhead 1.8 miles south of the bridge at Ripplebrook.

Memaloose Lake is a good goal for an easy day hike or a backpacking trip with kids. It's just 1.4 miles from Road 45 to the lake, but you can continue another mile to a former lookout site atop South Fork Mountain, with views from the Three Sisters to Mt. Rainier.

High Lake and the view on Fish

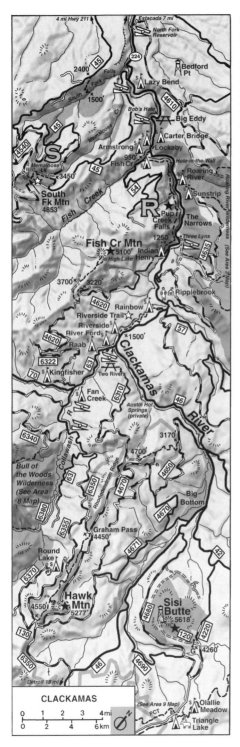

Creek Mountain are less visited because road washouts have made them harder to find. The new trail climbs 1.5 miles from Road 4620. When you reach an abandoned road on a ridgecrest, follow it north 0.5 mile to the pre-washout trailhead. Then it's 2.5 miles to High Lake or 2.2 miles to the summit.

The high point of the 10-mile Rhododendron ("Rho") Ridge Trail is Hawk Mountain, where a little lookout cabin has a great view of Mt. Jefferson. You can hike there in 2.1 miles from a trailhead to the south of the mountain. Drive to a 4-way intersection with Roads 6350 and 6355, go west on Road 6355 for 0.3 mile, and look for the trail opposite Road 130.

The area's best view, however, is atop Sisi Butte. Park at the gate of Road 120 and walk or bicycle 3 miles up the steep dirt road to the staffed lookout. Although the butte appears perfectly conical from the south, vanished Ice Age glaciers carved hidden bowls on the north flank. As a result there are actually two summits, 0.4 mile apart, and the tower is on the peak that's a foot shorter. So bushwhack northeast down to a forested saddle and then continue up to the taller summit, where open slopes allow views of Hood and Jefferson.

BOATING

Close to Portland, and famed for the Bob's Hole Whitewater Rodeo each spring, the Clackamas River is one of Oregon's most popular whitewater playgrounds. It's also the deadliest, averaging 5 to 10 fatalities a year.

The heavily used run downstream from the bridges at Three Lynx mostly has class 2 riffles, so many boaters are surprised by Hole-in-the-Wall, a class 4 chute that collides with a cliff and spins flotsam in an eddy. Beyond this lie a class 4 rapids at Carter Bridge and huge, fun waves at Bob's Hole.

Midway between Riverside and Indian Henry campgrounds is Killer Fang, an unrunnable, deadly suck hole.

7
TABLE ROCK

This pocket wilderness offers surprisingly quiet forest trails within a short drive of the populous Willamette Valley.

Climate

Summers are sunny, while other seasons are mild and wet (100 inches annual precipitation). Winter snows cover trails over 3000 feet from December to May.

Plants and Wildlife

The forests here are Douglas fir and western hemlock, with noble fir at higher elevations. Pink-blossomed rhododendron crowd upper slopes. The small, sparsely-petaled Gorman's aster found on rockslides is a federally-listed endangered species, as is Oregon sullivantia, a saxifrage of cliff seeps. White Clackamas iris, showy Washington lilies, and delicate calypso orchids are endangered primarily by flower pickers.

Geology

Fortress-shaped Table Rock is the remnant of a hard basalt lava flow that once capped the entire area. All local rocks date from the Old Cascades' eruptions 16 to 25 million years ago.

History

Table Rock was in the hunting

Location: 19 mi SE of Molalla, 50 mi S of Portland
Size: 9 sq mi
Status: 9 sq mi designated wilderness (1984)
Terrain: forested ridges
Elevation: 1300'-4881'
Management: Salem District BLM
Maps: Rooster Rock, Gawley Creek (USGS)

grounds of the Northern Molalla, a small tribe confined to the rugged foothills between the Willamette Valley and the High Cascades. Because the Molalla spoke a Sahaptin language similar to that of the Nez Perce, they are thought to have been driven from an Eastern Oregon homeland centuries ago to this unlikely range.

The east-west trail from the Molalla River to Pechuck Lookout is a remnant of a Molalla trail leading from the lowlands to Bull of the Woods and the High Cascades. Three archeological sites—evidently Molalla camps—have been identified in the area.

HIKING & BACKPACKING

Start with a 3.6-mile hike that gains 1500 feet to a sweeping wilderness viewpoint atop Table Rock's cliff. From the landslide on Table Rock Road, the route follows the closed road 1.3 miles. From there a trail heads into the woods, winds about the impressive columnar basalt cliffs of Table Rock's north face, and switchbacks up the gentler west slope. The panorama extends from Mount

Rooster Rock.

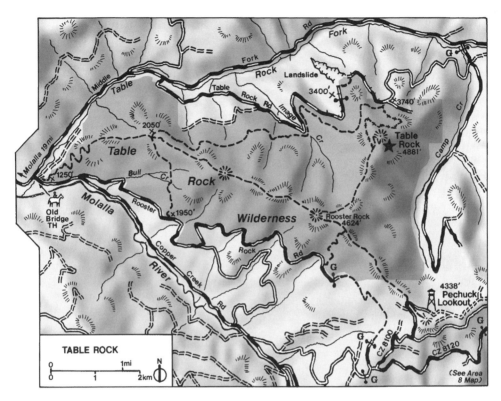

Rainier to the Three Sisters, including views into the Bull of the Woods Wilderness and the Willamette Valley.

Rooster Rock, an additional 1.4 miles by trail from Table Rock, affords similar views, and protrudes from a scenic heather-topped ridge. The hiker who has planned a car shuttle can continue past Rooster Rock on this ridge to the Old Bridge Trailhead on the Molalla River—an 8.8-mile trip in all. Pechuck fire lookout, a rare two-story stone structure from 1932, is another good goal.

There are no reliable water sources on the area's trails. Equestrians will want to avoid the rough rock talus slope directly north of Table Rock.

All trailheads are reached via the town of Molalla, 30 miles south of Portland. Take Highway 211 half a mile east of Molalla, turn south onto South Mathias Road for 0.3 mile, turn left on South Feyrer Park Road for 1.6 miles, and then turn right onto South Dickey Prairie Road. Follow this road past several jogs 5.3 miles to a poorly marked junction with South Molalla Forest Road. Turn right on a bridge across the Molalla River and follow the paved road 12.8 miles to a junction with Middle Fork Road. The low-elevation Old Bridge Trailhead is a stone's throw to the east. To find the upper trailhead, veer left onto gravel Middle Fork Road for 2.6 miles, and turn right on Table Rock Road for 4.4 miles to a landslide, the current trailhead. There are no parking fees.

Snowshoeing & Skiing

From December through March it is pleasant to drive to snowline on Table Rock Road, park to one side, and ski up the road and Table Rock trail to the base of Table Rock's ice-encrusted cliffs for the view. The distance varies from 3 to 4 miles, depending on the snow level.

8

Opal Creek & Bull of the Woods

Hidden high in the Cascade foothills, these adjacent wilderness areas feature ancient forests, subalpine mountains, wild rivers, and a dozen lakes. The rustic, free bath house at Bagby Hot Springs, with its cedar-log tubs, is the area's number one destination.

Sawmill Falls, on the trail to Opal Creek.

Climate

Only the Opal Creek Trail is usually open all winter. Other trails below 3000 feet are generally snow-free from April into December, and the highest trails are clear from June through October. Despite over 100 inches of annual precipitation, summers are sunny.

Plants and Wildlife

This area is one of the last great ancient forest reserves of Western Oregon. Towering Douglas fir, western hemlock, and western red cedar remain in the valleys, with a complex ecosystem of lichens, birds, insects, and mosses. Elegant white trillium and yellow-clustered Oregon grape bloom in the deep forest in April. Tangles of rhododendrons erupt in pink blossom in June.

Here the patient observer may sight a northern spotted owl, the huge, shy bird threatened by reductions in its old-growth habitat. By day the owl remains in its nest, high in the resprouted top of a broken conifer—or it may perch like an 18-inch-tall, earless statue on a branch near the trunk, where the owl's mottled, white-spotted feathers camouflage it perfectly against the tree's bark. At night, however, this owl glides through the forest on its three-and-a-half-foot wingspan, catching wood rats, mice, and flying squirrels. In the dark it answers readily to its own imitated call, a high-pitched "hoo, hoo-hoo."

Geology

Erosion has uncovered quartz veins containing small amounts of copper and silver in the 16- to 25-million-year-old "Old Cascades" here. The Elkhorn Mining District, which once brought a rush

Location: 68 mi SE of Portland, 64 mi E of Salem

Size: 80 sq mi

Status: 69 sq mi designated wilderness (1984, 1996, 2009)

Terrain: densely forested mountain ridges, valleys

Elevation: 2000'-5710'

Management: Mount Hood NF, Willamette NF

Maps: Bull of the Woods Wilderness (Geo-Graphics), Battle Ax (Green Trails)

of prospectors to the area, survives in the Jawbone Flats mining camp along Opal Creek. In the northern end of the wilderness, pioneer miner Robert Bagby blazed a trail from Bagby Hot Springs to his Pansy Blossom Mine, named for its colorful ore. The mine entrance is still visible above Pansy Lake.

Ice Age glaciation carved the area's many bowl-shaped lake valleys. A vanished Ice Age glacier carved Elk Lake's basin and polished the smooth bedrock visible along the trail on the eastern slope of Battle Ax.

Big Slide Mountain from Big Slide Lake.

HIKING & BACKPACKING

This wilderness has ample room for satisfying two- and three-day backpacking trips, yet it is small enough to be explored by day hikers as well.

Start with a stroll into the Opal Creek Wilderness from the locked gate on Road 2209, following an old mining road (now a broad trail) amid giant 400-year-old Douglas firs. After 2 miles, Merten Mill, a defunct sawmill's site, offers a campable meadow and a deep, swimmable pool by broad Sawmill Falls.

For a 7.1-mile loop, continue 0.2 miles past Merten Mill, keep right at a fork in the road, cross the river, and take the rough Opal Creek Trail 1.4 miles to an overlook of Opal Pool's scenic gorge. Then keep left to cross a footbridge and return on an old road through Jawbone Flats. Now an old-growth study center for the Friends of Opal Creek, the private cabins here, built 1929-1932, include four you can rent (*www.opalcreek.org*). For a longer hike up Opal Creek, continue upstream from Opal Pool 1.5 miles to Beachie Creek, just beyond a grove of ancient cedars, where the trail peters out.

To find the Road 2209 trailhead for Opal Creek, drive east of Salem 23 miles on Highway 22 to Mehama's second flashing yellow light, and turn left on Little North Fork Road for 15 paved miles and an additional 1.3 miles of gravel. At a fork, veer left on Road 2209 for 6 miles to the gate.

In the adjacent Bull of the Woods Wilderness, the most popular day trip is the easy, 1.5-mile hike through a huge old-growth forest to Bagby Hot Springs. Although the hot springs' shake-roofed bath house burned in 1979 when night bathers left a candle lit, the 8-foot cedar log tubs were too waterlogged to burn, and have been installed in an even larger bathhouse, built by volunteers. A resident ranger enforces a ban on camping from the trailhead to a quarter mile beyond the springs. Visit in mid-week to avoid crowds.

To find the hot springs' trail from Estacada, drive Highway 224 southeast 26 miles to the bridge by Ripplebrook Campground, veer right onto Road 46 for 3.6 miles, continue to the right on Road 63 another 3.5 miles, then turn left on Road 70 for 6 miles. Break-ins are not uncommon for cars left at this trailhead.

Pansy Lake is another rewarding, easy goal, also for backpackers. A 1.2- mile trail traverses a grove of big Douglas fir to the swimmable lake in a forested cirque. The drive starts out the same as to the hot springs, but follows Road 63 for 5.6 miles before turning left onto Road 6340 for 7.8 miles; then turn right onto Road 6341 for 3.5 miles,.

Several outstanding, but more strenuous, day hikes seek out viewpoints. Chief among these is Bull of the Woods, the only area peak still topped by a lookout tower. Here the view across beargrass-dotted meadows stretches from Mount Rainier to the Three Sisters. Staffed only in times of extreme fire danger, the tower also serves as an emergency shelter. The Pansy Basin Trail extends to the Bull of the Woods lookout—a 3.8-mile route in all—but the Bull of the Woods Trail from Road 6340 (past the Dickey Peaks) climbs 1200 feet less and is half a mile shorter.

Two craggy peaks contend for the title of best viewpoint in the southern end of these wilderness areas: Battle Ax and Mount Beachie. To reach either, drive Highway 22 to Detroit, turn north for 4.4 miles on Breitenbush River Road 46, turn left onto Road 4696 for 0.8 mile, turn left onto Road 4697 for 4.7 steep miles, and turn left for 2 rough miles to the Elk Lake Campground entrance. The 1-mile dirt track from the campground to the trailheads at Beachie Saddle is too rough for most vehicles. Park and walk.

To the north from Beachie Saddle, a 1.6-mile trail switchbacks up to the clifftop views at Battle Ax's old lookout site, gaining 1200 feet elevation. The lookout's old water trail continues north, making a loop trail possible back to the Elk Lake Campground—a pleasant 6.5-mile hike in all.

To the southwest from Beachie Saddle, a 5.6-mile trail traverses a lovely ridge topped by Mount Beachie, gaining just 900 feet to reach views of Elk Lake, Mount Jefferson, and beyond.

Whetstone Mountain, a former lookout site in the seldom visited northwest

The Bull of the Woods lookout tower.

edge of the wilderness, is the quietest viewpoint of all. The easiest route up, a 2.4-mile trail on the mountain's north flank, begins on Road 7020, 9 miles south of the Bagby Hot Springs trailhead.

A much more arduous trail up Whetstone Mountain—gaining 3000 feet in 4.5 miles—is the route of choice for some hikers because of its easier trailhead access from Salem. From the gate on Road 2209, hike half a mile up the old mining road toward Jawbone Flats and turn left up a spur road along Gold Creek half a mile to the trail.

Another good old-growth forest walk follows an easy 4-mile trail from Elk Lake to the site of the former Battle Creek shelter, where two woodsy streams join.

Just south of the wilderness, hike a mile up a closed road to the view at Gold Butte, where you can rent a restored 1934 lookout for $40 (*www. recreation.gov*).

Most of the small, scenic lakes in the Bull of the Woods Wilderness are just far enough from trailheads to be the destinations either of very challenging day hikes or pleasant overnight trips. For instance, the Welcome Lakes are 5 miles in and 2000 feet up from the Road 6380 trailhead—a rugged 10-mile day hike through old-growth forest. But backpackers can pitch a tent near Upper Welcome Lake and still have energy left to hike another mile up to the Bull of the Woods lookout, or to prowl the interesting ridges and meadows on nearby trails.

Likewise, Big Slide Lake is 5.5 miles in and 2300 feet up the rhododendron-lined Dickey Creek Trail from Road 6340-140. A base camp at the lake allows backpackers to continue out Big Slide Mountain's ridge to Lake Lenore's cliff-top cirque.

Another pretty lake destination is Silver King Lake. It's a 5.6-mile hike from Road 7020 along the Whetstone Mountain Trail's scenic ridgetop. Those who can arrange a short car shuttle can camp at the lake, then hike 7.7 miles down the Bagby Trail the second day through old-growth forest to Road 70, stopping at the hot springs for a dip on the way.

The Twin Lakes make a good hiking goal. Start out from Road 4697 near the Elk Lake Campground, climbing to a scenic ridgetop trail north of Battle Ax. Camp after 6.2 miles at Lower Twin Lake. The second day, stroll 5.3 miles to *Opal Creek.*

an easy camp at the site of the former Battle Creek shelter; then hike 4 miles farther for a loop back to Elk Lake.

Only the most determined bush-whackers can follow Opal Creek for 2 rough, trailless miles from Beachie Creek up to Opal Creek's headwaters at Opal Lake (not shown on the map), climbing around a spectacular waterfall below the lake's outlet. However, a much easier, 0.5-mile route to the marshy-edged lake follows a small trail down from gravel Road 2207. From Detroit, take French Creek Road 2223 for 4.2 miles and turn right on Road 2207 for 5 miles.

CLIMBING

Nasty Rock and a small unnamed pinnacle to the southwest offer some technical rock pitches. Many of the routes on these remote volcanic crags are untested. The rugged, up-and-down 4-mile trail route to Nasty Rock begins off Road 2209 a mile before the road's gate.

SNOWSHOEING & SKIING

Though roads are unplowed in winter, skiers park at snowline on Road 4697 and ski to Elk Lake. In spring the trip is usually 3 to 4 miles one way, with Beachie Saddle an additional 1.5-mile climb.

9
OLALLIE LAKE

In the shadow of Mount Jefferson, this forested plateau of 200 lakes and ponds is one of the more accessible portions of the Cascade's high country. Short, nearly level trails from seven developed campgrounds along Skyline Road 4220 lead to the larger lakes, while the open, lodgepole pine forests invite easy cross-country hikes to more remote lakeside campsites.

Monon and Olallie Lakes from Olallie Butte.

Climate

A very heavy winter snowpack keeps most trails, and Road 4220, closed from about mid-October to the first of July. As lingering snow melts during the peak wildflower month of July, mosquitoes are so profuse that headnets are advisable. By late summer, cross-country hikers may stumble on ground-nesting yellowjackets.

Plants and Wildlife

Huckleberry bushes provide a carpet beneath the forests of lodgepole pine and mountain hemlock. The best berries are in old burns. Watch for mink, otter, and eagles at the many fish-filled lakes.

Geology

This Cascade Range upland has been dotted by geologically recent cinder cones such as Olallie Butte and Potato Butte. A broad Ice Age glacial ice sheet left the many shallow lake basins. Look for glacier-polished bedrock at the north end of Monon Lake and along the PCT near Olallie Lake.

History

The Indians who once trekked here each fall to hunt deer and gather the abundant huckleberries named the largest lake Olallie—the Chinook jargon

Location: 80 mi SE of Portland, 69 mi E of Salem

Size: 36 sq mi

Status: 17 sq mi Forest Service scenic area, 14 sq mi Indian reservation

Terrain: forested, lake-dotted plateau

Elevation: 2100'-7215'

Management: Mount Hood NF, Confederated Tribes of Warm Springs

Maps: Olallie Scenic Area (USFS), Breitenbush (Green Trails)

Mt. Jefferson from Olallie Butte.

word for "berry." Seven bands of Central Oregon Indians were granted the eastern portion of this area when an 1855 treaty created the Warm Springs Indian Reservation.

HIKING & BACKPACKING

Short trails and frequent lakes make the area well-suited for beginning backpackers and families with young hikers. A good day hike for children is the 0.8-mile Russ Lake Trail from wildflower-filled Olallie Meadows. Hiking the shore trails around Olallie or Monon Lakes is also fun with children, and yields first-rate views of Olallie Butte and Mount Jefferson. It's 2.9 miles around Monon Lake (with 0.3 mile on a road), and 4.6 around Olallie Lake (including 1.6 miles along a road).

The pleasant 2.8-mile trail from Si Lake past cliff-rimmed Fish Lake and 73-foot-deep Lower Lake climbs 700 feet on its way to the Lower Lake Campground.

Good camping lakes appear at nearly every bend in the 5.7-mile Red Lake Trail between Road 380 and Olallie Lake. Worthwhile side trips to this east-west route are trails that climb to viewpoint peaks. It's 0.7 mile from Sheep Lake to the top of Potato Butte, and 1.2 miles from Top Lake to Double Peaks.

The most interesting section of the Pacific Crest Trail here is the 6.3 miles between Olallie Lake Guard Station and the PCT trailhead near Breitenbush Lake. At either end, this section follows cliffs and ridges with good views.

Olallie Butte has the best view of all, atop a trail climbing 2600 feet in 3.8 miles from an unmarked trailhead under the southernmost of three sets of powerlines. This is Indian land, so disturb nothing along the route. The former lookout site not only overlooks the entire Olallie Lake area, but it offers an eye-level view of Mount Jefferson and a long look into Central Oregon.

Cross-country hiking to trailless lakes avoids the crowds of the best hiking months, August and September. Beginners in the art of route-finding can practice their map and compass skills by bearing south from crowded Lower Lake to quiet Gifford Lake, or from Timber Lake to View Lake (the view is of Olallie Butte). Then try bushwhacking on compass bearings along the string of small lakes that form a 1-mile-diameter circle about the northern base of Double Peaks. It is difficult to become hopelessly lost anywhere in the area, because a trail or road is never more than a mile away.

Camping is prohibited within the

Olallie Butte from Olallie Lake.

Warm Springs Indian Reservation, except specifically at Breitenbush Lake. Anglers on reservation lands must have a state fishing license, a tribal fishing permit, and a copy of the Warm Springs fishing regulations. Violators are subject to a $200 fine or 90-day imprisonment.

To reach the Olallie Lake area from the north, follow Highway 224 and then paved Road 46 a total of 47.5 miles past Estacada. Turn left on paved Road 4690 for 8 miles, then turn right on gravel Road 4220 for 6 miles to Olallie Lake. Beyond Horseshoe Lake, Road 4220 becomes a very slow, badly rutted track, unsuited for trailer travel. The Fish Lake trailhead is only 6 miles from Highway 46; drive 3.4 miles up Road 4690, turn right on Road 4691, and follow signs.

Drivers approaching from Salem can take Highway 22 to Detroit, follow paved Road 46 for 17 miles, then turn right on treacherously rutted Road 4220 for 7.5 miles to Breitenbush Lake. Those without four-wheel drive should continue on paved Road 46 another 7 miles before turning right on Road 4690 toward Olallie Lake.

SNOWSHOEING & SKIING

Road 46, plowed in winter, allows cross-country ski access to the area's lakes via snowed-under Road 4220. Snowmobiles are allowed on these routes. The 7.5-mile distance to Breitenbush Lake makes an overnight trip in order, perhaps to one of the two shake-roofed, stone shelters beside the lake.

BOATING

A small resort at Olallie Lake rents rowboats, and Peninsula Campground offers a boat ramp. Canoeing is excellent because motors are prohibited on all of the area's lakes.

10
MOUNT JEFFERSON

Mount Jefferson is Oregon's second highest peak (after Mount Hood), and forms the centerpiece of Oregon's second most visited wilderness (after the Three Sisters). The top attractions are 150 mountain lakes, ranging from heavily visited, half-square-mile Marion Lake to the delicate tarns of Jefferson Park's popular alpine wildflower meadows. Three Fingered Jack, an impressive 7841-foot crag, dominates the southern end of the wilderness with its own collection of alpine lakes and meadows.

Mt. Jefferson's summit from the north.

Bald eagles are often sighted at lakes, waiting for an osprey to catch a fish — which the eagle will then steal.

Four forest types divide the area from west to east. The wetter western side has big Douglas fir in the lower valleys and mountain hemlock in the uplands. The dry eastern side of the range has lodgepole pine in the uplands and long-needled ponderosa pine in the Metolius Valley's lowlands.

The 2003 B & B Fire burned about a third of the wilderness, from Santiam Pass to Marion Lake, allowing wildflowers to bloom and huckleberries to prosper. Mountain hemlock and lodge-

Climate

Winter snows start early in November and total from 20 to 58 feet at Santiam Pass. The spring melt typically opens trails up to 3500 feet elevation by mid-May, up to 4500 feet by mid-June, up to 5500 feet by mid-July, and up to 6500 feet by August 1. Mosquitoes are troublesome for two to three weeks after the final snow melt in each region.

Storms occasionally interrupt clear, dry summer weather. The eastern slopes, with 40 inches annual precipitation, are often sunny even when the western slopes, with 100 inches precipitation, are lost in clouds.

Plants and Wildlife

Deer, elk, black bear, and coyotes are numerous enough to be seen frequently.

Location: 64 mi E of Salem, 37 mi NE of Bend

Size: 273 sq mi

Status: 174 sq mi designated wilderness (1968, 1984)

Terrain: glaciated peak, forested ridges, lake basins

Elevation: 2400'-10,497'

Management: Willamette NF, Deschutes NF, Mount Hood NF, Confederated Tribes of Warm Springs

Maps: Mt. Jefferson, Santiam Pass Winter Recreation (Geo-Graphics); Mt. Jefferson Wilderness (USFS); Mt. Jefferson, Whitewater River (Green Trails)

Entire areas of beargrass bloom every other year, perhaps synchronized by wildfires.

pole pine have reseeded their areas well on their own. Big ponderosa pines survived the fire, as they usually do. Except in the Eight Lakes Basin and at Square Lake, most lakeshore areas were too damp to burn. As a result, silver snags line the first mile or so of trails on the south and east sides of the wilderness, but most lake destinations are still green.

Fields of blue lupine and red paintbrush attract day hikers to Canyon Creek Meadows, Jefferson Park, the Eight Lakes Basin, and the Santiam Lake area in late July.

Also in July, the white, 4-foot-tall plumes of beargrass may be profuse, especially in open areas, old burns, and sparse lodgepole pine forests. This bunchgrass-like plant fills the wilderness with its fragrant blooms every other year. The two-year flower cycle may be a strategy to discourage seed-eating ground squirrels. Beargrass is a lily, and each bloom has hundreds of tiny, six-petaled flowers. Bears unearth and eat the plant's succulent root, which, when boiled, is said to make a substitute for soap. Indians gathered the plant's 2-foot-long leaves to weave baskets.

Geology

Mount Jefferson and Three Fingered Jack are both heavily eroded remnants of apparently extinct volcanoes. On Three Fingered Jack, only the hard lava plug, or central core, survives, flanked by ridges of the old volcano's subsidiary lava dikes. Mount Jefferson is also topped by a lava spire, but it is not the mountain's ancient plug. Glaciation has

removed the western third of the mountain, including the ancient summit. The current summit rock was once a flank lava flow.

Geologically recent cinder cones (including Pyramid Butte, South Cinder Peak, and Maxwell Butte) and two large 6500-year-old lava flows 6 miles southeast of Mount Jefferson prove that the area is not volcanically dead.

History

Lewis and Clark sighted Mount Jefferson from the mouth of the Willamette River in 1806 and named it after the president who had sent them on their expedition. Three Fingered Jack apparently won its name because its summit spires reminded pioneers of a renowned, mutilated cohort of California Gold Rush bandit Joaquin Murietta.

Two failed transportation routes across the Cascade Range left their mark on the wilderness here. Minto Mountain and Lake recall Salem pioneer John Min-

Three Fingered Jack from the PCT.

MT JEFFERSON

0   1   2mi
0   1   2   3km

N

Warm   Springs

Shitke

Camp Creek Butte

Lionshead 6110'

Whitewater

Bald Peter 6574'

Lava

Milk Cr

Parker Cr

Jefferson Cr

Lava

5905'

Indian   Reservation

L Sarah

Cr

River

Jefferson L

Hole-in-the-Wall Park

Harvey L

Kuckup Park

5470'
Table L

Patsy

Breitenbush Lk

×5650'

Jefferson Park

Whitewater Glacier

Waldo Gl

Goat Pk

The Table

Pacific

Pyramid Butte

Park Butte

6900

Russell

Scout L ×5800'

Jeff Park Gl

Mt Jefferson 10,497'

6100 ×

Cathedral Rocks

Hunts Cove

Hanks

4220

(See Area 9 Map)

Mt

Bays L

Russell Glacier

Jefferson

Hunts L

Bear Point 6043

Crest

Trail

5600'

Lizard

Ridge

Firecamp Lks

Claggett L

4852×

Crown L

3100×

R

Whitewater

Russell

Cr

4350'×

3884'

Pamelia Lake

Grizzly Pk 5799

Breitenbush

4700'

4080

Ridge

×4400'

3120×

Cr

Grizzly Cr

Minto Mtn

Minto Ridge

Bingham Cr

4685

S   Fork

×4400'

Cheat Cr

Boca Cave

2940

Woodpecker Ridge

040

2246

×4150'

2253

870

Spire Rk

5434'
Triangulation Peak

224

Creek

Pamelia

Marion Forks

Devils Pk ×4528

635

4960'
×

Whitewater

2450'

Breitenbush Hot Springs

2233

North   Santiam   River

Riverside

Estacada 60mi

46

Detroit 9mi

22

Detroit 9mi

(See Area 19 Map)

Camp Sherman

Canyon Creek $

Metolius R

1420

14

Abbot Creek $

12

1292

×3100'

Candle Cr

Sugarpine Ridge

Lava Cr

Cabot Cr

1230

Sheep Springs Horse Camp $

Jack Creek $

12

Sisters 12 mi

Canyon

1230

Head of Jack Creek

12

1210

Suttle Lk

G ×4570

Two Springs

1235

1234

4159×

1210

Bear Valley Cr

20

Cabot L

Brush Cr

5520' Carl L

Carl Lake 6380

FF

Rockpile

Jack Lake 5150' $

Round Lake 4500' $

Long L

PCT

Minto L

Wasco Lk

First Cr

Square L ×4800'

South Cinder Pk

HH

Minto Pass ×5400'

5500

CC Canyon Creek Meadows

Booth L

Wilderness

Swallow L

Three Fingered Jack 7841

PCT

Santiam

Prill L

Pass 4800'

Lake of the Woods

6500'

★

GG

P

BB ×4200'

Teto L

Eight Lakes Basin 5100'

5200'

Lower Berley L

Hogg Rk

Craig L

Marion Lake

Jorn Lk

Blue L

Red Butte

Santiam L

Lake Ann

Marion Falls

Marion Mtn 5351'

Mowich L 5077'

EE

Maxwell Butte 6229'

2255

×3360'

Temple L

Grenet L

Duffy L

Duffy Butte

Santiam R

Lost Lake $

Puzzle Cr

Turpentine Cr

Cleo L

Marion Cr

Gooch Falls

Swede Cr

P

Pine Ridge L 4526'

Twin Lakes

Camp Pioneer (Boy Scout)

4000' Mountain View Shelter

North Cr

20

126

Fir L

Santiam Cr

22

Albany 73 mi

2257

Fay L

2267

×3760'

Maxwell Sno-park

080

P

2261

Big Meadows Horse Camp $

22

(See Area 11 Map)

to, who urged in vain that a wagon road be built over Minto Pass in the 1870s.

The designated wilderness boundary between Santiam Pass and Lost Lake follows a bit of railroad grade built in 1888 by entrepreneur Colonel T. Egenton Hogg. Hogg dreamed of a transcontinental line from Corvallis east, but his London financiers doubted a crossing of Santiam Pass was feasible. Undaunted, he hired Chinese and Italian laborers to build 11 miles of grade, lay 300 feet of track, and pack a disassembled boxcar to the site. Mules pulled the car across the pass, allowing Hogg to tell his investors, straight-faced, that his train already had crossed the Cascades. The grade is still hikable from Santiam Lodge part way around the sheer cliffs of Hogg Rock.

HIKING & BACKPACKING

With 200 miles of trails, the Mount Jefferson area has room for plenty of day hikes and even week-long backpacking trips. The open high country and many off-trail lakes invite cross-country exploration as well—the surest way to find solitude.

At the most popular lakes, camping is permitted only at designated sites marked with a post. This restriction affects Square Lake, Duffy Lake, Pamelia Lake, and all the lakes in Jefferson Park. No campfires are permitted in Jefferson Park. Camping is banned altogether on Marion Lake's northwest peninsula, on the peninsulas of Scout and Bays Lakes, and within 100 feet of the high water mark of Marion, Pamelia, Hanks, and Hunts lakes. Campfires are banned within 100 feet of any water source. Livestock may not be tethered or picketed within 200 feet of any body of water. Wilderness rangers patrol the area. Camping is also banned within the Warm Springs Indian Reservation except at Breitenbush Lake. Hikers entering the reservation need written permission from the Confederated Tribes.

Among the easiest and most rewarding day hikes is the 2.2-mile trail from Road 2248 along a splashing creek under towering Douglas firs to Pamelia Lake. Because this trip is so popular with hikers and backpackers alike, this is the only part of the wilderness where visitors must obtain an entry permit in advance from the Detroit Ranger Station (call 503-854-3366 for details). Only 20 groups are issued permits for each day

Although fire burned over Duffy Butte in 2003, it left a ring of green around Duffy Lake.

Carl Lake is dammed on the east by a glacially carved, solid rock rim.

for the Pamelia Lake-Hunts Cove area, so plan ahead for summer weekends. In early June the lake is ringed with pink rhododendron blooms. The area's best mountain view is 2.8 miles beyond the lake, at the old lookout site atop Grizzly Peak, 1900 feet above the lake and breathtakingly close to Mount Jefferson.

Marion Lake is an easy 2.5-mile walk from Road 2255 along a wide and occasionally dusty path. Hikers can pack in inflatable boats or light canoes to sail the 360-acre, 180-foot-deep lake. Fishing is prohibited in inlet streams and in the outlet creek. Backpackers should not expect solitude anywhere near this lake.

Square Lake, in an area of silver snags with a dramatic view of Three Fingered Jack, is an easy 2.2-mile day hike either from the Pacific Crest Trail's Santiam Pass trailhead on Highway 20 or from the Round Lake Campground.

Wildflowers and a close-up view of Three Fingered Jack highlight the easy 4.5-mile loop to Canyon Creek Meadows from the primitive Jack Lake Campground at the end of Road 1234. To protect the fragile meadows, backpackers should pick campsites in the forest, out of sight of the trail. To limit encounters

on the trail itself, hikers are encouraged to hike the loop clockwise, returning past Canyon Creek's beaver ponds and a pair of 20-foot waterfalls. From the meadows, an additional 1.5-mile track leads steeply up a glacial moraine, past an ice-filled cirque lake, to a viewpoint saddle overtowered by Three Fingered Jack's summit pinnacles.

The fire lookout structures which once topped five peaks in this wilderness have been removed, but their panoramic views remain as enticing goals for invigorating day hikes. Bear Point's view of Mount Jefferson is 3.8 miles away, and 2900 feet up, from Road 4685, which joins Road 46 a mile east of Breitenbush Hot Springs.

Triangulation Peak is surrounded by several interesting rock spires and a cave. The huge mouth of Boca Cave, framing a view of Mt. Jefferson, can be reached by scrambling several hundred yards down the rugged east side of the summit. Because this protected archeological site is fragile, do not camp in the cave. Triangulation Peak is an easy 2.1-mile walk through the woods from the junction of Roads 2233 and 635. Some stout-hearted hikers prefer to start at the

Jefferson Park in April.

Cheat Creek trailhead on Whitewater Creek Road 2243 instead. The trail that begins there gains 2500 feet in 6.3 miles, passing a lovely meadow and a scenic ridge en route to Triangulation Peak.

Marion Mountain, the area's lowest lookout site, is a 2.8-mile side trip up from Marion Lake, or a 4.2-mile hike from the Camp Pioneer trailhead on Road 2261. Maxwell Butte, a cinder cone overlooking the Santiam Pass area, is 4.8 miles up from Road 080, off Highway 22 at the Maxwell Butte sno-park. At the dry trail's mid-point, Twin Lakes offer an irresistible swimming opportunity.

Another viewpoint worth the hike involves following the PCT 5.3 miles from Santiam Pass to Three Fingered Jack. After a 1600-foot climb the PCT crests a ridge with views south along the Cascades, then traverses almost directly below Three Fingered Jack's sheer west face.

Many of the wilderness' most spectacular areas are reached either by very long day hikes or by leisurely backpacking trips. The best example is Jefferson Park, a square-mile plain of lush wildflowers and swimmable alpine lakes set so close to Mount Jefferson that the snowy mountain seems to fill the sky.

Three routes reach Jefferson Park. The easiest trail climbs 5.1 miles from Whitewater Creek Road 2243 along a pretty ridge. The PCT also climbs to Jefferson Park, crossing 6900-foot Park Ridge along the way. That 5.6-mile route begins at the Skyline Road 4220 near Breitenbush Lake. A third, less used route to Jefferson Park climbs 6.2 miles along the South Breitenbush Trail from Road 4685.

Hunts Cove is a similar, but much smaller alpine basin on the south side of Mount Jefferson. The two main lakes, Hunts and Hanks, are 6.2 miles up from Road 2246 via Pamelia Lake. Hunts Cove is part of the Pamelia Lake limited entry area, so permits must be obtained

advance from the Detroit Ranger Station (call 503-854-3366 for details). Backpackers based at Hunts Cove can climb to the PCT and prowl the interesting crags of Cathedral Rocks.

Duffy, Mowich, and Santiam Lakes lie in a plateau of open lodgepole pine forests and small wildflower openings at the foot of Three Fingered Jack. From Road 2267, a 3.5-mile trail through mostly burned forest along the North Fork Santiam River reaches the unburned shore of Duffy Lake. Mowich Lake, with its large island, is another mile beyond. Santiam Lake is a 5.1-mile walk from Highway 20 at Santiam Pass.

Just 1.8 miles past Mowich Lake is the Eight Lakes Basin, a patchwork of meadows and silver snags renowned for its wildflowers, pretty lakes, and July mosquitoes. The five nearest trailheads are from 6.8 to 8.6 miles distant. If you arrange a car shuttle, you can see a different trail on the trip out.

Trails on the east side of the wilderness are often sunnier. They're also less used because of the longer gravel road access. A steep hike through burned woods gains 2100 feet in 5.4 miles to the PCT at Rockpile Lake, a lovely little pool with views and alpine rock gardens — and a popular stop for PCT backpackers. Start at the Bear Valley trailhead at

Mowich Lake from Red Butte.

the end of Road 1235 and keep right on the Two Springs Trail to the lake. For a 13.4-mile loop, return from the lake by heading south on the PCT 2.9 miles and keeping left.

Carl Lake, a forest-rimmed rock basin with lots of good backpacking campsites, is 4.7 miles up the Cabot Creek Trail from Road 1230. Hike 2 miles past Carl Lake to reach the sweeping viewpoint atop South Cinder Peak.

Table Lake lies at the center of a fascinating, rarely visited landscape of wildflower-filled mesas, sudden canyons, cinder cones, and lava flows. Backpack to Table Lake via Carl Lake (10 miles from Road 1230). Rougher, fainter routes to this lake include the long uphill climb of Sugarpine Ridge (10.5 miles

Mt. Jefferson from Table Lake.

from Road 1292) and the Jefferson Lake Trail (10.1 miles from Road 1292).

Another rewarding, longer backpack is the 20-mile circuit around Three Fingered Jack, following the Pacific Crest Trail from Santiam Pass and returning via Jack and Square Lakes.

For an even greater challenge try the 36-mile stretch of Pacific Crest Trail from Breitenbush Lake to Santiam Pass. After crossing Jefferson Park and skirting half way around Mount Jefferson, the wide, well-graded PCT follows a high, scenic ridgecrest south 10 miles to Minto Pass, passing lots of viewpoints, but no water. Then the PCT climbs high along the side of Three Fingered Jack before dropping to Santiam Pass.

CLIMBING

Mount Jefferson is the most difficult to scale of Oregon's Cascade peaks, both because of the relentless, 4000- to 6000-foot elevation gains required from base camps and because of the 400-foot summit pinnacle of crumbly lava, a class 4 climb in itself.

A dozen routes ascend as far as the summit pinnacle, with difficulties ranging from I-2 to III-5.2. The three easiest are from Jefferson Park across Whitewater Glacier to the ridge south of that glacier, from Pamelia Lake straight up the mountain's southwest ridge, and from the Pacific Crest Trail above Hunts Lake directly toward the summit.

In the 19th century Mount Jefferson was believed unclimbable. A reputed "first ascent" in 1888 probably did not reach the summit. When a group led by Salem lawyer Charles E. Robin really did scale the peak in 1899—but found that their photographer had put in his film backwards—skeptics drove Robin to climb it again a week later.

Three Fingered Jack, though much lower and easier, was first climbed on Labor Day, 1923 by six Bend boys, four of whom had been first to the top of Mount Washington the previous weekend.

Square Lake is a nice winter destination from Santiam Pass.

A popular, level I-4 route follows a well-defined climbers' trail up the south ridge, passes to the east of a gendarme spire at 7600 feet, and continues 300 feet to a rough, 40-foot recessed wall in the summit block.

The West Face Direct route is a level II-5.6-A1 climb, while a northeast route, above Canyon Creek Meadows, is rated III-5.4. Both cross dangerously rotten rock.

SNOWSHOEING & SKIING

Santiam Pass typically has enough snow for winter sports by late November. Starting from the Santiam Pass sno-park opposite Hoodoo Ski Area's entrance road, a marked trail leads 1 mile east through the woods to the snowed-under PCT trailhead. Following the PCT into the wilderness, you have three choices. If you veer right on the Square Lake trail, you'll reach that lake in 2.4 miles, where views of Three Fingered Jack emerge. If you continue straight on the PCT itself, you'll climb steadily up a forested ridge 3 miles to increasingly nice views that stretch from the Three Sisters to Three Fingered Jack. If instead you veer left on the old Skyline Trail you'll traverse across pleasant, rolling terrain for 3.3 miles to Lower Berley Lake (GPS location N44°27.57′ W121°52.38′), hidden in a basin that's notoriously easy to miss.

A 2003 forest fire made navigation on all of these wilderness routes much easier by opening up the view, but map and compass are still essential. Consult the Mount Washington entry for tours south from Santiam Pass.

The Mountain View shelter, a free, heatable cabin that sleeps 15 (no reservations required) is the goal of a 4.8-mile loop from the Maxwell sno-park on Road 080. Another option is the level trail 1.3 miles to Fay Lake (which passes Big Meadows, a large open area good for exploring). Only the hardy tackle the tough, unmarked route to the views on Maxwell Butte itself.

After December, routes lower in the North Santiam River canyon become accessible by ski or snowshoe. Marion Lake and Pamelia Lake are both dramatic goals. In midwinter, when the access roads are snowed in all the way down to Highway 22, Pamelia Lake is 6 miles and Marion Lake is 8. Most trekkers turn back halfway to the lakes at viewpoints along the snowed-under access roads. By late March the snow melts off these access roads and shortens the ski trip to the lakes. Spring brings corn snow with sunny, shirt-sleeved skiing weather.

11
MOUNT WASHINGTON

Sometimes called the "Black Wilderness" because of its 38 square miles of rugged lava flows, the Mount Washington area also features sweeping forests and scores of small lakes. Mountain vistas are everywhere, not only of Mount Washington's craggy spire, but of a half dozen snowpeaks in the adjacent Three Sisters and Mount Jefferson areas.

Climate

Santiam Pass, with an average snowfall of 20 to 58 feet, is plowed throughout winter. Highway 242 over McKenzie Pass is closed from November or December to May or June. Trails are clear of snow from mid June to mid October. Summers are warm and dry.

Plants and Wildlife

The barren lava fields support little more than an occasional, bonsaied

Location: 70 mi E of Eugene, 31 mi W of Bend
Size: 111 sq mi
Status: 82 sq mi designated wilderness (1964, 1984)
Terrain: lava plains, high forest, peak
Elevation: 2800'-7794'
Management: Deschutes NF, Willamette NF
Maps: Mt. Washington, Santiam Pass Winter Recreation (Geo-Graphics)

Rental rowboats at Clear Lake allow you to see the underwater snags of a drowned forest.

whitebark pine. But the high plains surrounding the lava are evenly covered by mountain hemlock and true fir on the west and by lodgepole and ponderosa pine on the east. Blacktail deer wintering in the Old Cascades and mule deer wintering in the Metolius Valley often make Mount Washington their summer range.

Geology

At least 125 eruptive centers have produced cinder cones and basalt lava flows in this area since the Ice Age—an average of one major eruption every century. The most recent flow, 1300 years old, streamed 12 miles from Belknap Crater's flank to bury the McKenzie River south of Koosah Falls, creating Tamolitch Pool.

Clear Lake formed 3000 years ago when a lava flow from a cone south of Sand Mountain dammed the McKenzie River and drowned a forest. The lake's water is so cold and clear that the unpetrified, branchless trees are still there, and can be seen as much as 100 feet below the lake surface — a source of fascination for boaters (no motors permitted) and wet-suited scuba divers. Rowboats can be rented at the Clear Lake Lodge.

The surface of the area's lava flows is intensely jumbled and almost uncrossable. As the crust of the flows cooled, it was broken up by the liquid lava that continued to flow underneath. Where molten lava flowed out from under an intact crust, lava tubes formed, such as Sawyer's Cave and Skylight Cave. Permanent ice and smooth lava stalactites can be seen in these long caves and in the collapsed lava tubes filling the summit crater of Little Belknap.

Though at least 100,000 years older than Belknap Crater, Mount Washington began as a similarly broad shield volcano. It went on to add a cone as large and symmetrical as any of the Three Sisters, but then was stripped to its central lava plug by glaciation.

History

The Santiam Wagon Road, built in 1866 to allow the grazing of Willamette Valley livestock in Central Oregon, has been reopened as a trail through the

Mt. Washington from the Pacific Crest Trail on the lava near Belknap Crater.

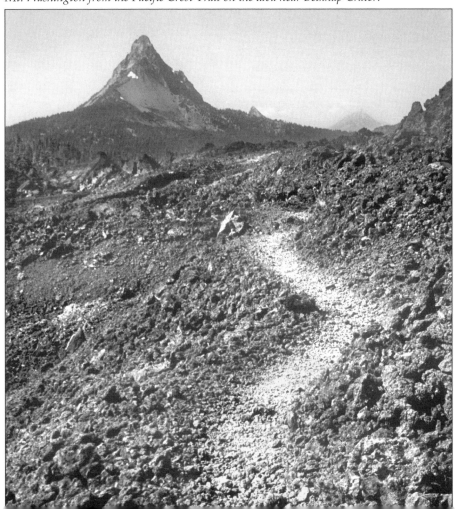

South Santiam's canyon, and survives as a rugged track along the north edge of the Mount Washington Wilderness, between Fish Lake and the 1896 Cache Creek Toll Station site.

On a cinder cone along that route, the Sand Mountain fire lookout tower burned in 1968. The lookout was rebuilt in 1990 by volunteers who staff the tower in summers and welcome visitors. A 1.3-mile loop trail passes the tower and tours the cinder cone's rim.

In 1871-72, John Templeton Craig built a wagon route over McKenzie Pass, arduously chipping and leveling a lava roadbed still visible in the rugged basalt flows around Hand Lake and near Dee Wright Observatory at McKenzie Pass. Craig contracted to carry mail across his road through the winter on skis. In an 1877 storm he froze to death in a cabin at Craig Lake. Since the 1930s, an annual John Templeton Craig ski tour and ski race has carried specially marked mail

Mt. Washington from the Patjens Lakes.

MT WASHINGTON

0   1   2mi
0   1   2   3km
N

Benson Lake, with Scott Mountain on the horizon.

on the 22-mile route across McKenzie Pass, usually on the first Sunday in April.

HIKING & BACKPACKING

One of the most popular day hikes near McKenzie Pass is the half-mile walk from Highway 242 through pine woods to the wildflower meadow at the Hand Lake shelter. For a longer hike, circle the lake on a 1-mile stroll alongside a lava flow.

Another very heavily used trail climbs 400 feet in 1.4 miles from photogenic Scott Lake (where you'll find a free, primitive campground and excellent reflections of the Three Sisters) to Benson Lake, a deep, blue jewel partly rimmed by cliffs. Beyond Benson Lake 1.1 mile are the similarly scenic and popular Tenas Lakes — also a good backpacking goal. Hikers seeking solitude should bring a compass and head for one of the many off-trail lakelets in this area. Because the entire Mt. Washington Wilderness lacks running water most of the year, campers should bring an approved filter to purify lake water. For a panoramic viewpoint, continue on the main trail past the Tenas Lakes 1.6 miles to the summit of Scott Mountain, a former lookout site.

The Patjens Lakes, with wildflower meadows and reflections of Mount Washington, are on a 6-mile loop through rolling forest from the end of paved Road 2690 at Big Lake. An equally swimmable, but far less visited lake is Robinson Lake, on an easy 0.3-mile trail from Road 2664.

Day hikers (and backpackers) often follow the Pacific Crest Trail south from Lava Camp Lake Campground to South Matthieu Lake, then take the old Skyline Trail back via North Matthieu Lake — a 6-mile loop through both lava and forest.

The lava fields at McKenzie Pass are so impressively rugged that many visitors merely walk the paved, half-mile Lava River nature trail around the Dee Wright Observatory's basalt-block hut. But the PCT climbs on a very good grade from a nearby trailhead through the heart of the lava's spectacular barrens. Hike to the panoramic view atop Little Belknap by taking the PCT 2.4 miles and turn right on a 0.2 mile spur that passes three small lava caves. From the junction, Belknap Crater's three distinct summit craters are a 0.7-mile cross-country climb to the west, mostly slogging up a cinder slope.

The view from Belknap Crater is good, but the best view of the Three Sisters is atop Black Crater, on a trail that climbs 2500 feet in 3.7 miles from Highway 242.

The PCT leads to views up and down the Cascades from wildflower meadows on Mount Washington's shoulder. Carry water on this dry, 12.4-mile section of the PCT north from McKenzie Pass to Road 811.

The many trailless lakes, often warm enough for swimming, invite cross-country exploration. Those surrounded by lava are among the most remote oases in the state. Wear gloves and carry a gallon of water if you bushwhack across lava—and expect to travel no more than half a mile per hour.

CLIMBING

Mount Washington's eroded lava plug offers several technical climbs. To take the level I-4 North Ridge route, pioneered by six boys from Bend in 1923, follow the PCT 2 miles south of Road 811. Follow tree blazes cross-country to the mountain's north ridge, then hike up the ridge to a small saddle at the base of the summit pinnacle. West of the saddle 25 feet ascend a 30-foot chimney, then climb 30 feet upwards and to the left on the rough, rotten rock of the "nose." Atop the nose, a steep hike leads to an additional 20-foot chimney and the summit.

A dozen additional climbing routes increase in difficulty to the foolishly dangerous, level III-5.7 East Face Direct and the west face's level II-5.8 Chimney of Space.

SNOWSHOEING & SKIING

Santiam Pass is a major Nordic skiing center, while McKenzie Pass offers a few longer, more remote trips. See area 10, Mount Jefferson, for routes north of

The Three Sisters from Hand Lake.

The Island Junction shelter at Santiam Pass.

Santiam Pass.

Santiam Pass' largest network of marked cross-country ski trails converges at the Ray Benson sno-park (a center shared with snowmobilers) near the Hoodoo ski area on Big Lake Road 2690. Three rustic, open-doored log shelters (not accessible to snowmobilers) make easy goals in the rolling terrain. Bear left for 1.8 miles to the North Blowout Shelter, bear right for 2.7 miles to the better view at the Brandenburg Shelter, or head east for 3.3 miles to the Island Junction Shelter. Snowshoe and ski rentals, lessons, and groomed trails are available for a fee at Hoodoo Ski Bowl nearby.

Another marked Nordic route climbs 1000 feet along a snowed-under road in 1.9 miles from the Road 830 sno-park (2 miles west of Santiam Pass) to the view atop Potato Hill. For a 3.8-mile loop with less of a climb, turn right off the Potato Hill route onto the Hash Brown trail.

The generally unplowed side roads from Highway 126 are skiable, especially Road 2664 to Robinson Lake (4 miles one way), and Road 2649 to Melakwa Lake (10 miles one way).

McKenzie Pass is typically plowed only a week or so past the first snowfall, usually in November. Once the snow gates close, trekkers prepared for a snow camp will find the 22-mile crossing of McKenzie Pass unparalleled in scenic splendor.

12
OLD CASCADES

Six separate roadless areas along Highway 20 remain to show the scale of the wild forests that once blanketed the western foothills of the Cascade Range. Here are broad ridges, subalpine meadows, and views of the High Cascades' snowpeaks, all within an hour's drive of the Willamette Valley.

Rabbit Ears in the Menagerie Wilderness.

Climate

The area's 80 annual inches of precipitation come as snow from December through March, and rain in spring and fall. Trails up to 4000 feet are usually clear of snow by May.

Plants and Wildlife

The Old Cascade's remarkable botanical diversity is best seen in early summer on the ridge between Echo Mountain and Iron Mountain ridge. A study of this site found 60 plant species that are rare or unusual in the western Cascades, including spectacular penstemon and other wildflowers. Nowhere in Oregon are there more varieties of conifers in such a compact area — 17 species, from water-loving western red cedar to drought-tolerant juniper and rare alpine Alaska cedar.

Lower elevation areas of the Old Cascades include pockets of old-growth western hemlock and Douglas fir. Higher elevations are dominated by flexible-limbed, snow-resistant Pacific silver fir and noble fir. Stumps in a 1986 clearcut 3 miles south of House Rock Campground indicate that the area held Oregon's oldest trees.

Fishing is banned in Hackleman Creek to protect that stream's unique strain of cutthroat trout.

Geology

The Old Cascades are a chain of volcanoes predating the peaks of the High Cascades by 10 million years. It was the Old Cascades which originally made Eastern Oregon the semi-arid area it is today, and which filled ancient inland seas with rhyolite ash, preserving the John Day area's famous fossils.

Time and erosion have reduced the Old Cascades' once-tall volcanic cones to a dissected canyonland, studded with the cliffs and pinnacles of resistant lava intrusions. The Menagerie is a collection of two dozen such rock spires, includ-

Location: 45 mi E of Albany

Size: 74 sq mi

Status: 8 sq mi designated wilderness (1984)

Terrain: densely forested ridges, ridgetop meadows, rock pinnacles

Elevation: 1230'-5830'

Management: Willamette NF

Maps: Menagerie Wilderness, Santiam Pass Winter Recreation (USFS); Bull of the Woods (Geo-Geographics)

Iron Mountain from Cone Peak's wildflower rock gardens.

ing three natural arches and a 300-foot tower called Turkey Monster.

History

The Santiam band of Kalapuya Indians once had a summer hunting and gathering camp at House Rock. White settlers built the Santiam Wagon Road through the area between Albany and Central Oregon in 1864-65. The state purchased the heavily used toll route by 1925. Construction of Highway 20 largely bypassed the old wagon route in 1939, but it has now been reopened as a recreation trail.

HIKING & BACKPACKING

All six of the Old Cascades' roadless areas have good hiking trails. In the east, follow the Old Cascades Crest Trail 1.1 easy miles from Road 508 to a collapsed bridge at Maude Creek, a good turn-around point for hikers with children. For a longer hike, continue 3.2 miles up across broad, grassy slopes of alpine wildflowers to the viewpoint atop Crescent Mountain, gaining 2200 feet of elevation. The Old Cascades Crest Trail continues a total of 27 miles, passing the Three Pyramids en route to the Middle Santiam Wilderness (see area 13).

The area's most popular trail climbs 1.7 miles past wildflower slopes to a railed deck at the former lookout site atop Iron Mountain, gaining 1400 feet. After a 1976 winter storm blew off the

original 1933 lookout building, the Forest Service used a helicopter to replace it with a similar structure from another peak, but removed it in 2008. Park at the Iron Mountain Trailhead just west of Tombstone Pass on Road 15 and hike up to the summit. To return on a 6.6-mile loop, keep right on the Cone Peak Trail, traversing even more spectacular wildflower fields on a gentler grade 3.3 miles down to Highway 20. Cross the highway and take the Tombstone Nature Trail 0.6 mile to the Tombstone Pass sno-park, where the Santiam Wagon Road leads 0.3 mile to your car. For a scenic cross-country side trip, leave the trail at Cone Peak and follow the open ridge east past Echo Mountain to North Peak.

Two trails lead to the fern meadows of Browder Ridge—the 4.5-mile

Iron Mountain in winter.

Viewpoint on Browder Ridge.

Browder Ridge Trail from Road 080 and the lovely 3.1-mile Gate Creek Trail from Road 1598. Where the routes join, take a faint spur trail 1 mile north and bushwhack up a meadow to the ridge's panoramic high point.

A portion of the historic Santiam Wagon Road has been reopened as a trail for hikers, bikers, and equestrians. The 19.5-mile trail begins opposite the closed Mountain House restaurant (on Highway 20 at Upper Soda), passes House Rock Campground, crosses Tombstone Pass, and continues to Highway 126 at the Fish Lake guard station. An interesting 0.8-mile loop sampling the historic wagon route starts at House Rock Campground, crosses the river, and passes a house-sized cave and a waterfall. For a longer hike, continue up from the waterfall 3.4 miles to a switchback near the 5-mile marker post, where a knoll overlooks the Sevenmile Creek.

The weird rock pinnacles of The Menagerie can be reached by two trails from Highway 20, both of which climb 2200 feet through Douglas fir forests. The 3.3-mile Trout Creek Trail begins near the Trout Creek Campground entrance, while the steep, 2.1-mile Rooster Rock Trail starts near Fernview Campground's entrance. From the viewpoint beside Rooster Rock's spire, a rough climber's path contours onward to Rabbit Ears' twin towers.

The wildflowers of Gordon Meadows are a good hiking goal. The brushy meadows are 4.3 miles through the old-growth forests of the Falls Creek Trail from Road 2032, or 3.6 miles from Road 230, past scenic Gordon Lakes and the cliffs of Soapgrass Mountain.

Moose Lake (GPS location N44°26.343' W122°22.09'), snow-free most winters, is particularly pretty in spring, when the moss of Moose Creek's boulder-strewn rapids glows a brilliant green. Reach the steep, 1-mile Moose Lake Trail by turning off Highway 20 onto the Moose Creek Road, 2.5 miles east of Cascadia. Promptly turn right on Road 2027 for 5.5 miles, fork left onto Road 720 for 0.2 mile, and park at a wide spot (GPS location N44°25.571' W122°22.177').

CLIMBING

The two dozen spires of The Menagerie provide popular technical climbing challenges. Rooster Rock's old lookout site can be reached with class 5.4 skills. Three other routes up that crag range in difficulty to level II-5.8. Nearby are Roosters Tail, Chicken Rock, and Hen Rock, with routes of similar difficulty.

Clustered a mile north of Rooster Rock, but composed of slightly lower quality rock, are two natural arches (Big Arch is a level II-5.7-A1 climb) and six additional spires, including 265-foot South Rabbit Ear (a III-5.7 climb) and North Rabbit Ear (III-5.7-A2). A climbers' trail accesses all of these destinations from a gravel road on the ridge above the Wilderness. Since the end of Road 850 has been closed, drive straight on Road 857 and then keep right at junctions to find the new trailhead at the end of Road 856.

A dozen other crags and spires dot the slope above Keith Creek, half a mile east of Rabbit Ears. The first of these is Turkey Monster, unclimbed until 1966. This 300-foot column has level III-5.6-A3 and IV-5.7-A3 routes. Other difficult spires include The Porpoise (I-5.8) and The Bridge (II-5.9).

Elsewhere in the area, the Santiam Pinnacle, above Highway 20, offers four routes of level I-4 to II-5.6 difficulty. And although a trail ascends Iron Mountain's west slope, the 400-foot cliff on the south face is a level I-5.6 climb.

SNOWSHOEING & SKIING

Plowed Highway 20 provides access to snowshoe and ski opportunities on trails and side roads in the Tombstone Pass area, notably the old Santiam Wagon Road to the east of the Tombstone Pass sno-park. Skiable snow can be expected from January to mid-March. Beginners often practice on Tombstone Prairie. Cross the prairie and the highway for an adventurous tour up to Cone Peak's scenic ridgetop meadows. Sno-parks at Lost Prairie and Lava Lake Road 2067 provide a half dozen marked tours and loops.

13

MIDDLE SANTIAM

One of Oregon's largest low-elevation, old-growth forests lies hidden along the remote headwaters of the Middle Santiam River, surprisingly close to the Willamette Valley. Great Douglas firs, western hemlocks, and western red cedars rise from the steep, mist-shrouded Middle Santiam canyon, where the green-pooled river cascades between mossy banks.

South Pyramid from Middle Pyramid.

Climate

Though the river's canyon seldom sees snow, access roads and trails cross higher elevations, and are blocked from about December through March. Annual rainfall averages 80 inches. Only summers are reliably dry.

Plants and Wildlife

Pockets of extremely old forest (over 450 years) throughout the area form a spectacular 200-foot-high canopy above a shady world of rhododendrons, lichen-covered snags, and huge rotting logs. Old-growth forests, now rare in Oregon, are the optimum habitat for 137 vertebrate species, including the spotted owl and 85 other types of birds.

Fallen old-growth trees across the Middle Santiam River create the river's silt-free, gravel-bottomed pools—the

spawning sites of a third of the Santiam drainage's Chinook salmon.

The Three Pyramids host higher-elevation plant species: noble fir and subalpine meadows of wildflowers.

Geology

In the east, the Three Pyramids are relatively recent volcanoes associated with the High Cascades. The remainder of the area consists of ancient, heavily eroded Old Cascades volcanics. Chimney Peak is an Old Cascades lava plug. Traces of gold and silver brought prospectors to Quartzville Creek in the 19th century.

Cliffs left by immense landslides extend from Scar Mountain to Knob Rock. One of these ancient slides dammed Donaca Lake. The area's steep, unstable clay soils made road construction so expensive that many of the unroaded old-growth forests could only be cut

Location: 56 mi E of Albany

Size: 40 sq mi (including the Pyramids)

Status: 13 sq mi designated wilderness (1984)

Terrain: densely forested river valley, rocky peaks

Elevation: 1300'-5618'

Management: Willamette NF

Maps: Bull of the Woods Wilderness (Geo-Graphics), Detroit (Green Trails)

Shelter Falls on the Middle Santiam River, near the Shedd Camp Shelter.

at a net loss. The southeast edge of the wilderness is rimmed with recovering landslides triggered by the Forest Service's abortive effort to punch logging roads into the area prior to wilderness designation in 1984. Adventurous hikers can follow an abandoned portion of Road 2041 past a half-mile landslide and the washed-out ruin of the road's bridge across Pyramid Creek.

HIKING & BACKPACKING

In the east, forest-rimmed Daly, Parrish, and Riggs lakes are each at the end of easy half-mile trails suitable for day hikes with children. Drive Highway 22 north of the Santiam "Y" junction toward Salem 7.5 miles to milepost 74 and turn west on Parrish Lake Road 2266 for 4.6, 5, or 6.5 miles, depending on which lake's trailhead you prefer.

Viewpoints and alpine rock gardens at the summit of Middle Pyramid climax a more challenging 2-mile trail that gains 1800 feet of elevation from Road 560. Drive Highway 22 north of the Santiam "Y" junction with Highway 20 for

4.8 miles. Between mileposts 76 and 77, turn west on Lava Lake Meadow Road 2067 for 1.9 miles, and turn right on Road 560 for 3.5 miles to its end. The Middle Pyramid trail serves as a link in the 27-mile Old Cascades Crest Trail. Backpackers or equestrians can continue south to Crescent Mountain (see area 12) or north past Scar Mountain and Knob Rock to the Middle Santiam Wilderness.

Chimney Peak, site of a former fire lookout, commands views across valley after valley of old-growth forests. The 6.1-mile McQuade Creek Trail leads to the peak, through deep forest and past a dilapidated shelter. The trail ends 100 yards below the summit. The final climb is a tricky scramble requiring caution and both hands. To find the McQuade Creek trailhead, turn north from Highway 20 onto the Quartzville Road 4 miles east of Sweet Home. After 24.7 miles, cross a bridge to a three-way fork. Keep right on Road 11 for 2.6 miles and turn right on Road 1142 for 4 miles.

The best sampler of the Middle

Santiam, however, begins off Road 2041 with an easy 0.7-mile hike down to the rustic, rain-proof Shedd Camp shelter, near a spectacular blue-green pool fed by a 20-foot waterfall. A pebbly beach here invites swimmers to a chilly dip. The main trail crosses the 30-foot-wide Middle Santiam River just upstream, without a bridge. By late summer, expert rock-hoppers can avoid wading.

On the far shore, the trail climbs 0.3 mile to a fork. To the right, the South Pyramid Creek Trail climbs 5.4 miles to the Old Cascades Trail at Road 572. To the left, the trail contours above the river 2 miles, fords Pyramid Creek, climbs 0.8 mile to an abandoned portion of Road 2041, and continues 2.7 miles to little, blue-green Donaca Lake. Backpackers will be able to camp at the lake and continue 6.2 miles to Chimney Peak, or perhaps take side trails up to Gordan Peak or the viewpoint at Knob Rock.

To find the trailhead off Road 2041, drive Highway 20 east of Sweet Home 24 miles. Just before the closed Mountain House restaurant (and after milepost 52), turn left on Soda Fork Road 2041 for 0.9 mile, and keep left at a fork for 7.1 miles to a 6-way intersection in Cool Camp's pass. Go straight on 2041 for 4.5 miles to a three-way fork, and take the middle route (Road 646) for 0.6 mile to its end.

A cross-country route to the Middle Santiam River begins at the landslide that now ends Road 2041. Adventurers can bushwhack from the bottom of the slide down to the river and follow the river's south bank downstream. Flats along the river feature towering Douglas firs, mossy bigleaf maples, and frequent glimpses of Chimney Peak and the Pyramids. West of Fitt Creek the canyon becomes too narrow even for bushwhackers.

14
MOUNT HEBO

The mossy forests ringing this broad peak harbor a pair of waterfalls and three lakes—rarities in the Coast Range.

Climate
Over 100 inches of annual precipitation sustain Mount Hebo's rainforest. Snow caps the summit briefly after winter storms.

Plants and Wildlife
Early summer wildflowers, thimbleberry, and bracken fern carpet the summit meadows, home to the rare silverspot butterfly. At lower elevations, Douglas fir, Sitka spruce, and alder dominate a green world of moss, sourgrass, sword fern, and trilliums.

Geology
Mount Hebo's flat top is a remnant of a Columbia River basalt lava flow that erupted 15 million years ago near Idaho, poured west through the Columbia Gorge, and puddled up in a seashore bay here. Subsequent uplifting of the Coast Range made this erosion-resistant basalt a plateau.

History
Tillamook settlers seeking a route to the Willamette Valley used an Indian trail across Mount Hebo from 1854 to

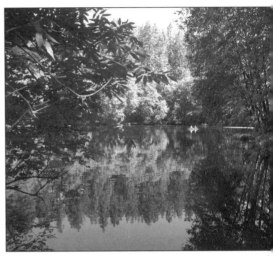
Hebo Lake.

1882. A portion of the route was restored in 1984 as the Pioneer-Indian Trail. Following massive fires in 1853 and 1910, the Forest Service replanted 12 square miles with Douglas fir in 1912. One of the earliest Oregon reforestation projects, the forest has grown slowly because the Douglas fir seedlings were imported from the Rocky Mountains, and were not adapted to the coastal climate. A World War II radar installation was removed from the west summit in the 1980s, but a small military reservation remains on the slightly taller east summit, near primitive Mount Hebo Campground.

HIKING & BACKPACKING
A 1-mile trail descends from Road 131 to a footbridge at the base of two waterfalls, Niagara Creek's 100-foot plunge and neighboring Pheasant

Location: 20 mi S of Tillamook, 26 mi N of Lincoln City

Size: 24 sq mi

Status: undesignated wilderness

Terrain: flat-topped mountain, steep forested flanks, lakes

Elevation: 200'-3176'

Management: Siuslaw NF

Maps: Niagara Creek, Hebo, Blaine, Beaver (USGS)

Creek's 80-foot fan.

An even easier, barrier-free path loops 0.5 mile around Hebo Lake from the Hebo Lake Campground, just off Road 14. The campground itself is gated closed for cars from November to mid-April, adding 0.2 mile to the hike.

For a more substantial hike, try the 8-mile Pioneer-Indian Trail. Starting at Hebo Lake, this route climbs 1200 feet in 2.9 miles to a crossing of paved Road 14. Continue on the trail a mile to a panoramic viewpoint with wild strawberries and red paintbrush—a good turnaround point for day hikers. For a longer trip, continue on the trail 1.4 miles through meadows to a junction near Mount Hebo Campground, switchback 1 mile down to brush-lined North Lake, and amble 1.7 miles to a campsite at South Lake.

A network of loop trails, designed primarily for equestrians, branches off the Pioneer-Indian Trail near Hebo Lake. The Hebo Plantation Trail, a 0.7-mile loop from Road 14 west of Hebo Lake, was built by the CCC in the 1930s to showcase reforestation methods.

Viewpoint on the trail along Mt. Hebo's summit plateau.

15
DRIFT CREEK

Drift Creek features the Coast Range's largest remaining stands of old-growth rain forest. The rock-strewn creek's steep-sided canyon gives the area a mountainous feel, although it is actually close to tidewater.

Climate
Temperatures are mild year round. Heavy rainfall can be expected from fall through spring (74 inches annually in the west, 120 inches at Table Mountain). Winter snow is rare even at high elevations.

Plants and Wildlife
Sitka spruce and western hemlock trees grow 7 feet thick many places in the area, particularly along the northern portion of the Horse Creek Trail. Creekbanks are overhung with bigleaf maple trees, their spreading branches cushioned by a 6-inch-deep layer of moss and licorice ferns.

In summer look for edible berries in the rainforest undergrowth: orange salmonberry, red thimbleberry, blue and red huckleberry, and dark blue salal. Sourgrass, or oxalis, is edible in small quantities and tart as a lemon. Its shamrock-shaped leaves often carpet the forest floor. Swampy areas brighten in April with the huge yellow spathes of skunk cabbage. Disturbed hillsides sprout 6-foot-tall spires of red and white foxglove throughout summer.

Several pairs of northern spotted owls and bald eagles, both endangered in Oregon, nest in the old-growth forest. It is not uncommon to find evidence of Roosevelt elk or black bear.

Though Drift Creek is not ranked as a river, it supports river-sized runs of native fish. Chinook salmon, coho salmon, steelhead, and cutthroat trout return each fall, while a much smaller Chinook

Old-growth trees at Drift Creek.

run comes in spring. Hatchery fish have never been stocked.

Geology
This area's crumbly sandstone and siltstone weather to slippery clay, making roads and trails susceptible to landslides. The rock began as oceanic deposits of mud and sand. The rise of the

Location: 12 mi E of Waldport, 57 mi W of Corvallis

Size: 18 sq mi

Status: 9 sq mi designated wilderness (1984)

Terrain: steep valleys, rain forest

Elevation: 80'-2100'

Management: Siuslaw NF

Maps: Tidewater, Hellion Rapids (USGS)

Coast Range lifted this section of sea-floor from the waves about 15 million years ago.

History

Drift Creek was once the hunting and gathering grounds of the Waldport Bay-based Alsea Indians. The creekside meadow on the Harris Ranch Trail is an abandoned homestead from the 1920s.

HIKING & BACKPACKING

Two paths descend through forest to the shady, green banks of Drift Creek. The trails can be connected by wading 20-foot-wide Drift Creek . By late summer, expert rock hoppers can sometimes accomplish the crossings dry-footed.

Rarely, after midwinter rains, the fords aren't passable at all.

The easiest route to the creek, the Harris Ranch Trail, starts out along a closed road for 0.8 mile and then descends 1200 feet in 2.2 miles to a large, campable meadow in a bend of Drift Creek. The exposed rock creekbanks here are great for sunbathing or wading. Red crawdads crawl in the shallows.

To find the trailhead, drive Highway 34 east of Waldport 6.9 miles (or west of Corvallis 57 miles) to an Alsea River bridge, and turn north on Risley Creek Road 3446, always taking the larger fork at junctions. You'll reach the Harris Ranch Trailhead after 4.1 miles.

Drift Creek from the campsite at the bottom of the Horse Creek Trail.

The other route to Drift Creek, the 3.6-mile-long northern portion of the Horse Creek Trail, descends 1500 feet in 3.8 miles through spectacular old-growth forest to a campsite on a forested bench 30 feet above the creek. Connecting to the Harris Ranch Trail is not easy, because you have to scramble down a steep 30-foot slope to the creek, ford across, and bushwhack downstream 0.2 mile to the Harris Ranch meadow. Even then, a car shuttle to the other side of the wilderness requires a 33-mile drive on twisty backroads.

Bushwhacking along other creeks and ridges is difficult enough to ensure solitude.

To find the northern Horse Creek trailhead, drive Highway 101 north of Waldport 7 miles to Ona Beach State Park, turn inland on North Beaver Creek Road 1 mile, fork left for 2.7 miles, turn right onto paved North Elkhorn Road for 5.8 miles, turn left on Road 50 for 1.4 miles, and fork right onto gravel Road 5087 for 3.4 miles.

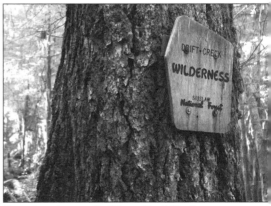

Boundary tree on the Horse Creek Trail.

16

CUMMINS CREEK & ROCK CREEK

On this wild stretch of coast, pristine rain forest canyons pour half a dozen clear creeks between the cliff-tipped headlands of 2000-foot-tall ridges. Hikers can prowl an old-growth forest, study tide pools, or picnic on a secluded beach.

The Oregon Coast Trail at Gwynn Creek.

Climate

Rainfall varies from 80 inches annually on the beach to over 100 inches in the interior. Cool fogs line the coast and fill the valley mouths most of summer. Winters are snowless. Fall and spring have the most clear days.

Plants and Wildlife

The ridge between Rock Creek and Big Creek is one of only three locations worldwide to support a stable population of the threatened, orange-and-brown mottled, Oregon silverspot butterfly. Cape Perpetua is a popular lookout from which to spot the spouts of migrating gray whales from December to May. Low tides expose sea urchins,

sea anemones, and other marine tide pool life on the rocky coastline between the Devils Churn and Gwynn Knoll.

Sitka spruce as large as 9 feet in diameter dominate the valley slopes within 2 miles of the ocean. Farther inland the forest shifts to hemlock and Douglas fir. The undergrowth of salmonberry (with edible salmon-colored fruit in summer), salal, and sword fern is so dense that tree seedlings often sprout atop rotting old-growth "nursery logs" to get started. Creeks are overhung with red alder, bigleaf maple, and autumn-reddening vine maple. Lily-of-the-valley carpets the forest with heart-shaped leaves.

The area supports larger native runs of salmon, steelhead, and cutthroat trout than any other similar-sized watershed in Oregon. A fish count in late June, 1979, found an average of 50 coho salmon per 100 feet on the lower 2 miles of Cummins Creek.

Location: 15 mi N of Florence

Size: 26 sq mi

Status: designated wilderness (1984)

Terrain: steep valleys, coastal rain forest

Elevation: 0'-2300'

Management: Siuslaw NF

Maps: Yachats, Heceta Head, Cummins Peak, Cannibal Mountain (USGS)

Geology

The area's basalt bedrock began as undersea lava flows. As upfaulting lifted the Coast Range from the ocean, creeks eroded the face of the fault block into steep, shallow-soiled canyons. Small oceanfront fractures have been widened by wave action into slot-shaped spouting horns and the Devils Churn.

History

Excavation of middens (shell piles) near the cape's tide pools show that humans have camped here to gather mussels for at least 6000 years—a tradition carried on by the Alsea tribe until the 1870s.

Explorer Captain Cook, sailing against stormy seas near here on March 11, 1778, complained that the same cape had been in sight to the north for five days. He named the perpetual landmark Cape Perpetua, in part because March 11 is the holy day of St. Perpetua, a faith-tested martyr.

HIKING & BACKPACKING

Five trails suitable for day hikes begin at the Cape Perpetua Visitor Center. The most heavily used of these are paved, and several are equipped with interpretive signs. An 0.8-mile loop ducks through a tunnel under Highway 101 to visit tide pools, shell middens,

Rock Creek.

and Cook Chasm's spouting horn (an optional 1-mile loop continues north to the Devils Churn). A different 1.5-mile trail from the visitor center crosses Cape Creek and climbs 700 feet to a spectacular viewpoint at a 1933 stone shelter atop Cape Perpetua. A 1-mile trail follows the south bank of Cape Creek, past the Perpetua Campground, to a giant spruce tree 15 feet in diameter. A more ambitious 5.8-mile loop starts from the visitor center's upper parking lot, climbs 2.3 miles along the Cooks Ridge Trail amid old-growth spruce, turns right to descend the Gwynn Creek Trail 2.5 miles, and then follows the Oregon Coast Trail right 1 mile along a pioneer wagon road to complete the loop.

A lovely, unofficial trail along Cummins Creek emerges at intervals from lush, valley-bottom rainforest to pass creekside gravel bars ideal for picnics. To start, turn off Highway 101 immediately north of Neptune State Park at a sign reading, "Cummins Creek Trailhead 1/4 mile." At road's end, park at a turnaround, walk 300 yards on the Cummins Creek Trail (an old roadbed), and fork to the right on a smaller path. After 250 yards this trail hops a small creek and then forks. To the right, a short path deadends at the creekbank. The left fork scrambles 0.6 mile upstream to a small creekside gravel bar.

For a scenic, 7.4-mile loop from the same trailhead, hike up the official Cummins Creek Trail 1.4 miles and turn left on a trail that climbs to a ridgecrest with occasional ocean views. Keep left at all trail junctions to return down Gwynn Creek and a portion of the Oregon Coast Trail to your car.

A 6-mile trail exploring the old-growth Sitka spruce forest on Cummins Ridge begins at the barricaded end of Road 1051. Hike the abandoned road (now a pleasant trail) 3 miles along the ridgetop to a cairn and veer right on a ridgecrest trail to Road 515, a short spur of Road 5694.

Explorers heading up Rock Creek start at the Rock Creek Campground and hike a rough scramble trail upstream. To continue more than half a mile, it's easiest to wear tennis shoes and walk up the middle of the chilly (average 56° F) creek.

A 5-mile-long elk trail traces the Rock Creek-Big Creek Divide from a saddle on Road 1055. Ridgetop meadows allow views of the valley forests on either hand.

The Oregon Coast Trail is being developed along the length of this shore. A new 1-mile section descends from Cape Perpetua's stone shelter toward Yachats.

Cape Perpetua from the stone shelter.

17

LOWER DESCHUTES RIVER

Roaring whitewater and cliff-rimmed canyons highlight the final 51 miles of the Deschutes River, popular for two-day float trips.

Climate

With just 10 inches of annual precipitation, this canyon boasts reliable sunshine. Summers are hot, but frost is common at night and in winter.

Plants and Wildlife

Sagebrush dominates this canyonland. Mule deer, coyotes, and rattlesnakes are common. The river's famous steelhead include a native Deschutes strain (6 to 8 pounds), which swim up the river from June to September, and a Clearwater River strain (up to 22 pounds), which visit the cool Deschutes seeking respite from the warmer Columbia River on their way to spawning grounds in Idaho.

Geology

The canyon walls are layered with 25- to 100-foot-thick lava flows belonging to the 13- to 16-million-year-old Columbia River basalts.

History

Warm Springs Indians maintain a

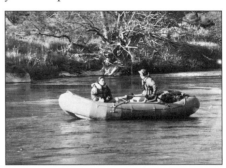

Rafting on the lower Deschutes River.

centuries-old tradition by dipnetting migrating salmon each spring and fall from rickety wooden platforms overhanging 15-foot Sherars Falls. Explorer Peter Skene Ogden lost five horses through an Indian bridge at the falls in 1826. A toll bridge built there in 1860 connected The Dalles with the rich Canyon City gold fields in Central Oregon. The old county bridge at Freebridge was apparently dynamited in 1912 by competing toll bridge owners.

Although an 1855 Army engineering survey reported that a railroad grade was impossible along the lower Deschutes, rivalry between railroad magnates James Hill and Edward Harriman resulted in two rail lines being built up the "impossible" canyon to Bend in 1909-11. Hill's Oregon Trunk Railway remains on the west bank; track has been removed from the east bank grade, now a path for hikers and bikers.

HIKING & BACKPACKING

The best trails start at Deschutes River State Park. For a 4.2-mile loop, hike the riverbank path to Moody Rapids,

Location: 14 mi E of The Dalles

Size: 38 sq mi

Status: federal wild and scenic river

Terrain: rimrock-lined river canyon

Elevation: 150'-2500'

Management: Prineville District BLM, Oregon Parks and Recreation Department

Maps: Wishram, Emerson, Locust Grove, Erskine, Summit Ridge, Sinamox, Sherars Bridge, Maupin (USGS)

climb to a viewpoint at Ferry Springs, and return on a portion of a historic wagon road. Also from the park, the old railroad grade, converted to a mountain bike path, leads 12 miles to Harris Canyon, and continues as an undeveloped route to Macks Canyon Campground. Backpacking campsites are plentiful along the river, but stays are limited to four nights, campfires are all but prohibited, and private land can block access, especially south of Freebridge (on the west bank) and Harris Canyon (on the east). Anglers should use barbless hooks and release all native fish.

An easy 0.3-mile trail from the Tygh Valley picnic area on Highway 216 visits three colossal White River waterfalls. A bushwhacking route continues downstream 2.2 miles to the Deschutes, but expect lush poison oak along the way.

BOATING

The popular 51-mile drift trip from Maupin to the Columbia River encounters three thrilling class 4 rapids, dozens of lesser riffles, and one impassable falls.

Four miles below the Maupin City Park boat ramp, class 4 Oak Springs Rapids split the river into three channels. Stop to look it over, and then avoid the right-hand channel. After another 3.5 miles, all craft must portage around unnavigable Sherars Falls. Just 150 yards beyond the portage, boaters are faced with class 3 Upper Bridge Rapids, and, in another 0.2 miles, the dangerous Lower Bridge Rapids. Scout this class 4+ whitewater from the right bank. Then paddle hard to stay in the smaller, right-hand channel.

Downriver 3.6 miles, class 3 Wreck Rapids introduce a 34-mile stretch of calmer water with a steady 5-mile-per-hour current, past some of the canyon's most spectacular basalt rimrock.

The pace picks up for the river's final 7 miles. First comes Washout Rapids, a boulder field created when a 1997 flash

The lower Deschutes River from the loop trail to Ferry Springs.

flood blasted rocks out of a side creek's twin culverts. A mile later is Gordon Ridge Rapids, a long, class 2+ ride with outcroppings of columnar basalt in mid-river. Scouting is required. A mile and a half downstream comes class 3 Colorado Rapids, with a treacherous standing wave and suckhole on the left-hand side. Class 4 Rattlesnake Rapids are only 1.2 miles farther. Three drownings testify to the danger of this narrows, where boaters must thread their way between rocks on the river's left side and a gigantic suckhole in the river's middle. Two miles farther on, the class 2 Moody Rapids delivers boaters to the backwater of The Dalles Dam.

All boaters must carry a Deschutes River Boater Pass, available at local sporting goods stores or online at *www. boaterpass.com* for about $2 per person per day (triple on weekends). The number of permits for weekends from July 1 to October 15 is limited. Fishing is prohibited from any floating device in the river. Campfires are permitted only in firepans, and only from October 16 to May 31. Campsites between Macks Canyon and Deschutes River State Park have a 4-night stay limit, and maximum group size is 16. No camping is allowed on islands. Boaters can recognize the beginning of private, off-limits shorefront by watching for posts marked with circles; posts with triangles signal the return to public lands.

Lower Deschutes float trips are often coupled with the two-day, 45-mile drift of the central Deschutes River, from the Highway 26 bridge near Warm Springs to the boat landing at Maupin. Jet boats and motors are banned on the portion of the river bordering the Indian Reservation and are restricted elsewhere.

Bicycling the Deschutes River Trail.

18
DESCHUTES CANYON

The Deschutes River roars through this 700-foot-deep canyon, beneath sagebrush mesas with views of the High Cascade snowpeaks.

The Deschutes Canyon below Steelhead Falls.

Climate

Sunshine is the rule in this steppe, which gets less than 10 inches of annual rainfall. Summers are hot, but frost is common at night and in winter.

Plants and Wildlife

Heavy grazing on the tablelands has converted a historic bunchgrass steppe to sagebrush, cheat grass, and tumbleweed. The steep canyons and The Island north of Cove Palisades Park, however, preserve native bunchgrasses and the original "desert crust," a complex ground cover of lichens and mosses. The river itself creates a narrow oasis dotted with ponderosa pine and vine maple. Golden eagles nest in the cliffs near Steelhead Falls. Coyotes and mule deer abound.

Geology

The canyon's layer-cake-style cliffs consist mostly of 5- to 25-million-year-old basalt lava flows from the Cascade Range. The Island, however, and other certain other terraces halfway up the cliffs, are remnants of the Intracanyon Basalt, a more recent flow that began 60 miles away at Newberry Volcanic National Monument. Slow cooling allowed many of the basalt layers to fracture into a distinctive pattern of hexagonal pillars. The slopes between cliff layers, sometimes eroded into multi-colored pinnacles, are composed of volcanic ash, gravel, and soil that accumulated between the devastating basalt floods, which were often 100,000 years apart.

History

Faint red petroglyphs under cliff overhangs along Whychus Creek testify to a long human presence here. Pioneers named the stream Squaw Creek. When modern tribes objected that this was demeaning, the name was changed in 2005 to Whychus, the Sahaptin word for "a

Location: 32 mi N of Bend

Size: 29 sq mi

Status: undesignated wilderness

Terrain: cliff-lined canyons, desert plateaus

Elevation: 1945'-2950'

Management: Crooked River National Grassland

Maps: Central Oregon (BLM); Steelhead Falls, Squaw Back Ridge, Round Butte Dam (USGS)

place to cross the water."

In the early 1990s a hermit bought a ranch in the creek's canyon and began threatening hikers headed to Alder Springs. Finally a hiker discovered that the recluse was actually using his ranch house as a meth lab. After a police raid, authorities confiscated the ranch, removed the house, and built a nicer hiking trail.

The Deschutes Arm of Lake Billy Chinook.

HIKING & BACKPACKING

Start with the Tam-a-lau Trail, which gains 550 feet in 1.3 miles from the far west end of the Cove Palisades' campground to The Peninsula. From there, a 3.6-mile loop trail skirts the edge of this arid mesa, with excellent views of the Billy Chinook Reservoir.

Steelhead Falls' thundering, 20-foot drop is a half-mile stroll from a primitive campground beside the Crooked River Ranch subdivision. Such easy access has made the falls a party site, particularly for daredevils who leap from a cliff 25 feet into the fall's chilly plunge pool—a stunt that is not recommended. From the falls, a good trail continues another 0.6 mile upriver. A scramble route continues, but a better side trail climbs 0.5 mile to viewpoints—and to unmarked trailheads on subdivision roads.

To find Steelhead Falls' main trailhead (GPS location N44°24.67′ W121°17.56′), drive Highway 97 north of Redmond 6 miles. Beyond Terrebonne half a mile,

The Island from The Peninsula.

turn left onto Lower Bridge Way for 2.1 miles. Then turn right on 43rd Street for 1.9 miles, turn left on Chinook Avenue for 1.1 mile, turn left on Badger Road 1.8 miles, turn right on Quail Road 1.2 miles, and turn left on River Road 1 mile.

Deeper in the Deschutes Canyon, the spectacular Scout Camp Trail loops 3 miles past striped cliffs and wildflowers down to the river. Drive as above, but stick to Chinook Drive for 2.4 miles. Then turn left on Mustang Road for 1.1 mile, turn right on Shad Road 1.4 miles, turn right on Peninsula Drive 3.3 miles,

Steelhead Falls.

turn left on Meadow Road 0.6 mile, and turn right on gravel Scount Camp Trail a quarter mile to road's end (GPS location N44°27.663' W121°19.294').

Striped cliffs also tower above Alder Springs, an oasis deep in Whychus Creek's desert canyon. Hike here on a delightful 1.4-mile trail that fords the creek (knee-deep in spring, but ankle deep in fall). If you're backpacking, note that fires are banned and tents must be 50 feet from water. Beyond Alder Springs the trail continues 1.6 miles to a scenic but uncampable deadend at the bouldery Deschutes River.

The road to the trailhead is gated closed each winter from November 1 to March 31 to protect wildlife. Drive Highway 126 from Sisters toward Redmond 4.6 miles, and turn left on Goodrich Road for 8.1 zigzagging, paved miles. At a marker for milepost 7, turn left on Road 6360 for 4.1 miles, and turn right to the trailhead.

BOATING

Big Falls and Steelhead Falls stop all whitewater boating on the Deschutes. Kayaks carried to the base of Steelhead Falls face 7.5 miles of unknown rapids.

19
METOLIUS RIVER

The Metolius is the most magical of all Oregon rivers. From the arid base of Black Butte it springs fully grown, at an identical temperature and volume year-round, then slides swiftly through 29 miles of rugged canyons before vanishing into the slack water of the Lake Billy Chinook reservoir. Along the way, the river twists through the Horn of the Metolius, a wilderness canyon.

Climate
Though mostly sunny and dry (20 inches annual precipitation), the area receives snow from about December to February. Snow lingers on Green Ridge till April.

Plants and Wildlife
Orange-trunked ponderosa pine and autumn-red vine maple flank the river. Bitterbrush and rabbit brush (bright yellow blooms in fall) form a sparse ground cover. On the eastern ridges, gnarled juniper are the only trees.

The river's name comes from the Warm Springs Indian *Mpto-ly-as*, "white fish." The light-fleshed salmon which prompted this name are gone, but introduced Kokanee salmon and abundant hatchery trout attract eagles, bears, and other anglers.

Geology
The geologically recent creation of Green Ridge, a 16-mile-long, 2500-foot-tall fault scarp, displaced the Metolius

The Metolius River.

River to the north and spawned Black Butte, a volcanic cone. Later basalt lava flows from the Cascade Range formed the adjacent Metolius Bench tablelands, with their dramatic rimrock.

HIKING & BACKPACKING
The 1.5-mile Shut-in Trail traverses a dense forest along the rushing Metolius River in a remote canyon called the Horn of the Metolius. Now that cars have been banned from 14.9 miles of the trail's badly rutted access roads, hikers, equestrians, and bicyclists can tour along the wild river undisturbed for a total of 16 miles from Lower Bridge Campground to Monty Campground.

The route's eastern trailhead at Monty Campground is reached by driving west from Madras through Cove Palisades State Park and Grandview to the gated end of Road 64. If you're coming

> **Location:** 45 mi N of Bend, 32 mi W of Madras
> **Size:** 17 sq mi
> **Status:** undesignated wilderness
> **Terrain:** steep, forested river canyon
> **Elevation:** 2000'-5050'
> **Management:** Deschutes NF
> **Maps:** Whitewater River (Green Trails)

from Sisters, drive 5 miles west on Highway 20, turn north onto Road 11 for 18
miles, turn right onto Road 1170 for 5
miles, and then take Road 64 to the left
for 8 miles to Monty Campground. Park
at the gate and hike (or bicycle) the old
road 4 miles to the Shut-in Trail.

To find the route's western trailhead,
take Highway 20 east of Santiam Pass 10
miles and turn north on paved Road 14
through Camp Sherman, passing many
campgrounds, for a total of 13 miles to
Lower Bridge Campground. From the
campground, hike (or bicycle) down a
gated road along the river for 9.4 miles
to the Shut-in Trail.

The Metolius River forms the southern boundary of the Warm Springs Indian Reservation. Entry to tribal lands is
completely prohibited here.

Excellent views of Mount Jefferson,
Castle Rock, and Five-Fingered Senti-
nel await cross-country hikers willing

to scale the persistent slopes of Green
Ridge. The open forest presents no obstacle.

A nice hike in the east of the area follows an unmarked half-mile-long trail
up Street Creek. To find Street Creek,
drive 2 miles past Perry South Campground on Road 64 to a sign reading,
"Monty Campground 3 miles." From
here the trail follows the creek's north
bank. At trail's end, adventurous hikers
can bushwhack another 1.5 miles upstream past ash formations and a cave,
hike north up a side canyon, and walk
east along the rimrock's edge to a viewpoint.

Similar ash deposits nearby created
the balancing rocks featured by the tele-
vision series "Oregon Field Guide." To
see them, drive 2 miles west of Perry
South Campground on Road 64, park at
a pullout, and hike a quarter-mile trail
to two overlooks.

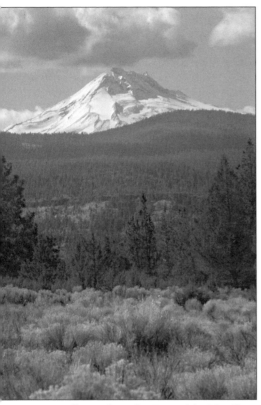

Mt. Jefferson from the Horn of the Metolius.

tween 5 and 10 miles per hour, providing plenty of whitewater thrills. In 26 miles of free-flowing water between Riverside Campground (1.5 miles south of Camp Sherman) and Lake Billy Chinook, the only unnavigable hazard is at Wizard Falls, 6.5 miles from the start. The "falls" itself is merely a reef-like ledge, but the dangerously low bridge beyond it requires a portage. The last bridge across the river, Lower Bridge, is at river mile 9. The Confederated Tribes of Warm Springs discourage boating beyond this point because the river borders the reservation here. To avoid trespassing and possible arrest, do not land on the left bank. Those who continue usually take out at Monty Campground, because the next public boat landing (at Perry South Campground) requires a 3.5-mile paddle across the reservoir.

The hiker-only East Metolius Trail follows the river 10.2 miles from Lower Bridge Campground to Riverside Campground—just short of the river's source at the Head of the Metolius' massive springs. This delightful but less wild hiking route (not shown on map) passes seven popular car campgrounds along the way.

The Metolius River at Shepard Tower.

CLIMBING

Shepard Tower of the Metolius, half a mile uphill from the road/trail along the Metolius River (6.5 miles from the Lower Bridge trailhead) offers four routes via chimneys and ledges. Difficulty levels are I-3 to I-5.4.

BOATING

Clear, deep, and cold (46° F year round), the Metolius races along at be-

20
SMITH ROCK

The orange rock walls and pinnacles of Smith Rock tower above an oasis-like riverbend at the edge of central Oregon's sagebrush plains. The spectacular formation is both a reliably rainless hiking destination and the best technical rock climbing site in Oregon.

The Crooked River loops around Smith Rock.

Climate

With just 8.5 inches of annual precipitation, Smith Rock is usually sunny even when the trails of the High Cascades are beset with rain or snow. Midwinter brings a few dustings of snow, and mid-summer brings blazing heat.

Plants and Wildlife

Visit in spring for high desert wildflowers. Admire but do not pick the riverbank's wild asparagus and wild onions. Climbers should take pains not to disturb birds of prey nesting on the crags.

Geology

The western vanguard of the Ochoco Mountains, Smith Rock is formed of welded rhyolite ash. This ash erupted from the Old Cascades, settled in a large inland sea, and was fused by heat and pressure to form rock. More recent lava flows pushed the Crooked River up against Smith Rock and left the basalt rimrock of the river's south shore.

HIKING & BACKPACKING

Drive to the park by turning east off Highway 97 at Terrebonne, 6 miles north of Redmond. Follow state park signs 3 miles, past Juniper Junction, a

Location: 9 mi N of Redmond

Size: 1 sq mi

Status: state park

Terrain: river peninsula with rock formations

Elevation: 2620'-3500'

Management: Oregon State Parks and Recreation Department

Maps: Redmond, Opal City, O'Neil, Gray Butte (USGS)

shop known for its refreshing huckleberry ice cream.

Park by the picnic area restroom, pay the park's $3-per-car fee at an automat, and walk to the right through the picnic area to find the 0.4-mile trail (a gated service road) down to a footbridge over the Crooked River.

Cross the bridge and turn left on a delightful riverbank path that skirts below orange cliffs. You'll soon round a bend and come to three side trails signed for The Dihedrals and Asterisk Pass; these climb up stairs and end at cliffs where climbers dangle, jangling their gear. Explore these side trails by hiking up one and down the next.

Then continue downriver. At the 2-mile mark the trail rounds the tip of a peninsula and soon offers the first view

ahead to Monkey Face, a 350-foot rock monolith topped by a remarkable natural sculpture of a monkey's head. Ignore a fork to the right for Angel Flight Buttress and continue along the river 0.5 mile. A bit beyond Monkey Face, and just beyond a house-sized boulder, you'll reach a trail junction. To the left, the river trail continues faintly another 0.3 mile before petering out at a collection of balancing rocks.

For a 4-mile loop hike, however, keep right on the main trail. This path switchbacks up past the base of Monkey Face to a ridge where views extend across Central Oregon to peaks from the Three Sisters to Mt. Hood. Contour 200 yards to the edge of Misery Ridge, where several steep staircases have taken the misery out of the switchbacking descent back to the Crooked River Bridge.

For a more challenging, 6.3-mile loop, bushwhack north from a trail switchback beside Monkey Face, climb to the ridge, and follow it for a mile to Burma Road. Turn right on this dirt track 0.7 mile to the start of a canal, and then take a side path down to the Crooked River.

The 5.8-mile Gray Butte Trail joins the Burma Road track at the top of Smith Rock's ridge, providing a quieter, backdoor route to this popular park. The two Gray Butte trailheads charge no parking fee and are open to bicyclists and equestrians (unlike the state park trails). To find the trailheads (not on the map), turn off Highway 97 at Terrebonne onto Smith Rock Way, but then stick to this paved road 5.9 miles, ignoring signs that point left to the park. At a T-shaped junction, turn left on Lone Pine Road for 3.4 miles, and then turn left across a cattle guard onto gravel Road 5710 for 1.1 mile. For the Gray Butte Saddle Trailhead, turn left on Road 5720 for 1.6 miles. For the McCoin Orchard Trailhead, continue straight on Road 5710 another 1.4 miles and turn left on Road 57 for 0.7 mile.

CLIMBING

With more than 3 miles of rock faces and nearly 1000 named routes, Smith Rock ranks first among Oregon's technical climbing sites, with routes to level IV-5.12 and beyond. Good weather and easy access add to the area's popularity.

Monkey Face

Climber at Smith Rock.

Heavy use, however, has necessitated several rules. Stay on established trails as much possible. Add no permanent anchors. Camp only in the designated bivouac area. Campfires are prohibited.

Large climbing classes and search-and-rescue practice groups should strive to minimize their impact by climbing in beginner areas. The 30-foot basalt rimrock cliffs on the opposite shore of the river from The Monument are easily accessible and offer technical pitches. Beginners intent on trying rhyolite will find a good practice boulder (named "Rope de Dope") on the riverbank opposite Morning Glory Wall.

The area's most spectacular challenge is Monkey Face, a 350-foot tower overhanging on all sides, first climbed on January 1, 1960. There are 27 routes and variations, including the level II-5.11 Monkey Space route behind the monkey's head, and the level II-5.7-A1 Pioneer Route past Panic Point, on the monkey's Mouth Cave.

Other major climbing areas include Picnic Lunch Wall (24 routes), Morning Glory Wall (56 routes), The Dihedrals (52 routes), The Christian Brothers (43 routes), Smith Rock promontory (43 routes), Mesa Verde Wall (23 routes), Red Wall (26 routes), Red Ryder Buttress (6 routes), Staender Ridge (6 routes), and Marsupial Crags (31 routes).

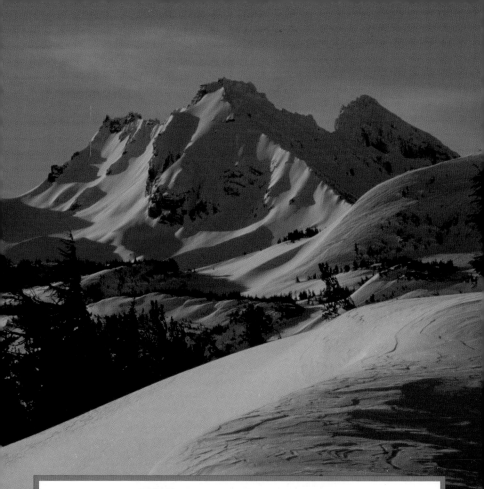

WILDERNESS
of
SOUTHWEST OREGON

Broken Top from the Chambers Lakes in April

THE THREE SISTERS

Oregon's most popular Wilderness has a cluster of volcanoes. Clockwise from above, the PCT near Scott Pass, , Scott Lake, North Sister, Middle Sister, South Sister from Camp Lake (Chambers Lakes), Talbot Bielefeldt and Broken Top in April, Tam Lake, Golden Lake, Wickiup Plain, and Broken Top from Moraine Lake.

SOUTH OF THE SISTERS

The Green Lakes (left) are a popular destination in the Three Sisters Wilderness. Goals to the south include (clockwise from top) Indigo Lake, Diamond Peak in February, Goodman Creek at Hardesty Mountain, Maidu Lake, and Howlock Meadows from Tipsoo Peak. Above: columnar basalt at the Soda Springs Trailhead of the Boulder Creek Wilderness.

CRATER LAKE & THE ROGUE

Oregon's national park, Crater Lake, stands at the head of the wild Rogue River, fringed by Wilderness. Clockwise from upper left: Crater Lake from Garfield Peak, Crater Lake from Sun Notch in April, Mule Creek Canyon on the Rogue River, Flora Dell Falls, the Elk River, Vulcan Lake, Biscuit Hill sunset, Lilypad Lake at Red Buttes, Hershberger Mountain, Devils Peak from Grass Lake, and Llao Rock at Crater Lake. Above: Marguerette Lake in the Sky Lakes Wilderness.

THE OREGON COAST

The state's Pacific islands are Wilderness, and varied coastal lands as well. Clockwise from upper left: Pacific City's Haystack Rock, Sea Lions near Cape Perpetua, the lower Rogue River at Copper Canyon, two sunset photos from the Oregon Dunes, and a wave at Cape Perpetua.

Map Key	Destination	Total miles	Easy-M-Diff.	Days	Est. Mos. Open	Uncrowded	Page
A	Sunshine/Obsidian Falls	10	D	3	VII½-X		127
B	Camp Lake/Chambers Lks	14	D	3	VIII-X½		127
C	Demaris Lake	11	M	3	VII½-X½	●	127
D	Park Meadow/Golden Lake	10	M	3	VII¾-X		127
E	Green Lakes	9	D	3	VIII-X½		130
F	Moraine Lake	7	D	2	VIII-X½		130
G	Sisters Mirror Lake	7	M	2	VII½-X		131
H	Horse Lake	7	E	2	VII-X		131
I	Mink Lake	17	D	3	VII-X	●	131
J	Cliff Lake	14	M	3	VII-X		131
K	Around the Three Sisters	44	D	5	VIII-X		131
L	Linton Meadow	19	D	3	VII½-X	●	134
M	Rosary Lakes	6	M	2	VI½-X		139
N	South Waldo Shelter	4	E	2	VI½-X		139
O	Waldo Lake Outlet	6	E	3	VI½-X		139
P	Erma Bell Lakes	4	E	2	VI½-X		142
Q	Salmon Lakes	6	E	3	VI½-X	●	142
R	Klovdahl Bay	8	D	3	VI½-X	●	142
S	Around Waldo Lake	20	D	3	VI½-X	●	143
T	Eddeeleo Lakes	9	D	3	VI½-X	●	143
U	Maiden Peak Shelter	13	D	3	VI½-X	●	144
V	Vivian Lake	8	D	3	VI½-X	●	147
W	Yoran Lake	10	D	3	VII-X	●	147
X	Diamond View Lake	11	D	3	VII-X	●	147
Y	Fawn Lake	7	M	2	VI¾-X		148
Z	Indigo Lake	2	E	2	VI¾-X	●	148
AA	Divide Lake	8	D	3	VII-X		149
BB	Around Diamond Peak	29	D	4	VII½-X	●	149
CC	Pine Bench	5	M	2	●	●	155
DD	Thielsen Creek Camp	11	D	3	VII¾-X		159
EE	Maidu Lake	8	M	2	VII¼-X		159
FF	Fish Lake	3	E	2	V-XII½		162
GG	Buckeye Lake	3	E	2	V½-XI	●	162
HH	Around High-Rock Mountain	15	M	3	VII-X	●	164
II	Seven Lakes Basin	10	M	3	VII¼-X		176
JJ	Heavenly Twin Lakes	5	E	2	VII¼-X		177
KK	Trapper Lake	13	D	3	VII½-X	●	177
LL	Pear Lake	7	M	2	VII¼-X	●	177
MM	Eb & Zeb Lakes	10	M	3	VII½-XI¼		180
NN	Sucker Creek Gap	7	M	2	VI¼-XI½	●	188
OO	Azalea Lake	13	D	3	VI½-XI½		189
PP	Boundary Trail	20	D	3	VI½-XI¼	●	189
QQ	Red Buttes	33	D	4	VI½-XI		189
RR	Babyfoot Lake	2	E	2	V-XI½		194
SS	Vulcan Lake	3	E	2	V-XI		194
TT	Pearsoll Peak	14	D	3	V½-X½	●	195
UU	Illinois River Trail	27	D	3	V-XI	●	195
WW	Rogue River Trail	40	D	4	●		200
XX	Siltcoos Lake	4	E	2	●		209
YY	Threemile Lake	6	E	2	●	●	209

SOUTHWEST OREGON

0   10   20   30mi   N
0 10 20 30 40km

Designated wilderness

Undesignated wilderness

Designated wilderness islands

Florence

Range

Eugene

36

126

OREGON DUNES **36**

37

DEVILS STAIRCASE

Drain

Reedsport Scottsburg

38

Ocean

Coos Bay

Coast

Roseburg

Table Rk

42

5

227

101

Canyonville

Tiller

Powers

GRASSY KNOB COPPER SALMON

Blanco Reef
Orford Reef

35

Port Orford

North Sisters Rocks

34

Agness

WILD ROGUE

Galice

Pacific

OREGON

Gold Beach

38

Grants Pass

199

Medford

Selma

ISLANDS

Arch Rock

KALMIOPSIS

33

Cave Junction

RED BUTTES

32

Brookings

Goat Is.

Siskiyou   Mtns

21
THREE SISTERS

A cluster of glacier-clad volcanoes highlights Oregon's most visited wilderness. This large area contains four very different geographic zones.

In the alpine region ringing the Three Sisters and craggy Broken Top, wildflower meadows alternate with lava formations. But to the south, the Cascade crest is a rolling forest of pine and mountain hemlock with hundreds of lakes. To the west, foggy, low-elevation canyons brim with old-growth Douglas fir. To the southeast, sparse forests of lodgepole pine and beargrass carpet arid lands beyond the Century Lakes.

Climate

Winter snow in the uplands drifts to depths of up to 20 feet. In the east the snow falls dry, providing some of the state's best powder skiing. Even the lowest trails remain blocked by snow until May. Trails up to an elevation of 5000 feet are clear by about mid-June and trails at 6500 feet are usually clear by August, though snowstorms can occur in any month.

The area's western slopes receive 90 inches of annual precipitation, but the eastern slopes receive just 20 inches a year. The Mink Lake and Horse Lake basins especially are plagued by mosquitoes in July and early August.

Plants and Wildlife

The area's size makes it a refuge for large, shy animals such as wolverine, mink, cougar, and bald eagle. Geographic diversity makes the area home to more plant species than any other Oregon wilderness.

Subalpine wildflower displays in July and early August include blue lupine and red paintbrush. Snowmelt zones teem with white avalanche lily, marsh marigold, and fuzzy pasque flower. Wet areas have red elephanthead, shooting star, yellow monkeyflower, columbine, and larkspur. Drier fields host fuzzy cats ears and wild sunflower.

Pink rhododendron displays brighten the lower western slopes in early June. Ripe wild huckleberries line forest trails in the 5000- to 6500-foot elevation range in late August.

Geology

Although a 1925 theory claimed the taller peaks were remnants of an exploded super-volcano, "Mount Multnomah," more recent study shows the mountains formed separately, all within the past 100,000 years, along the High Cascades fault zone.

Oldest peaks in the group are North Sister, which has lost a third of its bulk to glacial erosion, leaving its central plug as a summit spire, and Broken Top, eroded so severely it offers a good cut-away view of a composite volcano's interior structure—alternating red and

Location: 52 mi E of Eugene, 26 mi W of Bend

Size: 572 sq mi, including Century Lakes, Chucksney Mountain, and Macduff Peak

Status: 443 sq mi designated wilderness (1964, 1978, 1984)

Terrain: snowpeaks, lava, forests, lakes, valleys

Elevation: 1850'-10,358'

Management: Deschutes NF, Willamette NF

Map: Three Sisters (Geo-Graphics)

North and Middle Sister from Four-In-One Cone on the Scott Trail.

black bands of cinder and lava. Broken Top's violent past has left the area strewn with interesting, drop-shaped "lava bombs," football-sized bits of exploded magma that cooled in flight.

Middle Sister's Collier Glacier was once the state's largest, but a one-mile retreat since 1900 has transferred the honor to South Sister's Prouty Glacier. South Sister is geologically young enough to have kept its uneroded conical shape. Its summit crater cups the state's highest lake, Teardrop Pool. Mount Bachelor, another youthful volcano, harbors inner fires which create small snow wells on the mountain's north slope, a hazard for skiers.

Collier Cone erupted some 15,000 years ago directly in the path of the mighty Collier Glacier, commencing a battle of fire and ice. One of the cone's fresh-looking lava flows traced the White Branch valley for 8.5 miles, damming Linton Lake.

Flows of glassy, black obsidian are exposed both below Sunshine, near North Sister, and at Green Lakes, near South Sister. Another kind of high-silica-content eruption formed the frothy, lighter-than-water pumice of Rock Mesa. A California company's mining claim on Rock Mesa's pumice, which would have converted this prominent wilderness feature to cat litter, ended with a $2 million buyout by Congress in 1983.

Ice Age glaciers formed the steep, U-shaped valleys of the South Fork McKenzie River and Separation Creek. Sand-pile moraines left by retreating glaciers dammed most alpine lakes.

History

Once a popular autumn camp for Indians, the area provided huckleberries, venison, obsidian for arrowheads, and beargrass for basketry. Antler-shaped pictographs across the Cascade Lakes Highway from the east end of Devils Lake are federally protected.

Many place names in the area recall Chinook jargon, an Indian trade language once widely used by Indians and settlers of the Oregon frontier. Hikers can cross Skookum ("powerful") Creek, camp in Olallie ("berry") Meadows, climb Koosah ("sky") Mountain, and spot Cultus ("worthless") Lake.

Visitors to the area sometimes smile at the Three Sister's "family" of lesser peaks-the Little Brother, The Husband, and The Wife. Few realize there are also a Chinook aunt and uncle (Kwolh Butte and Tot Mountain) hiding behind Mount Bachelor. Other Chinook names in the area are Tipsoo ("grassy") Butte, Hiyu ("big") Ridge, Moolack ("elk") Mountain, Kokostick ("woodpecker") Butte, Talapus ("coyote") Butte, and Sahalie ("upper") Falls.

HIKING & BACKPACKING
EAST MAP

Free wilderness entry permits can be filled out conveniently at all of the trailheads except the Obsidian Trailhead, near North Sister's Sunshine area. To

North Sister and the Collier Glacier.

limit crowds in that popular area, permits are only issued for 20 groups a day, and the permits must be reserved in advance from the McKenzie Ranger Station. Call (541) 822-3381 for details.

The Three Sisters' popularity has brought other restrictions as well. In the Sunshine area, where several square miles of alpine meadows spread below North Sister, all campfires are banned and tents must be more than 100 feet from any water source or trail. Campfires are likewise taboo within a quarter mile of Husband or Eileen Lakes and within half a mile of other popular pools: Camp Lake, the three Green Lakes, the four Chambers Lakes, and Moraine Lake. At the Green Lakes, and at several other popular destinations, camping is allowed only at sites marked by a post. To avoid crowds, plan to visit in fall or in the middle of the week, or try striking off cross-country by compass; it's not hard through the high country.

Two of the area's easiest hikes are the 1-mile loop to feathery Proxy Falls and the 1.4-mile, relatively level trail to Linton Lake. Both paths start from the scenic, historic Highway 242 west of McKenzie Pass. Several other hikes in the dramatic McKenzie Pass area are described in area 12. For an easy hike near Sisters, take the 1-mile trail to 60-foot Chush Falls (known as Squaw Creek Falls prior to 2005) from a rough spur of Road 1514.

North Sister in winter from Soap Creek.

Special permits are required for the very popular 4.8-mile, uphill path to Sunshine Meadow that begins at the Obsidian Trailhead on Highway 242. Day hikers should not miss the loop past Obsidian Cliffs and Obsidian Falls. Following the Pacific Crest Trail in either direction from Sunshine makes for memorable backpacking trips. Two miles north, the PCT crosses a lava flow to Collier Cone and a viewpoint of the huge Collier Glacier. Five miles south of Sunshine, side trails of the PCT reach Linton Meadow, nestled between Middle Sister and the crags of The Husband.

The 7000-foot-high Chambers Lakes, surrounded by the glaciers of Middle and South Sister, often have drifting ice throughout summer. Wind-gnarled whitebark pines are the only trees. The dramatic lakes are 7.1 miles from the Pole Creek Trailhead at the end of Road 1524. From the town of Sisters, drive west 1.4 miles on Highway 242, then turn left onto Road 15 for 5 miles to Road 1524. Because the Chambers Lakes are relatively windy and barren, backpackers might consider heading 2 miles east to Demaris Lake instead, in more sheltered woods.

Park Meadow features views of four mountains. Nearby, easy cross-country hikes lead to Golden Lake and other wildflower havens higher on the slopes of Broken Top and South Sister. Backpackers here must remember not to camp in any meadow or within 100 feet of water; hide tents in the woods. Park Meadow is an almost level 4.9 miles from the end of pavement on Road 16, a road which begins as Elm Street in downtown Sisters.

The 500-foot cliff of Tam McArthur Rim has perhaps the best view of the Three Sisters. A 2.5-mile trail climbs from the turnoff to Driftwood Campground on Road 16 to the cliff's dramatic edge, where snow lingers through August. From there, the rim's above-timberline crest lures hikers on toward Broken Hand and more grand views.

A dozen popular campgrounds and

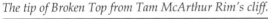

The tip of Broken Top from Tam McArthur Rim's cliff.

THREE SISTERS - EAST

0   1   2mi
0   1   2   3km

(See Three Sisters – West Map)

Bend 17 mi
Sunriver 14 mi
P
Swampy Lakes
Kapka Butte
P Edison Butte
Bridge Cr
Highway
45
Edison Ice Cave
P Vista Butte
Cascade Lakes
Tumalo Mtn
7775
5300
Dutchman Flat P
Mt Bachelor
6100
Kwolh Butte
7358
5900'
Sheridan Mtn
6890'
Mt Bachelor
9065'
Tot Mtn
Todd Lake
46
Century
4029
4525
Cr 5500
Soda Creek
Sparks L
Talapus Butte
Katsuk Butte
5200'
Lakes
Lava Lake
$ Little Lava Lake
Deschutes Bridge
$
Devils Lake
Mallard Marsh
South
Deschutes
R
Quinn Meadow Horse Camp
Hosmer
Lava L
4800'
5450
Red Crater
46
Crescent 36mi
4628
Elk Lake
$ Little Fawn
Lucky L
Kokostick Butte
Junco L
4950
6000'
G
Pacific
Point
Blow L
Williamson Mtn
Sisters Mirror
Koosah Mtn
Elk Mtn
Crest
Doris L
(See Area 22 Map)
Red Hill
Sisters
Wilderness
Goldeneye L
Top L
Colt
Senoj L
5800'
Leech L
Sixbit Pt
Lucky Butte
Horse Lake
4930
Sunset
Burnt Top
6250'
Mile L
Trail
Island
5450'
J
Moonlight L
Middle Horse L
Park
Sandy L
Dumbbell L
Krag L
Horseshoe
Horse Mtn
Lower Horse L
Nightshade L
Spy L
Cliff L
Mac L
Puppy L
Snowshoe L
Corner
Porky L
Long L
4800'
Upper Snowshoe L
Penn L
Packsaddle Mtn
5300'
I
(See Three Sisters – West Map)
Mink Lake
5034'

South Sister from the largest of the Green Lakes.

trailheads line the Cascade Lakes High-way. Opposite the turnoff to Mount Bachelor on this route is the trail to Tum-alo Mountain, a 1.8-mile path climbing 1200 feet up the conical, forested butte to a former fire lookout site.

The most heavily used trail in the area, and one of the most scenic, climbs 4.2 miles from Sparks Lake to the Green Lake Basin at the foot of South Sister. The route follows rushing Fall Creek around a blocky lava flow to these spectacular high lakes—which really are green, colored by finely ground silt from nearby Lewis Glacier. Campfires are banned within a half mile of Green Lakes, and tents are allowed only at 28 sites marked by posts. Weekend space is tight, and rangers issue tickets to illegal campers, so arrive early.

A more nearly level route into the Green Lakes is available by the start of August, when snowmelt opens Road 370 from Todd Lake to the Crater Ditch Trailhead. The 4.8-mile Ditch Trail from spur Road 380 contours around Broken Top, offering viewpoints at every turn. A worthwhile cross-country trip from

the same trailhead follows Crater Creek up to its head at an ice-filled lake inside Broken Top's ruined crater.

Scaling South Sister may sound too ambitious for a hike, but in fact Or-egon's third tallest mountain requires no technical climbing skills or equip-ment. The hike gains 4,900 feet in 5.5 miles to the view of a lifetime. Begin at the Devils Lake Campground and head directly for the summit. The trail steep-ens sharply at the edge of Lewis Glacier, continuing up snow and cinder slopes from there to the broad summit bowl. Do not attempt the trip in anything less than perfect weather.

A less ambitious goal is Moraine Lake, surrounded by an ancient, sandy glacial terminus. Climbers often biv-ouac here en route to South Sister, but note that tents are allowed near Moraine Lake only at sites designated by a post. If you arrive late in the day, plan on a dry camp at least half a mile away.

South Sister rises like a wall from the edge of Wickiup Plain, a square mile of cinders and bunchgrass located 2 miles by trail from Devils Lake. LeConte Crater, a perfect little cinder cone at the plain's upper edge, makes a fun climb. The scenic plain has no water, so the meadows a mile farther west, at Sisters Mirror Lake, see heavy camping use. This area is quite fragile; explore the interesting surrounding terrain for campsites well away from trailside lakes.

Horse Lake, an easy 3.3-mile hike west of the Cascade Lakes Highway at Elk Lake, is at the center of a broad basin of lakes. Backpackers at Horse Lake should bushwhack to the far (west) end of the lake and camp well away from the shore. Trails radiate from Horse Lake toward dozens of peaceful lake destinations. The forested lakeshores in this area lack views of snowpeaks.

Mink Lake is the largest of another cluster of forest-rimmed lakes. A popular 8.6-mile route to Mink Lake begins a mile south of Elk Lake. Expect crowds at the narrow gravel beach of Blow Lake, 1 mile along this trail, and at 90-acre Doris Lake, 1.4 miles farther. At a junction 5.4 miles from the trailhead, the PCT leads to other heavily used lakes: Mac, Horseshoe, Cliff, Island, and Dumbbell. Cliff Lake is a particularly scenic backpacking goal, with a rustic shelter and a cliff, but it's easy to miss the unmarked turnoff from the PCT. Hundreds of quieter lakes nearby offer solitude.

Equestrians should keep in mind that pack and saddle animals are not permitted within 200 feet of any lake in the designated wilderness except for watering, loading, or traveling on established trails.

Trails in the Century Lakes area, often used by equestrians, are also suitable for hikers. The 8-mile route from the Quinn Meadow Horse Camp to Soda Creek Campground passes Hosmer Lake, then dives back into the dry, lodgepole pine forest toward Sparks Lake. Trails from Hosmer Lake to Lava Lake, and from Lava Lake east, traverse unbroken forests of lodgepole pine, beargrass, and cinders. Carry water. Even the briefest cross-country travel in this 54-square-mile roadless area provides complete solitude. Explorers may search here for undiscovered lava tube caves.

The PCT offers a long-distance route the length of the Three Sisters Wilderness — 52 miles from McKenzie Pass to Taylor Burn Road. The area's most spectacular backpacking adventure, however, is the 44.1-mile loop around the Three Sisters, following 19.1 miles of the PCT's most scenic section. This breathtaking loop has been done in a single day, but deserves at least five.

Horse Lake.

Proxy Pt

6344'
Substitute Pt

(See Three Sisters – East Map)

Alder Springs

Proxy Falls

Tokatee Lakes

4250'

Rainbow

3500'

Separation

4100'

Dillon DL

Snow gate closed in winter

White Branch org. site

Louise

George

2700'

Harvey

Horse

242

Three

Sisters

Eugene

Foley

Ridge

Rainbow Falls

2643

2200'

Roney

Creek

Cr

Horse

Separation Creek

Mosquito

4800'
Olallie Mdws

1993

Limberlost

Santiam Pass 30 mi

2643

Castle

Taylor Castle

The Potholes

Wolverine Mdw

Pat Saddle

5700'
Olallie Mtn

4500
Lamb Butte

French Mtn

Paradise

2638

Avenue

5660'
Horsepasture Mtn

4650'
Horsepasture Saddle

4660'
Aspen

Pat

Foley Springs

McKenzie Br

1993

O'Leary Mtn

Olallie Cr

Lowder Mtn
5550'

2800'

Horse Creek

Harris

2800'

King Cr

Macduff Mtn

2500'

East Fork

French Cr

Old-growth forest

Bridge out

McLennan Mtn

1993

Walker Ridge

Sawtooth Ridge

Yankee Mtn

5200'

McKenzie Bridge

McKenzie R

Echo

2400'

2000'

Tipsoo Butte

1850
French Pete

Slide Creek

1980

3808
Castle Rock

126

2639

480

411

Cougar Reservoir

Dam

19

Terwilliger Hot Springs

Eugene 46 mi

Rainbow

THREE SISTERS - WEST

HIKING & BACKPACKING
WEST MAP

An often overlooked hike on the west side of the Three Sisters Wilderness is the 1-mile Rainbow Falls Viewpoint Trail. To find it, drive 3 miles east of the McKenzie Bridge Ranger Station on Highway 126 and turn right on Road 2643 for 6.5 miles.

Substitute Point's abandoned lookout site is the goal of another good viewpoint hike, through 5 miles of forest from the Foley Ridge Trailhead on a route popular with equestrians. Linton Meadows and the PCT are 4.5 miles past

Mt. Jefferson from Horsepasture Mountain.

Substitute Point, offering an excellent backpacking goal. Buck Meadows and the Honey Lakes are closer but less dramatic. To start, drive 4.8 miles past Rainbow Falls to the end of Road 2643.

Several day hikes in the Olallie Ridge Research Natural Area begin at Horsepasture Saddle. To find the trailhead, drive to the east end of the bridge in McKenzie Bridge, turn onto Horse Creek Road for 1.7 miles, and turn right onto Road 1993 for 8.6 paved miles. A path east from the saddle climbs 910 feet in 1.4 miles to a first-rate viewpoint atop Horsepasture Mountain. A 5-mile trail northwest from the saddle follows a ridge down 1800 feet before rejoining

Road 1993. A 4.5-mile hike west from the saddle traverses the ridgetop meadows of Macduff Mountain. Finally, a delightful 6-mile segment of the Olallie Trail leads southeast from Horsepasture Saddle, past viewpoints at Taylor Castle and Lamb Butte, to Road 1993 near Pat Creek.

The dilapidated, unlocked 1930s lookout building atop Olallie Mountain has a front-row view of the Three Sisters and eight other snowpeaks. From the Pat Saddle Trailhead on Road 1993, follow the Olallie Trail south 2.1 miles, then turn right on a path through beargrass meadows 1.5 miles to the summit. If instead you continue on the Olallie Trail 0.9 mile you'll reach Olallie Meadows, where a guard station stood until it was crushed by falling trees in 1996 and removed. Horse Lake is another 10.8 miles along the trail.

Castle Rock, a former fire lookout site, has a panoramic view of the McKenzie Valley. Depending on the trailhead you choose, you'll either climb 630 feet in 1 mile to the top, or 2600 feet in 5.7 miles. Both routes are open to mountain bikes. The short route begins at the end of gravel Road 480. The longer route begins from paved Kings Road 2639.

The meadow on Lowder Mountain's table-like summit offers eye-level views of the High Cascades. The best route there is the 2.8-mile trail from Road 1993. The Walker Creek Trail is a fainter, 6.5-mile climb. Backpackers should

Karl and Ruth Lakes from Lowder Mountain.

Broken Top in winter from the trail to the Chambers Lakes.

bring water for a dramatic dry camp on the summit to watch sunset on the Three Sisters.

Terwilliger Hot Springs (also known as Cougar Hot Springs) is a good place to wash off trail dust. An easy half-mile path leads to an old-growth forest canyon with a string of crowded natural hot pools (closed after dark). Expect a $5-per-person fee at the well-marked trailhead beside Cougar Reservoir on the paved Aufderheide Drive (Road 19).

The French Pete Creek Trail winds through a forest of massive old-growth Douglas fir. Day hikers starting from the French Pete Trailhead on Road 19 usually turn back at the 1.7-mile mark, where the first of two missing bridges demands a cold wade or an iffy crossing on wiggly logs. A car-shuttle option is to start at Road 1993 and descend Pat and French Pete creeks 9.8 miles to Road 19.

The Rebel Rock Trail climbs 3200 feet in 4.8 miles from Road 19 to a viewpoint and a cliff-edge lookout building (which is actually located 1 mile west of Rebel Rock's trailless summit). An easier trip is the 1.1-mile walk up the adjacent Rebel Creek Trail to its second bridge amid 400-year-old Douglas firs. Or connect both trails with a strenuous 12.3-mile loop.

Several routes popular with equestrians lead to the Mink Lake area from the west. The heavily used 7.8-mile Elk Creek Trail switchbacks uphill 1700 feet in its first 2 miles from Road 1964. The lesser-known Crossing Way Trail, along Roaring River Ridge from Road 1958, avoids the initial, grueling climb. The two trails join at Corral Flat. Equestrians often start at the Box Canyon Horse Campground.

Chucksney Mountain boasts long ridgetop meadows with sweeping views. A 10.3-mile loop trail along this scenic ridgecrest climbs 2000 feet from Box Canyon Horse Campground on Road 19. The trip is popular with equestrians and mountain bikers as well as hikers. With a car shuttle, it's possible to continue 5 easy miles from the end of the loop to Grasshopper Mountain's meadows.

Grasshopper Mountain can also be the goal of two shorter hikes, either along Hiyu Ridge 4 miles from Road 1927, or up the 1.4-mile trail from Road 1929. To reach the Road 1929 trailhead, drive 13 miles from Westfir (near Oakridge) on Road 19, turn left on Road 1926 for 3 miles, then turn right on Road 1927 for 2.1 miles, and finally turn right on Road 1929 for 5.5 miles.

SNOWSHOEING & SKIING

Powder snow and panoramic scenery make the Dutchman Flat-Swampy

South Sister in winter from Camp Lake in the Chambers Lakes group.

Lakes area near Mount Bachelor ideal for Nordic skiing. Highway 46 is plowed in winter to the Mount Bachelor ski resort, where snowshoe and cross-country ski rentals are available. Just across the highway, the Dutchman Flat sno-park has an extensive network of easy, marked trails through meadow and forest. Loop trips range from 1.4 to 8 miles. Snowmobiles are allowed in certain areas, notably Road 370 (see map on page 128) and the unplowed portion of the Cascade Lakes Highway.

Closer to Bend on the Cascade Lakes Highway, the Swampy Lakes and Meissner sno-parks access an even larger winter trail network, with eight rustic shelters serving as fun destinations and emergency refuges.

Popular trips from the Swampy Lakes sno-park include the easy 4.4-mile loop to the Swampy Lakes shelter, the 6.2-mile Emil Nordeen Shelter loop, and a 9-mile loop to the Swede Ridge shelter. The South Fork Trail descends to the Skyliner sno-park, a smaller Nordic center accessed by driving west of Bend on Galveston Street. An 8-mile trail connects the Dutchman Flat and Swampy Lakes sno-parks, climbing through forest behind Tumalo Mountain.

Skiers and snowshoers can climb 1400 feet up Tumalo Mountain to an outstanding view. Climb directly up the cone-shaped mountain from Dutchman Flat and then telemark or snowboard down through the sparse forest.

The open, high country between Broken Top and Tam McArthur Rim invites longer tours. From the Dutchman Flat sno-park, Broken Top's spectacular crater is 6 miles via the snowed-over Crater Creek Ditch. McArthur Rim is 8 miles. The Green Lakes are 9 miles. Carry emergency gear.

Paved Road 16 from Sisters is plowed in winter to the Three Creek sno-park. From there, a 4.9-mile ski tour reaches scenic Three Creek Lake. Very strong skiers can climb onward to astonishing views on the Tam MacArthur Rim trail.

Two 20-foot yurts and a wood-fired sauna, set up each winter at snowed-under Three Creek Lake Campground, offer backcountry skiers accommodations; check *www.threesistersbackcountry. com* for rates and reservations.

From mid-April to June, cars can drive from Sisters up unplowed Roads 15 and 1524 to the Pole Creek Trailhead, where dramatic (but unmarked) ski tours to Soap Creek's meadows below North Sister begin. Expert backcountry skiers can tackle a stupendous 3-day tour that traverses south from Pole Creek via the Chambers Lakes and the Green Lakes to a shuttle car at the Dutchman Flat sno-park at Mount Bachelor.

Winter tours in the McKenzie Pass area are described in area 12, but the Three Sisters maps cover two additional, easy trips on Highway 242. Park at the White Branch snow gate, where plowing ends, and trek 2.5 miles to see the ice cascades of the 1-mile Proxy Falls loop trail, or ski 4 miles to the 1.4-mile Linton Lake Trail.

CLIMBING

The Three Sisters and Broken Top are popular with climbers chiefly because of the very scenic setting. The rock itself is crumbly and the technical challenge is not great. In 2009 Mitch Thompson summited all Three Sisters in just 6 hours and 39 minutes, from the Pole Creek trailhead to Devils Lake. But people have died attempting similar feats. The area's changeable weather and the large number of novice climbers account for an above-average mountain rescue rate.

North Sister is by far the most dangerous, both because of the exposure and because the rotten rock is only completely stable after ice storms. For the easiest route (level I-4), hike from Sunshine to the col between Middle and North Sister. Follow the ridge toward North Sister, passing several gendarmes on the west at the 9500-foot-level. Skirt steep scree and snow slopes to the western base of the crown-shaped summit pinnacle, then scramble up a steep chute.

Of North Sister's eight additional routes, the two most difficult (levels II-5.2 and III-5.2) ascend the east face's couloir and arete. They have only been done in winter.

Middle Sister is frequently climbed from Sunshine. A trail from the meadow at Sunshine leads toward the col between North and Middle Sister, where climbers turn south and scramble to the top. An equally easy (I-2) route ascends the southeast flank's scree slopes. Climbers usually hike 4.6 miles from the Pole Creek Trailhead toward the Chambers Lakes, but then follow North Fork Whychus Creek to Middle Sister's southeast flank. Level II-5.2 and II-5.0 routes scale the east face glaciers' headwalls.

Broken Top is a I-3 climb, either from Green Lakes (via the peak's northwest ridge to a crumbly pinnacle), or from Crater Creek Ditch (ascending the Crook Glacier to the crater rim's lowest notch). The north face requires level II-5.2 skills.

The Husband, via the south ridge, is a I-3 climb.

Teardrop Pool in the summit crater of South Sister.

22
WALDO LAKE

Sailboats ply Oregon's second largest natural body of water, a brilliant blue lake so pure and clear that fish are visible 100 feet below the surface. The forests rimming Waldo Lake shelter hundreds of smaller lakes and a thorough trail network.

Climate

Snowfall from November to April accounts for most of the area's 60-75 inches of annual precipitation. Trails are generally clear of snow in late June. Headnets or repellent are necessary from early July to early August, when mosquitoes are plentiful.

Plants and Wildlife

Very few species live in Waldo Lake's renowned clear water, largely because the lake has no year-round inlet to bring nutrients for plant life.

The Charlton Butte-Cultus Lake area is frequented by bald eagles and the osprey which often roost at Crane Prairie Reservoir (a viewing blind is near Quinn River Campground). The Maiden Peak area, with the Pacific Northwest's largest stands of mountain hemlock, provides known habitat for the shy wolverine, threatened in Oregon. The

Waldo Lake from Fuji Mountain

meadows and high ridges west of Waldo Lake support a large Roosevelt elk herd. Black bear, cougar, bobcat, fisher, and marten are found throughout the area.

Sheepmen torched the forests of the Taylor Burn area around 1900 to encourage grass growth, but the result was a vast, even-aged stand of fire-resilient lodgepole pine.

Geology

During the Ice Age, sheet glaciers covered the entire Cascade crest here, creating the many lake basins. Maiden Peak, Charlton Butte, The Twins, and Cultus Mountain are the largest of the many geologically recent volcanoes in the east of the area. Irish Mountain is an older, heavily eroded volcanic plug.

Location: 59 mi SE of Eugene, 43 mi SW of Bend

Size: 148 sq mi, including Maiden Peak

Status: 58 sq mi designated wilderness (1984)

Terrain: lake-dotted upland forests

Elevation: 2480'-7818'

Management: Deschutes NF, Willamette NF

Maps: Waldo Lake Wilderness (USFS); Three Sisters, Willamette Pass X-C Ski Trails (GeoGraphics)

Pulpit Rock from Lower Rosary Lake.

History

Salem Judge John B. Waldo (1844-1907) and four companions were the first white men to travel the length of Oregon's Cascade Range from Willamette Pass to Mount Shasta, in 1888. Klovdahl Bay is named for an engineer who built a tunnel there in 1912-14 to tap Waldo Lake for irrigation and power, but the tunnel failed to work properly.

In the 1970s the Forest Service paved the lake's access roads and built large campgrounds with giant boat ramps to attract motorized recreation to Waldo Lake, one of the purest lakes its size in the world. Later studies showed the lake's clarity slowly decreasing, evidently because of fuel spills, campground runoff, and attempts to stock the lake with fish (at times dropped from aircraft). Motorboats are now limited (and are likely to be banned), pit outhouses have been removed, and fish stocking has ceased.

HIKING & BACKPACKING

Two of the most popular half-mile hikes are to Betty Lake (from Waldo Lake Road 5897) and to Upper and Lower Marilyn Lakes (via any of four paths

off Road 500). Both trips lead to views of Diamond Peak across the lakes.

The three Rosary Lakes nestle in a forest basin between Pulpit Rock's crag and the broad cone of Maiden Peak. A 2.7-mile section of the PCT from Willamette Pass leads to large Lower Rosary Lake, traversing an old-growth subalpine fir and mountain hemlock forest with glimpses of Odell Lake. Because this is a popular backpacking stop, especially for long-distance PCT hikers, overuse has stripped ground cover from several large campsites and much of the first Rosary Lake's shore.

Several short hikes sample Waldo Lake's shoreline. It's 1.7 miles from Shadow Bay Campground to a meadow by the rustic, 3-sided South Waldo Shelter, an easy backpacking goal. From North Waldo Campground, a 3-mile hike reaches the lake outlet, source of the North Fork Middle Fork Willamette River. This is the only place on Waldo Lake's north shore where camping is allowed, so it's a popular backpacking goal. The trail traverses miles of blackened snags from a 1996 fire, but pines, huckleberry bushes, and wildflowers

WALDO LAKE

0   1   2mi
0   1   2   3km

Hwy 58
16 mi

Davis L

W Davis L

4420

4660

4664

700

4950

Johnny L

Maklaks
Mtn

Maiden Pk
7818'

Found

Hidden L

Moore

The
Twins
7362'

Bobby L
5408'

Maiden L

Orphan
Cr

Hwy 97
22 mi

Crest

6600'

Maiden
Peak
Shelter

Trail

Rosary
Lakes

Princess
Cr

M

5897

Salt

6150'

U

Skyline

Cr

Eagle Pk

Odell L

5696

Betty L

Gold Lake Bog
Research
Natural Area

Willamette
Pass
5126'

Trapper
Cr

5100'

500

Lake
5414'

Mt Ray
7002'

Rhododendron Island

Shadow
Bay

N

Gold Lake

Marilyn
Lakes

Gold
Lake

Klovdahl
Bay

Waldo
Lake
Trail

S

R

Bingo L

6050'

JoAnn
L

Pothole
Mdw

Lorin

Island
Lks

Birthday
L

5894

Midnight
L

Nettie

Lillian
Falls

Black
Mdws

Fuji
Cr

Abernethy
L

Diamond

5760'

Wilderness

Fuji Mtn
7144'

6160'

Peak

2422

3400'

5650'

381

Fuji
Mdw

4700'

Wilderness
(See Area 23 Map)

Koch Mountain

2421

Black

5883

Eagle
Camp

Mt David
Douglas

Salt Cr
Falls

58

Oakridge
18mi

RR

P

are returning. After 2.3 miles, a sandy beach on the left invites swimming, though the water is chilly. For an 8-mile loop, return from the lake outlet via the Rigdon Lakes. They are flanked by a rocky little butte with a good view.

Lily Lake is an easy 2.4 miles, mostly on the PCT, from Road 4290. The route passes lily pad ponds in the lodgepole forest below Charlton Butte. Minimally maintained trails east of the butte provide a loop trip option.

Cultus Lake is big, but one can hike half way around it as a day trip. It's 3.7 miles from Cultus Lake Campground to West Cultus Lake trail camp. Those who plan a boat shuttle need only hike one way.

A waterfall connects popular, huckleberry-rimmed Middle Erma Bell Lake with its deep blue partner, Lower Erma Bell Lake. They're 1.7 and 2.1 miles along a nearly level, all-accessible trail from Skookum Creek Campground. Because this is such an easy backpacking distance, tents are allowed only at sites marked by a post at the three Erma Bell Lakes and nearby Otter Lake. Road access is via Oakridge; drive to Westfir and 32 miles beyond on Road 19 to the

Waldo Mountain's lookout is often staffed.

Skookum Creek turnoff.

Gander Lake, appropriately, is near Swan Lake and the Goslings. The downhill 1.2-mile trail to Gander Lake begins at the end of Road 2417. Follow paved Salmon Creek Road 24 east of Oakridge for 11 miles and fork left onto Road 2417 for 7.2 miles.

Waldo Mountain's fire lookout and viewpoint are the climax of a 3.2-mile trail that climbs 1900 feet. Drive to the trailhead as for Gander Lake, but turn off Road 2417 (onto Road 2424) after 6 miles. From the same trailhead, a much less strenuous 2.5-mile path veers to the right to Waldo Meadows' wildflowers. Backpacking campsites and a small waterfall are at the Salmon Lakes, half a mile to the right (south) of the meadow. For a loop trip, connect the Waldo Mountain and Waldo Meadows hikes on a 7.9-mile circuit.

Black Creek's impressive, 2000-foot-deep canyon is the start of a day hike with variety. After climbing past Lillian Falls, the 3.8-mile Black Creek Trail takes hikers to a good picnic spot or campsite on Waldo Lake's Klovdahl Bay. To reach the trailhead follow Salmon Creek Road 24 from Oakridge for 14.2 miles, then continue straight on Road 2421 for 8.2 miles to its end.

Interesting cinder formations and a view from Mount Hood to Mount Thielsen are the rewards at the former lookout site atop conical Maiden Peak. The 5.8-mile trail gains 2800 feet at a good grade from Road 500, half a mile south of Gold Lake Campground. A next-best viewpoint hike, atop The Twins' double summit, requires only a 3.3-mile hike (one way), gaining 1600 feet from paved Waldo Lake Road 5897.

Fuji Mountain is a cliff-topped old lookout site with an impressive view. A 1.5-mile trail reaches the peak from gravel Road 5883 (which joins Highway 58 east of Oakridge 15 miles), but many hikers prefer the 5.6-mile Fuji Mountain

An island near the north shore of Waldo Lake.

Trail from paved Waldo Lake Road 5897 near Gold Lake. This route gains 2200 feet of elevation but passes campsites at Birthday Lake along the way.

Two loop hikes tour the forest east of Fuji Mountain from paved Road 5897: the 9.7-mile trip from Gold Lake to Island Lakes, and the 9.5-mile circuit of Mount Ray past the South Waldo Shelter.

Irish Mountain has no trail to its summit, but the PCT skirts the small lakes about its base. The foot of the mountain is a 4-mile day hike on the PCT from Taylor Burn Road (numbered 600 and 514).

Extending deep into the wilderness, the Taylor Burn Road is a series of deep mudholes when wet and a rugged, high-centering track when dry. Vehicles able to survive 7 miles on this road can reach Taylor Burn Campground. From there, short hikes through the lodgepole pine forest lead to Wahanna, Upper Erma Bell, and half a dozen other lakes.

Many people enjoy hiking—or jogging or mountain biking—the demanding but scenic 20.2-mile Jim Weaver Trail around Waldo Lake in a single day. If 14.6 miles sounds better, plan a car shuttle between Shadow Bay and the North Waldo Campground. Shorten the trip further by arranging to meet a boat at Klovdahl Bay or the lake's outlet.

The Six Lakes Trail leads through deep woods to the two Quinn Lakes, Long Lake, and the three Eddeeleo Lakes. Expect rhododendron blooms in June, mosquitoes in July, and huckle-berries in August. From Road 254, it's 2 miles to the first lake and 6 miles to the last. Backpackers should bring stoves because fires are banned within 100 feet of lakes but brush makes it hard to tent outside the few established shore campsites. Longer backpacking trips can continue to Waldo Lake and the Rigdon Lakes. From Oakridge, drive Salmon Creek Road 24 for 11 miles, veer left onto Road 2417 for 10.9 miles, and turn left onto Road 254 for 0.3 mile to a wide spot on the right.

SNOWSHOEING & SKIING

Though snow at Willamette Pass is often wet, an abundance of trails and scenery make the area very popular. The Willamette Pass ski resort offers ski rentals and groomed trails for a fee, but the free trails to six nearby ski shelters

The Maiden Peak shelter can be hard to find.

provide more interesting goals. All of the shelters have woodstoves and are available free, without reservations, for overnight use, but only the Maiden Peak Shelter is fully enclosed and heatable.

Start at the Gold Lake sno-park on Highway 58, half a mile west of Willamette Pass. On weekends, Nordic ski patrol volunteers staff a little log cabin here, doling out advice, help, and sometimes even hot chocolate. For the easiest ski trip, start at the far right-hand end of the sno-park, ski along a snowed-under road, and keep left at junctions for 0.7 mile to the Westview Shelter. If you'd rather ski to the Bechtel Shelter (2.1 miles from the Gold Lake sno-park) start out along the same snowed-under road, but keep right at junctions instead.

The very popular, easy 2.2-mile ski trail to Gold Lake (and yet another 3-sided log shelter) begins across the highway from the entrance to the Gold Lake sno-park. Intermediate skiers can return from Gold Lake on side trails past the Marilyn Lakes.

The Salt Creek Falls sno-park has a snow play hill for sledders, but there's

Pulpit Rock from the middle Rosary Lake.

also an easy half-mile trail to the top of the 286-foot waterfall, Oregon's second tallest. For a tougher trip, cross Highway 58 at the sno-park entrance and climb 1500 feet in 4 miles on Road 5894 to the Fuji Mountain shelter, with its view of Diamond Peak.

The scenic basin of the Rosary Lakes is 2.8 miles from Willamette Pass, climbing gently on the PCT. Strong skiers can continue 3.7 miles on the PCT to the Maiden Peak Shelter, a fully enclosed, octagonal log cabin that sleeps fifteen, but is hard to find because it's hidden 100 yards from the PCT (GPS location N43°37.93′ W122°00.20′). Riding the ski area's chairlift to the top of Eagle Peak shortens the trek by half. The shelter serves as base camp for the challenging snowshoe or ski trek to the panoramic summit of Maiden Peak, gaining 1750 feet in 2.7 miles.

Snowmobiles are allowed on the snowed-under Waldo Lake Road 5897, but skiers sometimes tackle the 8.9-mile trek to the South Waldo Shelter and the Wilderness beyond.

Tours in the Diamond Peak Wilderness are discussed in that area's description.

BOATING

In the still of the morning, canoeists can watch fish as much as 100 feet below the surface of 417-foot-deep, 10-square-mile Waldo Lake. From about 11am to sunset, a steady southwest wind fills the sails of sailboats and creates sizable waves that keep canoeists close to shore. Note that dangerous rock reefs near North Waldo and Shadow Bay can be obscured by choppy water.

Davis, Odell, and Little Cultus Lakes have 10-mile-per-hour limits for power boats, and motorized trolling is banned on Davis Lake. Cultus Lake, on the other hand, has no speed limit, so it's abuzz with waterskiers. Only electric motors are permitted on Waldo Lake. Motors are prohibited on all other lakes.

23

DIAMOND PEAK

Diamond Peak isn't the only summit rising above this area's broad forests. Four other, less well-known crags top 7000 feet, each surrounded by its own scenic lakes and trails.

Climate

Snowfall from November through April accounts for much of the area's annual precipitation, which totals 80 inches in the west and 40 inches in the east. Most trails are snow-free by July 1, but hikers must cross snowfields on the PCT over Cowhorn Mountain and Diamond Peak until about August 1. Mosquitoes are a quite a problem from early July to early August.

Plants and Wildlife

Alpine scree slopes are habitat for pikas, guinea-pig-sized rodents that whistle at hikers in alarm. The slopes also provide footholds for lupine, penstemon, and heather. Dense mountain hemlock forests surround the peaks, leaving few openings for meadows. Lower forests are dominated by lodge-

Salt Creek Falls.

pole pine and beargrass in the east, and by Douglas fir, rhododendrons, and huckleberries in the west. Roosevelt elk are frequent until the first snows.

Geology

The tallest peaks are the eroded remnants of extinct volcanoes. Odell Lake and Crescent Lake fill the U-shaped gouges left by vanished Ice Age glaciers. The lakes prove the ancient glaciers were several miles wide.

History

John Diamond first climbed and named Diamond Peak in 1852 while

Location: 62 mi SE of Eugene, 64 mi SW of Bend

Size: 126 sq mi, including Cowhorn Mountain

Status: 82 sq mi designated wilderness (1964, 1984)

Terrain: snowpeak, forested uplands, lakes

Elevation: 4240'-8744'

Management: Deschutes NF, Willamette NF

Maps: Diamond Peak Wilderness, Willamette Pass X-C Ski Trails (Geo-Graphics); Diamond Peak Wilderness, Rogue-Umpqua Divide and Oregon Cascades Recreation Area (USFS)

leading an exploration party from Eugene that hoped to survey an Oregon Trail shortcut across the Cascades. Misled by word that the proposed shortcut was complete, 1027 people with 215 wagons left the usual Oregon Trail route in Idaho and followed Elijah Elliott through the desert to Central Oregon. There the "Lost Wagon Train" had trouble deciding which of the Cascade peaks was Diamond's landmark. They followed his sporadic blazes to Emigrant Pass at Summit Lake, arduously hewing a wagon route from the dense forest. In mid-October, the starving pioneers finally abandoned their wagons in despair. A rescue party found them on the Middle Fork Willamette River and led them down to the Willamette Valley, where they doubled Lane County's population.

HIKING & BACKPACKING

For a waterfall hike, start at the Salt Creek Falls picnic area off Highway 58, west of Willamette Pass 5 miles. Oregon's second tallest cascade, Salt Creek Falls drops 286 feet from the picnic area. Cross a footbridge, turn right, and keep right to find a 3.4-mile loop trail to lacy, 100-foot Diamond Creek Falls. For a longer hike, continue up the Vivian Lake Trail past several more falls for 2.3 miles to huckleberry-rimmed Vivian Lake, a backpacking goal with a reflection of Mount Yoran's monolith. An alternate route to Vivian Lake, with less elevation gain, passes Notch Lake from Road 23.

From Willamette Pass, an easy, 3.3-mile segment of the PCT leads through old-growth forest above Odell Lake to tree-rimmed Midnight Lake. Nearby, a trailhead opposite the Trapper Creek Campground serves as a starting point for two popular, ambitious day hikes to lakes with fine views of Diamond Peak. Yoran Lake is 5 miles on a steady uphill grade through forest, and Diamond View Lake is 5.4 miles up the Trapper Creek trail. Both Yoran Lake

Sawtooth Mountain from Indigo Lake, a backpacking goal easy enough for hikers with kids.

and Diamond View Lake are quieter, prettier backpacking destinations than heavily used Midnight Lake on the PCT.

Fawn Lake is also a popular destination for day hikers and backpackers, 3.8 trail miles from Odell Lake Lodge or 3.4 trail miles from the Crescent Lake Campground entrance. Worthwhile side trips lead 1.4 miles to shallow Stag Lake, at the foot of Lakeview Mountain's impressive cliffs, and 1.8 miles up to little Saddle Lake.

Trails fan out from Crescent Lake and Summit Lake to dozens of quiet lakes among the pines. The Windy Lake group is 3.9 miles from Road 60 at Crescent Lake; the Bingham Lake cluster is 3 miles from Road 60.

The PCT climbs unusually high over Diamond Peak and Cowhorn Mountain to sweeping vistas on slopes above timberline. On Cowhorn Mountain, the PCT comes within an easy 0.4-mile scramble of the craggy summit, 3.5 miles from Windigo Pass. The PCT's best viewpoints on Diamond Peak are 6 miles from Emigrant Pass — a long but rewarding day hike. Really energetic hikers can follow the PCT to timberline, then climb Diamond Peak's smooth

southern ridge cross-country to the exhilarating summit view. The 12-mile round-trip climb requires no technical skills, only stamina.

Sawtooth Mountain overtowers a scenic, less-visited network of trails. From Timpanogas Campground, hike an easy 1.9 miles to a stunning backcountry campground at Indigo Lake, directly below the mountain's cliffs. For an 9.2-mile loop around Sawtooth Mountain, turn left just before Indigo Lake and then keep right; this sometimes faint loop comes within an easy 0.4-mile bushwhack of the mountain's panoramic summit.

For a 9.9-mile loop from the Timpanogas Campground, hike left halfway around Timpanogas Lake, climb 1.1 mile to the Windy Pass Trail, and keep right at all junctions, returning past Indigo Lake. A 1-mile side-trip from this loop climbs 0.3 mile to the PCT, follows the PCT south 0.3 mile to the trail's high point, and then scrambles left along a ridge to Cowhorn Mountain's summit.

To reach the Sawtooth Mountain area from Oakridge, follow Highway 58 a mile east of town, turn right at a sign for Hills Creek Reservoir, follow paved

Road 21 for 31.2 miles, head left on Road 2154, and follow signs for Timpanogas Lake 9.3 miles.

Hidden on the less-visited west side of Diamond Peak are a collection of good day hikes—and prime huckleberry picking in late August. Some of the area's best wildflower meadows border Blue Lake (1 mile) and Happy Lake (3 miles) along an up-and-down trail from Road 23.

The former lookout site atop Hemlock Butte offers a panoramic view of Mount Yoran and Diamond Peak, and requires only a half-mile hike from Road 23. But for mountain views, few trails can match the 4-mile path from Road 23 to Divide Lake. The route passes narrow Notch Lake in a forest, then switchbacks up a ridge to a timberline valley of tiny lakes below Mount Yoran's sheer face. Divide Lake is a spectacular backpacking goal here, but tents must be at least 100 feet away from the fragile lake.

Trailheads on the west side of Diamond Peak are reached via Oakridge. Follow Highway 58 a mile east of town, turn right at a sign for Hills Creek Reservoir for 0.5 mile to an intersection, and go straight on Road 23

Long-distance hikers often choose the scenic, 28.7-mile section of the PCT from Willamette Pass to Windigo Pass, but there are other good routes as well.

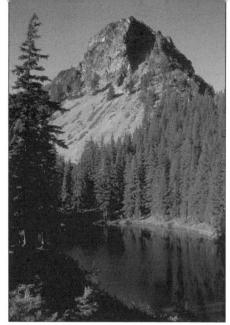

Mount Yoran from Divide Lake.

Most spectacular is the 29-mile circuit of Diamond Peak, passing Notch Lake, Divide Lake, and Rockpile Lake.

Cross-country hiking is not difficult in the high, open forests, and is particularly worthwhile in the lake-dotted forests between Yoran Lake and Willamette Pass, because the lakes directly along the PCT are overused.

CLIMBING

Diamond Peak is most easily summited from the south. If you've chosen a base camp at Rockpile or Marie Lake, hike half a mile east, take the PCT north 1.2 miles to a sharp corner, and bushwhack straight up a steep, open ridge a mile to a false summit. Then follow a hogback north 0.4 mile to the actual summit, using your hands to skirt three rocky gendarmes along the way.

Hikers hardly have to use their hands to summit Cowhorn Mountain and Sawtooth Mountain. Mount Yoran is a bit harder, requiring level I-3 skills.

SNOWSHOEING & SKIING

A network of cross-country trails centers on the Nordic ski patrol shelter at the Gold Lake sno-park. Tours north of this area are described under area 22. To the south, the well-traveled PCT leads

Indigo Lake from Sawtooth Mountain.

The PCT climbs south from Willamette Pass to Diamond Peak's timberline slopes.

2.7 miles at a modest grade through forest to Midnight Lake. Returning on a loop past the Bechtel Shelter is not much longer. The unmarked 6.3-mile trail to Yoran Lake and the 7.1-mile trail to Diamond View Lake are for skiers with route-finding skills and emergency gear.

Fawn Lake is a very popular, intermediate-level goal. One trail there climbs 3.8 miles from Odell Lake Lodge (ski rentals available). A slightly easier route from the Crescent Lake sno-park makes the climb in 3.4 miles. The additional side trip to Stag Lake is worth the extra 1.4 miles.

Redtop Mountain makes an excellent cross-country goal for advanced skiers willing to gain 2100 feet in 4 miles. The summit has a panoramic view of Diamond Peak, and the open, upper slopes are often draped with dry powder snow. From the Crescent Lake sno-park, ski half a mile toward Fawn Lake and then follow a compass bearing due east up through the woods.

Skiers should avoid the tempting railroad grade along Odell Lake because of frequent high-speed trains. Safer tours along Odell Lake follow forest roads above Sunset Cove.

Summiting Diamond Peak from the southwest is popular in April and early May when snowmelt clears Road 2149. Snowshoes or skins are required for the 6-mile, 4000-foot climb. The memorable run back down traverses a giant bowl of powder or corn snow.

Diamond Creek Falls in winter.

BOATING

High-elevation, 500-acre Summit Lake not only has a postcard view of Diamond Peak, but it also offers reliable afternoon breezes for sailboaters and an interesting shoreline for canoeists. Motors are permitted, but a 10 mile-per-hour limit prevails, and a rough dirt access road prevents crowds. Both Crescent Lake and Odell Lake have marinas with boat rentals.

24

HARDESTY MOUNTAIN

Soothing shades of green-moss, sword ferns, vanilla leaf-line the trails of Hardesty Mountain, where hiking is available year-round, just 30 minutes from Eugene.

Mount June from the Sawtooth Trail to Hardesty Mountain.

Climate

The ridges here are usually snow-free by mid-April, and lower trails are open year-round. Rain accounts for the

Location: 25 mi SE of Eugene
Size: 22 sq mi
Status: undesignated wilderness
Terrain: densely forested valleys, ridges
Elevation: 940'-4616'
Management: Willamette NF, Umpqua NF
Map: Mount June (USGS)

area's 55 inches of annual precipitation. Mount June's name commemorates a year when snow lingered there until that month.

Plants and Wildlife

In the area's lush old-growth forests of Douglas fir, western red cedar, and bigleaf maple, watch for rare Pacific giant salamanders. Shiny, 7 to 12 inches long, they are easily distinguished from the orange-bellied, rough-skinned newts common in Western Oregon. Also look for delicate calypso orchids on the forest floor in May and showy Cascade lilies and beargrass on ridges in June. Spotted owls and goshawks nest throughout

Falls on Goodman Creek.

the area, while osprey and bald eagles prefer lower elevations, nearer Lookout Reservoir. Whenever eagles nest in a tree within a quarter mile of a trail, the Forest Service closes that trail January through September.

Geology

Though dense forest obscures most rocks, ridgetop outcroppings reveal volcanic andesite typical of the Old Cascades, 16 to 25 million years old.

History

The Civilian Conservation Corps built most of the area's trails between 1933 and 1938 to access lookout towers on Hardesty Mountain and Mount June. Foundations of the towers remain.

HIKING & BACKPACKING

Three hikes begin at a well-marked parking area near milepost 21 of Highway 58. For a good kids' hike, walk up the Hardesty Trail 0.2 mile and turn right on the Goodman Creek Trail. This path contours 1.8 miles to a small waterfall and log footbridge, continues 2.2 miles through towering old-growth woods to a crossing of Road 5833, and continues as the 2.5-mile Eagles Rest Trail, climbing past the Ash Swale Shelter and crossing paved Eagles Rest Road before reaching Eagles Rest's 3022-foot summit viewpoint.

For a low-elevation walk from the same trailhead, hike 0.3 mile up the Hardesty Trail and turn left 5 miles on the South Willamette Trail to its end at the Eula Ridge Trailhead on Highway 58.

The Hardesty Trail itself gains 3300 feet in 5 steep miles to a partly overgrown lookout site. For a loop, return on the even steeper, 3.7-mile Eula Ridge Trail and the 5-mile South Willamette Trail. An easier, 0.9-mile route to Hardesty Mountain's summit begins on Road 550, an unimproved spur of Patterson Mountain Road 5840.

Mount June, a loftier former lookout site than Hardesty Mountain, commands a much better view, from Mount Jefferson to Mount Thielsen. A 1.2-mile trail switchbacks up to Mount June's cliff-edged summit opening. For a longer hike, continue eastward along meadow-topped Sawtooth Ridge on a trail lined with wildflowers, viewpoints, and rock spires. Hardesty Mountain is 3.6 miles past Mount June on this scenic route.

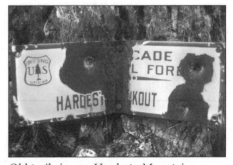

Old trail sign on Hardesty Mountain.

Bigleaf maple leaves.

top of Mount June in 4 miles; however, those seeking the easier 1.2-mile trail to Mount June's summit should continue 5.1 miles farther on this road, which soon turns to gravel. Then turn left on Road 1721 for 0.1 mile and turn left onto steep Road 20-1E-31.3 (alias Road 941) for 0.4 mile to the Mount June trailhead sign on the right.

To reach Mount June, drive 11.4 miles east from Interstate 5 on Highway 58 to Dexter Dam and turn right at a sign for Lost Creek. After 3.7 miles, turn left across a somewhat hidden bridge onto the signed Eagles Rest Road. Follow this paved, one-lane route 7.8 miles to a fork. Following a hiker-symbol pointer, keep left on Road 20-1-14 for a mile to a sign on the left identifying the Lost Creek Trail. This pleasant path does lead to the

Vine maple leaves.

25
BOULDER CREEK

Boulder Creek's swimmable pools and small waterfalls are the center of a broad, steep valley of old-growth forests with ponderosa pines. Because this wilderness is not in the High Cascades, it's often overlooked, yet it's one of the few Oregon wilderness areas hikable in winter. If you're eager to start the summer's backpacking in April or May, try Boulder Creek.

A viewpoint on the edge of Pine Bench overlooks Boulder Creek's valley.

Climate

Lower trails are generally snow-free all year. Winter and spring rains swell Boulder Creek, requiring knee-deep wading on trail fords. The area's annual precipitation is 60 inches.

Location: 47 mi E of Roseburg

Size: 33 sq mi

Status: 30 sq mi designated wilderness (1984)

Terrain: steep, forested valley

Elevation: 1600'-5600'

Management: Umpqua NF

Map: Boulder Creek Wilderness (USFS)

Plants and Wildlife

Pine Bench features an old-growth ponderosa pine forest with grassy openings, unusual so far west of the Cascade summit. Elsewhere, the forest is an interesting mix of gigantic sugarpine, Douglas fir, western hemlock, droopy incense cedar, and gnarled yew. A 1996 fire swept through nearly half of this wilderness, clearing out underbrush and leaving a healthier patchwork of old-growth trees. The rugged valleys are home to an estimated 30 black bear and 100 Roosevelt elk, but both species are shy.

Geology

Eagle Rock and other spires of the Umpqua Rocks are eroded remnants of 30-million-year-old Old Cascades volcanoes. Pine Bench's basalt plateau, however, is only a few thousand years old, part of a lava flow that originated 20 miles away in the High Cascades and poured down the North Umpqua River Valley, filling the canyon from wall to wall. Later erosion has left fragments of the old flow as pinnacles and benches along the river.

History

Several caves in the area preserve evidence of Indian camps. Arrowheads and other artifacts are federally protected.

HIKING & BACKPACKING

The most popular introduction to this wilderness is the 2.3-mile trail to Pine Bench's cliff-edge viewpoint. To find the Soda Springs Trailhead, drive High-

way 138 east of Roseburg 54.7 miles. Between mileposts 54 and 55, turn left at a sign for Slide Creek, and immediately turn left again onto gravel Soda Springs Road for 1.4 miles to the trailhead on the right. The path ducks under a 12-foot pipe that's carrying most of the North Umpqua River to a power station, and then climbs 1.3 miles amid 4-foot-thick Douglas firs and June-blooming rhododendrons to Pine Bench's plateau. Continue 0.6 mile across the mesa, turn right for 0.4 mile, and follow the sound of water left 100 yards to a gushing spring near several campsites. Climb out a rock promontory nearby for a breathtaking view of Boulder Creek's canyon.

For a longer day hike, follow the trail north from Pine Bench 1.7 miles to a log crossing of pebbly, 20-foot Boulder Creek. Explore upstream 100 yards to a waterfall and cold, swimmable pool. Backpackers can continue on the trail upstream another 2.9 miles, past good campsites and three easy creek crossings, to the forks of Boulder Creek. From there the trail climbs a ridge 3.9 miles to Road 3810 near Bear Camp.

Two of the area's best viewpoints are Mizell Point and Illahee Rock. The 1.2-mile route to Mizell Point requires bushwhacking now that the faint Perry Butte Stub Trail has been abandoned.

But access is good to Illahee Rock's trail, and the view is so good that the rock has two lookout towers—a 1925 cupola-style building and a 1958 tower still in use. To find the 0.7-mile trail to Illahee Rock, drive Highway 138 to the Dry Creek Store, turn north on Road 4760 for 8 miles, go straight on Road 100 for 1.3 miles, and turn left on steep Road 104 for 0.2 mile to its end. The nearby Wild Rose Trail starts from Road 100 and leads 1.4 miles to Wild Rose Point, a bluff strewn with wildflowers.

The well-built, 79-mile North Umpqua River Trail follows the river from its source at Maidu Lake in the Mount Thielsen Wilderness (area 26) to Swiftwater Park, just 22 miles from Roseburg. To sample the trail at Boulder Creek, where it's open to equestrians and bicyclists, start at the Soda Springs Trailhead and walk or drive the bumpy Soda Springs Road west 1.2 miles to a small trailhead. Then hike onward on the North Umpqua Trail 2.9 miles, below Eagle Rock's crags, to the Highway 138 river bridge.

CLIMBING

Eagle Rock is the largest of a cluster of rarely-visited andesite crags with challenging technical climbs. Eagle Rock was first climbed in 1958 via the northern Madrone Tree Route (level I-5.2-A2). The 400-foot South Face cliffs present a level II-5.6 challenge.

Old Man Rock, rated I-5.4-A1, remained unclimbed until 1963. The spire directly north of it, Old Woman, has I-5.2 and I-5.6 routes. Other crags in the area are easier, including prominent Rattlesnake Rock (I-3).

Lookout buildings from 1958 and 1925 remain on Illahee Rock.

26
MOUNT THIELSEN

The "Lightning Rod of the Cascades," Mount Thielsen's spire towers above the lakes, meadows, and high forests to the north of Crater Lake.

Climate

Snowfall from mid-October to April accounts for most of the area's 60 inches of annual precipitation. Most trails are snow-free by mid-June, but the Pacific Crest Trail may remain blocked until late July. Mosquitoes are plentiful for about four weeks following snow melt.

Plants and Wildlife

Nearly pure stands of lodgepole pine blanket the lower areas, where pumice and ash soils dry to dust in summer. Nearly pure stands of mountain hemlock cover the higher elevations, where lingering snow provides summer moisture. Clark's nutcrackers, gray jays, and golden-mantled ground squirrels are abundant. Look for elk and red-headed pileated woodpeckers. Diamond Lake originally had no fish, but is now stocked to provide 3 million trout annually.

Geology

A 5-foot-thick ground cover of lighter-than-water pumice rock remains as evidence that this area lay directly downwind of the cataclysmic explosion

Mt. Thielsen from Thielsen Meadow.

that created Crater Lake's caldera 7700 years ago.

Mount Thielsen, extinct for at least 100,000 years, was stripped to its central plug by the same Ice Age glaciers that carved the basins for Diamond Lake and Miller Lake. In 1965, after centuries with no glaciers at all, the peak was found to shelter two small moving ice masses on its northern flank.

Lightning strikes Mount Thielsen's spire so often that carrot-shaped "lightning tubes" and glassy, brownish-green fulgurites of recrystalized rock form at the summit.

Location: 72 mi E of Roseburg, 80 mi NE of Medford

Size: 126 sq mi

Status: 86 sq mi designated wilderness (1984)

Terrain: snowpeak, high forest

Elevation: 4260'-9182'

Management: Umpqua NF, Deschutes NF, Winema NF

Map: Mount Thielsen Wilderness (USFS)

HIKING & BACKPACKING

The most popular of the area's many viewpoint hikes is the Howlock Mountain Trail to Timothy Meadows. Starting from the horse corrals at North Diamond Lake,

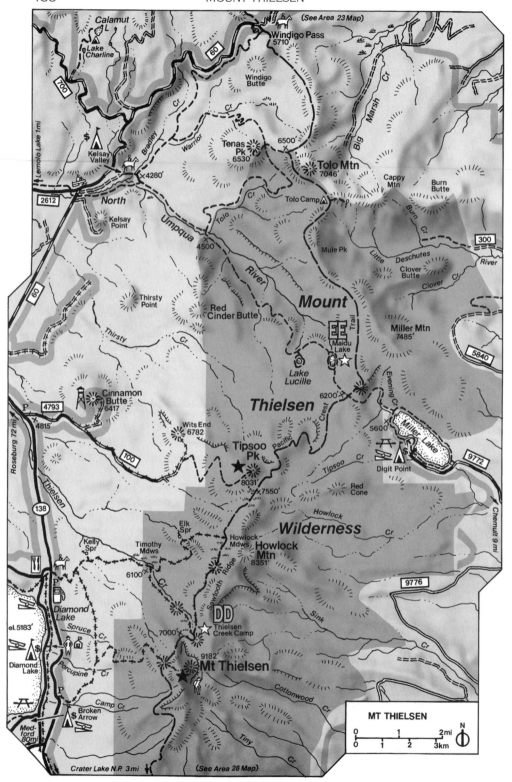

the route ducks through a tunnel under Highway 138 and climbs through viewless forests for 3 miles before reaching the meadows along splashing Thielsen Creek. Here are good picnicking swales with wildflowers and glimpses of Thielsen's summit. However, it's worth climbing 2.7 miles farther along the creek for the astonishing view at Thielsen Creek Camp, where the peak looms like the Matterhorn.

Once at Thielsen Creek Camp, there are two tempting alternatives to simply returning the way you came. It's 4.3 miles farther to make a loop to the north, following the PCT past serrated Sawtooth Ridge to Howlock Meadows and turning left back to Timothy Meadows. On the other hand, you'll only add 2.4 miles to your return trip if you make a loop to the south, following the PCT to far-ranging views on the flank of Mount Thielsen before descending to Diamond Lake via the Mount Thielsen and Spruce Ridge Trails.

Backpacking breaks these distances into shorter hikes. The only year-round water source on Mount Thielsen's flanks is Thielsen Creek. Be sure to camp in the forest well away from the fragile clearings at Timothy Meadows or Thielsen Creek Camp, and build no fire.

Tipsoo Peak is one of the few 8000-foot Cascade peaks with a well-graded trail to its summit. The view stretches from the Three Sisters to Mount Shasta, with Mount Thielsen front and center. The 3.1-mile trail up Tipsoo Peak gains 1780 feet of elevation from Wits End Road 100. From the top, it's an easy scramble down loose cinders to the alpine meadows along the PCT.

Those who have already climbed to Cowhorn Mountain on the PCT from Windigo Pass (see area 23, Diamond Peak) might try three rarely visited viewpoint goals south of the pass. Tolo Mountain and Tenas Peak are both 5 miles; Windigo Butte's little cone is a 1.5

Maidu Lake.

mile cross-country climb.

The most popular lakeside trail is the 11.5-mile paved bike path around Diamond Lake. It's easiest to start at the Diamond Lake Lodge, where you can rent bicycles. The path traverses 3 miles of campgrounds on the east shore, circumvents 2 miles of private cabins on the west shore, and delivers 2 miles of great mountain views on the north shore.

A much quieter, 5.1-mile lakeshore path circles Miller Lake from the Digit Point Campground. From the same trailhead, you can also climb 3.6 miles to a viewpoint on the PCT (where cliffs overlook Miller Lake), or cross the Cascade Divide to forest-rimmed Maidu Lake, a backpacking goal. Reach the trailhead via Road 9772, which leaves Highway 97 at a sign for the Chemult Recreation Site, between mileposts 202 and 203, half a mile north of Chemult.

Backpackers and equestrians have several long-distance trip options. The PCT covers 29.4 miles from Windigo Pass to the North Crater trailhead beside Highway 138, on the National Park boundary. Also, a popular 8-mile segment of the North Umpqua River Trail climbs to Maidu and Lucille Lakes from the Kelsay Valley trailhead.

Throughout the area, water sources are scarce. For solitude, carry enough water for a dry camp and strike off cross-country through the open, easily traversed forests.

Thousands of hikers climb—or nearly climb—Mount Thielsen each summer. Those without technical climbing experience must settle for the excellent view at the base of the near-vertical, 80-foot summit spire. Even this goal is 5 miles away from Highway 138 and 3700 feet up. From the Mount Thielsen Trailhead on Highway 138 above Diamond Lake, follow the path 3.8 miles up to the PCT, and continue straight up a ridgecrest on an unofficial trail 0.8 mile. When the path peters out above timberline, continue up dangerously slippery scree slopes 0.4 mile, spiraling slightly to the right, to a ledge at the eastern base of the summit pinnacle. The final 80 feet require the adept use of hands and feet to chimney up cracks in the rock.

Hikers who don't want to risk Mount Thielsen might consider scaling Mount Bailey instead (not shown on map). This broad, 8368-foot summit rises from the opposite side of Diamond Lake. A 4.9-mile trail climbs 3100 feet from Road 300, a spur from the southwest part of the road around Diamond Lake.

Mt. Thielsen from Diamond Lake.

CLIMBING

Mount Thielsen's summit pinnacle is a level I-3 climb from the southeast. A more difficult and extremely dangerous route to the summit, the III-5.7 McLoughlin Memorial, involves six rope lengths of technical work on rotten, east-facing cliffs, accessed via Thielsen Creek Camp.

SNOWSHOEING & SKIING

Resorts at North Diamond Lake and Lemolo Lake offer cross-country ski rentals and marked winter trails. All of the hiking trails between Diamond Lake and Mount Thielsen make good, if steep, cross-country routes. Perhaps the best level ski trail is the 11.5-mile bike path around Diamond Lake.

The fine view at Cinnamon Butte's lookout tower is 3 miles up from another Highway 138 sno-park. The reward for climbing 1600 feet on the lookout road's steady grade is a 2-mile downhill glide. For a backcountry adventure, ski 8 miles from Highway 138 to Tipsoo Peak and snow camp in the glorious, 7550-foot meadows along the PCT.

The area's best overnight ski/snowshoe destination is the Hemlock Butte Shelter (not shown on map), 2 miles southwest of Diamond Lake (GPS location N43°07.878' W122°11.296'). The heatable, 3-story A-frame log cabin sleeps 16 and is available for free by making reservations with the Diamond Lake Ranger Station (541-498-2531). To find it from Diamond Lake, drive Highway 230 toward Medford 3 miles to the Three Lakes sno-park, ski or snowshoe 2 miles northwest on a snowmobile road, turn right on a snowmobile route 0.2 mile, and turn left on a Nordic trail 1.4 mile, gaining 800 feet of elevation. From the cabin, a marked route to Mt. Bailey's summit gains 2200 feet in 2.2 miles.

BOATING

Diamond Lake and Miller Lake offer canoeing and sailing. Motors are permitted, but with a 10 mile-per-hour limit.

27

ROGUE-UMPQUA DIVIDE

Atop a high divide west of Crater Lake, this relatively undiscovered area boasts alpine meadows, interesting rock formations, and small lakes.

Climate

Snow covers most trails from mid-November to mid-May. Annual precipitation is 50 inches; summers are dry.

Plants and Wildlife

The ridges feature showy Cascade lilies and red paintbrush in June and ripe huckleberries in August. The bright red snow plant, a rare saprophyte, brightens the Fish Lake area as snow melts. Forests include sugarpine and ponderosa pine on the drier eastern slopes, true firs on the ridges, and Douglas fir on the western slopes. A park-like grove of old-growth incense cedars makes a nice stop along Road 800 north of the area.

Geology

The area belongs to the heavily eroded, 16- to 25-million-year-old Old Cascades. Glaciers broadened the valleys and left Buck Canyon, a mile-wide cirque. A massive landslide from Grasshopper Mountain dammed Fish Lake and created Fish Lake Creek Falls about

Muir Creek in upper Buck Canyon.

Location: 75 mi E of Roseburg, 56 mi NE of Medford

Size: 102 sq mi

Status: 52 sq mi designated wilderness (1984)

Terrain: high meadows, forested valleys, ridgetop rock outcroppings

Elevation: 2300'-6783'

Management: Umpqua NF, Rogue River-Siskiyou NF

Map: Rogue-Umpqua Divide Wilderness (USFS)

6000 years ago. Buckeye and Cliff Lakes fill hollows in the uneven surface of the old slide.

HIKING & BACKPACKING

Two trails lead to popular Fish Lake from Road 2840. This 90-acre lake, rimmed with forest and mountain views, was named by a group of 1889 explorers who caught 70 fish there in an hour, using venison for bait. A 3.8-mile route to the lake ascends Fish Lake Creek through an old-growth forest and passes within earshot of an 80-foot waterfall. The shorter Beaver Swamp Trail

Fish Lake.

from Road 2840 loses 700 feet through a regrowing burn area to reach Fish Lake in 1.5 miles. Head left around the lake for backpacking campsites away from the shore. With Fish Lake as a base, it's tempting to add a 5.6-mile loop past Cliff and Buckeye lakes, with their close-up views of Grasshopper Mountain's cliffs. Another excellent side trip climbs to the excellent views (and avalanche lilies) atop Grasshopper Mountain, 1.9 trail miles beyond Cliff Lake.

For a spectacular 12.6-mile loop from the Beaver Swamp Trailhead, hike past Fish Lake on the trail up Highrock Creek (amid 10-foot-thick Douglas firs) and keep left at all junctions to return on the Rocky Ridge Trail, a path lined with wildflowers, viewpoints, and rock pinnacles.

To find the Beaver Swamp Trailhead from Interstate 5, turn off at Canyonville, follow signs for Crater Lake 23 miles to Tiller, turn left onto Road 46 (toward South Umpqua Falls) for 24 miles, veer right onto one-lane, paved Road 2823 for 2.4 miles, fork right on gravel Road 2830 for 3.9 miles, and fork left on Road 2840 for 5.1 miles.

If your goal is Buckeye Lake (also great for backpacking), a shorter, kid-friendly 1.4-mile trail begins at the Skimmerhorn Trailhead on nearby Road 600. This is also the place to start a lovely 10.4-mile loop around Grasshopper Mountain that visits Buckeye, Cliff, and Little Fish lakes.

Elephanthead, a dramatic, elephant-shaped cliff on the shoulder of Abbott Butte, overlooks a lush wildflower meadow fringed with true firs and quaking aspen. It's a 4.3-mile hike along the Rogue-Umpqua Divide Trail from the summit of Road 68. Along the way you can detour 0.7 mile to the Cascade lilies, views, and abandoned lookout atop Abbott Butte. To find the trailhead from Medford, take the Crater Lake Highway north past Prospect 6 miles and turn left on Woodruff Meadows Road 68 for 4.9 miles of pavement and another 7.4 miles of one-lane gravel road to a trailhead pullout at a pass. To find the trailhead from Tiller, take Road 46 toward South Umpqua Falls for 5.3 miles, turn right on Jackson Creek Road 29 for 12.5 miles, and turn right at a "Huckleberry Gap" sign for 15 gravel miles.

Hershberger Mountain's restored 1925 fire lookout has a stunning view, accessed by a 100-foot trail from the end of very rough Road 530. Just half a mile

ROGUE-UMPQUA DIVIDE

down the road, a pullout at a switch-back serves as the trailhead for several day hikes. A nearly level 3-mile trail north to Hole-in-the-ground (a high meadow basin) provides a close look at Fish Mountain, tallest point in the Western Cascades. To the west of Hershberger Mountain, Grasshopper Mountain's viewpoint is 4.3 miles. The route passes Pup Prairie, the leaky Cripple Creek shelter, groves of huge Douglas fir, and Grasshopper Meadow.

No trail scales the area's highest peak, Fish Mountain, but a cross-country scramble to the top yields views from Mount Shasta to the Three Sisters. From the end of Road 870, walk the trail 0.3 mile south to a crest, then turn left 0.5 mile up an open, trailless ridge to the summit.

To explore the high basins at the foot of Fish Mountain, try the 7.7-mile hike through Alkali Meadows and down Buck Canyon. June wildflowers in the beautiful area's unfortunately cow-trampled meadows include fawn lilies, marsh marigolds, and pink kalmia. If you can't arrange a car shuttle for this hike (between Road 700 and Road 400), park at the end of Road 400 and content yourself with a hike to the top of Buck Canyon's meadows.

Whitehorse Meadows, in a pass overlooking the forests of Castle Rock Fork's broad valley, makes a good day hike goal. From the north, a 2.3-mile trail

Grasshopper Mountain from Buckeye Lake.

to the meadows from Road 950 offers a side trip to Wolf Lake. Reach Road 950 via Road 28, which joins the North Umpqua Highway 138 near Eagle Rock.

Another day-hike route to Whitehorse Meadows begins at Road 870 and traverses 4 miles along Rattlesnake Mountain. From this side, however, most hikers prefer instead to take a steep side trail up Rattlesnake Mountain (a fine viewpoint — with no rattlesnakes), making that summit's meadow their goal.

Several trips require backpacking gear. One of the best is the 13.4-mile trail loop from Fish Lake around the base of cliff-edged Highrock Mountain, passing Cripple Camp's meadow, Cliff Lake, and Buckeye Lake. Take a short detour to Grasshopper Mountain's viewpoint.

The Rogue-Umpqua Divide Trail follows a ridgecrest the length of the wilderness — 23.8 miles from Road 30 (not on map) past Abbott Butte, Jackass

Cascade lily at Abbott Butte lookout.

Mountain, and Fish Mountain to Road 37 — and even continues beyond toward Garwood Butte.

The 47.9-mile Upper Rogue River Trail parallels Highway 230 from Prospect to the northwest corner of Crater Lake National Park. Don't miss the dramatic section (not shown on map) that starts 1 mile south of Union Creek at the Natural Bridge trailhead, where the river disappears into a lava tube. South of this point the path follows the river 3.5 miles to a crossing of Road 68 at Woodruff Bridge Campground, and then continues another 4.6 miles to River Bridge Campground, passing the churning slot of Takelma Gorge along the way.

CLIMBING

Hershberger Mountain Road 6515 passes within 300 yards of the base of Rabbitears, a pair of 400-foot pinnacles first scaled in 1921. Both spires require level I-4 climbing skills. Some summers the road to Rabbitears is gated closed until August 15 to protect endangered falcons nesting on the spires.

SNOWSHOEING & SKIING

When snow levels are low, Nordic skiing is easy on the Upper Rogue River Trail. Try the 3.5-mile trail section north from the snowed-under Union Creek Campground, along the narrow, 50-foot-deep Rogue River Gorge.

For deeper snow, try unplowed Road 6560, at the 4000-foot level. Ski past Muir Creek Falls to Buck Canyon, below towering Fish Mountain. Advanced skiers with compass and survival gear can continue west on the wilderness trail system. Beginners can prowl the level meadows between Road 900 and Highway 230.

Elephanthead from Elephanthead Pond, near Abbott Butte.

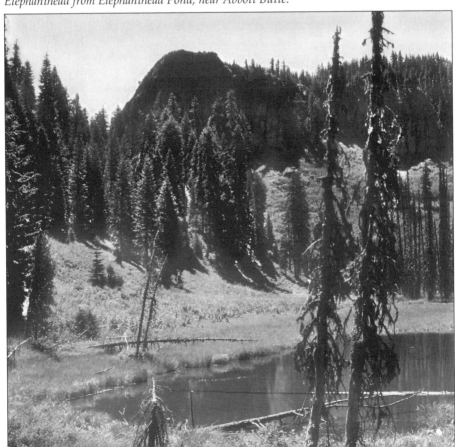

28
CRATER LAKE

Oregon's famous national park sees half a million visitors annually, yet away from the paved rim road the trails are only lightly used. On an average summer night, only a dozen backpackers camp in the area's 259 square miles of backcountry. In fact, the heaviest backcountry use comes in winter, when the snow is excellent for ski touring.

Location: 64 mi E of Medford, 49 mi NW of Klamath Falls

Size: 286 sq mi

Status: national park (1902)

Terrain: cliff-edged lake, high forest, pumice desert

Elevation: 3977'-8929'

Management: Crater Lake National Park

Map: Crater Lake (USGS, 25')

Climate

Average annual precipitation is 66 inches, largely measured by melting the area's 44 feet of snowfall. Snow closes most trails, and the rim road, from mid-October to mid-June. The eastern portion of the rim road past Mount Scott usually doesn't open until early July.

Plants and Wildlife

Virtually all life in the area was destroyed by Mount Mazama's eruption 7700 years ago. The 600 species of plants and many animals here are evidence of ongoing repopulation. Forests, largely of lodgepole pine, Shasta red fir, and mountain hemlock, have spread nearly everywhere but the Pumice Desert, where volcanic debris fell 200 feet deep. The Pumice Desert's cinder soil holds so little moisture that only occasional bunchgrass and dwarf lupine live there.

Most, but not all, Cascade wildflowers have reestablished themselves along the lake's alpine rim. Gnarled whitebark pines clinging to the rim withstand the cliff edge's fierce storm winds because their branches are so supple they can literally be tied in knots. The dominant animal species of the rim appear to be cute golden-mantled ground squirrels and raucous, swooping Clark's nutcrackers, both of which aggressively encourage visitors to defy the park's ban on feeding wildlife.

Biologists theorize that the toads, garter snakes, and chipmunks living on Wizard Island migrated there over land when the lake was lower. The crayfish in Wizard Island's ponds were introduced by early visitors.

The boat landing at Cleetwood Cove.

April is a good month to try the 31-mile ski or snowshoe tour around Crater Lake's rim.

Visitors sometimes sight black bears, especially in or near the Mazama Campground. If you stay there you must keep all food at night in the bear-proof lockers provided. Though the bears generally avoid backcountry camps, backpackers should hang all food 10 feet off the ground and 5 feet from a tree trunk at night.

Geology

Crater Lake fills the caldera of Mount Mazama, a volcano that collapsed after a cataclysmic eruption about 5677 BC.

Mount Mazama first began to form 400,000 years ago, when neighboring Union Peak and Mount Thielsen were already extinct. At its height, Mount Mazama was a broad, 12,000-foot mountain the size of Mount Adams. Ice Age glaciers gouged its flanks with valleys (still visible as Sun Notch and Kerr Notch). Smaller volcanoes sprouted on its sides (Timber Crater, Red Cone, and Hillman Peak). Its slopes oozed thick lava flows (visible in cross-section as The Watchman, Llao Rock, and Cloudcap).

Then, in an eruption 150 times as massive as the 1980 Mount St. Helens blast, Mount Mazama suddenly exploded 12.2 cubic miles of pumice and ash into the sky, emptying its subterranean magma reservoir. Ash fell 10 feet deep at Klamath Marsh, and a half inch deep as far away as Saskatchewan. As the hollowed mountain collapsed, a glowing avalanche of pumice and superheated gas raced down the slopes at freight-train speeds. Gas fumaroles in the fiery avalanche deposits welded pumice together around vertical vents. Later erosion exposed these as pinnacles along Annie and Sand creeks.

Later, two cinder cones erupted on the caldera floor. Wizard Island's cone still rises 764 feet above the lake, but Merriam Cone never saw the light of day and remains 486 feet underwater.

The deepest lake in North America, Crater Lake has no outlet but maintains its level by evaporation and seepage. The lake's 1943-foot depth and remarkable purity account for its stunning blue color.

CRATER LAKE

N

0 — 1 — 2mi
0 — 1 — 2 — 3km

Medford 70mi

Rogue River

6530

230

760

Lake West
5100'
★ Boundary Springs

Mt Mazama Viewpoint

National Cr

Crescent Ridge

6535

660

5600'

Spruce Cr

Copeland Cr

Oasis Spr
Oasis Butte

Bald Crater

Crater Springs
Sphagnum Bog

Crater Cr

Diamond Lake 1mi

Gaywas Pk

Desert Ridge

Desert Cone

Crater Lake

6265 ×

Red Cone Spr

Red Cone 7372'

Williams Crater

Pacific

6500 ×

Hiker Only

Pumice Desert

Crest Trail

North Entrance

5900 × P

138

9 mi Hwy 97

7015

2308

2308

Mt Thielsen Wilderness

Summit Rk

Timber Crater 7424'

Desert Cr

Sharp Pk

Cascade Spr

×6750'

Round Top

Mazama Rk

6800' ×

Cleetwood Cove

Pumice Pt

Boat Route

Hillman Pk

Llao Rk ★

Grouse Hill

Mt Scott
8929'

Pothole
Spr

Scott Bluffs

Cavern   Cr

Cr

Sand

The Pinnacles

Anderson Bluffs

Plaikni
Falls

Maklaks
Crater

Ridge

Sand

Ridge

Maklaks
Spr

6237

Lost
Creek

Wheeler

7700'

Cloudcap
8070'

Skell
Head

Kerr Notch

6000'

Grayback

Cr

Sun

Crater Pk
7263'

Creek

62

48 mi
Klamath Falls

3282

Crater
Lake
el.6176'

Phantom Ship

Dutton Cliff

Sun Notch

Vidae

Ridge

East   Fork

Annie Falls

Wilderness

Wizard
Island
6940'

Garfield Pk
8054'

Lodgepole

Scoria
Cone

Goose Nest

Rim
Village

Munson
Cr   Falls

Annie

Bear
Bluff

Pumice
Flat

x 6290'

Sky

The Watchman
8013'

Park
Headquarters

Munson Ridge

Lightning
Spr

7100'

Dutton Cr

Trapper

Park
Entrance

Mazama

Lakes

Pacific

Trail

Bald Top

Stuart
Falls

National

Creek

5870'

6200'

Crest

Whitehorse
Pond

Union Pk
7709'

Red Blanket

6205

3900'

Park

Castle Pt

62

Bybee Cr

Castle

Thousand
Springs

830

Medford
62mi

800

Union   Cr

HIKING & BACKPACKING

Popular day hikes lead to viewpoints on the lake rim and nearby peaks. The little-used backcountry trail system is largely dry and less scenic, but it's the best bet for backpacking because camping is prohibited within a mile of the Rim Drive, except in winter. Permits are required for backcountry camping. They are free and can be picked up at the Rim Village Visitor Center or at the Steel Center along the south entrance road.

Other park rules: Pets are prohibited on all trails. Saddle stock are limited strictly to the PCT and grazing is prohibited. Firearms and other hunting devices are forbidden. On the other hand, angling is permitted everywhere except Sun Creek, and no license is required to fish in the lake itself.

Only five hikes have views of the lake itself. Some of the best views are along the 1.7-mile trail switchbacking up 1010 feet from Rim Village to Garfield Peak, past alpine gardens of showy Davidson's penstemon, red paintbrush, and spreading phlox.

Hikers with less time can take the 0.8-mile path that climbs 413 feet from the Rim Drive to a lookout tower amidst twisted whitebark pines atop The Watchman. A trail from Rim Village along the caldera rim also leads to The Watchman — a 3.8-mile route that touches the highway four times.

Morning is the best time to scale Mount Scott for the farthest-ranging views in the park — from Mount Shasta to Mount Jefferson on a clear day. The 2.5-mile trail climbs steadily to the summit's 1952 fire lookout on this geologically recent stratovolcano.

The park's most used trail (500 hikers a day) is a steep 1.1-mile path from the Rim Drive down to Cleetwood Cove, where two-hour guided boat tours of the lake depart on the hour between 10am and 3pm from early July to early September. The really fun hike here, however, is to take the boat tour as far as Wizard Island, where you can climb a 1-mile trail to the cinder cone's summit crater or follow the lava shore 0.9 mile to the cold green water of Fumarole Bay. Just don't miss the last boat back to Cleetwood Cove, because camping is banned on the island.

An easy trailless ramble up Llao Rock leads to a quiet overlook of Crater Lake.

Phantom Ship from Sun Notch.

Craggy Union Peak lacks a lake view, but it commands a panorama of the rim peaks and of other Cascade summits. The 5.5-mile route there begins by following the PCT through a mountain hemlock forest south of Highway 62. Snow covers much of the route until mid-July.

Three other peaks make interesting hikes for those seeking respite from the rim's crowds. Plan a picnic to the wildflower meadow in the summit bowl of Crater Peak, a moderate 3.4-mile hike from the Vidae Falls picnic area. For views of Mount Mazama's other flank (and Cascade peaks as far north as the Three Sisters), try scaling Red Cone. It's an easy, obvious 1.5-mile cross-country hike from a turnout on the park's north rim access road, 1 mile north of the Rim Drive junction.

A third cinder cone, Timber Crater, is too well forested to offer views. Carry water on the 4-mile route from the Pumice Desert to the often snowy, flat summit—a crater filled to the brim by Mount Mazama's pumice. The final 2 miles are cross-country from the PCT.

Those staying at the popular Mazama Campground won't want to miss four short loop hikes nearby. The 1.7-mile Annie Creek loop trail from the campground passes abundant wildflowers and interesting gas-fumarole rock formations similar to those at The Pinnacles, in the park's distant southeast corner. Two miles farther up the south rim access road, the all-accessible 1-mile Godfrey Glen loop trail follows a cliff edge past more pinnacle formations. From the Park Headquarters, a half-mile loop tours the headquarters' historic area, and the self-guiding 0.4-mile Castle Crest wildflower garden nature-trail loop shows off the park's alpine flora.

Massive Boundary Springs, the sudden source of the Rogue River, is a 2.5-mile hike through riverside woods from the Mount Mazama Viewpoint, 5 miles west of the Diamond Lake junction on Highway 230. The hike starts at the beginning of the Upper Rogue River Trail, a path that continues 47.9 miles downstream to Prospect. No camping is permitted within a quarter mile of Boundary Springs.

Another long hike heads to Sphagnum Bog, a floating moss field with four carnivorous plant species, but the trip is chiefly of interest to botanists with mosquito headnets and hip waders.

The national park's portion of the Pacific Crest Trail is largely viewless, with no water north of Red Cone Spring or south of Dutton Creek. This is the only route in the park open to equestrians, but long-distance hikers should consider a more scenic alternative route that climbs Dutton Creek to the Rim Village and then traces the lake's rim north past the Watchman and Hillman Peak.

Day hikers can sample this route on a 12.9-mile loop. From Rim Village,

The view from Crater Lake Lodge's porch.

Crater Lake from Mt. Scott's fire lookout tower.

follow the trail north 2.3 miles along the lake rim, cross the highway, descend the Lightning Springs Trail 4 miles (passing the springs and a waterfall), turn left on the PCT equestrian bypass 4.2 miles to the wildflower meadow at Dutton Creek, and turn left for a 2.4-mile climb back to Rim Village.

The area's prettiest waterfall is not within the park at all. It's 40-foot Stuart Falls, at the head of Red Blanket Creek's scenic glacier-carved valley, in the Sky Lakes Wilderness. Crater Lake visitors can hike there from the Highway 62's Lodgepole picnic area on a dry, 5.4-mile route across forested Pumice Flat. But a shorter, more scenic trail reaches Stuart Falls from the west, passing 40-foot Red Blanket Falls on the way. The 4.3-mile trail from Road 6205 up Red Blanket Creek starts in a stately low-elevation forest and climbs 1500 feet. If you like huckleberries, add an extra 1.4 miles to the return trip by taking a fainter trail that loops past Lucky Meadow to Red Blanket Falls. To find the trailhead, turn off Highway 62 to the center of Prospect, take the Butte Falls Road 1 mile, turn left on Red Blanket Road for 0.4 mile, and fork left on gravel Road 6205 for 11.4 miles to its end.

SNOWSHOEING & SKIING

Within the park, Highway 62 and its short spur to Rim Village are plowed in winter, allowing skiers and snowshoers access to excellent tours on the snowed-under Rim Drive and surrounding terrain. Snowmobiles are out of earshot, restricted to the Diamond Lake area and the park's north access road. The lake itself is an unforgettable spectacle in winter. Park rangers offer free, guided snowshoe walks from the Rim Village cafeteria building on winter weekends, and even provide the snowshoes.

The area's premier challenge, the 33-mile loop around the lake, is usually a three- or four-day excursion, best attempted in March or April when winter's fiercest storms are over. The route is for experienced skiers and snow campers only. Because road cuts and slopes can calve avalanches, detours are marked around the two most dangerous areas. The Park Service recommends that ski parties carry avalanche beacons. Beware of approaching too closely to the rim, with its unseen cornice overhangs. By May, volcanic grit covers the snow, slowing progress and damaging skis. Free permits, required for snow campers, must be picked up in person.

When choosing day trips and tours away from the Rim Drive, remember that scenic routes on steep slopes are prone to avalanches. Map, compass, and route-finding ability are essential in the flatter areas, where viewless forests hide landmarks.

29
SKY LAKES

Hundreds of lakes hide among the mountain hemlock forests on the Cascade crest between Crater Lake and Mount McLoughlin, highest point in Southern Oregon.

Location: 36 mi NE of Medford, 22 mi NW of Klamath Falls

Size: 220 sq mi

Status: 177 sq mi designated wilderness (1984)

Terrain: lake-dotted upland forests, peaks

Elevation: 3520'-9495'

Management: Rogue River-Siskiyou. NF, Fremont-Winema NF

Maps: Sky Lakes Wilderness, Jackson Klamath Winter Trails (USFS)

Climate

The heavy winter snowpack blocks most trails until mid-June, and the Pacific Crest Trail until mid-July. Mosquitoes are so numerous after the snowmelt that headnets and zippered tents are advisable throughout July. Summers are dry, with occasional thunderstorms. Snows return in mid-October. Average annual precipitation is 55 inches.

Plants and Wildlife

The wilderness is heavily influenced by adjacent Upper Klamath Lake, which may shelter a half million birds at once during the October and March migrations. Bald eagles and osprey nesting near Klamath Lake's swamps commonly visit the high wilderness lakes. Pelican Butte is named for Upper Klamath Lake's white pelicans, unmistakable with their 7-foot wingspans.

The best time to view the teeming bird life on Upper Klamath Lake's marshy fringe is during the July and August nesting season, when a canoe put in at Rocky Point Resort (rentals available) enables birders to paddle 6 miles north up Crystal Creek on a marked canoe trail, past red-necked grebes, white-headed woodpeckers, and possibly even sandhill cranes.

Sky Lakes' profusion of July mosquitoes coincides with a profusion of mosquito-pollinated wildflowers and a profusion of tiny, mosquito-eating boreal toads.

In August the omnipresent huckleberry underbrush of the mountain hem-

Devils Peak from Cliff Lake.

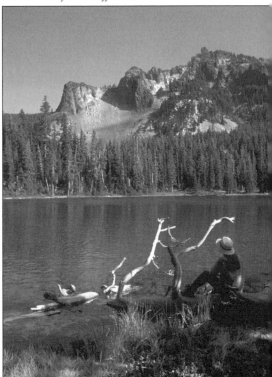

lock forest sags with ripe fruit—especially along the Wickiup Meadow trail. By September the huckleberry leaves turn scarlet, filling the uplands with color.

Geology

Mount McLoughlin presents a smooth conical face toward Medford and Klamath Falls but conceals a craggy glacial cirque on its northern side. Strata exposed there show the mountain was once a tall cinder cone like nearby Pelican Butte, then erupted an armor-like covering of andesite, and finally lost its original summit when a glacier (since vanished) cut through its northern shell.

Other Ice Age glaciers scoured out most of the lake basins and gouged the deep, U-shaped valleys of the Rogue River's many forks. Narrow Alta Lake and Long Lake did not result from glaciers, however. They lie along a possibly active fault that extends through the Mountain Lakes Wilderness to California.

Hiking & Backpacking

The area's most popular hike is also the most difficult: scaling 9495-foot Mount McLoughlin for a view of all Southern Oregon. No technical equipment is required, but you'll need enough stamina to gain 3915 feet in 5.3 miles and return.

From Road 3650 hike 1.4 miles to the PCT, where there's a short spur to Freye Lake. If the lake doesn't have a nice mountain reflection, turn back and try the climb in better weather. Otherwise, follow the ridgetop trail to a frustrating false summit at timberline. The true top's abandoned lookout foundations are another steep, trailless mile up a rocky ridge. Remember the route well. Most search and rescue calls come for hikers who return by romping south from the summit, missing the trail.

Other popular hikes prowl three clusters of forest-rimmed lakes: the Seven Lakes Basin, the Sky Lakes Basin, and the Blue Canyon Basin. Overused portions of some lakeshores are closed for rehabilitation, particularly near trails.

Craggy Devils Peak towers above the Seven Lakes Basin—especially Cliff Lake, where swimmers can dive from cliffs into deep water. An easy 4.7-mile trail to shallow Grass Lake from the Sevenmile Marsh trailhead on Road 3334 makes the entire lake basin accessible to day hikers, but the area deserves a two- or three-day trip, so bring a backpack.

For your second day in the Seven Lakes Basin, take the 6-mile loop trail over Devils Peak. Follow the PCT to a 7300-foot saddle, where a short, rugged spur trail heads for the peak's former lookout site and sweeping view.

Have another day to spend? Try an 8-mile loop to rock-rimmed Lake Ivern and slender Lake Alta. The route requires an easy half-mile cross-country traverse between the Lake Ivern Trail and the Middle Fork Trail. Follow a compass bearing northwest from the Bigfoot Spring spur trail turnoff. At Lake Ivern, be sure to take an easy quarter-mile side trip due north to a 500-foot cliff overlooking the U-shaped canyon of the Middle Fork Rogue River.

To reach the trailhead at Sevenmile Marsh, take Nicholson Road 4.3 miles west from Highway 62 at Fort Klamath, then continue on gravel Road 3334 to its end.

Less heavily used trails access the basin from the west. The shortest, a 5-mile path from Road 3780 to Cliff Lake, climbs 1600 feet over a ridge on its way. The longest, the 9.7-mile Middle Fork Trail from Road 3790 to Alta Lake, follows a splashing fork of the Rogue River through an old-growth forest with luxuriant, low-elevation greenery.

The Sky Lakes Basin makes up for a shortage of mountain views with an abundance of forest-rimmed lakes. In

Mt. McLoughlin from Fourmile Lake.

Lake Alta.

this basin, the aptly-named Heavenly Twin Lakes are just 2.4 miles from the Cold Spring trailhead, making this an easy day hike or a good backpacking trip with kids. It's worth the effort to continue on a 2.1-mile trail loop past deep Lake Notasha, swimmable Lake Elizabeth, and large Isherwood Lake. Another good extension to this hike heads 1.9 miles north to scenic Trapper Lake, in a cluster of lakes with views of Luther Mountain's rocky ridge.

Two quieter trails also make good routes into the Sky Lakes Basin. The Nannie Creek Trail from Road 3484 passes large, swimmable South Puck Lake after 2.4 miles (a good day hike goal for kids), then descends another 4.1 miles to Trapper Lake, a prime backpacking goal. The Cherry Creek Trail from Road 3450 arrives at that lake in 5.2 miles, but climbs 1300 feet, making the route a better choice for equestrians.

The popular lakes of the Blue Canyon Basin, nestled below Mount McLoughlin's snowy northern face, offer surprisingly few views of the nearby peak. Begin on the Blue Canyon Trail from Road 3770. It's 2.3 miles to deep, cold Blue Lake, with its cliff backdrop, and another 0.7 miles to Horseshoe Lake's peninsula. Trailside camps are closed here to allow the fragile flora to regrow. Best bets for backpacking solitude in the Blue Canyon Basin are off-trail Pear Lake and Carey Lake. Island Lake, largest of the group, is 5.5 miles from the Road 3770

trailhead. A rail fence at the lake protects the Judge Waldo Tree, inscribed in 1888 by the first pioneers to hike the length of Southern Oregon's Cascades. For a good swim, try nearby Dee Lake.

Fourmile Lake is dammed for irrigation, but it's still scenic and serves as the starting point for several top day hikes. The 3.7-mile route to Long Lake tours a snag-filled bay of Fourmile Lake (with views of Mount McLoughlin) and passes wildflower meadows near beautiful Badger Lake. To the west of the trailhead at Fourmile Lake's campground, a level trail through the woods leads 1.8 miles to Squaw Lake and another 1.1 mile to little Summit Lake, crossing the PCT along the way. Turn right on the PCT to complete a 14-mile loop around Fourmile Lake, returning via Long Lake.

Little-used trails in the north of this wilderness lead to McKie Meadow and Solace Meadow's cabin, both popular with equestrians. The 5.3-mile Tom and Jerry Trail to McKie Meadow from Road 600 offers a good cross-country side trip to the view atop Tom Mountain. An alternate route to McKie Meadow crosses Kerby Hill; it's steep, but features a spectacular view of the Middle Fork Rogue canyon.

The shortest route to Solace Meadow — 6.3 miles — follows the Middle Fork Trail from Road 3790, then switchbacks up the Halifax Trail through a rapid succession of botanical zones.

The nearly viewless 49.7-mile segment

The final pitch to Mt. McLoughlin's summit.

of the PCT between Highway 140 and Highway 62 in Crater Lake National Park manages to avoid all lakes and water sources, so savvy travelers detour off the PCT into the three major lake basins. Also be sure to take the 0.6-mile side trip to Ranger Spring, a welcome oasis. The Oregon Desert, on the northern part of the PCT route, is a lodgepole pine forest free of underbrush and notable for massive September mushrooms.

Cross-country hiking is easy and rewarding in all the upland lake basins, but particularly in the McKee Basin near Blue Rock and in the glacial cirque on Pelican Butte—areas lacking maintained trails.

SNOWSHOEING & SKIING

Marked Nordic ski trails radiate from several sno-parks along plowed Highway 140. Snowmobiles dominate snowed-under roads and are permitted on most non-wilderness trails (except the PCT and the Cascade Canal).

A good beginner tour off-limits to snowmobiles follows the Lake of the Woods shoreline 1.9 miles from Highway 140 to snowed-under Aspen Point campground. Another easy route, with good views of Mount McLoughlin, begins at the Fish Lake Resort and loops 3 miles on marked roads and trails south

of that lake.

The PCT offers routes both south of Highway 140, to viewpoints in the vast lava fields around nearby Brown Mountain, and north of the highway, where it climbs steadily 3.5 miles to Freye Lake's mountain view. A 1.5-mile trail connects the PCT with Fish Lake Resort, but a closer access to the PCT is the sno-park at the junction of Highway 140 and Road 3650.

Road 3650 and the parallel Cascade Canal provide a scenic, well-graded 9.7-mile Nordic route from Highway 140 to Fourmile Lake. A shortcut to that lake, along Road 3661, is shared with snowmobiles but allows snow campers quickest access to the wilderness trail system beyond.

The area's most challenging ski tour, to the summit of Mount McLoughlin, should only be undertaken in perfect weather by groups familiar with avalanche danger areas.

BOATING

Canoes and sailboats do well on Fourmile Lake, Fish Lake, and the marshy bays and creeks of Upper Klamath Lake. Motorboats are limited to 10 miles per hour in all of these areas. Note the canoe trail from Rocky Point, described under "Plants and Animals" above.

The Seven Lakes Basin from Devils Peak.

30
MOUNTAIN LAKES

This pocket wilderness is large enough that some of its alpine viewpoints and forest-rimmed lakes are best seen on backpacking trips.

Eb Lake.

Climate

Late summer brings occasional thunderstorms, but most of the area's 40 inches of annual precipitation comes as snow, which blocks trails from early November to late June. Mosquitoes are numerous in July.

Location: 38 mi E of Medford, 15 mi NW of Klamath Falls

Size: 45 sq mi

Status: 36 sq mi designated wilderness (1964)

Terrain: forested buttes, lake basins

Elevation: 4700'-8208'

Management: Fremont-Winema NF

Map: Mountain Lakes Wilderness (USFS)

Plants and Wildlife

Bald eagles, osprey, and a variety of ducks from nearby Upper Klamath Lake frequent the high lakes. The dense forests below 7000 feet are chiefly droopy-topped mountain hemlock and prim, Christmas-tree-shaped Shasta red fir. At higher elevations, only gnarled white-bark pines survive. Their seeds are a primary food source for the area's raucous Clark's nutcrackers.

Geology

This roughly circular upland was once thought to be the eroded remnant

Harriette Lake.

of a collapsed 12,000-foot volcano similar to Crater Lake's Mount Mazama. More recent research, however, has revealed the peaks here as a cluster of at least four overlapping volcanoes. Though glaciers have dissected them severely (Mount Carmine and Aspen Butte were once a single cone), they were probably never much taller than today. A feature of this volcanic hot spot is a swarm of faults running through the area—one of which aligned Seldom Creek's oddly straight glacial valley.

HIKING & BACKPACKING

Three trails climb to the 8.3-mile Mountain Lakes Loop, with its lakes and scenic passes. Because of the area's small size, groups are limited to ten—counting persons, saddle stock, and pack animals.

The most popular route into the wilderness is the Varney Creek Trail from Road 3664, which climbs among the creek's wildflowers (blooming in July) for 4.8 miles to Eb and Zeb Lakes. These heavily visited, scenic, but shallow lakes are often warm enough for swimming. If this is your backpacking base, look for tent sites well away from the lakeshores.

For the second day of your backpacking trip, head eastward on the Mountain Lakes Loop Trail 1.9 miles to very deep and very beautiful 40-acre Harriette Lake, passing Como Lake and shallow Silent and Zephyr lakes. Westward, the loop trail climbs 1 mile to a saddle, from which a 7708-foot summit with an excellent viewpoint is only a short cross-country hike away. Side trails from the 8.3-mile Mountain Lakes loop lead to seldom-visited South Pass Lake, the Clover Lake basin, and the Hemlock Lake basin. Those ready for a grander cross-country viewpoint hike can head northeast from Eb Lake up a 2.5-mile ridge to Mount Harriman.

To find the Varney Creek trailhead, drive Highway 140 west of Klamath Falls 21 miles. Between mileposts 46 and 47, turn south on Road 3637 for 1.8 miles, and turn left on Road 3664 for 1.9 miles to its end.

Another popular trailhead, on Road 3660 near Lake of the Woods, is the starting point of a 4.8-mile path up Seldom Creek's glacial valley to the Mountain Lakes Loop. After climbing 3 miles on this route, look for a spur trail to grassy Waban Lake, with its seasonal profusion of tree frogs.

A third path up to the Mountain Lakes Loop, the Clover Trail, is less used because it is shared with grazing cattle. It reaches small Clover Lake from Road 3852 in 2.5 miles. Some hikers veer right at the 2.4-mile point, following an unmaintained shortcut to the Mountain Lakes Loop Trail, to reach a ridgetop overlooking Harriette Lake. From here it's easy to strike off cross-country, following the alpine ridge up to the south past whitebark pines, dwarfed manzanita bushes, and showy Davidson's penstemons to Aspen Butte, whose summit view makes the strenuous 5.4-mile climb from Road 3852 worthwhile. Look for Crater Lake's rim peaks, Mount McLoughlin, and Mount Shasta.

Backpackers hiking the 8.3-mile Mountain Lake Loop Trail may also want to explore the 1.7-mile spur trail eastward down a forested, but increasingly arid glacial valley to large South Pass Lake.

SNOWSHOEING & SKIING

Ski or snowshoe trips can begin from plowed Highway 140 either at the Great Meadow sno-park near Lake of the Woods or at the Varney Creek Trailhead turnoff between mileposts 46 and 47. Carry map, compass, and emergency gear, because wilderness trails are not marked for winter use.

Great Meadow is a snowmobile center, but skiers leave noise behind when they leave Road 3660 for the Mountain Lakes Trail up Seldom Creek. Lake Waban, 4.5 miles from the sno-park, is a good goal.

From the Varney Creek Trailhead turnoff, skiers follow unplowed roads 3.7 miles to the trailhead. Eb and Zeb Lakes are an additional 4.8 miles uphill.

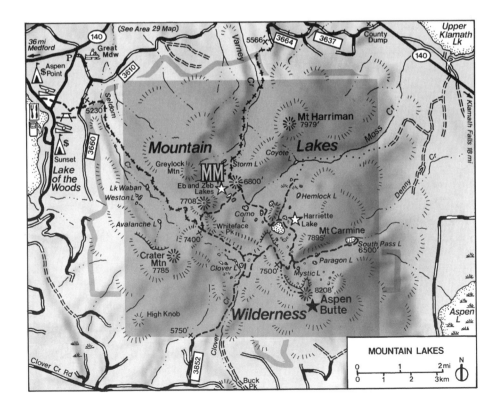

31
SODA MOUNTAIN

Soda Mountain stands at the center of the Cascade-Siskiyou National Monument, a biologically diverse area where the Cascade Range and the Siskiyou Mountains meet.

Mt. Shasta from Pilot Rock.

Climate

Moderate snowfall blocks the Pacific Crest Trail from about December to March or April. Annual precipitation varies from 40 inches in the upland forests to less than 20 inches on the dry, southern slopes, where summer temperatures can soar.

Plants and Wildlife

Soda Mountain stands at the apex of three biologic zones: the Cascades, the Siskiyous, and the high desert. Dark fir forests on the high, north-facing slopes resemble woods in the High Cascades. Droopy, canyon-bottom cedars and stiff-limbed manzanita brush remind one of the Siskiyous. Pungent sagebrush and juniper on the dry southern ridges belong to the Great Basin steppe's bioregion.

Location: 13 mi SE of Ashland

Size: 37 sq mi

Status: National Monument (2000), designated wilderness (2009)

Terrain: steep, mostly wooded slopes

Elevation: 2300'-6091'

Management: Medford District BLM

Maps: Siskiyou Pass, Soda Mountain, Parker Mountain, Hornbrook [California], Iron Gate Reservoir [California] (USGS)

The area is home to the showy Greene's mariposa lily (threatened in Oregon), though hikers are more likely to encounter trilliums and calypso orchids (in spring forests) or yellow-flowered rabbit brush (among fall sagebrush).

A large herd of blacktail deer from the Rogue Valley relies on the white oak grasslands of the lower southern slopes for winter browse. Other wildlife species include cougar, golden eagles, and quail. The area's unusual diversity allows desert species, such as kangaroo rats, to share habitat with forest species such as northern spotted owls and rough-skinned newts. The Monument supports one of the highest diversities of butterfly species in the United States.

The Soda Mountain lookout tower.

Geology

Soda Mountain is a block of the 16- to 25-million-year-old Old Cascades, wedged between the much older Klamath Mountains to the west and the much younger High Cascades to the east. Pilot Rock is an eroded volcanic plug of columnar basalt.

History

Pilot Rock's landmark basalt monolith once guided gold miners and trappers toward a low Siskiyou Mountain pass on the Oregon/California Trail. Train tracks built across Siskiyou Pass in 1887 filled the final gap in a rail line around the United States' perimeter. The area remained remote enough, however, to harbor Oregon's last known grizzly bear, the legendary, 8-foot-tall Old Reelfoot, which was shot near Pilot Rock's base in 1891. Later the D'Autremont brothers attempted a train robbery at Siskiyou Pass in 1923, murdering three men. They eluded a four-continent manhunt by camping under a deadfall tree beside Porcupine Creek.

HIKING & BACKPACKING

Interstate 5 travelers can stretch their legs with a 5-mile walk on the Pacific Crest Trail to the cliffs and views at the base of Pilot Rock. Take Interstate 5 to Mount Ashland exit 6, follow old Highway 99 south under the freeway 1.9 miles, and turn left on Pilot Rock Road 40-2E-33 for 2 miles to a huge parking area in an old quarry on the right. The trail ahead is an old road blocked by boulders. Climb 0.8 mile, turn left on the Pacific Crest Trail for 300 yards, and fork to the right toward Pilot Rock. Hikers should turn back at the rock's base, but cautious scramblers willing to use their hands can make their way straight up a steep chute to the top.

For a longer hike from the same trailhead, continue east on the PCT past Pilot Rock 6.5 miles to Soda Mountain's 1933 lookout tower, staffed each summer.

Pilot Rock.

For an easier route to the lookout, drive Highway 66 east of Ashland 14.5 miles. Just 200 feet before the Green Springs summit, turn right on Soda Mountain Road 39-3E-32.3 for 3.7 miles to a grassy pass with powerlines and small signs marking the PCT. Hike uphill to the right 1.1 mile, switchback to the left on a steep unmarked path 0.2 mile, and turn right on a road 0.8 mile to the lookout.

The best view of all is at Boccard Point's rocky promontory to the south. Hike the PCT 1.8 miles west of the Soda Mountain turnoff. At a pass where a dozen trails and roads connect, turn left on the second abandoned dirt road to the left. After 50 feet fork uphill to the left for 1.8 miles. At the old road's end, take a faint trail to the right on a broad ridgecrest 0.3 mile to the viewpoint.

Boccard Point also makes a good starting point for cross-country forays into the area's steep southern canyons. Trailless travel here is easiest through sagebrush and open grasslands along ridgetops, or along the creek's lush growth of moss and maples. Rock outcroppings and bands of nearly impenetrable scrub oak chaparral interrupt canyon slopes. Dutch Oven Creek's many small waterfalls make good goals.

The old Schoheim Road, a rough track traversing the southern edge of the national monument, has become a more attractive hiking route now that it is in designated wilderness, closed to motor vehicles and bicycles.

CLIMBING

Pilot Rock's columnar basalt tower offers seven mountaineering routes, including the scenic West Ridge (level I-5.3) and the South Face's broken basalt columns (rated II- 5.6). The West Gully, a class 3 scramble route to the summit, is commonly used by technical climbers as a descent route. A pinnacle 200 yards southeast of Pilot Rock requires level I-5.7 skills.

32
RED BUTTES

Straddling the rocky crest of the Siskiyou Mountains, this little-visited area's trail system extends along view-filled ridges and subalpine meadows from the Pacific Crest Trail to the Oregon Caves National Monument.

Climate

Snowfall closes high trails from about mid-November to mid-May. Summers are very dry. Annual precipitation measures 60 inches.

Plants and Wildlife

Expect signs of frequent wildlife on the trails: deer tracks, coyote scat, and the palm-sized paw prints of cougar and bear. This is also a prime spot for Bigfoot fanciers. Alleged sightings of ape men date to 1895. The Forest Service issued a special-use permit for a Sasquatch trap on Collings Mountain (west of Applegate Lake) in 1973, but to no avail.

The area teems with the unusual flora of the Siskiyous. Knobcone pines, resembling bumpy flagpoles, dot Figurehead Mountain. Droopy weeping spruce are common. Massive incense cedars, hollowed by fire, could serve as extra camping accommodations near Sucker Gap's shelter. A loop trail from the Oregon Caves leads to Big Tree, one

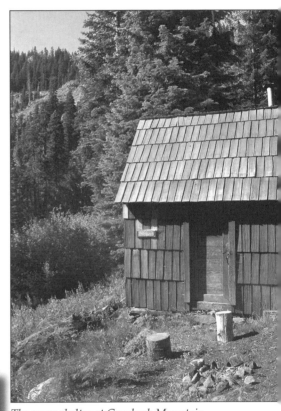

The snow shelter at Grayback Mountain.

Location: 34 mi SW of Medford

Size: 130 sq mi total; 42 sq mi in Oregon

Status: 31 sq mi designated wilderness; 6 sq mi in Oregon (1984)

Terrain: rocky buttes, forested ridges, small lakes

Elevation: 1300'-7055'

Management: Rogue River-Siskiyou NF, Klamath NF, Oregon Caves National Monument

Map: Red Buttes Wilderness (USFS)

of Oregon's largest Douglas firs. Some of the world's southernmost Alaska cedars grow on Mount Emily, while the world's northernmost Baker's cypresses grow on Steve Peak, a quarter mile east of Miller Lake.

June brings wildflowers familiar from the alpine Cascades as well as Siskiyou novelties, including two delicate, pink Lewisia species, best seen in Cameron

Sucker Gap's shelter.

Meadows or along the Fir Glade Trail to Azalea Lake.

Geology

Colorful rock cairns marking high trails here showcase these mountains' diversity. The rocks are up to 425 million years old (almost 20 times the age of the Old Cascades). Look for flat slate, shiny schist, green serpentinite, white marble, and speckled granite.

The Siskiyou or Klamath Mountains began as an island archipelago in the Pacific Ocean, but crustal movement "rafted" them to the edge of the North American plate about 200 million years ago, along with jumbled masses of seafloor rock — including the red peridotite that forms Red Buttes' twin peaks. The pressure of that collision also cooked limestone to marble, allowing later water seepage to create the white caverns of the Oregon Caves. Dripstone stalactites now grow in those caves at the swift rate of an inch per decade. Finally, hot granite intrusions melted out veins of mineral-rich quartz. Gold attracted swarms of prospectors in the 1850s. Mine tailings and washed-out, "hydraulicked" river bottoms remain.

HIKING & BACKPACKING

Start with a 4.1-mile hike along the Pacific Crest Trail from Cook and Green Pass to aptly named Lilypad Lake, at the foot of Red Butte's double peak. Along the way take a half-mile side trail down to Echo Lake, in a cliff-rimmed basin with blue gentians. Have energy for a longer hike? From Lilypad Lake, it's a nearly level 2.6 miles to Upper Devils Peak and a look at the Klamath River 4700 feet below. For a view toward Oregon, turn off the PCT at Kangaroo Mountain and head west 2.5 trail miles to the cliff- edged pass atop craggy Rattlesnake Mountain.

In much of this wilderness, dry, south-facing slopes confound cross-country hikers with impenetrable chaparral tangles of manzanita, snowbrush, and stunted chinkapin. Open forests on northern slopes, however, invite trailless exploration. A top cross-country trip from Cook and Green Pass takes off from Echo Lake and circles Red Buttes' ruddy double peak, passing wildflower meadows, springs, and five scenic cirque lakes on a sometimes rocky 5-mile traverse, returning via the PCT.

To reach Cook and Green Pass from Medford, take Highway 238 to Jacksonville and 8 miles beyond to Ruch. Turn left at an "Upper Applegate" pointer for 18.8 miles to a T-junction at the end of Applegate Lake, turn left on Applegate Road 1.2 miles to a big gravel intersection, go straight on Road 1050 for 0.9 mile, and fork right on one-lane Road 1055 for 10 miles.

Visit the wildflowers at Frog Pond and Cameron Meadows with a 5.8-mile

Red Buttes from the Pacific Crest Trail.

RED BUTTES

0 1 2 3mi
0 1 2 3 4km

N

loop hike from Road 1040. From the meadows, scramble up a ridge to the south for a good viewpoint. If you plan a short car shuttle between the two trailheads, you'll save a final 2.1-mile walk along Road 1040 back to your car.

Sucker Creek Gap, at the junction of the east-west Siskiyou Mountains and the north-south Grayback Range, is a great backpacking destination, a cool, grassy dale surrounded by giant old-growth incense cedars. Hike there from the end of Road 1030 on a 3.3-mile trail through Steve Creek Valley's deep forest. A shorter, less scenic 1.4-mile route to the Sucker Creek Gap shelter takes off from the end of Road 098. From Cave Junction, head toward Oregon Caves for 14.5 miles, turn south on gravel Road 4612 for 9 miles, and then turn right onto Road 098.

At the Oregon Caves National Monument it costs about $8.50 to tour the famous caves, but there's no charge to hike the 3.3-mile loop trail to Big Tree, a Douglas fir 13 feet in diameter. Midway along the loop, a side trail heads up a ridge 2.3 miles to a viewpoint atop Mount Elijah. An easier, 1.6-mile path to that goal begins on Road 070.

At Grayback Mountain, a steep 1.3-mile path from Road 1005 climbs to a wildflower meadow with a snow shelter that's open to the public for free. Lift the latch with a knife blade. Bushwhack uphill from the cabin through steep fields 1.1 mile to the mountain's summit for views from the ocean to Mount Shasta.

The swimmable Tannen Lakes, nestled in forest against a backdrop of Tannen Mountain's rockslides, are a popular day-hike goal. A 0.4-mile trail leads to the larger Tannen Lake from Road 041 East Tannen Lake is another 0.9 mile along a well-graded route that tempts hikers to continue 4.9 miles to Sucker Gap. From Cave Junction drive south 7 miles on Highway 199, turn left on Waldo Road 5 miles, and go straight on Happy Camp Road 12.5 miles to a pass. Turn left at a "Tannen Lakes" sign, fork to the right after 0.8 mile, left after 1.4 miles, right after 1.8 miles, right after 4.2 miles, and left after 7.5 miles to the

Phantom Meadows on the slopes of Figurehead Mountain.

Figurehead Mountain from Azalea Lake.

trailhead at mile 8.9.

Backpackers who make the 6.5-mile trek to Azalea Lake from the Fir Glade trailhead are rewarded with June wildflowers and views of rocky Figurehead Mountain. A half-mile shoreline trail loops around the popular little lake, with separate camp areas for hikers and equestrians. Continue to Cedar Basin and hike up to the rocky pass just south of Lonesome Lake for a look into the Klamath River country. Or bushwhack up Figurehead Mountain for wider ranging views.

To reach the Fir Glade trailhead from Grants Pass, follow signs south 6.5 miles to Murphy, continue straight on Highway 238 another 11.5 miles to a green steel bridge at Applegate, and turn right on Thompson Creek Road. After 14.7 miles turn right across a bridge and immediately fork left on Road 1030 for 5.2 miles. Then turn left on Road 400 (which becomes Road 1040) for 4.7 miles, and fork right on Road 800 for 0.6 mile to road's end.

Several long-distance backpacking routes surpass the PCT here, with its grueling, 4700-foot ascent out of Seiad Valley. The 20-mile Boundary Trail from Grayback Mountain to Tannen Mountain is a good choice. For a more thorough sampler of this wilderness, take a 33.5-mile loop backpack from Cook and Green Campground past Cook and Green Pass, Red Buttes, Rattlesnake Mountain, and Cedar Basin, returning via the Butte Fork Trail.

The Chateau at the Oregon Caves.

33
KALMIOPSIS

Cut by the green-pooled Illinois River's rugged gorge, the Kalmiopsis is Oregon's largest but perhaps least visited forest wilderness. Seen from one of the dry ridgetop trails, jagged canyonlands spread like a vast sheet of crumpled paper. This is a land of torrential winter rains and blazing summer heat, of rare wildflowers and shy black bears.

Hikers should expect challenge as well as beauty on the steep trails. Boaters on the wild Illinois must prepare for ten churning Class 4 rapids and the monstrous, Class 5 Green Wall.

Location: 33 mi SW of Grants Pass

Size: 672 sq mi

Status: 281 sq mi designated wilderness (1964, 1978); Illinois federal wild and scenic river

Terrain: steep, rugged canyons, sparsely forested ridges, river rapids

Elevation: 240'-5098'

Management: Rogue River-Siskiyou NF

Map: Kalmiopsis Wilderness (USFS)

Climate

Heavy rains from October to May (100 to 150 inches) swell the rivers, making crossings difficult in spring. There are no bridges. Snow usually covers trails over 4000 feet from December through March. Afternoon temperatures often exceed 90° F in virtually rainless July and August.

Plants and Wildlife

Unusual species have developed in the relatively isolated Klamath Mountains, and many have survived because Ice Age glaciers left most of the area untouched. Plant collecting is prohibited.

Carnivorous pitcher plants resemble green baseball bats sprouting from boggy land at springs. These plants make up for the area's poor soil by catching their own nutrients. A honey aroma lures insects into the plant's hollow stem, where tiny hairs prevent the insects from escaping and enzymes reduce the catch to liquid. Also at springs, look for brilliant blue gentian and white death camas.

Rare *Kalmiopsis leachiana* fills forests with pink blooms in June. This azalea-like shrub, found only in and near the Kalmiopsis, is best seen at Bailey Mountain, Dry Butte, Gold Basin, and Taggarts Bar.

The Biscuit Fire of 2002 overswept the entire Wilderness and much of the surrounding area, resetting the natural fire cycle that had been disrupted when

Illinois River footbridge near McCaleb Ranch.

Kalmiopsis hills from the trail to Babyfoot Lake.

intensive fire suppression began in 1940. In most areas the fire primarily burned manzanita, poison oak, and other underbrush, leaving large trees intact. Already, evidence of the fire can be hard to see. Perhaps the biggest impact has been the scientific community's new appreciation for the role of fire, sparked in part by OSU graduate student Dan Donato's 2006 *Science* article, "Post-Wildfire Logging Hinders Regeneration and Increases Fire Risk."

Forests are often Douglas fir and canyon live oak but include an odd mix of other species. Look for madrone, with peeling red bark, and chinkapin, with spiny fruit ("porcupine eggs"). Port Orford cedar and Brewer's weeping spruce, elsewhere rare, are common here.

Tail-twitching, orange Douglas squirrels scold hikers from trees. On rocky slopes, watch for western fence lizards, blue-tailed skinks, and the area's unaggressive rattlesnakes. Quiet hikers frequently surprise black bears foraging for sugarpine seeds, yellowjacket ground nests, or manzanita berries. The bears dislike dogs, but do all they can to avoid humans, typically climbing trees or fleeing on sight. Encourage this by wrapping smelly food tightly and hanging all food at night.

Geology

The Klamath Mountains began as a Pacific island archipelago with coral reefs and volcanoes, but the entire island chain crumpled against the advancing shore of North America about 200 million years ago when the continent began drifting westward at the speedy rate of an inch a year. The collision buckled up masses of sub-seafloor rock and folded Klamath strata like taffy.

Today, outcroppings of sub-seafloor rock (red peridotite and shiny green serpentinite) are so infertile they visibly stunt vegetation. They also provide the traces of rare, heavy metals which account for the area's many gold mining cabins and abandoned chrome mines.

Though new mining claims are prohibited in designated wilderness, recreational gold panning is allowed. To try, wash out heavy black sands gleaned from bedrock cracks in creekbeds. Be sure to avoid private claims, particularly in the Little Chetco River area. Rockhounds can also look for jasper along the Illinois River below Florence Creek.

HIKING & BACKPACKING

The 27-mile Illinois River Trail over Bald Mountain is well graded and maintained, but nearly all other paths in the area are steep, rocky miners' pack trails

KALMIOPSIS

0   1   2   3mi
0   1   2   3   4km

or bulldozed mining roads. Hikers may meet four-wheel drive vehicles even inside the designated wilderness, because miners with valid pre-1984 claims have keys to the road gates.

A few other cautions: Beware of shiny, autumn-red, three-leaved poison oak, which is prolific at lower elevations. Vast brushfields of tough, red-limbed manzanita stymie most cross-country travelers. The danger of stumbling onto illegal marijuana plantations has declined from the 1970s and 80s, when off-trail hikers sometimes encountered guarded marijuana patches, especially near creeks or springs within a mile or two of trailheads.

The two most popular short hikes lead to cirque lakes high in the mountain forests: Babyfoot Lake in the east of the wilderness and Vulcan Lake in the west.

An easy, 1.2-mile trail through a designated botanical area reaches Babyfoot Lake from Road 140. Most of the trees on this route burned in 2002, and the trailhead area was later logged by mistake, but big live trees surround the lake itself, an easy backpacking goal. For a 5.3-mile loop, bushwhack past the surprisingly green lake, contouring 0.5 mile, turn left on a mining road 1.8 mile to a cairn, and climb up to the left on a view-filled ridgetop trail. For even better views of the area's rugged canyonlands — and a glimpse of the distant ocean — head for Eagle Mountain or the abandoned lookout site atop Canyon Peak, both less than 4 trail miles from

The insectivorous pitcher plant Darlingtonia.

Babyfoot Lake. Reach the trailhead via Eight Dollar Mountain Road 4201, which branches off Highway 199 north of Cave Junction 5 miles.

Vulcan Lake, another good backpacking destination, is the same size as Babyfoot Lake (4 acres), but instead of being set in a burned forest, it fills a dramatic rock basin below broad Vulcan Peak. The red peridotite rock shores not only exhibit glacial scratch marks of interest to geologists, but they also make ideal sunbathing spots for swimmers. A well-maintained 1.4-mile trail from the end of Road 1909 crosses a scenic ridge on its way to Vulcan Lake.

Other trails near Vulcan Lake make good day trips. The old lookout site atop Vulcan Peak, with views of the Kalmiopsis and the Pacific coast, is up a 1-mile trail (gaining 1000 feet). A mostly level 4-mile ridgetop route passes Red Mountain on its way to austere Chetco Lake. Another trail with views from an open ridgetop heads north 3 miles to Dry Butte's fields of *Kalmiopsis leachiana*. Trailhead access is from Brookings; turn off Highway 101 at the north end of the Chetco River bridge, follow the road along the Chetco River 16.5 miles, and then turn right on Road 1909 to its end.

Where trails exist at all along the Chetco River's rugged inner gorge, they generally traverse canyon slopes several hundred feet above the green-pooled stream. A day hike from the western edge of the wilderness samples one such trail, a 3-mile route from a spur of Road 360 to a ford and chilly swimming hole at Boulder Creek Camp. From there, hikers can climb an extra mile to a view of the Big Craggies from Lately Prairie, or else continue 3 miles along the Chetco River for a look up Tincup Creek's gorge. To reach the trailhead, drive 23 miles up the Chetco River from Brookings, turn off Road 1376 onto dirt Road 360 for a mile, then switchback onto spur Road 365.

Illinois River Falls.

Several hikes begin near the McCaleb Ranch Boy Scout camp, on the Grants Pass side of the wilderness off Road 4103. For a short hike, cross a dramatic footbridge over the Illinois River and head cross-country upstream along the riverbank 0.8 mile to Illinois River Falls, a 10-foot chute with a deep green pool ideal for a swim on a hot day.

The other hikes in this area begin at Chetco Pass—a problem because the rutted, bouldery 5.1-mile road there from McCaleb Ranch is impassable to nearly all vehicles, and is sometimes gated closed altogether. It's simplest to cross the Illinois River suspension footbridge and walk the awful road up to the pass. Then you can either trek onward 4.2 miles on the closed road to the Chetco River ford or turn right on a 5.9-mile loop to the restored 1954 Pearsoll Peak fire lookout. Open for free public use (info at 541-592-2166), the cupola-style building is the highest point in the region and a nice backpacking goal.

To find the Illinois River suspension footbridge, drive Highway 199 south of Grants Pass 20 miles to Selma and turn right at a flashing yellow light onto Illinois River Road for 11 miles. At an "End Maintenance" sign look for a "Fall Creek Trailhead" pointer and turn left down steep Road 087 for 0.5 mile.

The popular 27-mile Illinois River Trail traverses wildflower-filled meadows on Bald Mountain's long crest, then descends through the wild Illinois River's remote inner gorge. Side trips to viewpoints at South Bend Mountain or to Collier Bar (a river ford passable from mid-June to November) can make the trip even more spectacular. Start at Briggs Creek, at the bumpy end of dirt Road 4103, and finish at a paved road 3 miles from Agness (see the Wild Rogue map, area 34). Those who can't arrange the long car shuttle can catch a Rogue River jet mail boat (available May 1 to November 1) from Agness to bus connections in Gold Beach.

Backpackers with a yen for solitude and rugged beauty will find both in the vast interior of the Kalmiopsis. The premier trip is a 42-mile trail loop around the Wilderness perimeter from Vulcan Lake past Dry Butte, Taggarts Bar, Emily Cabin, Doe Gap, and Chetco Peak. Beware of dehydration, because trails follow dry ridges and canyon slopes. Carry plenty of water and study maps carefully for trailside springs and perennial streams.

BOATING

Oregon's most difficult whitewater run, the Illinois River from Oak Flat to Agness packs 156 rated rapids into 35 miles. The setting is a breathtakingly stark, trailless, 4000-foot-deep canyon. The brilliant green river is so clear that mossy boulders 30 feet underwater seem within reach.

Only very experienced river runners in kayaks, narrow inflatables, or portageable hard boats should attempt the Illinois, and then only in April or May when water levels range between 600 and 1400 cubic feet per second (gauged at the Kerby station). The lower water of early summer turns the run to a gamut of rock dodging and boat bashing. Higher water after heavy spring rains converts Boat Eater and the Green Wall to deadly maelstroms.

Start the three-day trip at the unmarked Oak Flat launch site 13 miles west of Selma where Road 4103 dips close to the river. A box here contains free, unlimited, self-issuing permits. Drift an easy 3 miles before coming to Panther Creek and the first of many

View from the Illinois River Trail.

rapids that must be scouted. The next 2 miles wallop boaters with seven increasingly powerful class 3 and 4 rapids, culminating with York Creek Rapids, a 4+ churner with an underwater shelf and tall standing waves in the preferred left channel.

Boat Eater Rapids, 3 miles downriver at the mouth of Pine Creek, funnels the river past a cabin-sized boulder into a roaring suckhole with a record of trapping every third or fourth craft it meets. Boaters usually camp immediately after this class 4+ trial.

Ten miles of swift but manageable water the second day out lead to the big stuff. It starts with class 4 Fawn Falls, down a 10-foot chute into a boulder obstacle course. Hardly a half mile beyond, an ominous wall covered with green moss looms above the river, signaling all but daredevils to portage around the coming class 5 water.

The Green Wall Rapids drops boaters 50 feet in less than 300 yards. First comes a fast stretch of rocks and holes, then a drop through a barricade of truck-sized boulders, then another 12-foot cascade, and finally a possible crush against the wall itself.

Three-quarters of a mile farther, Little Green Wall's class 4 rocks hang up their share of boats. Whitewater is then nonstop for 2 miles to Submarine Hole's treacherous midstream boulder, which must be run on the left side (though this positioning requires strong rowing). Exhausted river runners will find no campsite for yet another 1.7 miles.

The third day is an easy drift to the Agness pull-out on the Rogue River. The car shuttle between ends of the run totals 120 miles over several poor roads (Oak Flat-Grants Pass-Galice-Agness). If this route is closed by lingering snow, plan on 150 miles via Crescent City and Gold Beach. Arrangements may be made by calling Whitewater Cowboys at (541) 479-0132.

34
WILD ROGUE

The irascible Rogue River, cutting through the mountains to the sea, is at times a string of sunny, green pools, lazily drifting past playful otter and circling osprey. But the river can also be misty mayhem, raging over Blossom Bar's boulders like a giant pinball game, swirling boats helplessly in The Coffeepot, and standing on edge in Mule Creek Canyon, a chasm so narrow boats sometimes bridge from wall to wall.

More than 20,000 visitors a year run the Rogue's famous whitewater. But the beautiful 40-mile Rogue River Trail is seldom crowded, and the rest of this river's rugged, 4000-foot-deep canyon remains virtually untrodden.

Climate

Toward the end of the reliably rainless, hot summers, river temperatures rise to 70° F, making the water attractive for swimmers, but driving fish into cooler tributaries. Intermittent rains from September to May total 90 inches in the damp western end of the canyon but only 50 inches in the east.

Plants and Wildlife

It's easy to spot wildlife attracted to the river: deer, merganser ducks, otters, mink, black bears (catching salmon), osprey (and their nests atop tall snags), great blue herons, kingfishers, swooping cliff swallows (with mud nests on overhangs), and water ouzels. Try iden-

Blossom Bar Rapids.

tifying the many tracks on the riverbanks each morning.

The river itself teems with salamanders, newts, and over 20 species of fish, including chinook salmon, steelhead, rainbow trout, sturgeon, shad, carp, lamprey, sculpin, stickleback, and dace. Among Oregon rivers, only the Columbia provides a higher annual fish catch.

Hikers encounter scurrying lizards, blue-tailed skinks, and occasionally rattlesnakes on the dry slopes. This is the northernmost habitat for the nocturnal ringtail, a tiny, big-eared relative of the raccoon once employed by miners to catch mice in mines.

The Douglas fir forests include lush red cedar and rhododendron in the west, but yield to canyon live oak and red-barked madrone in the more arid

Location: 27 mi NW of Grants Pass

Size: 224 sq mi

Status: 56 sq mi designated wilderness (1978); federal wild and scenic river

Terrain: steep, rocky, forested river canyon

Elevation: 140'-5316'

Management: Rogue River-Siskiyou NF, Medford District BLM

Map: Wild Rogue Wilderness (USFS)

WILD ROGUE

0 1 2 3mi
0 1 2 3 4km
N

(See Area 33 Map)

east. Brushfields of manzanita and chinkapin limit cross-country travel. May brings trailside blue iris and white beargrass blooms; expect blue lupine and California poppies in June.

Geology

Tough, 150-million-year-old lava restricts the Rogue River through much of its lower gorge. A massive landslide visible just west of Whisky Creek briefly dammed 15 miles of the Rogue in the

dians responded by killing Rogue Valley settlers and retreating to this remote part of the river canyon for winter.

The next April, soldiers tracked the Indians to Battle Bar and traded fire across the river before turning back. A month later, a Takelma band under Tyee John besieged an Army unit on a knoll at Illahe's Big Bend, killing eleven. Relief troops from the east fled when Indians rolled rocks on them from a hillside

1880s. Unusual kettle-shaped potholes in the riverbank rock, best seen near Clay Hill Rapids, form when floodwaters swirl pebbles in depressions, drilling them deeper.

History

The river's name comes from the Tututni and Takelma Indians, whom the early French trappers called coquins or "rogues." After white miners attacked a peaceful Indian village on a reservation near Medford in 1855, killing 23, the In-

near Brushy Bar, but a column of soldiers from Gold Beach broke the siege. More than 1400 Tututni and Takelma tribespeople were transported north to the coastal Siletz Reservation.

In 1926, author Zane Grey bought a miner's cabin at Winkle Bar, where he fished and wrote his popular Wild West books. Few unguided parties ran the river until the 1930s, when boatmen dynamited boulders in the most difficult rapids. Slim Pickens Rapids and Blos-

Hanging Rock on the northern rim of the Rogue River canyon.

som Bar dropped to Class 3 and Class 4 whitewater, respectively.

Until 1963, mules packed mail on the Rogue River Trail from Marial to Agness, where mail boats left for Gold Beach. Although pavement now extends up the canyon to Agness, jet-powered mail boats still make the run, carrying tourists.

HIKING & BACKPACKING

The prime trip here is the 40-mile Rogue River Trail backpack from Illahe to Grave Creek. Day hikers can sample scenic parts of the route. Because the sometimes rocky trail traverses steep slopes several hundred feet above the river, it is closed to horse use. Bring a backpacking stove because fires within 400 feet of the river are allowed only in metal fire pans that leave no trace.

A 4.3-mile walk from Illahe to Flora Dell Creek's shady glen reaches a trail-

The Whisky Creek cabin museum.

side waterfall. Those who drive the gravel road to Marial, at the Rogue River Trail's midpoint, can hike 2.1 miles downriver, past inspiring viewpoints of The Coffeepot and Slide Creek Falls to Blossom Bar, a good spot to photograph frantic boaters. East of the trailhead at Marial's Rogue River Ranch Museum, a 4.8-mile hike up the river trail leads to Zane Grey's log cabin at Winkle Bar. At the east end of the Rogue River Trail, from the Grave Creek trailhead, a 3.5-mile walk passes 15-foot Rainie Falls on the way to Whisky Creek, where an 1880 mining cabin is open as a museum.

Hikers should be alert for yellow-jackets, wood ticks, rattlesnakes, and prolific growths of head-high poison oak. Campers can expect nocturnal visits by the area's numerous black bears, particularly in the Brushy Bar-Clay Hill area. Here bears have grown bold from finding easy meals in boaters' cooler chests and hikers' backpacks. At such popular sites, campers are required to store food in the hoists and bear boxes provided. Elsewhere, hang food at least 10 feet above ground and 5 feet from a tree trunk.

Lodges along the trail at Clay Hill Rapids (*clayhilllodge.com*), Paradise Bar (*paradise-lodge.com*), Marial (541-474-2057), and Black Bar (*blackbarlodge.net*) offer meals and lodging by reservation. Scheduled daily jet boats take hikers from Gold Beach to some of these destinations between May 15 and October 15. Expect to pay about $90 for the boat trip and $120 per person for an overnight stay with meals. For boat reservations check *mailboat.com* or *roguejets.com*.

Surprisingly few day hikers have discovered the first-rate viewpoints on a ridgecrest high above the Rogue River's north shore. Two short hikes are tops here: a 1.4-mile path gaining 1160 feet up scenic Mount Bolivar, and a rhododendron-lined 2-mile trail from Buck Point to Hanging Rock (bring binoculars to spot rafters on Blossom Bar, 3600 feet below). For a longer trip, hike 10.5 miles along Panther Ridge from Hanging Rock to Bald Knob's rentable lookout tower ($35 at *www.recreation.gov*). Backpackers can tackle a 38-mile loop: Hike from Illahe on the Rogue River Trail to Marial, climb to Buck Point on a trail up the West Fork of Mule Creek, and return along Panther Ridge and Road 060.

The Illinois River Trail, south of Agness, offers an excellent 2.5-mile day hike (one way) to the craggy promontory of Buzzards Roost, with views in both directions along this green-pooled river's canyon. Backpackers will want to hike the entirety of the 27-mile Illinois River Trail (see area 33, the Kalmiopsis, for a description). Those who can't arrange the required car shuttle can make a base camp at Indigo Creek for forays to the meadows and old-growth ponderosa pines in the rarely visited Silver Peak and Indigo Prairie areas, swept by fire in 1987 and 2002.

One of the area's best kept secrets is a 1-mile trail to 60-foot Silver Falls, in the narrow, fern-draped gorge of Silver Creek. This hike is not shown on the map, and is difficult to locate because of missing signs and confusing, muddy roads. From Galice, drive 0.3 mile toward Merlin, turn west on paved Galice Access Road 23 (alias Bear Camp Road) for 9.5 miles to a 5-way junction, turn left on Road 35-9-1 for 4.2 miles, and fork left on rough Road 050 for 6 miles to its end.

BOATING

The 40-mile, wild stretch of Rogue River between Grave Creek and Illahe is Oregon's most famous and popular three-day whitewater trip.

Rafts, kayaks, and drift boats have hardly left the launch before they hit the spray of class 3 Grave Creek Rapids. Half an hour later the increasing roar of 15-foot-tall Rainie Falls warns boaters to portage by lining craft down the shallow fish ladder on the right. Large, well-constructed rafts of inner tubes sometimes succeed in running massive Rainie Falls, but such vehicles later often wedge side-to-side in Mule Creek Canyon or hang up on Blossom Bar's boulders.

Beyond the falls, pull in at Whisky

Inspiration Point in Mule Creek Canyon.

Creek for a quarter-mile side trip to a well-preserved mining cabin. Downstream 1.2 miles, pull out again to scout class 4 Tyee Rapids. Keep to the far right to avoid a suckhole and then a house-sized rock. Promptly thereafter come class 3 Wildcat Rapids, with a submerged, spiny-backed rock known as The Alligator.

After passing the historic Rogue River Ranch Museum at Marial on the second day (or third, for slower drifters), boats accelerate toward class 4 Mule Creek Canyon, a chasm so narrow and turbulent that it's easy to lose an oar just when the need is greatest. After spring floods, scout from shore for logs jammed sideways. Past the canyon's final, dizzying Coffeepot comes Stair Creek's lovely side waterfall—a good swimming area.

Blossom Bar, 1.3 miles beyond, requires scouting from the right. Following this treacherous, class 4 boulder field are the Devil's Stairs, where the river drops 30 feet in a 300-yard series of chutes. On the trip's final day, hike up to Tate Creek's shady waterfall pool, with a 25-foot natural slide of rock so smooth that swimmers can zip down its chute

sans suit.

Campers within 400 feet of the river must use stoves or bring their own firewood and metal fire pans. In summer, seek out solitude by camping away from side creeks on gravel bars or dry benches. Bring an approved pump to filter river water.

Perhaps the greatest challenge of the Rogue River is getting a permit to launch at all. During the restricted season from May 15 to October 15, only 120 permits are issued for each day, chosen by lottery from ten times that many applications. Apply for the lottery between December 1 and January 31 at *blm.gov/resources/recreation/rogue*. If you don't win a permit, you can pay for a commercially guided trip—at least $500—or plan a trip in the off-season's iffy weather. By October, skies turn a misty gray and the river grows chilly. During winter rainstorms, high water can make the river too dangerous to run. And when snow closes the 55-mile car shuttle route's twisty mountain roads (usually from November to May), the only alternative is to drive a 180-mile detour on highways via Crescent City.

The Coffeepot in the Rogue River's Mule Creek Canyon.

35

GRASSY KNOB
& COPPER SALMON

Fog drips from the tangled forests of these adjacent wilderness areas, where ridgetops provide surprising glimpses out to Cape Blanco's fringe of ocean islands.

Climate

Heavy winter rains push the average annual precipitation to over 130 inches. Summers are mostly sunny, because the area lies just inland of the coastal fog belt.

Plants and Wildlife

The rainforests here provide something precious in the heavily roaded southern Coast Range: pure, cold water. Close to 90 percent of the Sixes River's salmon spawn in Dry Creek and the South Fork Sixes River. Upriver clearcutting has pushed the Elk River's summer water temperatures to levels nearly fatal for fish, but the shady creeks of these wilderness areas offer a cool retreat.

Rare, old-growth Port Orford cedar grow as large as 6 feet in diameter here, with snaky limbs and characteristic white Xs on the underside of green leaf scales. Popular worldwide as a landscaping shrub, this fragrant cedar's

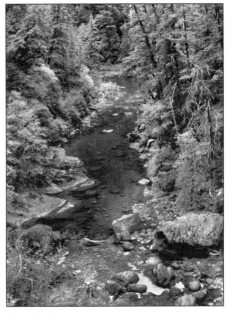

The Elk River.

small native range (five coastal counties) is shrinking rapidly. Japanese buyers have paid as much as $10,000 for a single tree, because its wood is a close substitute for Japan's highly prized, and nearly extinct, hinoki cypress.

The *Phytophthora* root rot fungus, accidentally introduced here from a Portland nursery in 1944, travels easily through ground water, killing every Port Orford cedar in an infected drainage. Because the fungus can be carried in dirt on tire treads, the roadless areas here may be the wild Port Orford cedar's last stand.

Location: 51 mi S of Coos Bay, 9 mi E of Port Orford

Size: 59 sq mi

Status: 48 sq mi designated wilderness (1984, 2009)

Terrain: rain forest-covered canyons and ridges

Elevation: 100'-3579'

Management: Rogue River-Siskiyou NF

Maps: Father Mountain, Mount Butler, Sixes, Port Orford (USGS)

Geology

Though largely hidden by forest, the area's rocks consist of heavily folded and compacted seafloor sediment scraped up by the Klamath Mountains in the past 200 million years while that range slowly moved westward, overriding the Pacific plate.

History

A reconnaissance plane for a Japanese submarine dropped a 170-pound incendiary bomb into the forest between Grassy Knob and Dry Creek in 1942 in an attempt to start a fire. Alarmed rangers at the mountain's lookout tower radioed the Army Air Force. Because of confusion about the lookout's location—south of the city of North Bend—U.S. fighters streaked to the Central Oregon town of Bend, where there were no submarines. Japanese pilot Nobuo Fujita landed his plane on pontoons, unbolted the wings, mounted the craft to his submarine's deck, and dived to safety. But the Japanese bomb failed to explode. Despite many searches, it has never been found.

HIKING & BACKPACKING

The Grassy Knob Trail was converted to a 30-foot-wide gravel road in the waning months of the 1984 wilderness designation battle. A local Forest Service supervisor with an anti-wilderness bias had ordered the road-building project to disqualify the area for wilderness status. Congress was so angry at this "legislation by bulldozer," however, that they declared Grassy Knob a wilderness nonetheless. In the next quarter century the rainforest thoroughly reclaimed the old roadbed. The Forest Service allocated money to restore the original trail in to Grassy Knob's lookout site in 2009.

Rainforest on Anvil Mountain.

To find the half-mile Grassy Knob Trail from Port Orford, drive 4 miles north on Highway 101 and turn right on Grassy Knob Road 196 for 7 miles.

Three trails climb to Barklow Mountain, a taller former lookout site in the Copper Salmon Wilderness. To find the shortest route, drive south of Powers 11.5 miles on Road 33 and turn right on Road 3353 for 11 miles. The trail climbs half a mile to a fork. A short spur to the right leads to the summit, while the left fork follows a ridge 0.4 mile to the ruin of an old shelter.

Photographers looking for emerald-green glens of waterfalls, autumn-red vine maple, and droopy Port Orford cedar will want to hike the passable cross-country route up misnamed Dry Creek. Another option is to ford the shallow Elk River and explore the mossy canyons of Sunshine Creek or Red Cedar Creek. For a different viewpoint, try the abandoned trail to Mount Butler from Road 390.

BOATING

The Elk River winds between narrow rock walls, alternating emerald green pools with lots of class 4 whitewater. Launch at unmarked Slate Creek Bar, 6.3 miles by road from the take-out point at the Elk River fish hatchery. Just 0.2 mile from the launch, beware of Nose Bender Rapids, especially in low water, when this 6-foot drop's rating increases from 3 to 4. Other class 4 rapids include Sluice Narrows, 90° Bend Drop, the scenic Lower Gorge, and Last Four Rapids.

To drive to the river, turn off Highway 101, 3 miles north of Port Orford. While driving to the launch site, scout the river for sweepers, the area's chief hazard.

36
OREGON DUNES

Sea and sand lovers take note: Here one can backpack through an oceanfront Sahara, hang glide off the top of 400-foot dunes, or gallop on 45 miles of beach. Bird watchers can count 247 species where meandering creeks cross the sand. And hikers can explore the wind-rippled sand hills that inspired Oregon author Frank Herbert to write the science fiction classic, *Dune*.

Climate

Marine air brings cool summers and wet, mild winters. Summer fogs occasionally burn off by afternoon. Spring and fall see the most sunshine. Average annual precipitation hits 75 inches.

Coastal dunes near Florence.

Location: Coos Bay to Florence
Size: 50 sq mi
Status: national recreation area (1972)
Terrain: sand dunes, ocean beach, lakes, forest
Elevation: 0'-1000'
Management: Siuslaw NF
Map: Oregon Dunes NRA (USFS)

Plants and Wildlife

On the beach itself, watch the waves for harbor seals and the spouts of gray whales (December to May). At creek mouths, bald eagles swoop for fish. Snowy egrets and great blue herons stand stilt-legged in the shallows. Canada geese migrating on the Pacific Flyway stop to forage wild grains in the estuaries. Hundreds of elegant tundra swans winter in the south Siuslaw spit's sandy marshes. In all, it's possible to tally 118 species of aquatic birds, 108 species of songbirds, and 21 species of birds of prey.

Rarest of the coastal birds is the small, chubby, western snowy plover, distinguished from sanderlings by its white shoulder yoke—and by its refusal to run piping along the beach's wet sand in search of food. Instead the plover finds sand fleas among driftwood and beachgrass near creek mouths, where it also scoops out its shallow sand nest in plain sight. Off-highway vehicles (OHVs) and nest-robbing crows have cut coastal plover populations to under 100, although about 900 birds of the same species eke out a living beside desert lake playas in southeast Oregon, where OHVs are also becoming a threat to their survival.

Plants and sand battle each other here on two fronts. To the east, winds shift the steep face of the high dunes 6 to 10 feet farther inland each year, burying forests alive. To the west, European beachgrass (originally introduced to stabilize sand near developments) has spread along the entire beachfront, creating a 30-foot-tall foredune that blocks sand from blowing inland. Behind the foredune, winds have stripped a broad "deflation plain" of sand, allowing a succession of brush and trees to gain a foothold.

In the deflation plain, watch for the insect-eating sundew plant, which traps prey in sticky drops of imitation dew. Among the alder and coast willow of the forest drainageways, look for yellow skunk cabbage and eight of Oregon's fifteen salamander species. In the spruce and hemlock forests, admire white trilliums in March, 20-foot-tall pink rhododendrons in April, and chanterelle mushrooms in October.

Geology

Most of Oregon's coastline is too steep and rocky to collect much sand, but here winds have repeatedly pushed waves of dunes inland across a coastal plain. Each fresh onslaught of sand buries forests, peters out, then sprouts with brush and trees of its own.

However, European beachgrass stabilized a wall-like oceanfront foredune in the 1950s, blocking off the area's sand supply. The present high dunes are expected to run out of sand and stop their eastward march within 90 to 200 years. Because the stubborn European beachgrass regrows when burnt or plowed, the Forest Service has experimented with breaching the foredune with bulldozers to set the dune-formation cycle in motion again.

The broad mudflats at the mouths

European beachgrass creates a foredune.

of Oregon's coastal rivers are indirect products of the Ice Age. When enlarged polar ice caps converted much of the earth's water to ice, oceans dropped 300 feet and rivers cut their valleys deeper to match. When the ice melted 6000 years ago, the ocean rose into the widened river mouths. Sand and river silt have since converted these fjords to shallow estuaries.

History

The United States Army established Fort Umpqua on the Umpqua River spit in 1856 to watch over Indians of the

Sanderlings like to run along wet sand. Endangered snowy plovers prefer dry sand.

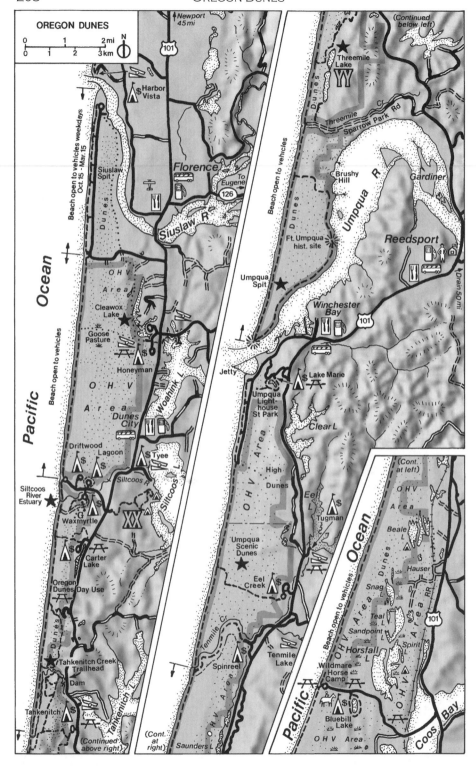

OREGON DUNES

0   1   2 mi
0   1   2   3 km
N

Siletz Reservation to the north. After a visiting paymaster in 1862 found every officer away on a hunting trip, the fort was permanently closed.

Before completion of a coast highway in the 1930s, stagecoaches traveled the hard sand beaches of low tide between Florence, Reedsport, and Coos Bay. This led to public ownership of all Oregon beaches under the Department of Transportation. Beaches are now park land.

HIKING & BACKPACKING

Short forest trails lead to the open sand, where hikers can explore dunes, tree islands, and lakes without need of marked routes. Remember that walking in dry sand takes twice the time and energy of a hike on solid ground.

Off-highway vehicles (OHVs) are allowed in about half of the area. The noise, tracks, and danger of speeding dune buggies in these areas reduce their appeal to hikers. Beaches are subject to varying vehicle closure rules (see map) but warrant hiking regardless. The following hikes, listed from north to south, are outside OHV areas unless otherwise noted.

Swimmers at Cleawox Lake slide down a 100-foot sand dune into the clear water. This extremely popular lake borders Honeyman Park, a 355-unit state campground. While OHVs are banned near the south end of the lake, expect motor traffic when prowling over the dramatic dunes toward the area's interesting tree islands, Goose Pasture (a brushy bird-watching site), or the beach.

The short Siltcoos River meanders through campgrounds and dunes. A 0.7-mile, self-guided nature trail loops around Lagoon Campground, touring an oxbow slough of the river. From Waxmyrtle Campground, a trail leads 1.3 miles along the river past open dunes to the beach. To make a pleasant 3.1-mile loop, wade the warm, calf-deep river at its mouth and return on a road past Driftwood Campground.

Want a break from sun and sand? Hike inland from Highway 101 on a 4.3-mile loop through a cool, lush forest of ferns and Douglas firs to several primitive campsites on the shore of Siltcoos Lake.

Marked by posts in the sand, a fun 4.8-mile loop trail through the dunes and along the beach to Tahkenitch Creek begins at the Oregon Dunes Day Use Area.

Some of the quietest and most spectacular sand landscapes lie between Tahkenitch Creek and remote Threemile Lake. From the Tahkenitch Creek Trailhead (between mileposts 202 and 203 of Highway 101), a 1.6-mile loop explores the creek's estuary. From Tahkenitch Campground, a 6.4-mile loop trail climbs 2.9 miles along a forested ridge to backpacking campsites at the edge of the dunes overlooking Threemile Lake. The loop path then follows posts to the

Tahkenitch Creek's estuary.

The Siltcoos River's estuary.

beach and north 1 mile before returning through the dunes.

Clams, huckleberries, dunes, and views lure hikers to the 6.5-mile-long Umpqua River Spit. For a scenic route to this vast sand peninsula, cross by boat from nearby Winchester Bay. Otherwise, park at the end of gravel on the Threemile Creek Road (100 yards short of the beach), hike south a mile on the beach, and follow a dune-buggy road inland to the dunes. Look for late August huckleberries on Brushy Hill; very low tides expose clamming mudflats along the Umpqua River below the hill. The long, rock jetty at spit's end is a good spot to watch pounding waves and ocean-going ships.

An easy warm-up hike near Winchester Bay loops half a mile around forest-lined Lake Marie at Umpqua Lighthouse State Park. Top the walk with a visit to the adjacent lighthouse.

OHVs dominate Oregon's tallest dunes, south of Lake Marie. Hikers bent on exploring these 400-foot sand mountains should watch for the red flags OHVs display atop 9-foot antennas, because dune buggies often zip blindly over dune crests.

The 280-foot-tall Umpqua Scenic Dunes provide a 4-square-mile sand playground off limits to OHVs. A 2.4-mile trail from Eel Creek Campground leads through woods to the open sand and continues to the beach.

Long-distance hikers can tramp the beach 23.7 miles from the tip of the Siuslaw Spit to the tip of the Umpqua Spit, but more interesting routes alternate beach hiking with dune exploration.

Throughout the Oregon Dunes, hikers should heed a few tips: Carry plenty of water. When hiking cross-country to the beach, mark the return route through the foredune with a stick in the sand. The open dunes have few landmarks, especially in the frequent fogs. When lost, simply listen—the sound of surf or traffic will point the way to the ocean or Highway 101. Camp well above the beach's driftwood line (night has its high tide too), and bring a sleep-

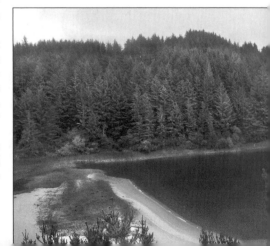

ing pad (sand is rock hard). Fires on the beach are discouraged, and fires in piles of driftwood are banned.

Equestrians often begin beach rides at Wildmare Horse Camp near Bluebill Lake Campground, though many other beach access points are also feasible.

BOATING

The coastal dunes have dammed dozens of large, many-armed freshwater lakes. Sinuous shorelines make for interesting canoe paddling. Steady west winds provide first-rate sailing conditions but can create large waves on summer afternoons. Warm water makes windsurfing practical.

Cleawox Lake, with its steep sand dune shore and long, narrow arms is the most popular non-motorized boating site. Launch at crowded Honeyman Park.

Launch at Tyee Campground to canoe up the Siltcoos River to 5-square-mile Siltcoos Lake. For an overnight trip, paddle to the lakeshore campsites on the Siltcoos Trail loop.

Tahkenitch Lake covers 3 square miles, but has nearly 100 miles of shoreline worth exploring by canoe. Launch at a boat ramp on Highway 101. Carry a canoe 160 yards down the Tahkenitch Creek Trail to launch there and paddle the lazy creek 2 miles to its mouth. Both Tahkenitch Lake and Siltcoos Lake are

Footprints in the open dunes.

heavily used by fishermen for warmwater bass and easily caught yellow perch.

WIND SPORTS

Reliable west winds and unobstructed landing sites make the 400-foot-tall High Dunes an excellent practice area. Hike 1 mile east from the last parking lot south of Winchester Bay on the jetty road. Watch for OHVs.

Threemile Lake is a nice backpacking destination between dunes and forest.

37
DEVILS STAIRCASE

In this forgotten Coast Range valley, Wassen Creek splashes over the stairstep falls of the mysterious, remote Devils Staircase. Side streams tumble from steep slopes of sword fern and salmonberry. Rain drips from the great, drooping branches of age-old red cedar and Douglas fir.

Adventurers exploring the nearly trailless, twisting canyons often find it easiest to wade along the creekbed itself — the route of the canyon's cheery water ouzels.

Climate

Torrential winter rains boost annual precipitation to 90 inches. The dry summers are free of the coastal fog that socks in Highway 101 just a few miles west.

Plants and Wildlife

In the deep forest look for white trillium and yellow Oregon grape in early spring. Rhododendrons put out pink blooms in April. By early fall both blue and red huckleberry are ripe for picking.

Expect great blue herons and Pacific giant salamanders at Wassen Lake. In old-growth woods, watch for the red top-feathers of pileated woodpeckers and the dark eyes of silent spotted owls. Bald eagles soar above the creek canyon. Sea-run fish cannot leap the falls at the Devils Staircase, leaving the upper creek to small trout and bright red crawdads.

Geology

This part of the Coast Range began as mud-covered seafloor 50 million years ago. It lay directly in the path of the North American continent, which was crunching westward over the Pacific seafloor at the geologically speedy rate of an inch a year. However, a fracture in the Pacific floor lifted the Coast Range above the waves, where it became the

Wassen Creek loops through the rainforest in a steep canyonland (photo by David Tvedt).

Snags and waterlilies in Wassen Lake.

Location: 13 mi E of Reedsport
Size: 24 sq mi
Status: undesignated wilderness
Terrain: steep, densely forested creek valley
Elevation: 20'-1760'
Management: Siuslaw NF, Coos Bay District BLM
Maps: Scottsburg, Smith River Falls, Deer Head Point, North Fork (USGS)

western edge of the advancing continent.

As a result, Wassen Creek now flows over layers of weak sandstone and nutrient-poor, washed-out red clays that originated on the bottom of the sea. The area is roadless in part because roadcuts in such soils send entire hillsides sliding toward the creek. Wassen Lake itself formed when a slump dammed the creek's headwaters about 150 years ago. Snags of drowned trees still stand in the 5-acre lake.

Wassen was the name of a local homestead family of Coos tribal descent.

HIKING & BACKPACKING

Trails are in short supply, but the

valley's solitude and beauty inspire cross-country exploration. Canyon slopes are so steep and rugged that many visitors wear tennis shoes and wool socks, and simply wade along the creekbed itself. Wading is most pleasant in the warm weather of summer and early fall. Since the sandy creek bottom has some slippery mudstone, a walking stick is essential, and hikers with packs may want two sticks. If you do plan to hike on ridges and canyon slopes, consider going when the salmonberry brush loses its leaves in winter, making it easier to bushwhack and see around.

Wassen Lake is a good place to sample the area, partly because the driving route is entirely paved. Drive Highway 38 (between Reedsport and Drain) to the Scottsburg fire station a quarter mile west of milepost 19. Turn north on Wells Creek Road (BLM 22-9-7.0) for 2.2 miles, fork left onto paved Fern Top Road (BLM 21-9-32.0) for 3.3 miles, veer right on paved Wassen Lake Road (BLM 21-9-10.0) for 3.7 miles, and park at a bulldozed 2-car pullout on the left (GPS location N43°44.842' W123°47.546') where boulders block an old roadbed.

Walk 200 yards down this overgrown track to Wassen Lake's shore. Rimmed with alder and old-growth conifers, the shallow lake teems with rough-skinned newts. There is no trail around the lake, so the circuit requires a tough, half-mile bushwhack. Following Wassen Creek downstream from the lake outlet is an even more difficult option because low-hanging brush spans the creekbed here.

The best trail to Wassen Creek descends 0.7 mile from the end of Road 119. This is the route to take if your goal is the Devils Staircase — a series of a dozen stair-stepped falls totalling 22 feet.

From Wassen Lake, drive north on paved Wassen Lake Road (BLM 21-9-10.0) for 1.2 miles and turn left on gravel Road 21-10-12.1. The sign here may be missing, and the road itself becomes crowded with brush that can scratch car paint. After 5.4 miles turn left at a fork onto Road 119 for 0.6 mile to its end. A rough trail descends to the left through a regrown clearcut on a ridgecrest for 0.3 mile before entering ancient woods.

After 0.5 mile the route crashes down a very steep slope and then follows a small creek gully 200 yards to Wassen Creek, where wading becomes the only feasible option. If you're prepared, 6-foot Folly Falls is 2 miles downstream and the Devils Staircase is an additional 1.8 miles. A grassy gravel bar below this legendary waterfall makes a good campsite — and you'll need it, too, because the trek here is too difficult for a day trip.

The Devils Staircase lies deep in Wassen Creek's winding canyon (photo by David Tvedt).

38
Oregon Islands

Nesting sea birds and lolling sea lions crowd the nation's smallest and least accessible designated wilderness—the surf-pounded islands scattered along the length of Oregon's Pacific shore.

Climate
Wet, frost-free winters and cool, fog-shrouded summers push annual precipitation from 60 to 100 inches. In summer, north winds generally bring fair skies, while south winds presage storms. In winter, storms come from all angles, battering the islands with 40-foot waves and high winds. Six- to twelve-foot tides submerge many rocks twice daily.

Plants and Wildlife
The islands' fascinating bird and sea mammal colonies are best observed from mainland viewpoints, particularly with the aid of binoculars or a spotting scope. Access to wilderness islands is generally impossible, but it is banned nonetheless, and boats are allowed no closer than 200 yards to islands included in the federal wildlife refuge. In many areas, island wildlife has already been severely hurt by people who venture within 200 yards by boat, sailboard, kayak, jet ski, scuba gear, or airplane. The approach of hu-

Sea lions on Shell Island at Cape Arago.

mans startles seabirds, allowing their eggs to fall from nests and break. Similarly, human contact can cause sea lions and seals to abandon their pups.

From April to August, thousands of murres crowd the rocks to nest—the only time these black-and-white, loon-like birds visit land. Also in summer look for tufted puffins (with unmistakable, red-and-orange-striped bills) and their close relatives, the virtually neckless little auklets and murrelets.

When these birds leave for winter, other species arrive: long-necked loons, scoters (small sea ducks), and grebes (resembling clumsy, dark-backed swans). Year-round residents include five species of sea gulls and two kinds of black, crook-necked cormorants.

The brown dots one sees on these islands from a distance are often 600- to 2200-pound Steller's sea lions. Smaller harbor seals among the waves often watch humans with a curiosity rivaling our own. Also look for the spouts of gray whales, which pass here from Decem-

Location: along Oregon coast

Size: 1477 islands/groups (1.2 sq mi)

Status: 56 islands/groups (0.8 sq mi) designated wilderness and national wildlife refuge (1970, 1978)

Terrain: small, wave-swept, rock islands

Elevation: 0'-327'

Management: Coos Bay District BLM, U.S. Fish and Wildlife Service ber to February as they migrate toward Mexico, and from March to May as they return to Alaska. Sea otters, whose fur first brought regular European trade to these shores, were driven to extinction in Oregon by 1911. An attempt to reintroduce sea otters near Cape Blanco in 1970 failed. Since then a few otters have shown up on their own, although these may be visitors from populations in California and Washington.

Most islands support few plants beyond sea palms and bobbing kelp seaweed. Others are topped with brushy salal, twinberry, and stunted spruce. Seacliff stonecrop, a thick-leaved flower threatened in Oregon, is known only from these islands.

The best wildlife viewing sites are at the Yaquina Head lighthouse 3 miles north of Newport, on the Cape Meares Loop Road west of Tillamook, at Cape Kiwanda near Pacific City, at the state park on Cape Blanco, at Boardman State Park north of Brookings, and from the shore at Brookings itself.

Geology

Wave erosion separated these islands' resistant rock from the softer rock of the mainland, much as tides reduce a sand castle to the pebbles that once topped its towers. All islands along the northern half of the Oregon Coast, from Astoria to Seal Rock, consist of tough, black Columbia River basalt. This lava welled up near Idaho about 15 million years ago and poured west 300 miles through the Columbia Gorge to the ocean in a series of long lava flows.

The islands south of Bandon are 20

Island at Blacklock Point near Cape Blanco.

times older, belonging to the ancient Klamath Mountains. Many of these islands consist of heavy, resistant blueschist, a rock prized for use in jetties.

History

Two of Oregon's offshore islands have been inhabited. Sea lion bones and clamshells remain from an Indian camp on Zwagg Island beside Brookings. Dutch hermit Folker Von Der Zwaag, who moved to the island in 1889 with his dog Sniff, is remembered for the trolley he devised to retrieve fresh water from the mainland automatically.

A lighthouse built with great difficulty on Tillamook Rock in 1879 was abandoned in 1934 and sold as surplus government property in 1957. After shifting ownership several times, the island ended up with Eternity at Sea, a funeral business that helicopters out urns with the ashes of people who want to be buried in the lighthouse when they die.

Though an estimated 2 million birds used Oregon's offshore rocks in 1940, their numbers have declined to fewer than 500,000 because of development along the coast.

The nation's first designated wildlife refuge protected 17 acres of islands at Three Arch Rocks, near Oceanside in Tillamook County, in 1907. Today the islands are also wilderness.

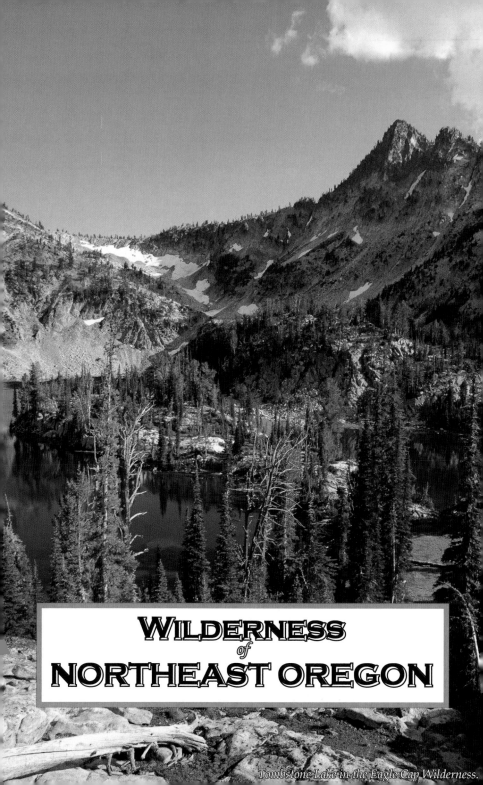

WILDERNESS
of
NORTHEAST OREGON

Tombstone Lake in the Eagle Cap Wilderness.

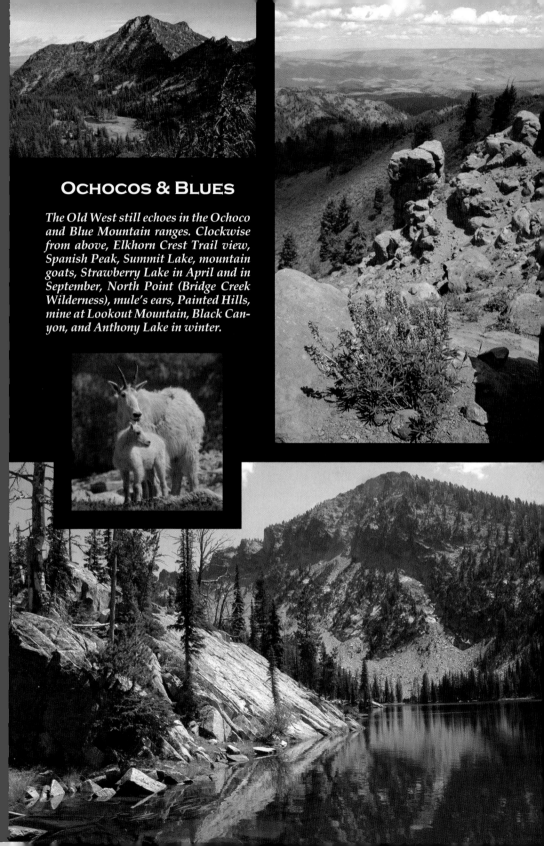

OCHOCOS & BLUES

The Old West still echoes in the Ochoco and Blue Mountain ranges. Clockwise from above, Elkhorn Crest Trail view, Spanish Peak, Summit Lake, mountain goats, Strawberry Lake in April and in September, North Point (Bridge Creek Wilderness), mule's ears, Painted Hills, mine at Lookout Mountain, Black Canyon, and Anthony Lake in winter.

THE CANYONLANDS

Hells Canyon may be the nation's deepest gorge, but it's not the only big canyon in Northeast Oregon. Clockwise from above: the Imnaha River canyon from Buckhorn Viewpoint, the Imnaha River Trail, Gem Lake in the Seven Devils, Freezeout Saddle's view, a cactus on the Snake River Trail, Hells Canyon, red paintbrush, and horseback riders. At left: fireweed in the Seven Devils.

THE WALLOWAS

The popular Eagle Cap Wilderness' Wallowa Mountains resemble a fragment of the Alps or the Rockies. Clockwise on this page from upper left: Eagle Cap, Tombstone Lake, Cornucopia Mountain near Summit Point, the Pine Lakes, McCully Basin, and Aneroid Lake from Aneroid Mountain. Clockwise on the right page from the top: Cusick Mountain from Mt. Nebo in winter, skiing up Big Sheep Creek, Arrow Lake, sunset, Frances Lake, horses at Wallowa Lake, and a water ouzel.

Frances Lake inlet, Wallowa Mountains.

Map Key	Destination	Total miles	Easy-M-Diff.	Days	Est.Mos.Open	Uncrowded	Page
A	Spring Basin	3	M	2	●	●	229
B	Mill Creek to Belknap Creek	6	E	2	IV½-XI	●	234
C	Rock Creek to Fir Creek	8	E	2	IV¾-XI½	●	242
D	Black Canyon	12	M	3	V¾-XI½	●	242
E	Strawberry Lake	3	E	2	VII½-X		250
F	Slide Lake	8	M	2	VII-XI½		250
G	High Lake	2	E	2	VII¾-X		250
H	Wildcat Basin	5	E	2	VII¾-X		250
I	Hotel de Bum	14	D	3	VII½-X¼	●	251
J	Around Strawberry Range	13	D	3	VII¾-X		252
K	Strawberry Range Crest	42	D	4	VII¾-X	●	252
L	Little Malheur River	7	M	2	VI¾-XI	●	256
M	Dutch Flat Lake	8	M	2	VII-X	●	261
N	Elkhorn Crest Trail	23	D	3	VII-X	●	261
O	Twin Lakes	10	M	2	VII½-X	●	264
P	Baldy Lake	13	M	2	VII-X	●	265
Q	Dupratt Spring	10	M	2	VII-X	●	265
R	North Fork John Day R	25	D	4	IV-XI	●	265
S	Lost Lake Loop	20	M	3	VII-X	●	266
T	Wenaha River to Crooked Cr	13	M	3	●	●	273
U	Wenaha Forks	9	M	2	VI-XI	●	275
V	Wenaha River Trail	31	D	3	VI½-XI¼	●	275
W	South Fork Walla Walla R	7	M	2	VI½-XI¼	●	276
X	Eureka Bar	8	M	3	●	●	286
Y	Deep Creek	9	M	3	●	●	286
Z	Kirkwood Ranch	12	M	3	●	●	286
AA	Oregon Snake River Trail	56	D	6	IV-XI	●	288
BB	Seven Devils Loop	25	D	4	VII-X½	●	288
CC	Aneroid Lake	12	D	3	VII½-X		292
DD	Ice Lake	15	D	3	VII½-X		292
EE	Horseshoe Lake	18	D	3	VII½-X		293
FF	Glacier Lake Loop	27	D	3	VII½-X		293
GG	Minam Lake	12	D	3	VII½-X		293
HH	Mirror Lake	15	D	3	VII½-X		296
II	Steamboat Lake Loop	29	D	3	VII½-X		296
JJ	Bear Creek	10	M	2	V-XI	●	296
KK	Reds Horse Ranch	15	D	2	VI½-XI	●	297
LL	Minam River	55	D	6	VII½-X	●	297
MM	Catherine Creek Mdws	8	M	2	VI-XI½	●	298
NN	Echo Lake	11	D	2	VII½-X		298
OO	Tombstone Lake	18	D	2	VII½-X		298
PP	Eagle Creek Meadow	9	M	2	VII-X½		298
QQ	Arrow Lake Loop	19	D	3	VII½-XI	●	299
RR	Hidden Lake	16	D	2	VII½-X	●	299
SS	Pine Lakes Loop	18	D	3	VII½-X	●	299
TT	Bonny Lakes	8	M	2	VI½-X	●	300
UU	McCully Basin	11	M	2	VI½-X	●	300

Designated wilderness
Undesignated wilderness

Washington

Richland

Kennewick

Pasco

The Dalles

Wasco

Heppner

Condon

Ukiah

Dale

JOHN DAY
RIVER

39

Fossil

Clarno

Antelope

SPRING
BASIN
CLOSE-UP

Service
Creek

Monument

Madras

PAINTED
HILLS
40

MILL
CREEK **41**

Mitchell

BRIDGE
CREEK

43

44 OCHOCO
CANYONS

Dayville

John Day

Mt. Vernon

45

ALDRICH
MOUNTAINS

Redmond

Prineville

42
LOOKOUT
MOUNTAIN

Paulina

Bend

Ochoco
Mountains

39
JOHN DAY RIVER

The Spring Basin Wilderness lures explorers with scenic desert canyons. Boaters on the John Day River float through an even deeper desert gorge.

Climate

The hot summers are virtually rainless. The freezing winters accumulate no snowpack. With just 10 inches of annual rainfall, this portion of the John Day only flows as a river because of precipitation in the distant Ochocos and Blue Mountains.

Plants and Wildlife

The sagebrush steppe here features hedgehog cactus (blooms red in April) and mat-like prickly pear cactus. Look for rare yellow hairy paintbrush in May. Junipers dot upper slopes, while creeks harbor wild rose, red osier dogwood, and snowberry.

Golden eagles and prairie falcons patrol the canyon skies. Canada geese, mergansers, goldeneyes, and green-winged teals paddle ahead of boaters.

The trail to Clarno Arch.

The river's salmon runs died in 1889 with construction of a since-demolished grist mill dam. Steelhead trout, bullhead, and suckers remain. Smallmouth bass, introduced in 1971, thrive.

Hikers should be alert for scorpions and rattlesnakes, though chances are greater of meeting cattle, wild horses, mule deer, coyotes, and startled, partridge-like chukars.

Geology

Fossils from the Clarno Unit of the John Day Fossil Beds National Monument indicate this area was a coastal rainforest 34 million years ago. Primitive rhinoceroses and tapirs flourished alongside ferns and avocado trees.

The creation of the Cascade Range 16 to 33 million years ago not only dried up this area by blocking moisture from the sea, but it also buried the landscape repeatedly with volcanic ashfalls, preserving countless fossils, including the skel-

Location: 41 mi SE of The Dalles

Size: 93 sq mi

Status: 13 sq mi designated wilderness (2009), federal wild and scenic river

Terrain: sagebrush canyonlands, river rapids

Elevation: 540'-3600'

Management: Prineville District BLM

Maps: Muddy Ranch, Clarno, Chimney Springs, Bath Canyon, Shoestring Ridge, Horseshoe Bend, Indian Cove, Harmony, Esau Canyon (USGS)

etons of saber-toothed tigers and small, three-toed horses. The many layers of red, buff, and green volcanic ash form the "painted hills" visible on the west riverbank 4 miles north of Clarno. Vast floods of Columbia River basalt 13 to 16 million years ago capped the area with a rimrock of black lava. Cliffs exhibit basalt's characteristic hexagonal pillars.

History

Numerous Indian housepit sites and painted rock carvings testify to over 4,500 years of human habitation along the river. From 1866 to 1930 white settlers built the remote riverside ranches whose abandoned buildings remain. All artifacts are federally protected.

HIKING & BACKPACKING

The area's best marked trails are interpretive nature paths at the John Day Fossil Beds National Monument's picnic area on Highway 218, east of the Clarno bridge 3 miles. A 0.3-mile connector path leads from the picnic area west to a parking pullout where two trails begin. The Trail of the Fossils is a 0.2-mile loop on a slope with boulders containing leaf and branch fossils. The Clarno Arch Trail climbs 0.2 mile to a viewpoint by a massive cliff with a dainty, 10-foot natural rock arch.

Trails in the Spring Basin Wilderness consist of ancient, closed roads. The open terrain invites cross-country exploration, but be sure to bring a map, a compass, and route-finding skills. Wear sturdy shoes and carry plenty of water.

To reach Spring Basin from Clarno, drive 1.5 miles east on Highway 218, turn right onto a dirt road for 3.1 miles, park, and hike 1.2 miles up a road track to the east. At a T-shaped road junction in a pass continue straight, bushwhacking northeast down into Spring Basin's juniper-dotted upper canyon—a good backpacking destination. Springs flow here at times, but don't count on them.

From Spring Basin, bushwhack east

0.8 mile up Horse Mountain to a viewpoint above small rock pinnacles. For a longer loop head down Spring Basin's canyon and follow roads to Eagle Canyon's twisty, narrow, mile-long chasm.

Nearly 50 square miles of land just north and east of the Spring Basin Wilderness are owned by the Confederated Tribes of Warm Springs, managed as wilderness, and open to the public.

Along the John Day River, cross-country hikes prowl side canyons and bluffs in the BLM-owned land between Clarno and Cottonwood Bridge. Because the only public access to these remote lands is by boat, hikes must be planned in conjunction with float trips.

CLIMBING

The John Day Fossil Beds National Monument near Clarno offers several small blocks and towers, ranging from the level I-4 Steigomonster to the II-5.2-A3 Hancock Tower.

BOATING

Plan for four lazy days by raft or three thrilling days by open canoe to drift the 70 scenic miles between Clarno and Cottonwood Bridge. Timing is critical, because this undammed river varies from an unnavigable maelstrom in winter to an unfloatable dribble in September. The river is technically runnable between 800 and 23,000 cubic feet per second (measured at the Service Creek gauging station), but expect the easiest levels (3000-7000 cfs) from April to July and again in November.

The river's wildest water, Clarno Rapids, begins 4.4 miles downstream from the Clarno Bridge launch site. This class 3, canoe-swamping rapid becomes a class 4 canoe-wrecker at water levels above 4000 cfs. Scout or portage on the left, remembering that Lower Clarno Rapids (class 2) lies just downstream. Beyond, however, the only serious whitewater is class 2+ Basalt Rapids, 15.9 miles from Clarno Bridge.

Expect good camping spots in the Basalt Canyon, a 4-mile-long gorge below Basalt Rapids. Then look back upriver to spot Arch Rocks' twin hoops atop a cliff. Just before Horseshoe Bend, watch the right bank for two wagons used in a movie filmed here in 1928. Then, a mile past Horseshoe Bend, stop at Potlatch Canyon on the right to observe (but not touch) the cliff's petroglyphs. Cave Bluff's river-level cavern makes a fun stop 3.5 miles further downstream. Another 10 miles along are Hoot Owl Rock, an owl-shaped clifftop pillar, and Citadel Rock, a fortress-shaped palisade. Cottonwood Bridge is the last public take-out site before a falls and the tamed Columbia's backwaters.

Many who float the John Day launch 44 miles upriver from Clarno at Service Creek, where the BLM maintains a recreation area with campsites. The two- to three-day run to Clarno includes class 2 rapids located 6, 15, and 23 miles downriver from Service Creek.

40
PAINTED HILLS

Oregon calendars often feature photographs of the John Day Fossil Beds' colorfully striped ash hills, so many people are familiar with this small national monument's short nature trails. But few have explored Sutton Mountain, in the vast roadless country surrounding the monument.

Climate
With just 12 inches of annual rainfall, these arid hills feature blue skies that are rarely troubled by thunderclouds during the hot summers or snowstorms in the cold winters.

Plants and Wildlife
No plants grow on the soft, fast-eroding clays of the painted hills, but the surrounding rimrock plateaus host cheatgrass, bitterbrush, bunchgrass, and sagebrush. A sparse juniper forest clings to Sutton Mountain's slopes, with surprising patches of ponderosa pine and even Douglas fir in the draws.

Geology
The rounded, colorfully striped Painted Hills began as ash that erupted from the ancestral High Cascades volcanoes 33 million years ago and settled in a vast lake here. The resulting yellow claystone was colored by trace minerals—red from oxidized iron and black from manganese. The soil is so soft that

footprints last for years, so please stay on designated paths.

Vast floods of Columbia River basalt 13 to 16 million years ago capped the area with a rimrock of black lava. Erosion has uncovered the colorful ash in the Painted Hills' valley, but half a dozen layers of rimrock remain as Sutton Mountain's tilted plateau.

History
When gold was discovered near John Day in 1862, entrepreneurs built a military road, stagecoach line, and supply route from The Dalles to Canyon City.

Location: 40 mi NE of Prineville
Size: 77 sq mi
Status: 4 sq mi national monument
Terrain: colorful badlands, sagebrush rimrock
Elevation: 1750'-4694'
Management: Prineville District BLM, John Day Fossil Beds National Monument
Maps: Sutton Mountain, Painted Hills, Mitchell, Toney Butte (USGS)

The Painted Cove Trail.

The road followed Bridge Creek past the Painted Hills. The U.S. government granted the builders a checkerboard of land along the route as payment for their work. Not until the 1990s did the Bureau of Land Management reacquire the alternate square miles of private land on Sutton Mountain, opening the area for public use and for study as a designatable wilderness. Cattle grazing is still permitted on the northern two-thirds of Sutton Mountain.

Shortly after the stagecoach road opened in the 1860s, frontier minister Thomas Condon recognized the Painted Hills as a remarkable source of fossils. Condon later became the University of Oregon's first paleontologist and organized excavations here that drew international attention. At Leaf Hill in the 1920s, excavators unearthed over 20,000 leaf fossils in less than 100 cubic feet of shale.

HIKING & BACKPACKING

A grassy picnic area and four short hiking trails are the top attractions of the Painted Hills Unit, one of three widely separated parts of the John Day Fossil Beds National Monument. Start by following signs to the Painted Hills Overlook parking area. From there, a 0.3-mile path strolls south along a broad ridge to panoramic views of the colorfully striped clay slopes. For an even better look around, hike the 0.8-mile Carroll Rim Trail, which starts opposite the parking area's entrance road and climbs 400 feet to a viewpoint atop a lava rimrock cliff. Then drive west to visit two short (0.2-mile) interpretive nature loops, the very scenic Painted Cove Trail and the interesting Leaf Hill Loop.

Sutton Mountain presents a nearly unscalable rimrock cliff to the west, but the eastern side of this tilted plateau is much gentler. Several routes climb to the summit rim, where hikers can amble cross-country along the cliff edge for views of the colorful Painted Hills valley. The easiest route, a 3.4-mile abandoned roadbed that gains 1580 feet to the top, begins at a driveway near milepost 15 of Highway 207. Park along the highway and cross Girds Creek on the driveway to a "Road Closed" sign marking the public roadbed.

A different route to the summit begins at the paved road along Bridge Creek and follows an abandoned roadbed up Meyers Canyon. Keep left for 3.6 miles to the track's end at a spring and then bushwhack up a forested ridge 1.5 miles to the top. A third route to the summit plateau follows cattle trails up narrow, cliff-lined Black Canyon from the paved road to Twickenham.

Sutton Mountain from the Painted Hills.

41
MILL CREEK

Mill Creek is a wholly-preserved Ochoco Mountain valley with forest trails, rock climbing sites, and sweeping viewpoints. Considering that this valley lies just one hour's drive east of Bend, it's surprising Mill Creek is a little-known wilderness in a generally overlooked mountain range.

Climate

The area receives only 25 inches of precipitation annually, primarily as winter snow. Summers are dry and fairly hot. Late spring and fall are pleasant.

Plants and Wildlife

Mill Creek preserves one of the Ochocos' few remaining climax forests of ponderosa pine and bunchgrass. Wildfires traditionally cleared such forests of underbrush. Decades of overzealous fire suppression have allowed an understory of Douglas fir to grow, enabling fires to reach above the large ponderosa pines' fire-resistant trunks to their flammable crowns, as happened in 1995 when a fire burned 2 square miles at the headwaters of Belknap Creek.

Livestock grazing in some areas limits native flora. Other animals include Rocky Mountain elk, mule deer, bobcat, cougar, and an occasional black bear.

Geology

The Ochoco Mountains formed as a string of coastal volcanoes 40 to 50

Twin Pillars.

million years ago, before the Cascade Range existed. Twin Pillars remain as the plug of an eroded volcano. When the Ochoco volcanoes subsided and the Old Cascades roared to life 25 million years ago, massive ash deposits covered Eastern Oregon, collecting in lakes and rivers. Rhyolite ash deposits subsequently welded together to form the resistant tuff outcropping at Whistler Point and the 350-foot tower of Steins Pillar. At Whistler Point, in the Ochoco Agate Beds off Road 27, look for baseball-sized thundereggs. Oregon's state rock, the thunderegg forms when small cavities in the tuff fill with quartz and agate.

HIKING & BACKPACKING

For an introduction to this wilderness, take the Twin Pillars Trail from Wildcat Campground through an old-growth ponderosa pine forest along East Fork Mill Creek. To reach Wildcat Campground from Prineville, follow Highway 26 east 10 miles to the far end of Ochoco Reservoir and turn left for

Location: 20 mi NE of Prineville

Size: 27 sq mi

Status: designated wilderness (1984)

Terrain: forested upland valley

Elevation: 3725'-6240'

Management: Ochoco NF

Maps: Mill Creek Wilderness (USFS)

Mill Creek.

10.7 miles on Mill Creek Road 33.

The first 2.9 miles of the creekside path are nearly level, but include several bridgeless crossings. By summer the crossings can usually be accomplished dry-footed, and even in spring's high water it is possible to avoid wading by staying entirely on the creek's south bank, using short scramble trails between crossings. After 2.9 miles, there's a nice campsite in a grassy glen at the junction of the faint Belknap Trail.

For a longer hike, continue straight on the Twin Pillars Trail, gaining an additional 1400 feet in 2.6 miles, to a viewpoint at the base of Twin Pillars' 200-foot rock towers. A shorter but less scenic 2.6-mile route to Twin Pillars begins at a different trailhead, on the northern edge of the wilderness on Road 27.

For other hikes, Wildcat Campground is nearly always the endpoint, because it's 2000 feet lower than other trailheads. One 8.6-mile route starts at the White Rock Campground, on the shoulder of Wildcat Mountain. Another route to Wildcat Campground, from Whistler Point on Forest Road 27, is 13.1 miles. Potential backpacking campsites are plentiful throughout. Only creeks named on the map are year-round water sources.

An easy 2-mile trail to 350-foot Steins Pillar (shown in the lower left of the map) features views, flowers, and ponderosa pines. From Highway 26 at the east end of Ochoco Reservoir, drive Mill Creek Road 33 for 6.7 miles and turn right on Road 500 for 2 miles to a gravel turnaround on the left, 0.2 before road's end.

CLIMBING

Twin Pillars are a pair of vertical-sided, 200-foot andesite plugs at 5400 feet. Though quite scenic and challenging (rated II-5.7), they are rarely climbed because of the proximity of the more challenging Steins Pillar. This 350-foot, overhanging spire of welded tuff, unscaled until 1950, offers routes from difficulty III-5.6-A3 to IV-5.7-A4.

SNOWSHOEING & SKIING

Ochoco Divide on U.S. Highway 22

Twin Pillars.

offers good cross-country skiing and snowshoeing from January through March. The highway is plowed in winter, allowing access to unplowed roads along the eastern edge of the wilderness. View Point makes a scenic goal, 5 miles up Road 27.

Steins Pillar.

42
LOOKOUT MOUNTAIN

From the wildflower-spangled sagebrush meadows of Lookout Mountain's plateau, views stretch beyond the forested Ochoco Mountains to a string of High Cascades snowpeaks.

Ruins at the Independent Mine Trailhead.

Climate

Winter snow accounts for most of the area's 30 inches of annual precipitation. Summers are dry and warm.

Plants and Wildlife

An amazing variety of wildflowers bloom on the vast summit plateau in June, including desert parsley, mountain bluebells, balsamroot, wild peony, paintbrush, and yellowbell.

This is prime elk, wild horse, and mule deer range. Watch for herds in the high meadows during summer, and in the cover of low-elevation forests during winter. Open, parklike forests of ponderosa pine invite cross-country travel, while wetter northern slopes host Douglas fir and grand fir. Storm-stunted subalpine fir struggle in the summit meadows.

Geology

A lava flow forms the flat top of Lookout Mountain. This basalt oozed from vents north of the John Day River about 25 million years ago, smothering most of the Ochoco Mountains. Out-croppings of older Ochoco rock in the valleys prompted an 1873 gold rush. The abandoned buildings and mineshafts near the Independent Mine Trailhead are off-limits because the cinnabar once mined there has contaminated the area with poisonous mercury.

HIKING & BACKPACKING

Half a dozen trails climb to the vistas atop Lookout Mountain. Three of the best paths fan out from the Independent Mine Trailhead on Road 4205, making possible nice 4.6- to 7-mile loop hikes to the summit. The original lookout is gone, but the building's stone corral remains atop a panoramic rimrock lip. Just 400 yards east is a three-sided shelter (GPS location N44°19.637' W120°22.234'), built in 1989 primarily as a winter retreat for skiers and snowmobilers.

From Prineville, drive Highway 26 east for 17 miles. Near milepost 35, fork to the right at an "Ochoco Creek" sign for 8.2 miles to the closed Ochoco Ranger Station. Continue 0.3 mile, veer right

Location: 25 mi E of Prineville
Size: 26 sq mi
Status: undesignated wilderness
Terrain: forested ridges, sagebrush plateau
Elevation: 3793'-6926'
Management: Ochoco NF
Maps: Lookout Mountain, Gerow Butte (USGS)

The cliffs at Lookout Mountain's summit viewpoint.

on paved Road 42 for 6.8 miles to a pass, and turn right on Road 4205. If you're driving a delicate passenger car, park at the Round Mountain Trailhead near the start of this bumpy road and hike a trail 0.9 mile up to the Independent Mine Trailhead; otherwise, drive on up.

The more difficult, 7.3-mile Lookout Mountain Trail begins at a roadside pullout 200 yards east of the closed Ochoco Ranger Station and climbs nearly 3000 feet along a forested ridge to the summit, passing viewpoints at Duncan Butte and North Point along the way.

The Line Butte Trail, a backdoor route to Lookout Mountain's plateau, gains 1000 feet in 3.9 miles from Road 257 to South Point's rimrock viewpoint. Drive as to the Independent Mine but continue straight on Road 42 an extra 7 miles to Big Summit Prairie, turn right on Road 4215 for 9 miles, turn right on Road 4220 for 1 mile, and turn left on Road 257 for 1 mile to the Fawn Creek Trailhead.

From Road 42, the well-marked Round Mountain Trail climbs 4.1 miles through open woods and wildflowers to a crest. From there, either take a side road 0.3 mile to Round Mountain's summit, or continue straight 4.6 miles down the north side of the mountain to popular Walton Lake Campground.

SNOWSHOEING & SKIING

Cross-country skiers can drive up Road 42 to snow level and ski up the marked loop trail (shared with occasional snowmobiles) past the Independent Mine. The reward is great, for Lookout Mountain's high, 2.5-mile-long summit meadows have the Ochocos' best snow and superlative views.

43
BRIDGE CREEK

At the edge of the Ochoco Mountains' summit plateau, North Point's 600-foot cliff overlooks Central Oregon and Cascade peaks from Mount Adams to the Three Sisters.

Climate

The area receives 30 inches of precipitation annually, primarily as winter snow. Summers are dry and hot.

Plants and Wildlife

Mixed conifer thickets of Douglas fir, grand fir, and larch dominate the area, with bands of lodgepole pine and ponderosa pine. Openings of sagebrush, bunchgrass, and sparse, gnarled mountain mahogany break up the plateau forests.

Mule deer and elk find good cover and browse here year round, but especially when hunting season drives them from roaded areas. Watch for prairie falcons, goshawks, and the large, red-headed pileated woodpeckers which, because of their reliance on forest snags, are an indicator species for old-growth Ochoco forests.

Geology

North Point's cliff of pillar-shaped

Location: 39 mi E of Prineville
Size: 8 sq mi
Status: designated wilderness (1984)
Terrain: forested plateau, cliffs, slopes
Elevation: 4320'-6816'
Management: Ochoco NF
Map: Mount Pisgah (USGS)

basalt columns is the edge of a lava flow capping most of the Ochoco crest. Vents north of the John Day River produced this lava about 25 million years ago.

HIKING & BACKPACKING

There are no maintained trails in the Bridge Creek Wilderness. Still, the breathtaking view at North Point is a 1.2-mile bushwhack up an old, closed jeep track from the Bridge Creek cross-

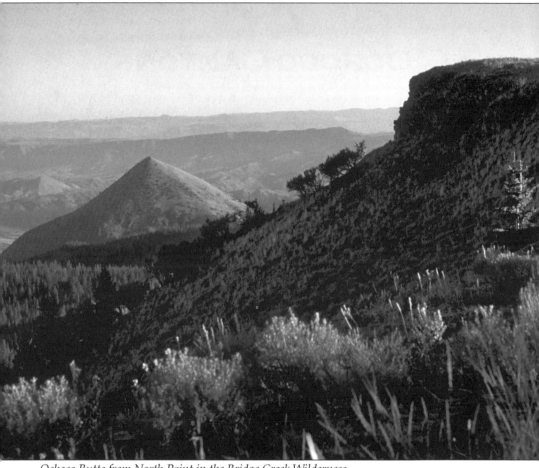

Ochoco Butte from North Point in the Bridge Creek Wilderness.

ing of Road 2630 near Pisgah Spring. To reach the starting point from Prineville, follow Highway 26 east 16 miles, at a sign for Ochoco Creek turn right for 8 paved miles to Ochoco Ranger Station, continue straight on paved Road 22 for 8.5 miles, turn left on Road 150 for a half mile, and turn right on Road 2630 for 7 miles (the last 2 miles are rough and rutted).

Conifer thickets stymie most off-trail hikers in this wilderness, but frequent winds at North Point have stunted vegetation there, allowing easy and interesting cross-country hiking along the cliff edge for a mile on either side of the point. Bushwhacking becomes increasingly difficult—but possible with map and compass—for hikers intent on making a loop trip by continuing west to Thompson Spring, or along the cliff rim southeast to Bridge Creek.

East Point's rounded knoll offers lesser views. It is 1.5 miles along an arrow-straight jeep track from Road 2630.

The trail to Bridge Spring has been abandoned to the cattle that graze this sparse wilderness range each summer. Although the watershed is the domestic water supply for the town of Mitchell, Bridge Spring and Bridge Creek usually are churned to mud by hooves.

44

Ochoco Canyons

Three major canyons—each with its own trail system and splashing creek—provide scenic examples of the Ochoco Mountains' remarkable transition from dense forests to sagebrush lowlands.

Climate

Summers are hot and dry. Snowfall from November to April brings annual precipitation to a sparse 20 to 30 inches.

Plants and Wildlife

Water determines where there will be forest and where sagebrush dominates in these steep mountains. Exposed ridgetops and sunny south slopes are brown and bald. Green swaths of forest cling to shady north slopes and fill the steep canyons—like biological glaciers winding downhill to the arid lowlands, where all melts to brown again.

A hike through the forest reveals bands of lodgepole pine, ponderosa pine parklands, and dense thickets of Douglas fir and grand fir. At creek's edge, expect an oasis of solomonseal, coneflower, snowberry, wild gooseberries, and delicate twinflower.

Black bears, coyotes, mountain lions, deer, and elk are common year round.

Watch for migratory cranes and geese passing overhead on their way to the Malheur Refuge to the southeast.

Geology

Black Canyon's winding, cliff-lined lower gorge, and the similar canyon of the adjacent South Fork John Day, resulted when these streams cut through the basalt lava that once flooded much of central Oregon. In Picture Gorge, 12 miles to the north, the John Day River has cut through 17 layers of this basalt. The lava, now characterized by rusty

Location: 77 mi E of Prineville, 40 mi W of John Day

Size: 54 sq mi

Status: 21 sq mi designated wilderness (1984)

Terrain: steep, forested canyons, sagebrush slopes, rocky creeks

Elevation: 2840'-6871'

Management: Ochoco NF

Maps: Central Oregon (BLM); Aldrich Gulch, Wolf Mountain, Six Corners, Antone, Day Basin, Dayville (USGS)

specks of weathered olivine, erupted from vents north of Dayville 16 million years ago. This outpouring was dwarfed a few million years later when Oregon's next round of basalt floods filled much of the Columbia River Basin.

History

When miners found gold flakes in the dry hills north of Spanish Peak in the late 1800s, E. O. Waterman built a water flume from Rock Creek to help miners wash out the gold. The ditch was converted to a hiking trail in the 1970s.

In the early 1920s, rangers built a "crow's nest" fire lookout platform in the top of a tall tree on Wolf Mountain. No longer climbable, the lookout tree offers good views of Black Canyon from the tree's base. The nearby replacement lookout, a 107-foot tower built in the 1940s, is still staffed in summer.

Boeing Field's name recalls a B-18 bomber that crashed on Wolf Mountain

Rock Creek.

during a World War II transit flight.

HIKING & BACKPACKING

The area's best trails are not in the designated Black Canyon Wilderness, but rather in the undesignated Rock Creek area next door. The best view, for example, is atop 6817-foot Spanish Peak—or perhaps on the peak's shoulder, where a spectacular trail traces a

Spanish Peak from the rim cairn.

cliff-edged rim marked by rock cairns. Although it's possible for rugged high-clearance vehicles to drive to the peak's summit, it's safer to skip the rugged final 1.7 miles of Road 200, park at a small pullout, and start hiking on a trail from there.

The trail from Road 200 contours 1.4 miles through high meadows and fir woods to a junction. From there, Spanish Peak's summit is 0.8 mile to the right, and the rim cairn viewpoint is 2 miles straight ahead.

The area's best streamside path starts at Road 38 and follows Rock Creek downstream through lovely meadows and stands of lodgepole pine. After 2.4 miles the path begins to follow the nearly level route of an abandoned water flume. A good turnaround point (and backpacking campsite) is another 1.4 miles along this Ditch Trail at Fir Tree Creek.

For a longer trip, continue another 3.2 miles on the Ditch Trail to a well-marked junction and turn right on a switchbacking trail that climbs 2.5 miles to the rim cairn on Spanish Peak. A 17-mile loop is possible here, but because the final leg follows 1.9 miles of faint paths down an open ridgecrest and 2.2 miles of gravel

Road 3820, it is best for equestrians.

To find these trailheads from Mitchell, drive Highway 26 east 13 miles, turn right on Road 12 for 15.4 miles to a crossroads, turn left on Road 1250 for 3.9 miles to another crossroads, and turn left on Road 38 for 1.7 miles to the Rock Creek Trailhead on the left (GPS location N44°21.322' W119°46.957').

For other trailheads, continue east on Road 38 another 3.1 miles to a 4-way junction. From this intersection, the Boeing Field Trailhead for the Black Canyon Wilderness is 1.2 miles to the right on Road 5810 (GPS location N44°20.560' W119°43.872'). The trailhead on Spanish Peak, however, is 3.5 miles to the left on rough, rocky Road 200. Where a Jeep road joins from the right, look for rock cairns marking the Spanish Peak trail on the left (GPS location N44°23.985' W119°45.511').

The backpackable 11.9-mile Black Canyon Trail descends along a rushing stream from the forests on Wolf Mountain to a narrow, cliff-walled gorge at a ford of the South Fork John Day River. Along the way, the trail crosses Black Canyon Creek 17 times without bridges. Generally, only the ten crossings in the final 1.8 miles require wading. Most

Boeing Field, the upper trailhead for the Black Canyon Trail.

people access the upper end of the trail on a shortcut from gravel Road 5820 at Boeing Field (see driving directions above). The field itself is a broad meadow of June wildflowers: mules ears, desert parsley, larkspur, and owls clover.

The lower end of the Black Canyon Trail is separated from Road 47 by a ford across the South Fork John Day River (GPS location N44°20.023' W119°33.909'). The river is uncrossable in high water from January to March, but idles along only calf-deep in summer.

The South Prong Trail also accesses Black Canyon, dropping 5.6 miles from Mud Springs Campground to Big Ford.

Cottonwood Creek meanders through the most isolated canyon of all. A lovely forest trail drops 1500 feet in 3 miles to the forks of the creek. Downstream, the trail ends in 0.8 mile at an off-limits, private dirt road leading to the Mascall Ranch at Picture Gorge; upstream, 8 miles of creek await exploration by hardy bushwhackers. The trailhead is at the junction of Road 38 and spur Road 700.

SNOWSHOEING & SKIING

Snowed-under ridgetop roads provide quiet routes for winter tours. Spanish Peak makes the most challenging and spectacular goal. Expect sufficient snow from mid-December to late March. Roads are unplowed, so you have to drive to snow level and park.

The lower portion of Black Canyon.

45
ALDRICH MOUNTAINS

This little-known range between the Ochoco and the Strawberry mountains preserves two wild areas. In the west, the Aldrich Mountain lookout rises above the forests and sagebrush gulches of the Murderers Creek Wildlife Area. In the east, a dozen peaks with bare, 2000-foot-tall shoulders cluster along the 13.9-mile McClellan Mountain Trail.

Location: 11 mi W of John Day

Size: 91 sq mi

Status: undesignated wilderness

Terrain: broad mountains, sagebrush slopes, forest

Elevation: 2649'-7363'

Management: Malheur NF, Prineville District BLM, Oregon Department of Fish and Wildlife

Maps: McClellan Mountain, Big Weasel Springs, Aldrich Mountain S, Aldrich Gulch, Aldrich Mountain N, Dayville (USGS)

Climate

Most of the area's scant 20 annual inches of precipitation fall as snow from November to April. Hot summer afternoons may bring thunderstorms.

Plants and Wildlife

Bighorn sheep are a highlight of the Murderers Creek Wildlife Area, between the South Fork John Day River and the Aldrich Mountain summit. Once hunted to extinction here, the wild sheep were reintroduced in 1978. They prefer Smoky Gulch and Oliver Creek's upper canyon. Sleek pronghorn antelope summer along Murderers Creek and winter in the north of the area. Elk rely on the timbered areas for winter cover, and mule deer come from as far as Strawberry Mountain for winter forage. Mountain lions, coyotes, rattlesnakes, meadowlarks, and mountain cottontails are also in the area. Bald eagles winter near Dayville.

Sagebrush, bunchgrass, juniper, and yellow-bloomed rabbitbrush dominate the lower elevations and south-facing slopes. Douglas fir and grand fir forests cling to north slopes and cap Aldrich Mountain. Near McClellan Mountain, canyon bottoms are forested with stately ponderosa pine and larch. Bitterroot and phlox bloom on bare ridges in June.

The Cedar Grove Botanical Area preserves a biological oddity—60 acres of Alaska cedar, isolated 130 miles from other Alaska cedar stands. An easy 1-mile trail from Road 2150 leads to the grove.

Geology

The Aldrich Mountains began as the

The view east from Fields Peak.

mud, sand, and reefs of a Pacific island chain 190-230 million years ago. The Earth's crustal movements "rafted" this island rock to Oregon's coast 150 million years ago. The later eruption of the Ochoco volcanoes, and then the Cascade volcanoes, left the Aldrich Mountains progressively farther inland.

HIKING & BACKPACKING

A steady 2.3-mile climb reaches the area's highest point, Fields Peak, a former lookout site with panoramic views of the John Day Valley and beyond. Although all-terrain vehicles are allowed on this route, they are rare, and they are banned from other parts of the McClellan Mountain Trail. Find the trailhead by turning south from Highway 26 on Fields Creek Road 21 (the junction is 13 miles east of Dayville or 18 miles west of John Day). Follow this one-lane paved road 8.6 miles, turn left on gravel Road 115 for 0.4 mile, turn right on Road 2160 for 200 yards, and fork left on rough Road 041 for 1.2 miles to its end.

For a longer hike without risk of ATV noise, start out toward Fields Peak for 1.5 miles, but then keep right on the Mc-

Clellan Mountain Trail. For the next 7.6 miles the path threads through high, scenic passes, traversing the crest of the range to Bear Flat. Along this route, bare side ridges invite cross-country detours to the scenic summits of Moon Mountain and McClellan Mountain. Beyond Bear Flat the trail angles down into Riley Creek's gorge and then follows the stream up through ponderosa pine woods to a more remote trailhead.

To find the Riley Creek Trailhead from Highway 26, drive Fields Creek Road 21 for 13.7 miles to Murderers Creek, turn left to continue on Road 21 for 6.4 miles, turn left on Road 2190 for 5.6 miles (keeping right at unmarked junctions) to road's end.

A topographic map, compass, and water are essential for cross-country hiking on the steep, western flanks of Aldrich Mountain where wildlife observation is best. To spot bighorn sheep in winter, park on the South Fork John Day Road 47 between Smoky and Oliver Creeks and hike up the ridge to an excellent viewpoint at Bottle Rock. In summer, start at Aldrich Mountain and hike down.

Lookout foundations atop Fields Peak.

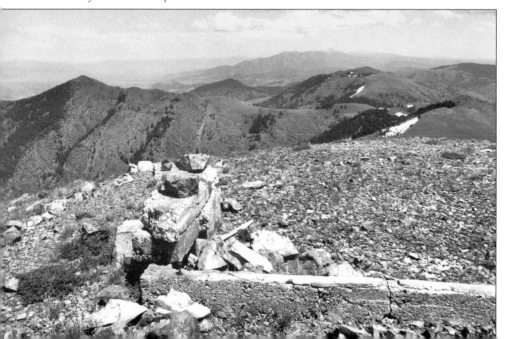

46
STRAWBERRY MOUNTAIN

For a lesson in Eastern Oregon's diversity, visit the Strawberry Range. Above the John Day River's alfalfa fields, and above an arid band of sagebrush and juniper, dense conifer forests rise past blue lakes, waterfalls, and alpine wildflowers to palisades of snow-draped crags.

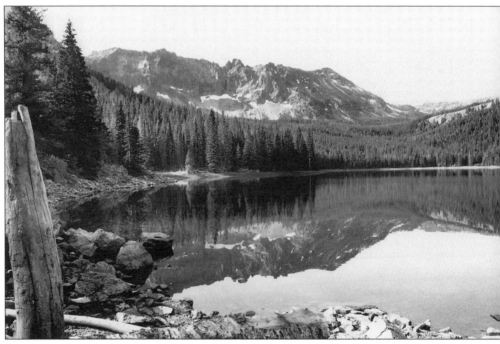

Strawberry Lake.

Location: 4 mi SE of John Day

Size: 123 sq mi

Status: 107 sq mi designated wilderness (1964, 1984)

Terrain: snowpeak, forest valleys, high meadows, lakes

Elevation: 3570'-9038'

Management: Malheur NF, Prineville District BLM

Map: Strawberry Mountain Wilderness (USFS)

Climate

Because most of the wilderness is above 6000 feet in elevation, snow closes trails from November to June and snow patches linger in high passes until August. Summers are fair and warm, with some thunderstorms and freezing nights. Snow flurries may interrupt October's typically cool, clear Indian summer. Annual precipitation measures 40 inches.

Plants and Wildlife

Five of the United States' seven major biologic zones are packed into this relatively small mountain range. Larch, the only native conifer to lose its needles in winter, spangles the high forests with autumn gold. Other trees include Engelmann spruce, white pine, Douglas fir, grand fir, lodgepole pine, and ponderosa pine. The area's name derives from the wild strawberries rampant in mid-elevation forests. Watch for their fruit in July and their bright red leaves in October.

Bighorn sheep, reintroduced here after local extinction, now thrive on Canyon Mountain. Look for them up Sheep Gulch from Highway 395. Rocky mountain elk and mule deer summer here in profusion, and seek shelter during autumn hunting season. Other wildlife include black bears, coyotes, mountain lions, bobcats, ground squirrels, and golden eagles.

Geology

The western half of the Strawberry Range is a chunk of seafloor sediments and island debris buckled up from the Pacific by the westward drift of North America 200 to 250 million years ago, before the creation of the Cascades and Coast Range made this an inland area. Canyon Mountain consists of reddish peridotite, greenish serpentinite, and crumbly brown basalt—all indicative of oceanic crust.

The eastern half of the Strawberry Range, beginning at Indian Creek Butte, consists of much younger volcanic rock. About 15 million years ago, volcanoes here spewed out immense amounts of ash and lava, burying the southern Blue Mountains. Rabbit Ears is the eroded plug of one vent. Above Wildcat Basin, colored ash deposits have weathered

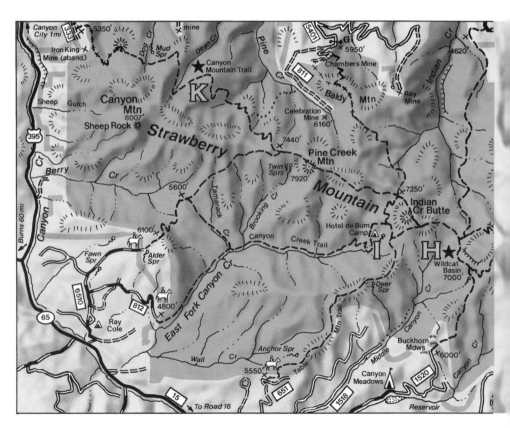

into a scenic badlands.

Ice Age glaciers carved the many broad, U-shaped mountain valleys. They also left sandy moraines (visible in Indian Creek Canyon) and cirque lakes. Strawberry Lake formed when glacial ice retreated and the remaining, steep valley wall collapsed, blocking Strawberry Creek with a landslide.

History

Traces of gold in Canyon Mountain's peridotite launched a decade of intense placer mining in 1862, when Canyon City began as a tent town of 10,000 men. Pioneer Oregon poet Joaquin Miller wrote and served as county judge in the boomtown between 1863 and 1869.

HIKING & BACKPACKING

This compact mountain range features rugged alpine scenery and a thor-

Knoll along the Canyon Mountain Trail.

ough trail system with room for backpacking treks. Mountain lakes are rare in Eastern Oregon, so the seven in this area are popular. Do not camp within 100 feet of lakeshores.

From Strawberry Camp, a 1.3-mile uphill walk reaches Strawberry Lake, a

Wildcat Basin's ash cliffs.

 popular backpacking base camp with a photogenic backdrop of snowy crags. Another 1.2 miles up the valley Strawberry Falls cascades 40 feet onto boulders glowing with moss. Don't turn back yet, because an additional 0.6-mile, level walk takes you to a spectacular lunch spot at Little Strawberry Lake.

Climbing to Strawberry Mountain's panoramic viewpoint requires a demanding 6.3-mile hike from trailhead to summit, gaining 3300 feet in elevation, but the trail grade is good and after all, this is one of Oregon's tallest peaks. Hike to Strawberry Falls and keep right at junctions.

To find the Strawberry Camp trailhead turn south off Highway 26 on Prairie City's Main Street for 0.4 mile to a T-shaped junction, turn left for two blocks, and turn right onto Bridge Street (Road 60) for 10.7 miles.

Slide Lake, in an amphitheater of stripey cliffs, is another popular destination for day hikers and backpackers from the Strawberry Camp trailhead. It's 3.9 miles, with Little Slide Lake just a short distance beyond.

For a shortcut to the top of Strawberry Mountain, start at a trailhead on the southern side of the wilderness, 0.4 mile from the end of Road 1640 above Indian

Springs Campground. From there, a 3.6-mile trail climbs just 1100 feet to the top.

If you drive the extra 0.4 mile to the end of Road 1640, you'll find the trailhead for High Lake. A good trip for kids or for beginning backpackers, the trail ambles 1.3 miles down to the lake's scenic basin. Those who continue 1.6 miles past High Lake up to a pass are rewarded with a view of Slide Lake's glacier-carved valley. For an even broader view, hike cross-country from this pass up a cliff-edged ridge past Rabbit Ears' rock pillars to Indian Springs Butte.

To reach the trailheads on Road 1640 take Highway 395 south of John Day 9.7 miles, turn left on paved county Road 65 (which becomes Road 15) for 13.6 miles to a stop sign, turn left on Road 16 for 2.5 miles, and turn left on gravel Road 1640 for 10 miles.

 Wildcat Basin's ash badlands and July wildflowers also make a good goal for a day hike or a backpack. Take the 2.4-mile trail up from Buckhorn Meadows, at the end of Road 1520. Follow Road 65 from Highway 395 for 8.9 miles, turn left on Road 1520 for 4 miles to Canyon Meadow Campground, and continue 3 rough miles to road's end.

Baldy Mountain's broad ridge of wildflowers and views is one of the

Strawberry Mountains' least discovered scenic destinations. From John Day, drive Highway 26 east 6 miles, turn right on Pine Creek Road 54 (later 5401) for 8 miles to a gated trailhead parking area, walk up the closed road 0.3 mi, turn left up the abandoned Chambers Mine road 0.5 mile to the second switchback, and strike off on a genuine trail through meadows 1.1 miles to the ridge's crest. The path continues 3.9 scenic miles, traversing to the Canyon Mountain Trail junction at a pass beside Indian Creek Butte.

Two uncrowded trails on the south side of the wilderness follow creeks to mountain lakes. One trail heads up Lake Creek 3.7 miles to High Lake, and the other follows Meadow Fork 3.2 miles, past a waterfall, to Mud Lake. With a car shuttle, hikers can either combine the two hikes or else start out at the high-elevation Road 1640 trailhead and make the trip into an easy downhill romp. From Highway 395, take Road 65 for 13.6 miles, turn left on Road 16 for 6.5 miles to Logan Valley, then turn left on Road 924 to Murray Campground. From there the Lake Creek trail begins 1.5 miles ahead at the end of Road 924.

For the Meadow Fork Trailhead to Mud Lake, turn right from Murray Campground for 0.5 mile on Road 1648, turn left on Road 021 for 1.4 miles, and turn left on rough Road 039 for 1.6 miles.

The East Fork of Canyon Creek splashes through a stately forest in a deep canyon. Backpackers and equestrians often use the trail along this stream when trekking into the range's high country, especially to the small meadow and spring at Hotel de Bum Camp, 7.3 miles from the Road 812 trailhead. Day hikers will find the creekside path soothing, but may have trouble deciding when to turn back.

The Canyon Mountain Trail offers a different challenge. Blasted into the rugged upper slopes of the Strawberry Range, this route offers lots of scenery, but very few campsites. For 15 miles between Dog Creek and Hotel de Bum there is only one reliable creek, and the flattest tent sites are in possibly windy passes. Still, the route's start makes a first-rate day hike, and it's the closest trail to Canyon City, although the access road is very steep. At the Grant County Museum in downtown Canyon City, turn uphill on Main Street

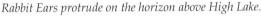

Rabbit Ears protrude on the horizon above High Lake.

Strawberry Falls in winter.

Skyline Trail's forested ridge in the east, where trails are faint.

SNOWSHOEING & SKIING

There's plenty of winter snow in these mountains. The challenge is to get to it, because most access roads are unplowed. From January to March, when snow covers low-elevation roads, one solution is to drive 15 miles south of John Day on plowed Highway 395 to the Starr Bowl winter sports area, with its network of snowmobile and ski trails among non-wilderness hills.

Paved county road 62 south of Prairie City is also plowed as far as the Huddleston sno-park at the road's summit (elevation 5899 feet). From there, snowmobiles roar onward along the snowed-under road to Logan Valley and Road 16, along the southern edge of the Strawberry Range. Cross-country skiers and snowshoers, however, can trek from the Huddleston sno-park west on Road 101 and the woodsy Skyline Trail into the Strawberry Mountain Wilderness. A steeper tour heads east up Road 994 and the trail to Lookout Mountain

Another midwinter option is to park 1.9 miles up Canyon City's Main Street and trek on backroads for 2.8 miles to the Canyon Mountain Trail. The first 2.4 miles of this trail are not too rugged, yet offer excellent viewpoints.

Strawberry Lake in winter is worth a journey. Expect snow to block the unplowed access road 2 to 4 miles short of the trailhead. A spectacular goal is to climb past frozen Strawberry Falls to Little Strawberry Lake.

Some of the best snow, and best views, are atop Baldy Mountain. Access is via Pine Creek Road 54 (alias Road 5401). Although this road is not plowed, it is seldom blocked by snow more than 2 or 3 miles before the Chambers Mine, where a spur climbs left to treeless upper slopes. The Pine Creek Road joins Highway 26 east of John Day 6 miles.

1.9 miles, turn right on paved Gardner Road 77 for 0.3 mile, curve right onto an oiled road for 0.3 mile to a fork, and go straight on a gravel road 2.2 miles, ignoring dirt spurs. When gravel ends in a saddle at a junction at the 2.2-mile mark, go straight on a dirt road 200 feet to a blazed pine tree and turn left for 300 yards to road's end (GPS location N44°21.75' W118°55.565').

A complete circuit of the area's high lakes makes a fun two- or three-day backpacking trip. The 13.3-mile loop from the Road 1640 trailhead passes Strawberry Mountain, Strawberry Lake, Slide Lake, and High Lake. Add 2.3 miles if starting from Strawberry Campground. Allow time for side trips.

To really experience the Strawberries, try backpacking the entire length of the mountain range's crest. It's 42 miles, starting with the Canyon Mountain Trail's rugged slopes in the west to the

47
GLACIER MOUNTAIN & MONUMENT ROCK

At the southern edge of the Blue Mountains, this area's subalpine, once-glaciated ridges offer views across much of Eastern Oregon. The dense canyon forests shelter reclusive wildlife.

Climate

The John Day Valley funnels winter storms and summer thundershowers eastward to the mountain ridges here. As a result the area receives 40 inches annual precipitation, twice as much as the surrounding lowlands. Expect snow to block trails over 6000 feet from November to late June. Summer brings hot days and chilly nights.

Plants and Wildlife

A wolverine sighted west of Table Rock in 1980 provides rare evidence that this unusual animal still exists in Oregon. Named "skunk bear" for its habit of scenting uneaten food, and *Gulo gulo* (Latin, "glutton glutton") for its diverse appetite, the wolverine resembles a small, bushy-tailed, gray-headed bear. Though only 18 to 42 pounds, its ferocity successfully drives coyotes, bears,

Monument Rock.

and even mountain lions away from contested carrion.

Wolverines and mountain lions are among the few predators that dare to eat porcupines, a locally abundant species. Watch for porcupines during the day on low tree limbs (where they gnaw on bark and sleep), and at night in human campsites (where they eat sweaty backpack straps and fishing rod handles for the salt).

The unstocked Little Malheur River preserves a population of rare red-banded trout. The area's 70 bird species include the creek-loving water ouzel and the red-headed pileated woodpecker.

Ponderosa pine and juniper sparsely

Location: 26 mi E of John Day, 52 mi SW of Baker City

Size: 91 sq mi, including Wildcat Creek area

Status: 31 sq mi designated wilderness (1984)

Terrain: steep, forested canyons, open ridges

Elevation: 4300'-8033'

Management: Malheur NF, Wallowa-Whitman NF

Maps: Monument Rock Wilderness (USFS)

forest the lowlands and dry south-facing slopes. Topping the high ridges are subalpine meadows, June wildflowers, and spire-shaped subalpine fir. Thickets of mixed conifers crowd other areas.

Geology

Glacier Mountain, Lookout Mountain, and Little Baldy Mountain are glacial horns, their sides steeply scalloped by the U-shaped valleys of vanished Ice Age glaciers. That the equally high Monument Rock area shows so little of this scenic glacial topography remains a puzzle.

The rocks are mostly 15-million-year-old lava and ash from vents near Strawberry Mountain, but an outcropping of much older, more mineralized rock on Bullrun Mountain and Mine Ridge has spawned several small mines.

History

The lichen-covered 8-foot cylindrical stone monument atop Monument Rock was mostly likely erected by pioneer Basque sheepherders in the early 1900s. The Snake Indians who once roamed here have no tradition of building megaliths, but Basques do. Likewise the tribe has no tradition of rock paintings, so the ancient petroglyphs on a natural rock arch at Reynolds Creek may belong to an earlier culture.

HIKING & BACKPACKING

The area's high ridges feature easy trails to dramatic viewpoints. Even the road to the Lookout Mountain trailhead, dirt Road 548, provides thrilling views as it traces a narrow ridgeline from Sheep Mountain. From Road 548's gate, the tops of Lookout Mountain and Glacier Mountain are a half hour's hike away, but require some cross-country scrambling. A popular day hike continues past the gate on the abandoned road (now maintained as a trail) along the nearly level ridgeline 3.6 miles to Little Baldy Mountain's summit meadow, and the best view of the John Day Valley.

All-terrain vehicles are uncommon but allowed on the closed road.

Reach Road 548 from Prairie City by turning south on Main Street. At a stop sign after 0.4 mile, turn left onto what becomes Road 62 for a total of 20 paved miles, turn left on gravel Road 1665 for 4 miles, turn left on very rough Road 548 past Sheep Mountain a total of 6 miles to the gate at Lookout Mountain.

The fire lookout tower on Table Rock

is a good place to begin a visit to the Monument Rock area. After taking in the view, backtrack half a mile down the lookout road and take a level, 2-mile stroll along an ancient dirt road to Bullrun Rock's 150-foot cliffs. Scramble to the top for a good view. A faint fork of the abandoned road winds close to Monument Rock. About 0.4 mile of easy bushwhacking through open sagebrush is required to climb to the monument itself. Adventurers can continue 3.5 miles to Lone Rock.

To reach the Table Rock lookout from Highway 26 in downtown Prairie City, turn south on Main Street 0.4 mile, turn left at a stop sign, and then keep straight on what becomes Road 62. After 8 miles, turn left on paved Road 13 for 11.7 miles, turn left on gravel Road 1370 for 4.4 miles, fork left to stay on Road 1370 for another 1.5 miles, and turn right at a

"Table Rock" sign to continue on Road 1370 (now much rougher) for 4.8 miles. If you're coming from Unity, drive west of downtown up the South Fork Burnt River 16 miles following Road 6005, turn left on Road 2652 for 2 miles, and then take Road 1370 to the left.

Several streamside trails in deep forest offer cool retreats during summer's heat. The 1.4-mile path up Reynolds Creek traces this moss-banked, splashing stream well into its shady canyon. The final 0.2 mile follow a rough path through the canyon's narrows. At that point, just after a major gulch appears on the left, adventurers can scramble steeply 0.2 mile up a ridge to the left to a large basalt outcrop with a natural rock arch, some petroglyphs, and a nice view of the valley (GPS location N44°25.449' W118°29.082'). Do not camp near the arch, and touch nothing, because the petroglyphs can be damaged even by the oil of a fingerprint.

To find the Reynolds Creek trailhead from Highway 26, turn south on Prairie City's Main Street 0.4 miles, turn left at a stop sign, and then keep straight on what becomes Road 62. After 7.5 miles, turn left on gravel Road 2635 for 4.3 miles.

A 7.4-mile trail descends the Little Malheur River from the river's source at Elk Flat. A good turnaround point for day hikers—and one of many possible campsites for backpackers—is where South Bullrun Creek joins the river. Although the trail crosses the creek seven times, logs and rocks allow hikers to avoid wading. To find the Elk Flat trailhead from Highway 26 in Prairie City, turn south on Main Street 0.4 mile to a stop sign, turn left on what becomes Road 62 for 8 miles, turn left on Road 13 for 11.7 miles, and turn left on Road 1370 for 5 miles. The lower trailhead, on rough Road 457, can be accessed by high-clearance vehicles via Roads 16 and 1672.

Sheep Creek's trail is most often used by equestrians, but day hikers who arrange a car shuttle can easily make the trip one-way downhill. It's 5.2 miles from the Road 548 gate at Lookout Mountain to Road 13 at the bottom. In October the creek's broad glacial valley glows with bright orange quaking aspen and larch.

A good route up to Bullrun Rock is conveniently accessed via Unity. From Highway 26 in downtown Unity, head west on Road 6000 for 7.2 miles and turn left on Road 6010 for 5.2 miles. Trail 1973 gains 1300 feet in 4.3 miles to the rock.

The Little Malheur River.

48
DIXIE BUTTE

This prominent, cone-shaped butte overlooks a broad slope of pristine forestland—an island in an otherwise heavily roaded and logged portion of the Blue Mountains.

Dixie Butte.

Location: 26 mi NE of John Day, 50 mi W of Baker City

Size: 19 sq mi

Status: undesignated wilderness

Terrain: forested butte and bench cut by creek valleys

Elevation: 4000'-7592'

Management: Malheur NF

Maps: Bates, Dixie Meadow (USGS)

Climate

Snow blocks the Davis Creek Trail from about Thanksgiving to late April, the same period that the Dixie Mountain Ski Area operates. The 30 inches of annual precipitation are chiefly snow. Summers are dry.

Plants and Wildlife

Mule deer and elk rely on the area for browse, and for cover during fall hunting season. Larch trees and creekside golden currant bushes provide orange foliage in October. The virtually

The Stump Dodger Railroad Trail.

unbroken forests are mostly Douglas fir and grand fir, with some ponderosa and lodgepole pine.

Geology

Though shaped like a volcano, Dixie Butte was born of water. The peak's rocks are seafloor sediments and Pacific island debris buckled up by the westward-moving seacoast of the North American continent 200 to 250 million years ago. Lava flows from the Strawberry Mountains 15 million years ago cover the plateau below the Davis Creek Trail.

History

During the Civil War, Southern gold prospectors christened Dixie Butte and (Jefferson) Davis Creek to spite the Union men who named the area's new county for Ulysses S. Grant.

In 1910, the narrow-gauge Sumpter Valley Railroad opened a line past Dixie Butte, linking Prairie City with Baker City. Known as the "Stump Dodger" because it was used to log the area's forests, the railroad closed this portion of the line in 1947.

HIKING & BACKPACKING

For a quick break while driving Highway 26, stop at milepost 184 at Dixie Summit (opposite Dixie Campground) to hike a 0.2-mile interpretive trail that explores the abandoned track of the historic Sumpter Valley Railroad. The paved loop trail is accessible for wheelchairs.

The Davis Creek Trail contours 7.8 miles through Dixie Butte's forests. Small log bridges cross three creeks. Elk often show themselves along the way. After the hike, plan to drive to the Dixie Butte lookout tower for an overview of the trail's route, as well as a bird's eye view of the snowy Strawberry Mountains across the John Day Valley.

SNOWSHOEING & SKIING

The snowed-under roads looping through the foothills of Dixie Butte are ideal cross-country ski trails. Start at the Dixie Mountain Ski Area, where there's a warming hut and rope tow. In midwinter, park at Austin Junction for a nearly level, 3.2-mile jaunt along Road 2614 to icy Davis Creek.

The area's premier challenge is the 5.5-mile climb up Road 2610 to the summit's unmatched winter view. Beware of avalanche danger on steep roadsides.

49
NORTH FORK JOHN DAY

The largest wild area in the Blue Mountains, this sprawling complex of wilderness lands encompasses two entire mountain ranges—the craggy Elkhorns and the Greenhorns—as well as a major river, the North Fork John Day. Here roam a good share of the Blue Mountains' 52,000 elk and 150,000 mule deer.

Though separated by paved or well-graveled roads, each of the three units of this wilderness has plenty of room for day hikes or long backpacking trips. Anthony Lake is a scenic center for hikers in summer and skiers in winter.

Climate

Snowfall is heaviest in the Elkhorn Mountains, where the Anthony Lake Ski Area usually operates from Thanksgiving to April 15. Snow blocks hiking trails over 7000 feet until early July, but the lower part of the North Fork John Day River Trail is clear as early as April.

Annual precipitation hits 45 inches in the Elkhorns, but drops to 20 inches in the western canyons. Summers are dry. October, though generally pleasant, may bring sudden snowstorms. Night temperatures can dip below freezing even in summer.

Plants and Wildlife

This is elk country, where 800-pound bulls with 5-foot-wide antlers bugle

Mountain goat in the Elkhorn Range.

challenges to rival males each fall. More than twice as large as mule deer, elk bulls assemble harems of up to 60 cows during the August to November rut. In this season, listen at dawn or dusk for the bulls' bugles: snorts that rise to a clarinet-like whistle and end with several low grunts. Also look for saplings stripped of bark to mark territory, and elk wallows—small bogs dug by hooves and laced with urine as a bull's private orgy site.

Many of the area's deer and elk winter in the Bridge Creek Wildlife Area south of Ukiah (not shown on map), but others remain, able to survive in this high country's heavy snows by shifting daily between north- and south-facing slopes. Dense conifer thickets on north-facing canyon slopes provide shelter from snow and wind. South-facing slopes are sparsely forested, allowing

Location: 61 mi S of Pendleton, 13 mi W of Baker City

Size: 617 sq mi

Status: 190 sq mi designated wilderness (1984)

Terrain: snowy mountain ranges, rugged river canyons, forested benchlands, cirque lakes

Elevation: 3356'-9106'

Management: Umatilla NF, Wallowa-Whitman NF, Malheur NF, Prineville District BLM

Maps: www.digital-topo-map.com or similar Internet site

winds to expose the dried grass important to elk for food.

The highest of the Elkhorns' glacial lakes appear to have just been released from a glacier's grip, while others have filled in to become marshy wildflower meadows. Lower basins have grown over with subalpine fir and Engelmann spruce. Reintroduced mountain goats have become so common near the range's highest point, Rock Creek Butte, that they sometimes nibble on backpackers' gear for salt.

Recovering from occasional dredging of stream gravels for gold 1920-54, the North Fork John Day River now provides spawning grounds for 70 percent of the John Day River's steelhead and 90 percent of its Chinook salmon. The fish runs, which peak in late August, help feed a population of bald eagles.

Geology

The granite and scrambled sedimentary rock here reflect the Blue Mountains' history as a volcanic island archipelago in the Pacific Ocean 210 to 270 million years ago. The Earth's crustal movement "rafted" this oceanic debris onto the advancing North American continent about 200 million years ago. Later bubbles of relatively light granitic rock (known as batholiths) rose through the sediment to form the granite cores of the Elkhorn and Greenhorn Ranges. When magma cools slowly to form large-crystaled granitic rock, gold and silver tend to collect along the rock's quartz veins—hence this area's colorful mining history.

Columbia River basalt flows buried the area about 15 million years ago. Basalt rimrock remains on the western benchlands, but erosion has stripped this lava from the rising Elkhorn and Greenhorn Mountains. Relatively recent Ice Age glaciers scalloped the ranges with scores of U-shaped glacial valleys.

History

Sumpter, Bourne, Granite, and Greenhorn are picturesque mining boomtowns from 1860s gold strikes. Ancient prospects, tailings, and a few small active mines dot hills near the towns, though the easy placer diggings are gone. Part

Anthony Lake, accessible by a paved road, is a popular entry to the wilderness beyond.

of the North Fork John Day River Trail follows an abandoned mining ditch once used to bring water to gold sluices.

A floating gold dredge, now restored as a visitable state heritage site in Sumpter, once churned many valleys in these mountains to gravel wastelands.

Near Sumpter's dredge museum is the depot for the Sumpter Valley Railroad. Known as the "Stump Dodger" because it logged ponderosa pines from these valleys in the 1890s, the narrow-gauge railroad has been restored by volunteers. A steam locomotive pulls passengers on 5 miles of restored track on summer weekends. For rates and schedules check *www.svry.com*.

HIKING & BACKPACKING

The most popular day hikes explore the Elkhorn Mountains' alpine scenery. Anthony Lake, ringed with rugged peaks, is easily accessible from Interstate 84, making it the only destination in the entire area likely to be crowded.

For starters, take the 1-mile trail around Anthony Lake. A worthwhile 0.9-mile side trail skirts rugged Gunsight Mountain to Black Lake. Another easy side trail loops 2.3 miles from the south end of Anthony Lake, ascending Parker Creek to the Hoffer Lakes and returning down a ski area service road. From the Hoffer Lakes loop, however, the area's best view is just another 1.3 miles away and 900 feet up; hike up the service road to a pass and keep left on a path up a craggy ridge to The Lakes Observation Point.

For an excellent sample of the high Elkhorns' scenery, take the 8.2-mile loop trail from Anthony Lake entirely around Angell Peak and Gunsight Mountain. The well-built path gains only 1300 feet along the way, passing views of Crawfish Meadow. To turn this loop into a backpacking trip, detour a mile to campsites at Dutch Flat Lake.

Other lakes make good goals. Pretty Crawfish Lake is 1.3 or 1.4 miles from

Road 73, depending on the trailhead. From Crawfish Lake, it's easy to bushwhack 1 mile due east along the inlet creek up to Crawfish Meadows' wildflowers. Van Patten Lake, in an alpine cirque, is a steep 1.5-mile hike from the defunct Little Alps Ski Area 2.6 miles east of Anthony Lake on Road 73; the hike begins up an old service road. Nearby, the 7-mile trail to Dutch Flat Lake ascends a cattle-grazed, U-shaped glacial valley from Road 7307.

The spectacular Elkhorn Crest Trail contours from pass to pass for 22.8 miles along the granite backbone of the Elkhorn Range from Anthony Lake to Marble Pass. By sticking to the crest, the trail narrowly misses a number of pretty alpine lakes, so plan on taking a few short detours, especially if you are backpacking. Day hikers starting from the Elkhorn Crest Trailhead on paved Road 73 near Anthony Lake can aim for Black Lake (0.9 mile), Dutch Flat Lake

NORTH FORK JOHN DAY

0   1   2   3   4mi
0   2   4   6km
N

Hwy 244
10 mi

River

51

Grande
Ronde

Grande

Woodley

Ronde

River

La Grande
Watershed

Marion
Pt

43

51

5185

Anthony
Butte
6805'

43

411

I-84 at
North
Powder
6 mi

Grande
Ronde Lake

Mud
Lake

73

4980

7307

Anthony Lake

Bulger
Flat

Anthony
Lake

Van
Patten

7810'

Angell Pk
8646'

Dutch Flat L

Dutch Flat Cr

Twin
Mtn

Rock Creek

Crawfish L

Elkhorn

N Fk Powder R

Haines 4 mi

North Fork
John Day

73

380

5550'

7800'

5850

Lost

M

7301

Red Mtn L

5520

5200'

N Fk John Day
Wilderness

Baldy Cr

Mt
Ruth

6150'

Red Mtn

Summit
Lake

Killamacue
L

Hunt Mtn

Crane
Flat

73

7345

Cable
Cove
Area

7500'
Cracker
Saddle

Rock Cr

7088

Mining

Cracker Cr

5505

Elkhorn

Crest
Trail

N

Rock Creek
Lake

Pine Cr

(See Elkhorn Mountains Close-up)

Baldy
Lake
P

Ireland
Mtn 8321'

Downie L
6650'

Bourne

Rock 9106
Cr Bu

Pine Cr
Reservoir

Goodrich
L

Granite

6010'

130

Twin Lakes

Elkhorn Pk
8934'

Baker
City
14mi

Boundary

7370

Mountains

7542'

030

6510

6550

Marble
Pass

McCully
Forks

73

Deer
Creek

Lake Cr

Blue
Spring

Sumpter

Dredge

Railroad

Hwy 26
23 mi

7

Baker
24 mi

Twin Lakes and Rock Creek Butte, at the southern end of the Elkhorn Crest Trail.

(4.3 miles), Lost Lake (6.4 miles), or even Summit Lake (10 miles).

The Marble Pass Trailhead at the southern end of the Elkhorn Crest Trail is accessible only by rugged, high-clearance vehicles. From Baker City, drive 10th Street north a mile, turn left on Pocahontas Road for 7.6 zigzagging miles, and go straight on gravel Marble Creek Road 6510 for 7.8 increasingly awful miles to the pass. From there, a lovely 4.8-mile hike leads to Twin Lakes, a backpackable destination in a gorgeous alpine bowl below Rock Creek Butte. For a view across Baker City's valley to the distant Wallowas, continue an extra mile along the Elkhorn Crest Trail and scramble cross-country up 0.8 mile to reach Rock Creek Butte's summit. Ex-

Baldy Lake from Ireland Mountain's lookout.

pect mountain goats along the way.

If you don't want to risk your vehicle on the rugged road to Marble Pass, access the southern end of the Elkhorn Crest Trail via the Twin Lakes Trailhead on Road 030. To find it, drive Highway 7 east of Phillips Lake. Between mileposts 28 and 29, turn north on Deer Creek Road for 4.2 miles, and go straight on Road 030 for 3.8 miles to its end. From there, a 3.1-mile trail gains 2270 feet to Twin Lakes.

Repeated forest fires have left snags along the faint trails that begin at the 1934 Peavy Cabin on Road 380. Still, it's fun to rent the historic log cabin ($40 a night; check *www.recreation.gov* for reservations). To tackle an adventurous 10.8-mile loop, follow the faint Peavy Trail from the end of Road 380 up 1700 feet in 3.6 miles to Cracker Saddle, turn left on the Elkhorn Crest Trail for 4.4 scenic miles, and return to Peavy Cabin on the steep, 2.8-mile Cunningham Trail.

Rock Creek Lake fills a breathtakingly stark, treeless cirque, backed by the cliffs of the Blue Mountains' highest peak, 9,106-foot Rock Creek Butte. The 3.5-mile trail to this beautiful lake would be more popular, but the trailhead access up Rock Creek Road is miserably rough. Likewise, the nice hiking routes to scenic Pine Creek Reservoir, Killamacue Lake, and Red Mountain Lake all require horrific drives on steep, rocky roads. Drive only as far as you feel comfortable; then park and walk.

On the west side of the Elkhorns, a quiet 6.3-mile trail up Baldy Creek from Road 73 leads to Baldy Lake, a backpacking destination overtowered by Ireland Mountain. A 1.2-mile shortcut path to the lake begins off Road 7345, but requires some route-finding skills.

For a hike to Ireland Mountain's staffed lookout tower, drive 12.2 miles west of Sumpter on Road 73, turn right on Road 7370 for 3 miles (keeping left at unmarked forks after 0.6 and 2.4 miles), and turn right on Road 100 for 0.3 mile to a trailhead sign. Hike up abandoned Road 130 for 240 yards to a confusing junction and continue straight up a ridgecrest path 2 miles to a signpost. The lookout is 1.1 mile up to the left, while Downie Lake is 1.3 miles down to the right.

The Greenhorn Mountains, dotted with small, active mines, offer trails and old mining tracks among broad, subalpine summits. Start with the lovely 4.8-mile trail from the Olive Lake Campground past Upper Reservoir's marshy meadow and Saddle Camp to Dupratt Spring's pass, a campable site on a rocky ridge between deep, glacier-carved valleys. For a 360-degree view, scramble a half mile east to Ben Harrison Peak. For a loop, follow an old road-trail 2.3 miles northeast and fork left on a 2.9-mile path through Lost Meadow to a Road 10 trailhead. From there you can either walk the road 1.4 miles back to the Olive Lake Campground or return on a 1.7-mile connector trail that follows a portion of a historic redwood pipeline.

To explore more of the Greenhorn Mountains, park where Road 45 bridges South Fork Desolation Creek and hike a creekside path 7 miles to the head of that glacial valley. Or start at primitive Head O' Boulder Campground, just below Indian Rock's staffed lookout tower, and either follow the level Princess Trail 6 miles east to Dupratt Spring's pass, or take the Squaw Rock Trail 3.1 miles north, descending Big Creek to Road 45.

The winding, 24.6-mile North Fork John Day River Trail traces a rimrock canyon with new vistas at every bend. Forests plunge down 1000-foot slopes into the brawling stream. The dilapidated log cabins of gold mining claims remain along the trail have mostly returned to public ownership, but often have backpacking campsites nearby.

Day hikers can easily sample this impressive canyon trail at several points.

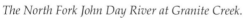

The North Fork John Day River at Granite Creek.

The "Bigfoot Hilton," an old mining cabin on the North Fork John Day River Trail.

The most popular route follows Granite Creek 3.3 miles from Road 1035 to a footbridge across the North Fork John Day and a meadow with a log cabin ruin. At the canyon's eastern end, hikers starting from the North Fork John Day Campground can follow the river 2.6 miles to a bridge across rushing Trout Creek near a small, public log cabin known as the Bigfoot Hilton. For a 13.5-mile loop, continue 4 miles downriver to a cold, deep ford, turn left on the Crane Creek Trail to a trailhead on Road 73, and follow the 2.6-mile North Crane connector trail back to your car. At the canyon's western end, Road 5506 provides another river-level access to the North Fork John Day River Trail, but this remote road is far rougher than the other access routes.

Those unable to arrange a car shuttle for end-to-end backpacking trips along the Elkhorn Crest or North Fork John Day River Trails should consider several loop hike alternatives. A 19.8-mile, figure-eight-shaped loop from Anthony Lake follows the Elkhorn Crest Trail south to Cracker Saddle and returns via Lost Lake. A 31-mile loop from the Granite Creek trailhead climbs from Dixson Bar to Moon Meadows before returning via China Meadows and the upper portion of the North Fork John Day River Trail.

CLIMBING

The Elkhorn Mountains feature 300-foot-tall granite cliffs, rare in Oregon. All peaks have walk-up sides. Perhaps the most scenic and convenient place to test the granite is on the giant tilted rock faces beside the Hoffer Lakes, 1.5 miles south of Anthony Lake.

SNOWSHOEING & SKIING

The Anthony Lake Ski Area charges a fee to use their 10 kilometers of groomed Nordic trails, including the 1-mile loop around Anthony Lake and the scenic side trip to the Hoffer Lakes' basin. However, Nordic skiers and snowshoers have many other options. Start with a 1.5-mile jaunt past the east edge of Anthony Lake to Black Lake.

Van Patten Lake, set in a narrow basin below Van Patten Ridge's cliffs, is a steep 1.7-mile climb from plowed Road 73. Iced-over Crawfish Lake and broad, snowy Crawfish Meadow are also good destinations. Ski to these goals cross-country from the top of the Anthony Lake ski lift, or else ski 4.3 miles along Road 73 (unplowed west of Anthony Lake) to spur Road 216 and follow a 1.6-mile trail to the lake. The two routes can be connected to make a loop.

Take the Anthony Lake chairlift to start the dramatic, 7-mile loop around Angell Peak. Pass up this challenging trip, however, if weather or avalanche danger threatens—or if you find a cornice blocking the pass on the Elkhorn Crest Trail east of Angell Peak.

BOATING

The North Fork John Day is not generally considered navigable through its wilderness portion due to boulders and low water levels. Raft and kayak trips on the North Fork commence at Dale and follow 40 miles of class 2+ whitewater to Monument.

Only boats without motors are allowed on small, scenic Anthony Lake.

50
NORTHERN BLUE MOUNTAINS

One of the roughest barriers confronting Oregon Trail pioneers in the 1840s and 1850s, the northern Blue Mountains still harbor enough wilderness to challenge hikers and hide elk.

Climate

Autumns are renowned both for delightful Indian summer weather and surprise blizzards. Shade is at a premium during summer's heat, especially on the unforested, south-facing slopes. Annual precipitation—mostly winter snow—ranges from 30 inches in the canyons to 45 inches on the tablelands. The ski season at Spout Springs runs from mid-November to mid-April.

Plants and Wildlife

Road building and logging have largely been confined to the area's plateaus, leaving wilderness in the steeply dissected canyonlands. There, only the relatively wet and shady north-facing slopes support forests—chiefly grand fir and Douglas fir. As a result, nearly every ridge offers a view to the south of forest and a view to the north of seemingly uninterrupted, dry grasslands,

Bull elk.

giving the illusion that one is always on the edge of a steppe.

The low-elevation creekbanks sprout lush foliage, with sword fern, wild ginger, Oregon grape, yew, alder, wild cherry, stinging nettle, and snowberry. Look for beaver ponds and gnawed trees along the North Fork Umatilla. Expect to find boggy wallows made by bull elk along the North Fork Meacham and Five Points Creek.

Geology

The northern Blue Mountains do not

Location: 26 mi E of Pendleton, 9 mi NW of La Grande

Size: 233 sq mi

Status: 32 sq mi designated wilderness (1984)

Terrain: plateaus cut by steep, partly forested canyons.

Elevation: 2000'-6064'

Management: Umatilla NF, Wallowa-Whitman NF

Map: North Fork Umatilla Wilderness (USFS)

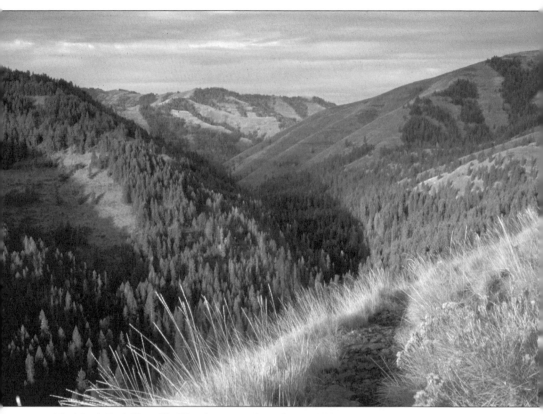

The North Fork Umatilla River's canyon from Coyote Ridge.

resemble the southern part of the same range. Forty miles to the south the Blue Mountains are craggy, granite peaks. Here the range consists of dissected basalt tablelands.

The difference is that when the Columbia River lava flows spread out from the Grande Ronde area 17 million years ago, the lava floods mostly spared the southern Blue Mountains. Here, flow upon flow of lava buried the landscape 4000 feet deep. Even where subsequent uplifting has allowed creeks to cut the leveled terrain into a jagged canyonland, the older rock presumably below has still not been exposed.

History

This mountain range once divided the Cayuse and Nez Perce Indian tribes.

Lookingglass Creek commemorates Nez Perce leader Apash-wa-hay-ikt, dubbed Chief Lookingglass because he often carried a hand mirror.

The first white men here were crossing the continent to establish a fur-trading post at Astoria in 1812. In 1827 botanist David Douglas hiked to the Blue Mountain crest and found 4-foot-tall yellow lupine blooming—possibly the rare Sabine lupine, found only in these uplands.

In 1836, missionaries Marcus and Narcissa Whitman rode on horseback across the range on a primitive route now interpreted by the Forest Service as the Whitman Route (south of Mount Emily, across Five Points Creek and Meacham Creek, then down Horseshoe Ridge toward Walla Walla). Marcus

← Weston 10 mi
Woodward
Tollgate
Bear Cr
Pendleton 26 mi →
204
3715
Coyote Cr
Woodward Cr
040
041
3719
Lookingglass Creek
8306
Luger Spr
Grouse Pt
Bingham Springs
Corporation
Lick Cr
4400'
Coyote Ridge
5100'
Spout Springs 5448'
Woodland
Eagle Cr
Umatilla River
Umatilla N Fk
2356'
Umatilla River
North Fork Umatilla
Ninemile 5120'
Johnson Cr
3728
3725
Bobsled Cr
4000'
Bobsled Ridge
River
32
Wilderness
Buck Cr
4400'
330
High Ridge
31
Ridge
South Fork
2591'
4560'
Buck Mtn
Elk
2850'
4540'
Thomas Cr
3150
3128
Umatilla
South Fork
Goodman
Shimmiehorn Cr
The Shimmiehorn
3133
Ridge
3130
Black Mtn
Dusty Saddle Canyon
Ruckel Junction
32
204
Elgin 2 mi →
3128
Hellhole Cr
31
Thimbleberry Mtn
Big Saddle
Trap Cr
158
5411
N Fk
Meacham
Huckleberry Mtn
Poll Cr
2600'
Hoskins Cr
The Knob
Gray Rock
3316
31
Bear Creek
3113
Green Mtn
Herron Ridge
3720
Summit
4800'
Points Cr
I-84 at Kamela 11 mi →
31
Five
4000'
Grandview Spr
Mt Emily
6064'
Summerville
Imbler 2 mi →

NORTHERN BLUE MOUNTAINS
0   1   2   3mi
0 1 2 3 4km
N

Whitman returned in 1843 leading a wagon train. Within five years, 9,000 settlers had followed on what became the Oregon Trail, winching their wagons onto the tablelands west of La Grande to avoid the brushy canyon bottoms.

HIKING & BACKPACKING

A cluster of campgrounds near the forks of the Umatilla River form the hub of eight radiating hiking trails. All of these paths gain some 2000 feet in elevation on their way to progressively higher and more compelling canyon viewpoints. The trails that follow creeks climb gently at first, while the ridge trails start out briskly.

Only three of the eight trails connect, so up-and-back day hikes are customary. Those who wish to hike the trails only downhill must arrange car shuttles to the remote upper trailheads.

The most heavily trafficked trail follows the North Fork Umatilla River for 2.7 nearly level miles from a trailhead near Umatilla Campground to a good picnic spot in an old-growth fir forest at the mouth of Coyote Creek. Here crowds thin out, because the trail then climbs another 1.6 miles along the river and switchbacks 4.8 miles up grassy Coyote Ridge to Road 041 on Tollgate's plateau.

Several less crowded trails nearby also feature rushing streams. One traces the South Fork Umatilla River 1.8 miles before petering out in brush. Another, the Lick Creek Trail, charges up Lick Creek's ravine 2.3 miles and then follows a ridge 1 mile to an upper trailhead on Road 3715; an alternate spur

Ninemile Ridge.

follows a ridgecrest to end at Grouse Mountain's viewpoint.

Three paths begin at the Buck Creek Trailhead. If you go straight on the well-built Buck Creek Trail, you'll amble upstream 3 miles to a ford and climb a ridge 3 miles to a four-way junction with the Umatilla Rim Trail, a connector route for loop hikes. If you start at the Buck Creek Trailhead but keep right on the faint, rough Buck Mountain Trail, you'll zoom up 2100 feet in 2.2 miles. At the top, the path contours along the canyon rim 5.7 miles (crossing clearcuts and logging roads) to the four-way junction mentioned above, making a 13.9-mile loop possible.

The third, and perhaps prettiest, trail from the Buck Creek Trailhead veers left and switchbacks up Ninemile Ridge at a good grade. The route extends 6.5 miles to the Umatilla Rim Trail, but most people turn back at a summit after 3.6 miles. As with all of the local ridgeline hikes, the first mile has most of the elevation gain while the remaining miles follow an open, view-filled crest with wildflowers (cat's ears, paintbrush, balsamroot).

The 4.9-mile trail up Bobsled Ridge starts out with a tricky ford of the deep Umatilla River, then rockets uphill.

For canyon solitude, try the Lookingglass Creek area, east of Highway 204. After floods obliterated the original creekside trail in the 1990s, the Forest Service built a new trail system along the canyon's rim and ridges. These trails are open to mountain bikes. The Lookingglass Rim Trail starts at the Spout Springs ski area's parking lot and contours along the rimrock's edge for 3.9 miles, largely on abandoned roads.

The Eagle Ridge Trail starts at the Woodland Campground entrance, crosses Road 3725, and follows a ridge 4.9 miles down to a footbridge across Lookingglass Creek at the mouth of Eagle Creek—a good turnaround point.

Clarkia, a wildflower named for William Clark of the Lewis & Clark expedition.

On the far shore, the path climbs 1.2 miles to the primitive Luger Spring Campground on a spur of Road 6306.

The area's largest roadless tract has been named Hellhole by the Forest Service—a name that misrepresents the area's lovely canyon scenery. For proof of this, search out the long-abandoned trail down Bear Creek from the Summit Guard Station. The route gradually descends 6 miles through a cool, old-growth forest, then follows the clear North Fork Meacham Creek 2.5 miles to a grassy campsite at Pot Creek before climbing 3.5 miles to flat-topped Thimbleberry Mountain.

SNOWSHOEING & SKIING

Highway 204, plowed in winter, provides Nordic skiers and snowshoers with access to snowed-under roads on the tablelands fringing the North Fork Umatilla Wilderness. Expect competition from snowmobiles on routes near Tollgate. A good strategy is to find quieter routes along the rims of wilderness canyons. Top bets are the Lookingglass Rim Trail from Spout Springs, the Eagle Ridge Trail from the sno-park opposite Woodland Campground, and the Umatilla Rim Trail from Andies Prairie sno-park at the junction of Road 3728 and Highway 204.

Warm up at Spout Springs, a winter recreation center with three lifts, two day lodges, and a restaurant.

51

WENAHA-TUCANNON

This huge canyonland on the Oregon-Washington border supports the nation's highest elk population density. The excellent trail network, popular with equestrians, has room for extended backpacking trips.

The Timothy Springs Guard Station.

Climate

Snowfall from late November to April averages 8 to 12 feet at Oregon Butte and 1 to 2 feet along the Wenaha River. Trails to 4000 feet elevation clear of snow by early May, but higher routes may be blocked until June. August afternoon temperatures often exceed 100°F, while fierce winters bring weather as cold as -40°F and occasionally freeze the Grande Ronde River. Sudden snowstorms may interrupt autumn's cool, clear weather.

Plants and Wildlife

Elk dominate the area, but whitetail deer and big-eared mule deer are also plentiful. The herds move down from the mountains in winter to the Wenaha Wildlife Area, where the state supplies them with supplemental feed. These feeding stations are probably the best spot in Oregon to observe elk and deer. For a look at the herds, drive the road from Troy along Eden Bench from mid-January to late May.

Other mammals include whistling marmots, Columbia ground squirrels, snowshoe hares, black bears, mountain lions, coyotes, bobcats, and martens. Moose and wolves established footholds in Oregon here in 2008. Bald eagles winter along the Grande Ronde River. Chukar and grouse startle hikers by bursting out of trailside brush.

The trailside brush with elegant white berries is snowberry. When Lewis and Clark passed north of here they collected snowberry seeds and brought them to Thomas Jefferson, who delighted in the "very handsome little shrub" and presented a bush to Lafayette's aunt in Paris as a gift from America. Snowberry is now considered an invasive alien weed in some European gardens.

Old-growth cottonwood, fir, and ponderosa pine line the Wenaha River. Sparse bunchgrass covers the steep canyons' dry, south-facing slopes. Dense

Location: 50 mi N of Enterprise, 28 mi E of Walla Walla

Size: 363 sq mi total; 122 sq mi in Oregon

Status: 277 sq mi designated wilderness; 104 sq mi in Oregon (1978); Grande Ronde and Wenaha federal wild and scenic rivers

Terrain: steep, partly forested river canyons, dissected plateaus

Elevation: 1700'-6401'

Management: Umatilla NF

Map: Wenaha-Tucannon Wilderness (USFS)

The Wenaha River.

mixed conifer forests cover other slopes and tablelands. Expect wildflowers in June and the beautiful red foliage of nonpoisonous sumac bushes in October.

Geology

This area was the main source of the Columbia River lava flows that buried the landscape from Utah to Astoria 15 million years ago with up to 5000 feet of basalt. For proof of this look in the canyons, where stream erosion has cut deep into the old lava plain. Running vertically through the basalt layers are occasional, wall-like outcroppings of jointed rock, looking almost like stacked cordwood. These are dikes, formed when the lava oozed up from the earth and squeezed into cracks on the way.

The distinctive red layers between rimrock levels are old soil horizons, indicating that forests had time to grow for thousands of years between lava eruptions.

History

The Nez Perce name "Wenaha" signifies that this area was once the "ha" (domain) of Wenak, a Nez Perce chief.

HIKING & BACKPACKING

Part of the wonder of this area is its enormity. Even day trips open vistas of seemingly endless canyonlands, wild rivers, and rugged ridges.

Troy (population 58) offers the only river-level trailhead on the Oregon side. Start here for a 6.4-mile walk up the Wenaha's arid, winding canyon to a footbridge and backpacking campsites near the mouth of Crooked Creek. The trail begins 0.4 mile from downtown at a switchback of the Bartlett Road toward Pomeroy.

The two best driving routes to Troy are not shown on the map. An all-year paved road to Troy follows the Grande Ronde River up from Boggan's Oasis, Washington, which is 32 miles south of Lewiston on Highway 129. To reach Troy from the Oregon side, take Highway 3 north from Enterprise for 35 miles, turn left at a sign for Flora, and follow a steep gravel road (icy in winter) for 15 miles to Troy.

WENAHA - TUCANNON

A good way to sample the area's rugged scenery is to hike from a canyon rim down to one of the rivers. Of the many possible routes, here are three that are neither too steep nor too long: The Hoodoo Trail switchbacks 3 miles from Road 6214 to a river ford in a narrow part of the Wenaha River's chasm near Fairview Bar, losing just 1400 feet. A 3.5-mile route from the Three Forks trailhead loses 1600 feet on its way to Crooked Creek. And finally, those who prefer a longer, gentler trail through forest might try the 4.6-mile path from the Elk Flats Campground down 2100 feet to a knee-deep ford at Wenaha Forks. The canyon-bottom flat at Wenaha Forks features big cottonwoods, snowberry and gravel bars with campsites.

Other day trips follow ridgelines to high viewpoints. Start at Indian Campground on Road 64 for a 3.4-mile walk to Round Butte and a view down the length of the Wenaha River; the final quarter mile to the summit is cross-country. A different day trip climbs to the fire lookout on Oregon Butte, the wilderness's highest point, with a view worth the 2.2-mile hike from Tepee Campground.

Trailheads on the southwest side of the wilderness are best reached via Walla Walla or Tollgate. From Walla Walla, take Highway 12 east 3 miles and turn right onto paved Mill Creek Road, which becomes Road 65. From Tollgate (located on Oregon Highway 204 halfway between Weston and Elgin) take gravel Road 64 for 11.5 miles to the popular Jubilee Lake Campground, shown on the lower left corner of the map.

Much of the vast backcountry can only be reached by overnight trips. A classic trip follows the 31.4-mile Wenaha River Trail from Timothy Spring Campground to Troy. This path fords small, calf-deep streams at the 2.3-mile and 4.5-mile marks, but requires no fords of the tricky Wenaha River itself.

Of the many possible loop trips, here are three suggestions for exploring the wilderness's interior. An 18.2-mile route begins at the Twin Buttes trailhead on Road 300, follows Grizzly Bear Ridge's mesa to the Wenaha River, then returns to Twin Buttes via Wenaha Forks and Slick Ear Creek. For a 29.2-mile loop, start at Diamond Peak, follow the ridge to Indian Corral, descend Trout Creek and Crooked Creek, then return via the trail up Melton Creek. A spectacular 41-mile loop visits Oregon Butte, Weller Butte, Moore Flat, Crooked Creek, and Indian Corral. Access this loop from any of the eastern trailheads.

Just west of the Wenaha-Tucannon area, the South Fork Walla Walla River rushes through Box Canyon, a rocky gorge where stream-loving water ouzels dip and sing. Day hikers can reach Box Canyon by switchbacking down 1900 feet in 3.3 miles from a trailhead near Mottet Campground. This scenic path crosses the river on a footbridge by a small backpacking campsite. Keep left and amble downstream a mile or two to viewpoints in the narrowest part of Box Canyon. In all, the South Fork Walla Walla Trail extends 18.4 miles from Road 65 downstream to Road 600, although the lower portion of this route shows evidence of all-terrain vehicle use.

SNOWSHOEING & SKIING

The best access to winter snow is via Dayton, Washington. Take Fourth Street to plowed Road 64 and the Ski Bluewood ski area. From there, ride the lift to the canyon rim and set out on snowshoes or cross-country skis. Snowed-under Roads 46 and 300 provide well-defined, nearly level ridgetop routes with views into the North Fork Wenaha River canyon. The trail along narrow Buck Ridge stays level for 2 miles and then descends dangerously. Another tour from Road 46 climbs slightly for 2.5 miles to Burnt Flat's plateau.

BOATING

The Grande Ronde River winds through a 2400-foot-deep canyon of steep forests and interesting basalt formations. Canoeists can navigate the river except in high water, from April to June, which kayakers often prefer. Low water grounds most craft in September.

The run begins at Minam on Highway 84, follows the Wallowa River 8.5 miles to Rondowa, then continues down the Grande Ronde River 28.5 miles to Powwatka Bridge, 8 miles south of Troy. All rapids in this section can be scouted by boat. The most serious of these is the (class 3) Minam Roller, 1.5 miles below the Minam put-in.

From Powwatka Bridge, boaters can continue 26 miles to Boggan's Oasis (on the Enterprise-Lewiston highway), and then another 26 miles to Heller's Bar on the Snake River. In low water The Narrows, below Boggan's Oasis, poses a class 4 hazard.

Troy, at the mouth of the Wenaha River.

52
JOSEPH CANYON

Birthplace of the Nez Perce tribe's famous Chief Joseph, this stark canyon features the same kind of awe-inspiring scenery as the larger Hells Canyon nearby.

Climate

The canyon's wildflowers bloom and the bunchgrass greens April to June. In summer, temperatures top 100° F. Fall is dry, infrequently interrupted by brief snowstorms. Winter temperatures remain below freezing for weeks at a stretch. Highway 3, though plowed of snow, is often icy and treacherous from December to March. Annual precipitation is an arid 15 inches.

Plants and Wildlife

The canyon's sides are corrugated with steep gulches. Forest grows only on north-facing gulch slopes, while bunchgrass grows on dry south-facing slopes. The result is the distinctly stripy vegetative cover popular with elk, who need to shift between shelter and grazing areas, especially in winter.

Every decade or so a wildfire sweeps through the canyon, performing the maintenance work traditionally reserved for fire here—clearing out deadfall, brush, and mixed conifer thickets, while leaving the old-growth ponderosa pine intact.

Bring binoculars to distinguish raptors in flight—golden and bald eagles, goshawks, Cooper's hawks, and sharp-shinned hawks. All of these nest here, as do blue grouse, ruffed grouse, and chukars. Joseph Creek and its tributaries provide spawning grounds for salmon and steelhead.

Geology

This canyon exposes some of the state's most interesting basalt formations. The area was a major source of the colossal Columbia River basalt flows 15 million years ago. Not only are dozens of horizontal basalt flows visible in cross-section, but basalt dikes show as vertical stripes, formed when the upwelling lava squeezed into cracks. The basalt has eroded into cliffs, caves, and crags, including domed Haystack Rock.

When the land here began to rise about 13 million years ago, creeks swiftly cut canyons into the lava plain, following the areas' north-south fault lines.

History

Chief Joseph, leader of the Wallowa band of the Nez Perce, was born in a cave along this portion of Joseph Creek. The original 6.5-million-acre Nez Perce Reservation of 1855 included Joseph Canyon. A divisive 1863 treaty left the tribe with only a small tract of land in Idaho. The Wallowa band refused to sign the treaty or to recognize it. President Grant upheld their right to the Wallowa Valley and Joseph Canyon in 1873, but under mounting pressure

Location: 20 mi N of Enterprise

Size: 39 sq mi

Status: undesignated wilderness

Terrain: steep, sparsely forested canyon

Elevation: 2400'-4920'

Management: Wallowa-Whitman NF

Maps: Table Mountain, Roberts Butte, Sled Springs (USGS)

*Joseph Canyon
from the Highway 3 viewpoint.*

JOSEPH CANYON
HELLS CANYON - NORTH

0   1   2   3mi
0   1   2   3   4km   N

Hellers Bar
15 mi

250
1450
840

Cook
Hot
Spr

×1950'

Cherry

Snake

Dry

Frog Pond
Butte

4680

Cold Spring Ridge

Cook Cr

Cr

Deadhorse

2300'×
Cherry Cr
Camp

Salmon Bar

Mountain Sheep
Rapids

Salmon R

I d a h o

River

5210'

Five Points

Ridge

5350'
×

Oldman Cr

Knight Cr

950'

Imnaha
Rapids

Warm Springs
Rapids

Box
Spr

788

Eureka Bar

4260

2700'
×

Dug Bar

4625

760

Eureka
Cr

Ridge

×4530'

Imnaha
River Trail

Nee Me Poo
(Nez Perce) Trail

1023

×1840'

1870' ×

Dug

Hells

46

Cemetery

Tulley Cr

R

Cow Cr
Ranch

Canyon

Deep Cr

Buckhorn
Spring

G

Imnaha Bridge

Wilderness

780

5331'
Buckhorn
Viewpoint

1170'×

G

Summit

(See Hells Canyon
Center Map)

Imnaha

Cow Cr

Ridge

46

Lightning Cr

Thorn
Creek

Litch
Ranch

Thomason
Meadow

5220
×

Corral Cr

4260

Zumwalt 8 mi
Enterprise 33 mi

Imnaha 14 mi

G

from settlers, the Army in 1877 ordered the Indians to leave, setting in motion the Nez Perce's famous, ill-fated march toward freedom in Canada. After his capture in Montana, Chief Joseph was never allowed to return to his Oregon homeland.

In 1997, the Bonneville Power Administration admitted that its dams had decimated fish runs pledged to the Nez Perce by treaty, and offered the tribe financial compensation. The Nez Perce used the money to buy the canyon's 10,300-acre Joseph Creek Ranch, to be managed for wildlife and cultural values.

HIKING & BACKPACKING

Begin with a visit to the Joseph Canyon Viewpoint on Highway 3. West of

Joseph Creek below Table Mountain.

the highway stretches an unassuming plain of forest and wheatfields, while to the east the land suddenly falls away into a gaping, 2100-foot-deep chasm.

The Davis Creek Trail offers the gentlest route into this canyonland. Drive 9 miles south of the Joseph Canyon Viewpoint (or 21 miles north of Enterprise). Between mileposts 23 and 22, turn east on Road 174 and keep left for 0.3 mile to the Chico Trailhead. The trail angles down through park-like stands of old-growth ponderosa pine, losing 900 feet in 1 mile to Davis Creek. Intensive cattle grazing has hammered the canyon bottom here. The official trail then crosses Starvation Ridge 2.3 miles to Swamp Creek (gaining 700 feet and losing 1250 feet), but it's also possible to follow cattle trails 9 miles down Davis and Swamp Creeks downstream to Joseph Creek.

Adventurers with good shoes and sound knees can hike to the bottom of Joseph Canyon in just 2 miles by following the steep, abandoned Wilder Trail down from the Joseph Canyon Viewpoint on Highway 3. To avoid the cliffs below the viewpoint, first hike north along the canyon rim 0.2 miles, then descend a rounded ridge past the remains of a log cabin. The faint trail heads southwest halfway down, but is easy to lose.

At the bottom, another unmaintained route follows the winding creek through its cliff-edged gorge—a narrow oasis of green shaded by stately ponderosa pines. Bring creek-wading sneakers because the cold, calf-deep creek crosses the narrow canyon often. Private land blocks creek bushwhackers 2.3 miles downstream from the Wilder Trail terminus and 6.8 miles upstream at the Joseph Creek Ranch.

The grassy edge of Table Mountain's forested plateau affords a sweeping view of the entire canyon and the distant Wallowa Mountains. Haystack Rock provides an easy cross-country goal across the grassy slopes from Road 4650.

53
HELLS CANYON

The deepest river gorge in the United States, Hells Canyon inspires awe for its sheer size. From the gentle wildflower meadows on its rim, this chasm gapes like the ragged edge of a broken planet. Basalt rimrock and stark, treeless terraces alternate downward toward a tiny curve at the bottom: the brawling whitewater of the mighty Snake River, over a vertical mile below. And stacked 9000 feet high on the Idaho rim loom the crags of the snowy Seven Devils Mountains.

Climate

Two different climates prevail here at once. Heavy snows drape the subalpine rim from November to May or June, while the relatively balmy, arid canyon bottom receives less than 10 inches of precipitation in an entire year. Summer temperatures often hit a sweltering 100° F along the river but remain in the 60s on the rim, where nights can freeze in any season. Spring and fall are pleasant in the canyon.

Plants and Wildlife

Bring binoculars to spot big-eared mule deer and herds of up to 100 elk from miles away in this open canyonland. Also watch for mountain goats, with shaggy coats and spike horns, and

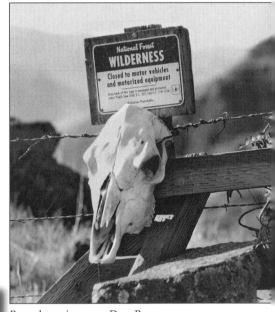

Boundary sign near Dug Bar.

Location: 80 mi E of Baker City, 36 mi E of Enterprise

Size: 761 sq mi

Status: 336 sq mi designated wilderness (1975, 1984), Snake and Imnaha federal wild and scenic rivers, national recreation area

Terrain: immense unforested chasm, whitewater river, forested tablelands, snowpeaks, lakes

Elevation: 840'-9393'

Management: Hells Canyon National Recreation Area, Wallowa-Whitman National Forest

Maps: Hells Canyon NRA, Wild and Scenic Snake River (USFS)

bighorn sheep, with curling horns. The black bears in Hells Canyon are a distinctive cinnamon brown.

Wolves had long been extinct in the Pacific Northwest, but they were reintroduced in Idaho in the 1990s and have since begun crossing Hells Canyon into Oregon on their own.

Birds include herons and non-migrating geese, enticed to year-round residency by the river's mild climate.

The Snake River itself provides rare habitat for giant white sturgeon up to 12 feet long. Sea runs of salmon and

The Nez Perce crossed the Snake River at Dug Bar — now the route of the Nee-Me-Poo Trail.

steelhead died forever from the entire upper Snake River system when the Idaho Power Company built the Hells Canyon, Oxbow, and Brownlee dams in 1958-64 with inadequate fish-passing facilities. The company has since built a hatchery on the Rapid River in an attempt to perpetuate Snake River strains of fish in the free-flowing Salmon River system.

In April and May the canyon slopes glow green with bunchgrass. Flowers include tiny pink phlox and prickly pear cactus. In June, red paintbrush and yellow desert parsley carpet rim meadows.

The canyon turns brown in summer, but balsamroot brightens river benches with miles of little sunflowers. Summer is the only likely time to spot rattlesnakes. By October most gulches flame with the beautiful scarlet leaves of (nonpoisonous) sumac bushes. Sumac's relative, poison oak, grows in low-elevation creek bottoms.

Geology

This enormous chasm did not exist as recently as 16 million years ago. For proof of this, note that Columbia River basalt flows of that age are continuous across the Oregon and Idaho rims.

Surprisingly, Hells Canyon was not carved by the Snake River. The ancestral Snake flowed across Southern Oregon to the sea. When Great Basin faulting lifted large chunks of Eastern Oregon about 13 million years ago, the Snake backed up, creating a lake that covered most of southern Idaho. Meanwhile, north-south fractures from the Great Basin faults allowed Columbia tributaries to cut deeply into the new Northern Oregon uplands, carving the parallel canyons of the Imnaha, Salmon, and an unnamed creek that dead-ended in Hells Canyon. When this unnamed creek cut its canyon to the edge of the huge lake in Idaho, the waters suddenly poured northward to the Columbia, and the Snake River raged into Hells Canyon.

The canyon cuts through 4000 feet of Columbia River basalt to expose the older surface below. This light gray rock, forming the Snake's rugged Inner Gorge, consists of jumbled sedimentary and volcanic strata that began as a Pacific Ocean island chain 280 to 220 million years ago, and was scraped up as an ancient coastal range by the westward-moving North American continent.

At first it seems puzzling that the tablelands bordering Hells Canyon slope upward to the canyon's edge. Consider, however, the Earth's crust floats on a molten mantle. When Hells Canyon's erosion removed some 500 cubic miles of rock here, the crust floated upward like an emptied gravel barge. This in turn caused the river to cut the canyon still deeper. The Seven Devils Mountains, between the vast, empty canyons of the Salmon and Snake, have bobbed highest of all.

Ice Age glaciers ground out the many lake basins in the Seven Devils Mountains and rounded the valleys of the Imnaha River, Rapid River, and upper Granite Creek.

History

Pit house depressions along Tryon Creek testify to ancient habitation, as do petroglyphs at Willow Bar and elsewhere. Vandalism by pottery- and basket-seekers threatens study of the estimated 160 to 200 archeological sites in the canyon. All artifacts are federally protected, including arrowheads and old bottles.

Nez Perce Indians under Chief Toohoolhoolzote established domination of the canyon by obliterating a Shoshone village at Battle Creek. In 1877, U.S. Army negotiators took Toohoolhoolzote hostage in an attempt to convince the Nez Perce to move to a small Idaho reservation. The Wallowa band's Chief Joseph led 400 Indians and several thousand head of Appaloosa horses and cattle toward the reservation. The tribe marched down the Imnaha River and managed to cross the Snake in flood stage by using horsehide bundles as rafts. A 4.1-mile portion of the amazingly rugged route they followed is preserved as the Nee-Me-Poo (Nez Perce for "the real people") Trail. A shoot-out near the reservation, however, sent the tribe on a four-month tactical retreat, ending with defeat just 30 miles short of permanent sanctuary in Canada.

Hells Canyon frustrated pioneer explorers seeking a navigable river route west, including an 1811-12 overland expedition to Astoria. Once, in 1870, a full-size steamboat built on the upper Snake River ran the canyon downriver, but lost 8 feet of its bow in the process.

A largely fictitious copper and gold strike at Eureka Bar in 1900 brought regular steamboat service from Lewiston to the mouth of the Imnaha River. A 125-foot ship winched herself up the river with the aid of giant iron rings still visible in the cliffs above Wild Goose and Mountain Sheep Rapids. The ship lost power on a 1903 run, drifted backward into Mountain Sheep Rapids, bridged the 62-foot-wide canyon there, and broke in half. Visible at Eureka Bar are remains of the steamboat landing and a huge, never-completed ore mill.

In 1887, a group of seven Idaho cowhands robbed and murdered 32 Chinese gold miners panning river gravel at Deep Creek. The robbers buried their loot at the scene. One vial of gold dust turned up there in 1902.

Homesteaders built hardscrabble ranches in the canyon bottom during 1910-30. The Forest Service later acquired the abandoned ranches and has restored the Kirkwood Ranch's clapboard ranchhouse and log bunkhouse as a museum of that era.

HIKING & BACKPACKING

Nearly all of the trails crisscrossing this huge, open canyonland provide shake-your-head-in-wonder viewpoints. The area is so remote, however, that trailheads require long drives on poor roads. Many of the rugged trails involve wearying elevation gains of up to 6000 feet. And expect that rarely used paths (not described here) will be faint and hard to follow.

Several lookout towers reachable by

Mine entrance at Eureka Bar.

The Buckhorn lookout.

car provide good starting points. Most popular is Hat Point, near the top of the Hells Canyon-South map. Day hikers can savor views of the Seven Devils from wildflower meadows along the start of the trail switchbacking down from Hat Point. Drive Highway 82 to Joseph, then continue 30 miles to pavement's end at Imnaha (general store, no gas). Hat Point is an hour beyond Imnaha on 23-mile-long, one-lane gravel Road 4240.

Buckhorn Viewpoint, on the northern part of the Oregon rim, overlooks the jumbled canyonlands at the mouths of the Imnaha and Salmon Rivers (see the map for area 52). To drive to Buckhorn Point, take Highway 82 east of Enterprise 3.2 miles, turn left on Crow Creek Road for 1.1 miles to a fork, veer right to stay on Crow Creek Road another 3.9 miles, fork right onto Zumwalt Road for 32 gravel miles, and turn right on Road 780 for 1 mile to the Buckhorn Lookout's short spur road on the right (GPS location N45°45.232′ W116°49.401′). For the best view, however, hike or drive an extra 1.2 miles out Road 780 to a gate and walk on out Cemetery Ridge.

The most popular viewpoint on the Idaho side is the Heavens Gate lookout (on the south map), close to the Seven Devils' crags. From Highway 95 at Riggins (Idaho) take gravel Road 517 for 17 miles to the trailhead at Windy Saddle, then drive north 1.5 miles to the lookout.

Only a few hikes in the area are short enough and level enough to qualify as day trips. Perhaps the most accessible begins at the south end of the canyon near the Hells Canyon Dam. A 1.2-mile river trail from the Hells Canyon Creek boat launch site (just past the dam) reaches Stud Creek before the path is stopped by cliffs. To find this trailhead from Baker City, take exit 302 of Interstate 84, drive 65 miles east on Highway 86,

Hells Canyon from Stud Creek, just below the Hells Canyon Dam.

HELLS CANYON - CENTER

0   1   2   3mi
0   1   2   3   4km

(See Area 52 Map)

Imnaha
River
Trail

Cow Cr
Ranch

Imnaha
Bridge

4250

Summit Ridge

Deep Creek

1023'

2170'

Deep Cr
Ranch

Dorrance
Ranch (aband)

1680'

Roland Cr

Copper
Cr Lodge

Idaho

Snake River

Square
Mtn

Cow Ridge

Haas Ridge

Lightning Cr

Litch
Ranch

2160'

2850'

Snake
River
Trail

Rhodes
Cr Ranch

4500'

Fingerboard
Saddle

West Fk

4700'

Tryon
Saddle

Lookout

Tryon Cr

Ranch

Hells

Camp Cr

1092'

2400'

Deep Creek

Lord Flat

Winter's Gulch

Airstrip

Englishman
Hill
3050

White Bird
14 mi

2460'

Haas Ridge

Sleepy Cr

Sleepy Ridge

Mormon Flat

Cow
Camp

Canyon

Somers
Pt
5676'

Pittsburg

4000'x

Pittsburg
Landing

Easternmost point
of Oregon

95

Horse Cr

Jakey Ridge

Medicine Cr

Windy Ridge

Wing Ridge

Parliament

Somers Cr

High Trail

Salt Cr

Wilderness

Kirkwood Ranch
Museum

517

5440'

070

Bald
Knob

Tepee
Spr

Summit Ridge

Rim

Grave

Ninemile
Saddle
6080'

Wisnor
Place
2800'

Hominy Cr

Creek

High Cr

1360

Brockman
Ranch

Dry Gulch

Suicide
Point

Saw Pit
Saddle

Caribou Cr

2060

4240

Western Ridge

Grassy
Knoll
6515'

Temperance Cr

3920

Quartz Cr

Game
Commission

Willow Bar
Petroglyphs

Low
Saddle
5300'

Idaho

Horse Creek
Viewpoint

6250'

345

Hat Pt
3 mi

Warnock
Corral

6700'

High Trail

4240

Sand Cr

Johnson
Bar

(See Hells Canyon - South Map)

Clarks Ridge

Imnaha 6 mi

Imnaha 20 mi

cross the bridge at Oxbow (Copperfield), and turn left (north) on the Idaho side of the river 24 miles to the dam.

Another three day-hike trails are in the north end of Hells Canyon. All of these begin with a grueling 21-mile drive north of Imnaha on the horribly rough, dirt Lower Imnaha Road 4260 (see the map for area 52). Park at the Cow Creek Bridge on the Imnaha River to hike a delightful, nearly level, 4.2-mile trail down the raging Imnaha River through a cliff-edged defile to the Snake River at Eureka Bar's mile-long gravel beach—a nice backpacking destination. Here you can prowl the ruins of Eureka's gold mill and watch boats run Eureka Rapids.

The Nee-Me-Poo Trail, tracing Chief Joseph's route, begins 2.8 miles past the Cow Creek Bridge on Road 4260. This faint 4.1-mile path climbs 900 feet to the excellent view at Lone Pine Saddle before descending to the road near Dug Bar.

Road 4260 ends at Dug Bar, but the last 11.4 miles of road (past Imnaha Bridge) are too rough for trailers and most cars. From the primitive camping area and boat launch at Dug Bar, a 4.3-mile portion of Oregon's Snake River Trail climbs over a ridge to Deep Creek's bar, where an old Chinese miners' camp overlooks the Snake River and cliffs. It's still a spooky backpacking destination.

The Imnaha canyon from Freezeout Saddle.

Pittsburg Landing, the only road access to the middle of Hells Canyon, is the start of the Idaho shore's Snake River Trail. A hike along the rugged trail's first 6 miles penetrates the narrows opposite Oregon's easternmost point and reaches the museum at Kirkwood Ranch, a good goal for a backpack or a tough day trip. To drive to the trailhead from Highway 95 at White Bird, Idaho, take gravel Road 493 for 16 miles to Upper Pittsburg Landing.

Backpacking or horseback trips are needed to reach most of the trails in this enormous wilderness. Maximum group size is eight people and sixteen head of stock. Keep in mind that open fires are banned within a quarter mile of the Snake River. Fragile streambank and lakeshore areas see such heavy use that visitors are advised to keep campsites and stock 200 feet away from water.

The commercial jet boats roaring up and down the river detract from the wilderness atmosphere but provide backpackers with an alternative to dusty trailheads. For about $140 per person, any of several jet boat outfitters will take backpackers from Lewiston to the Idaho shore at Pittsburg Landing or Johnson Bar and back. Prices from Pittsburg Landing to Johnson Bar are about $50. The short run from Hells Canyon Dam to Wild Sheep Rapids (where hikers can join either the Idaho or Oregon Snake River Trails) costs about $50. Most outfitters require reservations. Some operate only from Memorial Day to September 15. For names and schedules, check *www.hellscanyonadventures.com.*

The Idaho Snake River Trail is not only spectacularly scenic, it's nearly level for 35 miles from its start at Pittsburg Landing to its end at Brush Creek, 3 miles short of the Hells Canyon Dam. Still, the path is too faint and rugged for a trip with small children. At Suicide Point, the trail has been blasted from sheer cliffs nearly 500 feet above the

HELLS CANYON - SOUTH

0   1   2   3mi
0   1   2   3   4km
N

College Creek
Imnaha 15 mi
Imnaha 11mi
Memaloose
4230
4240
Freezeout
Imnaha River
3955
Morgan Ridge
Squirrel Prairie
X3500'
5980'
Freezeout Saddle
Saddle Creek
High Trail
6895
Bear Mtn
Cache Cr
Saddle Cr
Hat Pt
6982
Sacajawea
X4640'
Sluice Cr
Snake River
Idaho
Johnson Bar
Rush Creek Rapids
Waterspout Rapids
6000
X4000'
Lower Bernard Rapids
Bernard Cr
1351
2960'
Dry Gulch
Dry Diggins
7828
Bernard Lks
Heavens Gate
Granite Creek Rapids
AA
Hells   Canyon
1440'
Little Granite Cr
Gem L
BB
7580 Windy Saddle
517
Seven Devils
Sheep L
She Devil
CannonL
Riggins 16 mi
6730'
Wild Sheep Rapids
Lookout Mtn
6792'
Battle Cr
Barton Cabin
5743'
Echo L
6660
Baldy
Lk
Potato Hill
Devils Farm Cr
He Devil
9393'
Devils Throne
Seven Devils Mountains
Twin Imps
Dog L
Wilderness
Granite Creek
Brush Cr
Granite Mtn
7840
Horse Heaven
Barton Heights
Summit Ridge
Hells
Stud Cr
Hells Canyon Creek
Saulsberry Saddle
5800'X
Launch Site
1490'
Hells Canyon Dam
Cliff Mtn
Stevens Saddle
6350'
Rapid River
W Fk
Ruth
Trail Cr
Summit Cr
8 mi Road 39
Powerline
PO Saddle
Steamboat Cr
Deep
Oxbow Cr
Casey Mtn
Monument Pk 8956'
Crystal
3965
Buck Point Overlook 6141'
McGraw
6 mi Rd 39
Cr
Hells Canyon Reservoir
Sheep Rock
Emmet Mtn
Six Lake
Basin
Emerald L
Black Lake
White Mtn 8514'
7700'
89
111
Idaho
106
Leep Cr.
Copperfield 14 mi
Copperfield 17 mi
Cuprum 6 mi
Cuprum 12mi
Council 35 mi
Smith Mtn

(See Hells Canyon Center Map)

river. Four major side trails climb 6000 feet into the Seven Devils Mountains, increasing the options for longer treks.

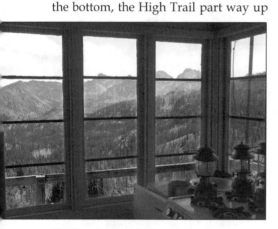

The Oregon shore's Snake River Trail is also scenic, but longer (56 miles from Dug Bar to Battle Creek), and climbs sharply away from the river on five occasions. Backpacking this route takes a week if you have a shuttle car. If you don't, use the route's many side trails to create your own loop. While studying the map for loop ideas, note that the Oregon side of Hells Canyon has three long trails that run lengthwise through the gorge—the Snake River Trail near the bottom, the High Trail part way up

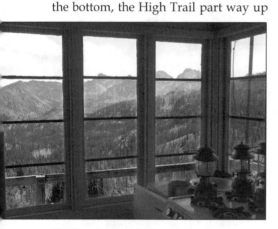

The Dry Diggins lookout tower.

the slope, and the Western Rim Trail at the top. These routes are connected by steep trails that run cross-wise from top to bottom of the canyon. Most notable of these connector trails are the route up Dry Gulch to the High Trail, trails from Sluice Creek and Saddle Creek to Hat Point, the Saddle Creek Trail to Freezeout Saddle, and the Battle Creek Trail to Saulsberry Saddle.

The Western Rim Trail hugs the plateau edge. Somers Point's remote view is 14.7 miles (mostly on an old road) from the Warnock Corral trailhead north of Hat Point. South of Hat Point, the Summit Ridge Trail continues another 15 miles from Road 4240 to PO

Saddle. Side trails lead to photogenic Snake River vistas atop Bear Mountain and Barton Heights. To reach the PO Saddle trailhead from Joseph, drive toward Imnaha 8 miles, turn right onto Road 39 for 31 paved miles, then turn left onto Road 3965 for 16 miles to its end, passing the Hells Canyon Overlook, the McGraw lookout tower, and several other viewpoints along the way.

The High Trail zigzags through the canyon halfway up, passing grassy slopes, big ponderosa pines, and tumbling creeks. Try a portion of this route for variety on a longer trek, or hike along this rugged bench the length of the canyon, 63 miles from the Freezeout Creek trailhead to Dug Bar, via Freezeout Saddle, Englishman Hill, Tryon Saddle, and Deep Creek.

Arguably the best Hells Canyon view is on the Idaho side at the Dry Diggins fire lookout (open for free use). The most scenic backpacking loop is almost certainly the trail circling the Seven Devils Mountains. A 25-mile hike combines these two attractions. From Road 517 at Windy Saddle, a 7-mile trail to the lookout building at Dry Diggins dips 1000 feet crossing Sheep Creek's glacial valley. Continue south to the spectacular Horse Heaven lookout. Return to Windy Saddle along the range's east face. The trail passes only the Bernard Lakes, but worthwhile side trails climb to Sheep, Echo, Baldy, and Cannon lakes.

BOATING

Huge canyon scenery and several huge rapids make the Snake River a popular float trip. Plan on two to eight days from the boat ramp below Hells Canyon Dam, depending on whether the goal is Pittsburg Landing (32 miles), Hellers Bar at the mouth of the Grande Ronde River (79 miles), or Asotin, Washington (104 miles). Be forewarned that all the big whitewater thrills jam into the first 17 miles below the dam. For

Jet boat at Eureka Bar.

this stretch, ranger-issued permits are required all year. Mondays, Tuesdays, and Wednesdays are usually reserved for non-motorized craft in summer. Self-issuing permits suffice for the slower water below. For permit information call (509) 758-1957 or check *www.fs.fed.us/hellscanyon/*.

Wild Sheep Rapids, 6 miles below Hells Canyon Dam, can easily flip 18-foot rafts. This class 4 whitewater, the longest on the river, concludes with big diagonal waves that must be run head-on. Two miles beyond lie Granite Creek Rapids, where a large submerged rock in the river's center creates a variety of unpredictable class 4 turbulence (class 5 at high flow levels).

Lower Bernard Creek Rapids, at river mile 12 below the dam, is a 6-foot, class 4 drop that washes out in high flows. Beyond it 1.3 miles, Waterspout Rapids develops a class 4 suckhole, especially at low levels; better scout it. The final rapid requiring scouting is Rush Creek, at river mile 16, with a boat-hungry, class 4 hole on the Idaho side.

This is no river for open canoes or rafts under 12 feet, although jet boats and rafts with up to 30 passengers are allowed. Camping is not allowed at the Hells Canyon Dam. Each year landing beaches grow smaller as upriver dams silt in, blocking the supply of fresh sand. Open campfires are banned within a quarter mile of the river. Bring camp stoves or use firepans that contain all fire and ashes. There is no firewood along the river.

The Snake is runnable year round, with 70° F water and low flows in summer, chilly water and some squalls in fall, cold weather in winter, and very challenging high water in spring.

The Snake River at the mouth of Saddle Creek, below Hat Point.

54
EAGLE CAP

This wilderness in the Wallowa Mountains encompasses Oregon's largest single alpine area. Here are wildflower meadows and ice-bound lakes. Of the 31 mountains in Oregon over 9000 feet tall, 18 are here. Presiding at the hub of eight radiating valleys rises 9595-foot Eagle Cap.

Horseshoe Lake in the Lake Basin.

Climate

Wettest area east of the Cascades, the Wallowas collect up to 100 inches of precipitation each year. Heavy winter snows close most trails from about the end of October to the start of July. Snowdrifts cling to high passes into August, but the lower Minam River Trail clears of snow as early as April. High water from snowmelt can make river fords difficult in May and June.

Mosquitoes can be thick in lake basins throughout July, when wildflowers are at their peak. Come prepared for brief afternoon thundershowers in July and August. September often brings clear Indian summer weather with freezing nights.

Plants and Wildlife

Rocky Mountain bighorn sheep were reintroduced here in 1971 after local extinction. In winter, bring binoculars to spot them on the slopes above the Lostine River near Pole Bridge Picnic Area. In spring they lamb on high ledges, where the young's only predators are golden eagles. In summer these curly-horned sheep range into the high country, where males butt heads during the November rut. Also watch for the area's spike-horned mountain goats which winter on Sacajawea Peak. Easier to find, however, are mule deer, especially in winter when they browse the moraines of Wallowa Lake.

The little, round-eared "rock rabbits" whistling warnings to each other from the Wallowas' alpine rockslides are pikas. These cute, industrious animals clip and sun-dry large piles of grass and wildflowers, then store them in tunnels under rockslides, where the pikas winter without hibernating. One of their few predators here is the weasel-like marten, which likewise does not hibernate. The marten may travel 15 miles a night through treetops in pursuit of squirrels.

Location: 7 mi S of Enterprise, 21 mi E of La Grande

Size: 715 sq mi

Status: 560 sq mi designated wilderness (1964, 1972, 1984)

Terrain: snowpeaks, high lakes, alpine meadows, valley forests

Elevation: 2700'-9845'

Management: Wallowa-Whitman NF

Map: Wallowa Mountains (Imus Geographics), Eagle Cap Wilderness (USFS)

Aneroid Lake.

Chipmunks and cinnamon-colored black bears are numerous enough that food must be hung at night for safe keeping. Campers also report nighttime visits from porcupines that chew fishing rod handles and sweaty backpack straps for their salt.

Wallowa Lake attracts geese, ducks, and occasional tundra swans in winter. Summer birdwatchers can watch for the rare Wallowa gray-crowned rosy finch. Known chiefly from just three locations—Glacier Lake, Petes Point, and a tarn near Tenderfoot Pass—this finch feeds on numbed insects that have fallen onto high snowfields. Its winter home remains a mystery.

July brings an impressive show of wildflowers to the area's many alpine meadows—notably at the Bonny Lakes south of Aneroid Mountain. Blue gentian, yellow monkeyflower, and purple elephanthead brighten wet areas, while drier fields host blue lupine, aster, scarlet gilia, and heather.

Douglas fir and lodgepole pine dominate the forests. The twisted trees at timberline are whitebark pine and limber pine, both of which sport five-needle clusters and limbs so flexible they can literally be tied in knots. Limber pine, identified by its longer cones, grows nowhere else in Oregon but the Wallowas.

Geology

The predominantly granite Wallowas have been called America's Little Switzerland, and in fact resemble the Alps geologically.

Many of the Wallowas' jumbled strata began as sediment from a string of volcanic islands in the Pacific Ocean. The greenstones that form the peaks south of Wallowa Lake are 250-million-year-old metamorphosed basalt. The stunning white marble and contorted limestone of the Matterhorn and Marble Mountain began 200 million years ago as compacted coral reefs. Dark outcroppings are usually slate and shale that began as seafloor mud.

All this island debris was buckled up from the Pacific by the advancing North American continent and then cooked by magma bubbling up from below 100 million years ago. The magma cooled slowly to form granite. Next, erosion

The Matterhorn from Ice Lake.

must have nearly leveled the mountain range, because Columbia River basalt flows 15 million years ago successfully blanketed the entire area with lava. Shortly afterwards, Great Basin faulting lifted the Wallowas as much as 5000 feet above the surrounding plain, allowing stream erosion and glaciers to strip the basalt from most of the range. Basalt rimrock still tops ridges along the lower Minam River.

Ice Age glaciers ground out U-shaped valleys and basins for the area's 58 named lakes. The last major glacial advance left the smooth moraines which dam Wallowa Lake on three sides. Global warming in the late 1900s eliminated Eastern Oregon's last glacier, the Benson Glacier above Glacier Lake.

History

The Wallowa band of the Nez Perce occupied a summer village on the site of the present Wallowa Lake State Park until their flight in 1877 under Chief Joseph. The names of Joseph and his U.S. Army adversary, General Howard, now grace opposing mountains across Wallowa Lake. A lakeside monument near Joseph contains the remains of Joseph's father, the elder Chief Joseph.

The 1885 boomtown of Cornucopia produced $15 million in gold before its mines closed in 1941.

HIKING & BACKPACKING

Ninety percent of all visits by horseback riders and hikers begin at just three adjacent trailheads: Wallowa Lake State Park, Hurricane Creek Campground, and Two Pan Campground. As a result, trails in this central area are crowded, camping space is tight, and some lakeshores are roped off altogether for restoration. For solitude, skip the Lake Basin. The Wallowas have four other lake clusters and 400 miles of quieter trails.

Scenic Wallowa Lake offers only a few paths short enough for day hikers. For an easy panoramic view, ride the gondola of the Wallowa Lake Tramway to the top of Mount Howard ($19 for adults, $12 for children). From the top, a 1.9-mile loop circles the summit, but adventurers can bushwhack south along an open ridge 2 miles to 9380-foot East Peak.

Perhaps the most popular day hike from the heavily used Wallowa Lake area, is the dusty, 6-mile climb to the rustic log cabins at the far end of beautiful Aneroid Lake. A resident caretaker often allows backpackers to use these private cabins for free, but plan on using public tent sites north of the lake.

Other trail destinations from the Wallowa Lake Trailhead are a little too far for day hikers, and so are mostly left to backpackers. Ice Lake is 7.5 miles away and 3300 feet up a switchbacking trail. Backpackers use Ice Lake as a scenic timberline base for hiking up Oregon's

Cabin at Aneroid Lake.

Glacier Peak from Glacier Lake.

sixth and seventh tallest mountains, the Matterhorn and Sacajawea Peak. Though high enough to warrant caution, the route from the lake gains only 1900 feet and requires no special gear or use of hands. A ridge between peaks allows ambitious hikers to reach both summit viewpoints on the same trip.

Horseshoe Lake, at the start of the Lake Basin, is 9.2 miles from the Wallowa Lake trailhead and 2500 feet up. Most level, wooded ground in the Lake Basin is closed for restoration. Expect to search away from trails or lakes for a low-impact campsite.

Stark, island-dotted Glacier Lake climaxes a 12.1-mile trail ascending the West Fork Wallowa River past Six Mile Meadow, through a rocky gorge, and past Frazier Lake. For a scenic 27.3-mile loop trip, continue north from Glacier Lake across a pass (with a sweeping view) and return through the Lake Basin.

To appreciate the enormity of the Matterhorn's 1800-foot, west-facing marble cliff, park at the end of Hurricane Creek Road 8205 and hike up Hurricane Creek 4.9 miles to a ford with a view of the mountain's base — or, better yet, climb an additional 3 very steep miles to Echo Lake for a bird's eye view across the valley.

Chimney Lake is one of several good day hike goals from the dirt Lostine River Road 8210 south of Lostine. The 5.1-mile route from the Bowman Trailhead to Chimney Lake climbs 2400 feet, but it's worth continuing another mile to Hobo Lake in order to scramble to the view atop 8831-foot Lookout Mountain.

Frances Lake fills an alpine valley in the midst of bighorn sheep country, where open slopes tempt hikers to scramble up nearby 9000-foot peaks. The 8.9-mile trail from Road 8210 (near the Bowman Trailhead) gains a staggering 3340 feet in well-graded switchbacks before dropping 900 feet to the lake.

The switchbacking 3.8-mile trail from Shady Campground up to Maxwell Lake is much shorter, and also quiet.

Two popular trails start from the Two Pan Campground at the end of Road 8210. One path climbs 5.8 miles to large Minam Lake, a campsite for trekkers heading deeper into the wilderness.

EAGLE CAP

0   1   2   3mi
0 1 2 3 4km

N

Forest Service Vis Ctr

3 *Lewiston 87 mi*

Enterprise

Imnaha 17 mi

82 *Joseph*

Chief Joseph Grave

Ruby Pk

Hurricane Creek

8205

Ferguson Ridge

39

Sawtooth Pk 5040'

Legore

Hurricane

Twin Pks

7680'

Frances L

Chief Joseph Mtn

7400'

Wallowa Lake

Wallowa Lake Tramway

5900'

8256'

Mt Howard

McCully Cr

3920

4640'

Shady

Sacajawea Pk 9833'

DD

East Fk

CC

East Pk

UU

McCully Basin

6120'

Salt Creek Summit

Echo L

Two Pan

Ice Lake

Aneroid Lake 7500'

Aneroid Mtn 9702'

×8700'

Wing'd Ridge

100

Matterhorn 9845'

EE

7200'

West Fk

Petes Pt

×8430' *Bonny Lakes*

II

6800'

Sheep Cr

200

39

Lick Cr

Lick Creek

015

Glacier Mtn

HH

Lake Basin

7600'

FF

Glacier L

Mt Nebo

Lick Cr

6100'

Indian Crossing

3960

GG

8450'

Blue L

Eagle Cap

(See Lake Basin Close-up)

North Fork

Imnaha Falls

4700'

Blue Hole

Minam R

Hidden L

RR

Cusick Mtn

7600'

Boner Flat

South Fork

Imnaha R

Mountains

QQ

8150'

Eagle Lake 7500'

River Head

6280'

Marble Mtn

Deadman Pt

6430'

Twin Lakes

NN

8500'

Traverse L

Arrow L

PP

Bear L

Blue Cr

6880'

66

Heart L

Culver L

Gull

Clear Cr

Falls

Lookingglass L

Crater L

7600'

Red Mtn 9555'

Queen Mine

Fish Lake

Krag Pk

Little Kettle Cr

Pine Lakes

W Fk

E Fk Trail

5280'

Boulder Park 4990'

8000'

SS

Cornucopia 4800'

Pine Cr

Two Color

4330'

Elk Cr

6610

68

7755

7740

Two Color

East Fork

7732

Amalgamated Mine

7006'

Summit Pt

4190

7715

Halfway 8 mi

G

Maxwell Lake.

Another path from Two Pan climbs to the Lake Basin and Eagle Cap itself. For a day hike on this route, turn back after 2.8 miles when you get a view of Eagle Cap across the East Lostine River's beautiful meadows. If you're back-packing, continue another 4.6 miles to crowded Mirror Lake, strike off into the woods, and find a campsite well away from lakeshores or trails. From Mirror Lake a good trail climbs 1950 feet in 2.7 miles to Eagle Cap's summit. This is not the area's tallest peak, but its view is unsurpassed. A register box at the top immortalizes those who make the trip.

Steamboat Lake and North Minam Meadows highlight a less crowded region of peaks, lakes, and winding glacial valleys. For a 29.3-mile loop from Two Pan Campground, climb 2900 feet along Copper Creek and descend past gorgeous (misnamed) Swamp Lake to Steamboat Lake, with its ship-shaped rock formation. Continue 5.3 miles down to North Minam Meadow, and turn right through the Wilson Basin to the Bowman Trailhead. If you haven't left a shuttle vehicle here, you'll have to walk 3.2 miles up Lostine River Road 8210 to your car.

For a look at the vast canyonlands in the northwest of the wilderness, climb the steep, 1.9-mile trail from a spur of Road 8250 to Huckleberry Mountain's former fire lookout site. Below Huckleberry Mountain, river-sized Bear Creek drains the northwest corner of the wilderness. A 5-mile day-hike follows the stream from the Boundary Campground to a historic log cabin that served as a guard station in the early 1900s. Good campsites are nearby.

Or, farther west, take a relatively

Traverse Lake.

level 5.1-mile trail from Bear Wallow Spring through a 1990s forest fire zone to Standley Guard Station's 1932 cabin. Don't expect canyon views until you've gone a mile south past the cabin. Drive to Bear Wallow Spring via Big Canyon Road 8270, which leaves Highway 82 at milepost 35.

Day hikers can sample the lower Minam River's rugged, V-shaped canyon by hiking down the canyon's side 3.4 miles from Rock Spring on Road 62 to a derelict, long-abandoned lodge at a riverside meadow.

The Wallowas' most popular equestrian trailhead, Moss Springs Campground, accesses a network of dusty canyon trails on the southwest side of the wilderness—notably a 7.6-mile path

down the Little Minam River to Reds Horse Ranch, a closed lodge and huge meadow with the only bridge across the Minam River for miles. Although the public cannot stay overnight in the ranch buildings, the Forest Service caretaker often gives tours, and plenty of campsites are nearby.

Want to track a river to its source? Take the Minam River Trail 46 miles to Blue Lake's alpine cirque. The rugged lower canyon is V-shaped, while the valley's forested upper canyon has been cut to a U shape by vanished glaciers. Start at the Rock Springs or Moss Springs trailheads, head for the Minam River bridge at Red's Horse Ranch, and continue upriver. From Blue Lake, hike past Minam Lake another 8.6 miles to the

The outlet of Frances Lake.

Two Pan trailhead, where you'll want to have left a shuttle car in advance.

The less heavily used North Catherine Creek trailhead is the starting point for a 4-mile hike up a curving glacial valley to campable Catherine Creek Meadows and a small, public log cabin (GPS location N45°09.245' W117°36.931').

On the south side of the Wallowas, the Mule Peak lookout offers a view extending to the Blue Mountains. A steep, faint 11.4-mile loop trail from Road 600 includes the 3700-foot climb to the abandoned lookout.

The headwaters of Eagle Creek fan

Blue Hole on the Imnaha River.

out in U-shaped valleys to a dozen granite-rimmed lakes in high mountain bowls. From West Eagle Meadow on Road 77, hike 5.4 miles to cliff-backed Echo Lake, gaining 1800 feet on countless, gentle switchbacks. Even more spectacular Traverse Lake is 1.3 miles beyond and another 500 feet up. Both make nice backpacking goals.

Another fork of the trail up West Eagle Creek crosses a pass to Tombstone Lake. The trek gains 2770 feet in 7.2 miles to the pass, and then loses 780 feet in 1.7 miles to the lake—actually a series of four pools with enough woods to hide a dozen tents. Granite slabs here are as white and smooth as tombstones. Part of the appeal of scenic Tombstone Lake is the difficulty of getting there. It's 8.9 miles from any of the three closest trailheads, and all routes cross high passes.

From the Main Eagle Trailhead (beside Boulder Park Campground at the end of Road 7755), a 4.4-mile climb takes you to Eagle Creek Meadow, a popular backpacking base camp for trips to half a dozen high lakes. Do not to camp in the fragile meadow itself, but rather hide your tent in the nearby woods. Goals from Eagle Creek Meadow include Lookingglass Lake (2.7 miles), Bear Lake (2 miles), and Eagle Lake (3 miles, in a bare granite bowl rimmed by 9000-foot peaks). Unfortunately, small irrigation dams have converted Eagle Lake and Lookingglass Lake to reservoirs, giving these two largest lakes "bathtub ring" shorelines.

Dollar Lake, in the pass above Aneroid Lake.

For a 19.1-mile loop, visit Eagle Lake, Cached Lake, and Arrow Lake before returning to the Main Eagle Trailhead.

The trail up East Fork Eagle Creek's valley is long enough to call for an overnight trip. Head for the alpine meadows, tarns, and campsites near Hidden Lake, 8.3 miles upstream.

Start near Cornucopia, a semi-abandoned mining boomtown, for the 7.4-mile hike to Pine Lakes. From the Cornucopia Wilderness Pack Station, walk through the horse ranch on a road that soon becomes the Pine Lakes Trail. In a vast granite bowl, the green lakes shimmer amid rock gardens of heather, gentian, paintbrush, and monkeyflower.

For an 18.2-mile loop trip, circle Cornucopia Mountain by continuing over Nip and Tuck Pass and keeping left through Little Eagle Meadows back to a different Cornucopia trailhead, a mile from your car. From Baker City, take exit 302 of Interstate 84, head east 52 miles to Halfway's Business Loop, keep straight on Main Street (Cornucopia Road 4190) for 12.3 miles, and turn right 0.5 mile to the pack station.

The eastern edge of the Wallowa Mountains remains relatively uncrowded. A nearly level path follows the rushing Imnaha River from Indian Crossing Campground on Road 3960 for 2 miles to Blue Hole's 50-foot-deep river slot. Continue 3.7 miles and listen for the

The south side of Eagle Cap from Hidden Lake, at the head of the East Eagle valley.

roar of whitewater to find churning, 10-foot Imnaha Falls, 100 yards off the trail. To reach to the trailhead from Joseph, drive 8.3 miles toward Imnaha, turn right on paved Road 39 for 32 miles, and turn right on Road 3960 for 9 miles.

Most hikers headed for the wildflower fields above Aneroid Lake trudge up the long trail from Wallowa Lake. But an easier route to the same alpine area begins at the little-used Tenderfoot Trailhead on Big Sheep Creek at the end of Road 100. From there, you can either hike 3.9 miles to the Bonny Lakes, or 5.6 miles to scenic, treeless Dollar Lake in the pass above Aneroid Lake.

Looking for an even less visited wildflower patch? Try McCully Basin, 5.3 miles up from Tucker Down Road 3920. Only adventurers discover the best meadows here, hidden a few hundred yards west of the trail at the valley's head. This is also an excellent base camp for non-technical climbs of Aneroid Mountain, Oregon's ninth tallest peak.

Backpackers and equestrians in the wilderness should note camping is

Mt. Nebo, near Big Sheep's rental ski camp.

banned within 200 feet of any lake. Stock cannot be grazed or confined within 200 feet of lakes. Group size is limited to six in the Lake Basin and twelve elsewhere in the wilderness. Campers are not allowed to cut firewood from standing trees, alive or dead. Downed firewood is scarce; bring a camp stove.

CLIMBING

Although all peaks have walk-up sides, granite cliffs provide technical challenges in Yosemite-like rock. The Matterhorn's 1800-foot marble west face is toughest of all. Winter ascents of the Matterhorn and Sacajawea can be undertaken with snowshoes or even skis from Ice Lake.

SNOWSHOEING & SKIING

A good warm-up jaunt for snowshoers and Nordic skiers traverses the snowed-under park and shore of Wallowa Lake at the end of plowed Highway 82. The small Ferguson Ridge Ski Area, 6 miles east of Joseph, opens when snow levels permit. A sandwich-board sign on Main Street in Joseph announces when the rope tow is running.

Avalanche danger makes backcountry tours into the Wallowas' U-shaped valleys risky. Hurricane Creek won its name from the swaths of broken trees left not by windstorms but by snowslides. Snow shovels, avalanche beacons, and training are essential.

Wing Ridge Ski Tours offers trips to rental tents at Big Sheep Creek (elevation 6220 feet) and Wing Ridge (7220 feet) in the mountains' northeast corner for about $55 per person per night. Powder snow in this area can rival that found in the Rockies. The large tents have wooden floors, cots, pads, woodstoves, kerosene lamps, and cooking facilities. For information call 800-646-9050 or check *www.wingski.com*. Road 39 is plowed as far as the Salt Creek Summit sno-park, the starting point for the Wing Ridge tours.

WILDERNESS
of
SOUTHEAST OREGON

The Owyhee River at Hole in the Ground.

SOUTHEAST OREGON

Blue Mountains

Ironside

26

84

Ontario

395 Vale

Drewsey Nyssa

Harper 20

Snively
Hot Springs 201
Juntura (free) 95

Burns
Hines

Princeton Crowley LOWER
78 OWYHEE
RIVER
Follyfarm 65
Diamond
205 Jordan
Valley
Frenchglen 63 95
STEENS MOUNTAIN
Rome
STEENS Burns
CLOSE UP Junction
Three
Forks
66
UPPER
OWYHEE
RIVER
Whitehorse
Ranch
Fields 95
64
PUEBLO TROUT CREEK
MOUNTAINS MOUNTAINS
Denio McDermitt

Nevada

Idaho

Map Key	Destination	Total miles	Easy-M-Diff.	Days	Est. Mos. Open	Uncrowded	Page
A	Around Paulina Lake	8	E	2	VII½-X		*316*
B	Antler Springs	9	M	3	VII-X	●	*326*
C	Blue Lake	5	E	3	VII-X		*330*
D	Barnhardi Basin	7	M	2	VII-X	●	*338*

Map Key	Destination	Total miles	Easy-M-Diff.	Days	Est. Mos. Open	Uncrowded	Page
E	Wildhorse Lake	3	M	2	VII½-X½		*348*
F	Big Indian Gorge	13	D	3	VI-XI½	●	*348*
G	Little Blitzen Gorge	8	M	3	VI-XI½	●	*349*
H	Pueblo Mtns / Desert Trail	22	D	3	VII½-XI½	●	*354*

Steens Mountain from the Alvord Desert.

Little Blitzen Gorge on Steens Mountain.

THE HIGH DESERT

Alkali lakes, mountain oases, and geologic oddities sprinkle the arid uplands southeast of Bend. Clockwise from above: Fort Rock, two views of Summer Lake, (center of page: the Sycan River above Winter Rim and Gearhart Mountain from Blue Lake), Newberry Caldera from Paulina Peak (lower right), Paulina Peak, Paulina Lake, Summer Lake refuge canal, and Crack In The Ground. Below: Summer Lake mud cracks.

CLIFFS & HOT SPRINGS

The faults that lift cliffs from Oregon's high desert also fire hot springs. On this page, clockwise from below: Poker Jim Ridge, hummingbird moth, Hart Lake, the Warner Lakes, and Abert Rim. On the opposite page, clockwise from upper right: tortoiseshell butterfly on corn flower, hot springs algae, Mickey Hot Springs, Borax Hot Springs, Summer Lake Hot Springs, and Borax Hot Springs.

STEENS MOUNTAIN

A 50-mile block uplifted from the desert, Steens Mountain is cut by cliffs and gorges. On this page, clockwise from below: Kiger Gorge, Wildhorse Lake in August, Steens' summit in April, and the Alvord Desert. On the opposite page, clockwise from upper right: Little Blitzen Gorge, Riddle Ramch, Kiger Gorge, waterfall at the head of Little Blitzen Gorge, bighorn sheep, and Steens' summit from the Alvord Desert.

THE OWYHEE

The colorful canyons of this desert river snake across three states. Clockwise from below: Three Forks, penstemon, dwarf monkeyflower, the Honeycombs, hot springs at Three Forks, and bitterroot.

55

BADLANDS

Just 10 miles from sprawling Bend, but a world apart, this maze of lava formations, ancient juniper trees, and hidden sandy basins is a wilderness retreat.

Climate

Cold, windy winters give way to pleasant spring weather as early as March. Summers are dry and blazing hot, but fall arrives cool and clear. Annual precipitation is just 12 inches.

Plants and Wildlife

A sparse, old-growth forest of scenic, gnarled juniper dots these rugged lava lands, increasing the feeling of isolation by blocking most long-range views. Sagebrush adds its pungent desert smell. Bright yellow and orange lichens encrust many rocks. Spring brings the daisy-shaped blooms of Oregon sunshine and the tiny purple blossoms of miniature monkeyflower. Watch for mule deer, lizards, and coyotes. Evening brings bats from lava tube caves. Badlands Rock and the Dry River Canyon are closed in spring and summer to protect nesting falcons.

Geology

The fresh-looking lava here erupted 10,000 years ago, puddled up in a prairie, and then buckled into thousands of

Petroglyphs in the Dry River's channel.

ten-foot-tall pressure ridges, in much the same way that paint can wrinkle when it dries. The low spots filled with volcanic sand after Mt. Mazama's cataclysmic eruption powdered the area 7700 years ago.

During the wetter climate of the Ice Age, a lake in Millican's broad valley spilled northwest across the lava here to the Crooked River. Today the lake is gone and its outlet, the Dry River, is a waterless canyon.

HISTORY

Faint red petroglyphs at the base of rock overhangs in the Dry River's colossal canyon and its smaller channel must be thousands of years old, because the symbols evidently remain from a time when people camped beside a flowing river, perhaps to fish.

HIKING & BACKPACKING

Start at the Flatiron Trailhead, 16 miles east of Bend on Highway 20 toward Burns. At milepost 16 turn left

---

Location: 10 mi E of Bend

Size: 46 sq mi

Status: designated wilderness (2009)

Terrain: juniper-forested lava plain, sandy basins, dry river canyon

Elevation: 3400'-3865'

Management: Prineville District BLM

Maps: Alfalfa, Horse Ridge, Millican, Horse Butte (USGS)

Ancient juniper in the Badlands.

1.6 miles on the Flatiron Trail (also an old road) to Flatiron Rock, a 30-foot-tall lava outcrop that resembles a castle in the desert (GPS location N43°59.362′ W121°02.748′). Explore the rock's ramparts on a half-mile loop, watching for three small natural windows in the walls.

Another good starting point is the Badlands Trailhead, near the gate marked with a "G" on the map. Drive Highway 20 east of Bend 18 miles to the bottom of a hill and turn left on an unmarked, paved road for a mile to a dirt parking area on the left (GPS location N43°57.216′ W121°00.883′).

Hike a dirt road/trail 0.3 mile to a fork where a small wire fence marks an early 1900s homestead site. Veer right 0.9 mile to three boulders on the right (GPS location N43°57.788′ W121°00.286′), take a small trail to the right 150 yards, and keep right to explore the Dry River's channel, flanked by 40-foot walls.

The much larger Dry River Canyon is open only from September through January. Drive Highway 20 to the low point near milepost 18, turn left across a cattle guard onto a paved road, immediately turn right, and keep right through a cluster of gravel piles to find a dirt road that ends at a trailhead in half a mile. Hike up the dry wash 2.2 miles to a 300-foot rock wall covered with bright yellow lichen. Turn back here because the path peters out and enters private land.

across a yellow cattle guard to the rough dirt parking turnaround (GPS location N43°57.454′ W121°03.086′). Bring lots of water, avoid midday heat, wear a big sun hat, and choose loose, long-sleeved clothing. If you stray from the old roads that serve as trails in this wilderness it's easy to be disoriented, so pack a compass or GPS device.

From the Flatiron Trailhead, the Ancient Juniper Trail loops 3.3 miles through the gently rolling terrain of twisted trees and weird lava blocks. At a large, triangle-shaped trail junction at the far end of the loop, detour north

56
NEWBERRY CALDERA

Oregon's national volcanic monument features the remnants of an ancient volcano, Mount Newberry, which collapsed in Crater Lake fashion to form Newberry Caldera and the Paulina Mountains.

Climate

Patches of snow remain in the campgrounds and ice still fringes the lakes when crowds arrive for the opening of fishing season here in late May. Snow blocks the higher Rim Trail until July. By August all streams are dry except Paulina Creek. Winter snows, commencing again in November, account for most of the area's 15 to 30 inches annual precipitation.

East Lake from the Rim Trail at Cinder Hill.

Plants and Wildlife

Lodgepole pine forests cover most of the area, but big ponderosa pines grow at lower elevations. The woods harbor wildlife typical of both the Cascades and the high desert. Raucous gray jays and inquisitive golden-mantled ground squirrels seem prevalent. The state stocks East Lake and Paulina Lake with 300,000 trout annually.

Geology

This volcanic hot spot marks the western end of the Brothers Fault Zone, a line of recent eruptive centers running from here to Idaho. This major fault, and the jumble of Great Basin faults south of it, resulted from the North American continent's shearing collision with the Pacific seafloor's plate. Oregon is being stretched diagonally, and lava is leaking through the resulting cracks.

The remains of the Newberry volcano form one of Oregon's most massive and least noticed mountains. Countless thin basalt lava flows stack here into an enormous shield shape 25 miles in diameter, rising 4000 feet above the surrounding plain. From the highways at the mountain's perimeter, however, the overall silhouette seems low. People mostly notice the mountain's 100 parasitic cinder cones, which dot the slopes like giant molehills.

After the Newberry volcano had been built of basalt, the magma became richer in silica, causing more violent eruptions of pumice. Hollowed by massive lava outpourings, the volcano collapsed. Eruptions continued inside the caldera.

Location: 23 mi S of Bend

Size: 51 sq mi

Status: National Monument

Terrain: forested peaks, high lakes, lava flows, cinder cones

Elevation: 4750'-7984'

Management: Newberry National Volcanic Monument

Maps: Paulina Peak, East Lake, Lava Cast Forest, Fuzztail Butte (USGS)

Paulina Peak from the Paulina Lake Trail near Little Crater Campground.

Two obsidian flows and the 1900-year-old Central Pumice Cone have since separated Paulina and East Lakes.

At the Lava Cast Forest, a fluid basalt flow surged through a stand of large trees, then ebbed, leaving the trees encased with lava up to the flow's highest level. The trees burned, but their lava shells retain even the checked pattern of the wood.

The Newberry volcano is still very much alive. The mountain has bulged four inches in the past 70 years. Geothermal energy speculators who drilled a 3000-foot-deep well on the volcano in 1981 hit such hot rock that the drill bit melted. A shortage of ground water

Pumice Desert east of the Big Obsidian Flow.

deep enough to produce steam, however, made energy production impractical.

HIKING & BACKPACKING

A paved, 1-mile interpretive trail loops through the Lava Cast Forest. The road there joins Highway 97 just opposite the turnoff to Sunriver.

For other hikes, drive up Road 21 to the monument's entrance fee booth and buy a Northwest Forest Pass for your car (if you don't have one already). For a lovely 7.5-mile hike around Paulina Lake, drive past the fee booth 1.5 miles and park in the Paulina Lake Day Use Area on the left, opposite a small visitor center and just before the Paulina Lake Campground. The lake's loop trail passes an obsidian flow, two camping areas on the north shore (accessible only to boaters or backpackers), and a beach with warm springs. The springs are bathable when lake levels are low enough to scoop a pool in the black sand.

Drive Road 21 beyond the Paulina Lake visitor center 2 miles to find the Big Obsidian trailhead, where a partly paved, 0.8-mile path climbs a staircase and loops across a square-mile flow of glassy obsidian that erupted about 800 AD. Views range to the Three Sisters.

A 1.5-mile loop from Paulina Lake's Little Crater Campground climbs to views on the rim of a small cinder cone.

A lovely 8.5-mile trail follows Paulina Creek from Paulina Lake's outlet down to the Ogden Group Horse Camp (not shown on map). To find the horse camp from Highway 97, drive 2.8 miles up Road 21 toward the entry fee both. Both ends of the trail along Paulina Creek make for easy day hikes. You can either walk the lower 2.8 miles (open year round) up to a 15-foot waterfall at McKay Crossing Campground, or you can hike the trail's topmost section down to 100-foot Paulina Creek Falls.

The easiest way to see Paulina Creek Falls is to stroll a few hundred yards from a signed parking area on Road 21, just east of the monument's entrance booth. For a longer hike from the same trailhead, continue upstream 0.3 mile, cross the lake outlet, and hike back downstream to a quieter viewpoint of the waterfall from the opposite shore.

Gravel Road 500 climbs to the area's most popular view and highest point, Paulina Peak. Here the vista extends from the peaks of the Cascades to Fort Rock in the high desert. A path from the top drops 1500 feet in 2.2 miles to a lower trailhead on Road 500. Then the path crosses the road and continues a mile to the visitor center near Paulina Lake's outlet.

The 21-mile Rim Trail passes several other viewpoints — all less crowded than Paulina Peak. Take the trail north from the bridge by Paulina Lake Lodge for increasingly fine views of Paulina Lake. At the 4-mile mark, make an easy cross-country side trip to the summit of North Paulina Peak for a view of Bend and possibly even Mount Adams.

Those who prefer to climb less for their views can join the Rim Trail at the 7009-foot-level, where it meets Road 21 above East Lake. From this pass, head north along the broad, nearly level rim top, or cross Road 2127 and hike the scenic rim west toward Paulina Peak,

Paulina Lake from Paulina Peak in winter.

5.9 miles away. Hikers on the rim must carry water, and backpackers must plan on dry camps.

SNOWSHOEING & SKIING

Clear weather, dry snow, and plowed access make these mountains attractive to snowshoers and Nordic skiers, despite the presence of snowmobiles. To avoid the snow machines, either visit on a weekday or steer clear of their favored haunts — the snow-covered humps of the Big Obsidian Flow, the road up Paulina Peak, and the lakeshores.

From the uppermost sno-park on Road 21, follow the snowed-under road 2.5 miles to the Paulina Lake Lodge, open year round (*www.paulinalakelodge. com*). Explore the lakeshore or head north up the Rim Trail for viewpoints. Don't miss icicle-draped Paulina Creek Falls, 0.5 miles below the lake.

If Road 21 is heavily trafficked, two much quieter, parallel routes also lead to the lake. Just north of Road 21, a snowed-under dirt road follows powerlines to the lodge. Still farther north, confident trackers can cross Paulina Creek and search for the Paulina Creek Trail.

BOATING

Paulina Lake and East Lake are both large enough for sailing and scenic enough for rowing or canoeing. Sail over the hot springs near the southeast shore of East Lake. Squalls and choppy water can appear quickly. Motors are allowed.

Paulina Peak from the trail to Paulina Lake.

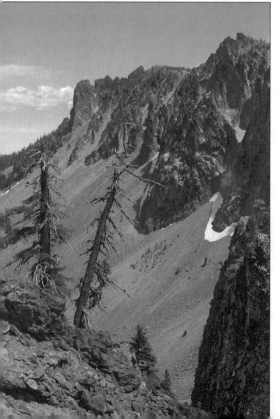

57
FORT ROCK
& LOST FOREST

The high desert here is full of curiosities: Oregon's largest inland sand dunes, Fort Rock's imposing citadel, Hole In The Ground's enormous crater, Crack In The Ground's fissure, a "lost" forest of ponderosa pine, a lava cave with "skylights", and three large lava beds.

Climate

Studies of tree rings in the Lost Forest show that the current, bleak 9 inches of annual precipitation has been the average here for over 600 years. Up to a foot of snow may fall in very cold December and January. In July and August, afternoon heat can be withering. Clear skies are the rule.

Plants and Wildlife

The Lost Forest's puzzle is how a 5-square-mile stand of ponderosa pine thrives in a sagebrush steppe with barely half the rainfall usually required for such stately trees. There are no other ponderosas for 40 miles. The answer is that during the wetter climate of the Ice Age, pines grew throughout Southeast Oregon. This relict grove survives where rainfall collects in windblown

Location: 64 mi S of Bend
Size: 263 sq mi
Status: undesignated wilderness
Terrain: high desert plain, lava beds, sand dunes
Elevation: 4290'-5585'
Management: Lakeview District BLM
Maps: Cougar Mountain, Sixteen Butte, Fox Butte, Hogback Butte, Crack In The Ground, Fossil Lake, Sand Rock, Moonlight Butte, Mean Rock Well (USGS)

sands underlain by the impermeable hardpan of an ancient lakebed. The odd forest also has Oregon's largest juniper, with a trunk 18 feet in circumference.

More than a century of intense cattle

Fort Rock is a volcanic crater that erupted in an Ice Age lake.

grazing cleared the high desert savanna of its original grassy cover, allowing sagebrush and juniper to spread. Ungrazed "islands" within lava flows here provide a rare look at the old bluebunch wheatgrass savanna.

Bald eagles winter here for carrion, relying on mule deer that die during harsh weather. Local and migratory birds gather at Cabin Lake Campground's spring; a public blind there provides first-rate birdwatching. Throughout the area, bobcats and coyotes hunt jackrabbits, cottontails, and kangaroo rats.

Geology

The fresh-looking volcanism here is a result of an east-west fault zone extending from Newberry Caldera to Idaho. When the Ice Age brought heavy rains, a 170-foot-deep lake collected in the Fort Rock and Christmas Lake Valleys. Eruptions during that time met surface water and exploded in blasts of steam and rock, leaving rimmed craters, or maars. Mile-wide Hole In The Ground looks like a meteorite crater, but is actually a maar. Fort Rock, another explosion crater, lay in water deep enough that waves eroded its once-sloping rim to sheer, 320-foot-tall walls. Maars at Flat Top and Table Mountain later filled to the brim with basalt.

Bones preserved at Fossil Lake reveal that this enormous Ice Age lake attracted camels, elephants, horses, and a profuse bird population of flamingos, gulls, and cormorants. Winds have collected the vanished lake's sands into miles of dunes as tall as 60 feet near Fossil Lake.

Fort Rock's Homestead Museum.

Most of the Devils Garden Lava erupted from a low, U-shaped vent in the extreme northeast of the flow. When the basalt's crust hardened, lava flowed on underneath, leaving lava tubes like Derrick Cave. South of Derrick Cave, a line of small vents formed circular spatter cones 5 to 30 feet across—as well as two larger cones, the 400-foot-wide Blowouts. The soupy, pahoehoe lava of this flow left a relatively smooth surface with ropy wrinkles. In the south of the flow, collapsed lava tubes left sinuous depressions and circular dips that filled with pumice from the eruption of Newberry Crater 1900 years ago.

Both the Squaw Ridge Lava Bed and the Four Craters Lava Bed consist of much more rugged, blocky, aa lava. Crack In The Ground, at the edge of the latter flow, is a 2-mile-long tension fissure that formed along the edge of a broad valley. The valley was created when the Four Craters' eruptions emptied an underground magma chamber and the ground sank.

History

Archeologists here rocked the scientific world in 1938 with the discovery of more than 70 sandals over 9000 years old, pushing back estimates of man's arrival in North America. The sandals, woven from sagebrush bark, were found in a cave a mile west of Fort Rock. Flourishing wildlife at the area's once-huge Ice Age lake apparently attracted early hunters. Artifacts found in caves on nearby Cougar Mountain date back 11,900 years.

The federal government opened this region to homesteading in 1906, and settlers staked out hundreds of dry-land farms. Nearly all were abandoned after the drought of 1913. In the village of

Derrick Cave has natural skylights.

Fort Rock, an outdoor museum (open 10am-4pm, Friday through Sunday in summer) has collected many of the homesteader's buildings.

HIKING & BACKPACKING

From the picnic area at Fort Rock State Natural Area, climb 0.1 mile to a viewpoint below the rock's east cliff to see the wave-cut terrace there. Cliff swallows swoop from nests in the rock, watched by prairie falcons. Continue on abandoned road beds for a 1-mile loop around the inside of the "fort's" open center for June wildflowers and views across the valley. For a longer hike, bushwhack 1.9 miles around the outside of Fort Rock's cliff. In the evenings, owls sail out from perches on the eastern rim.

The Lost Forest and nearby sand dunes offer easy and rewarding cross-country hiking. In the Lost Forest, climb Sand Rock, a small basalt outcropping near the forest's center, for a view. Then trek southwest into the dunes' vast Saharan landscape to explore the sand—but watch out for the noisy, dangerous dune buggies that plague this area, particularly on summer weekends.

To reach the area, drive east 8 miles on paved Road 5-14 from the village of Christmas Valley, turn left on paved Road 5-14D for 8 miles to a T intersection, take gravel Road 5-14E right 3.3 miles to a corner, and go straight on a dirt track past a "Rough Road Ahead" sign for 4.4 miles. This sandy road can be impassable in wet weather. Park at a wood rail fence at a T junction. The dunes are 0.4 mile to the right. For the Lost Forest, drive left 0.3 mile to another T junction and turn right for 2.2 miles of rough, sandy road to Sand Rock, an orange bluff with the area's best view.

Crack In The Ground is a 2-mile-long basalt slot 10 to 70 feet deep and often so narrow that it is bridged by boulders. From the far east end of the village of Christmas Valley, drive 7.2 miles north on gravel to a parking lot. A trail leads 0.2 mile to the crack's northern end and traces the slot 0.3 mile south before petering out. North of the crack, adventurers can cross a rugged lava flow to four prominent cinder cones.

The Devils Garden Lava Bed attracts both hikers and volcanologists. Drive 5.8 miles east of the village of Fort Rock, turn left on paved Road 5-12 for 9.1

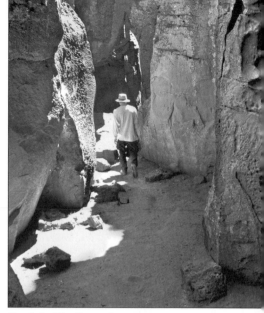

Crack In The Ground.

miles to a guard station entrance, and continue straight on gravel 6.1 miles. Stop here to explore a row of giant spatter cones on the left. Then drive another 0.7 mile to Derrick Cave's parking area. Bring lanterns and warm clothes to explore this 0.2-mile lava tube. Above ground again, hike a mile southwest of Derrick Cave over rough lava to reach The Garden, an old lava dome island in the fresher basalt flow.

For an overview of the smoother, southern part of the Devils Garden flow, make the short climb up Cougar Mountain. Then head north from that summit across the lava to find small sandy openings and desert solitude.

The highest point and best view in the area is atop Lava Butte, 3 miles from a road over the extremely rugged Squaw Ridge Lava.

Hikers should carry plenty of water. Fort Rock and Cabin Lake Campground have the only public sources of drinking water. All lakes and streambeds are dry. Wear sturdy boots when hiking on the area's sharp, rugged lava flows. Expect dirt roads to be badly rutted, slow, and unsigned. Side roads can be confusing, and after a rain, mud can stop even four-wheel-drive vehicles.

58
SUMMER LAKE

Birds thrive in the marshes of Summer Lake's refuge. To the east, Diablo Mountain's 1800-foot cliff overlooks desert hills and salt lakebeds.

Climate
July and August afternoons top 100° F. Intensely cold December and January bring light snows. Spring and fall are pleasant. Annual precipitation is a scant 9 inches.

Plants and Wildlife
Marshes north of Summer Lake attract bald eagles and tundra swans in winter, migratory species in spring and fall, and white pelicans, Canada geese, and sandhill cranes in summer. The most commonly sighted birds are ducks (7 species), song sparrows, marsh wrens, blackbirds, herons, egrets, terns, American avocets, black-necked stilts, curlews, and gulls. The best bird-watching is in March and April.

Unusually salt-tolerant plants survive in Summer Lake's vast alkali flats, including three spiny shrubs: greasewood, shadscale, and hopsage (blooms brilliant orange in July). Sagebrush dominates Diablo Mountain, but May brings wildflower shows of yellow, orange, and red paintbrush.

Bobcats and badgers are common in uplands, but they're shy. Bighorn sheep were reintroduced in 1990. Watch for sage grouse and flocks of western bluebirds. Raptors nest in rimrock.

Geology
Great Basin faults left the impressive, east-facing scarps of Winter Rim and Diablo Mountain. Summer Lake, with no outlet, is the salty remnant of a 40-mile-long Ice Age lake.

History
In 2008, a team of archeologists from

Summer Lake from Winter Rim.

the University of Oregon and Denmark announced that 14,300-year-old human DNA had been isolated from dried feces found in the Paisley Caves southeast of Summer Lake. The find proved nearly as revolutionary as Luther Cressman's 1938 announcement that sandals from a Fort Rock excavation predated Mt. Mazama's eruption. Carbon dating of

Location: 73 mi S of Bend, 49 mi N of Lakeview

Size: 757 sq mi

Status: 29 sq mi wildlife refuge; undesignated wilderness

Terrain: marshes, high desert rimrock, brush-covered sand, alkali flats

Elevation: 4130'-6145'

Management: Lakeview District BLM, Oregon Department of Fish and Wildlife, Fremont-Winema NF

Maps: Diablo Peak, Ana River, South of Ana River, Loco Lake, Sharp Top, Bull Lake, St. Patrick Mountain (USGS)

Marshes in the Summer Lake Wildlife Refuge.

the Paisley Cave coprolites (dried feces) verified that these are the oldest known human artifacts anywhere in the Americas, pushing back arrival dates of humans in this hemisphere by more than 1000 years. Perhaps more important, the DNA analysis showed that Oregon's first people are related to Siberians (lending strength to the theory of migration via an Alaskan land bridge) and are in fact the ancestors of Indian tribes throughout the Americas.

At Picture Rock Pass, ancient petroglyphs mark a car-sized boulder 200 feet west of the crest of Highway 31.

Summer Lake and Winter Ridge were named by Captain John Fremont, sent by the U. S. government to explore the Or-

Ponderosa pine along the Fremont Trail.

egon Trail and the West in 1843. Guided by Kit Carson, Fremont's troop dragged a cannon west across the Rockies to The Dalles. Then they struck south toward California. When they crested a snowy rim on December 16 and saw a sunny lake 2700 feet below, the names "Winter" and "Summer" sprang to mind. In their haste to descend the steep slope their pack mules must have slipped several times. Coins from the early 1840s recovered on the slope by archeologists are now on display in the Forest Service ranger station in Silver Lake.

Summer Lake Hot Springs opened a rustic bathhouse at the south end of the lake in 1928, piping geothermal springs to an indoor 102° F pool. Stop to swim in the original bathhouse at a funky, wind-swept resort with geothermally heated cabins (*www.summerlakehotsprings.com*).

HIKING & BACKPACKING

Start with a level 2.3-mile walk along a wildlife refuge dike through the bird-rich marshlands to a culvert where the Ana River enters Summer Lake. Drive Highway 31 to the refuge headquarters near milepost 70, follow "Wildlife Viewing Area" pointers 1.6 miles to a T-junction, turn right for 0.9 mile to a camping area, and walk out Windbreak Dike.

The 147-mile Fremont Trail traces the crest of Winter Ridge (known as Winter Rim to locals) through ponderosa pine woods with wildflower meadows and spectacular views across Summer Lake's valley. Much of the route here is faint and best suited to equestrians, but hikers can sample an easy-to-follow segment from Road 29 north for 3.4 miles. To find it, drive Highway 31 to milepost 82, turn west on gravel Road 29 at a sign for Government Harvey Pass, and drive 9.5 miles up to a T-shaped junction at the pass. Turn right on Road 2901, driving slowly for just 0.1 mile until you spot a tiny trail marker on a pine tree to the right. Park on the shoulder here (GPS location N42°42.183' W120°47.910') and hike up to the right.

Diablo Mountain's breathtaking, 1800-foot cliff deserves an overnight trip, but a 5.5-mile (one way) day hike also reaches the summit. Drive east from the Summer Lake Store 7 miles to a fenceline. Hike east and north around the fenceline to the peak.

Wildcat Mountain is the best viewpoint in the south, a 1-mile cross-country hike from either of two dirt roads. In the north of the area, drive past the area's only brushless dunes to the base of Rocky Butte, then explore cliff-rimmed Sand Canyon.

SNOWSHOEING & SKIING

Although Road 29 at the south end of Summer Lake is not plowed in winter, this gravel route to Government Harvey Pass is steep enough that drivers reach snow level fairly suddenly. Park at the snow line and trek up the road. Three miles before the pass, a marked trail on Road 017 leads south 1.5 miles to the Slide Lakes (not shown on map), overtowered by the cliffs of 7762-foot Slide Mountain.

BOATING

Canoes are perfectly suited for exploring the sinuous meanders of the

Winter Rim's Slide Mountain from the Slide Lakes at the south end of Summer Lake.

Ana River and the maze-like marshlands north of Summer Lake. Bring binoculars for birdwatching. Motors are prohibited. Summer Lake itself is too shallow and windy for boating.

59
YAMSAY MOUNTAIN

Like a misplaced High Cascades peak, this solitary 8196-foot cone rises from the ponderosa pine forests 40 miles due east of Crater Lake.

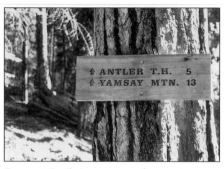

Fremont Trail sign on a ponderosa pine.

Climate

Snow caps Yamsay Mountain from November to early July. Summer and fall are pleasant, with the hottest days cooled by afternoon thundershowers. Annual precipitation tops 40 inches.

Plants and Wildlife

Lodgepole pine thickets cloak the lower slopes of the mountain, with meadows and park-like ponderosa pine groves in creek canyons. Above 7000 feet the forests shift to mountain hemlock, white fir, and weather-gnarled whitebark pine.

Geology

Like Newberry Crater to the north, Yamsay Mountain is a shield volcano, but its cliff-rimmed crater was formed by ice, not fire. An Ice Age glacier on the shady north face gouged the crater-like cirque and Jackson Creek's canyon.

History

Klamath Indians called this mountain Yamsi, "the north wind," and believed it to be the home of Kmukamtch, a supreme deity who sometimes took the weasel-like form of Marten. The area is still sacred to the tribe. Respecting this, the Forest Service has kept Yamsay Mountain wild and undeveloped.

HIKING & BACKPACKING

The Fremont Trail climbs 16.6 miles from Silver Creek Marsh Campground to a top-of-the-world view on Yamsay Mountain. The path's lower 2 miles were rerouted after a wildfire and are a little faint due to brush. Look for a trail sign on the side of Road 27 directly opposite the entrance to Silver Creek Marsh Campground. After 2 miles you'll regain the old route and follow the splashing North Fork of Silver Creek up 2.8 miles to Road 3038.

For a backpack trip, follow the Fremont Trail's upper 8.6 miles from the Antler Trailhead on Road 038 up a broad ridge to the summit. Antler Springs, 0.2 mile off the trail along abandoned Road 024, offers a logical camp stop. Cross-country explorers can strike off from the springs to find the idyllic meadows in

Location: 87 mi S of Bend, 75 mi NE of Klamath Falls

Size: 40 sq mi

Status: undesignated wilderness

Terrain: forested mountain, canyons, streams

Elevation: 5840'-8196'

Management: Fremont-Winema NF

Maps: Yamsay Mountain, Gordon Lake (USGS)

Scarlet gilia.

Buck Creek's basin.

For these hikes, drive Highway 31 a mile west of the town of Silver Lake. Between mileposts 46 and 47, turn south onto paved Road 27, and follow signs for Silver Creek Marsh Campground or the Antler Trailhead.

On the west side, a road once led to a lookout tower on Yamsay Mountain's summit. With the tower gone, the abandoned road has become an alternate trail to the top, climbing 3.4 miles from the end of Road 4973.

Though trailless, Jackson Creek's open forests and creekside meadows invite bushwhacking—especially along the 4-mile section from Road 130's crossing to the creek's forks in a bowl-shaped cirque below the summit cliffs.

To find westside hiking routes, drive Highway 97 to the Klamath Forest Wildlife Refuge sign near milepost 228, turn east on the Silver Lake Road for 21 paved miles, and turn right on Road 49 for 5 miles to Jackson Creek Campground.

SNOWSHOEING & SKIING

Jackson Creek Campground, accessed by plowed Road 49, is a winter Nordic ski and snowshoe center with 25 miles of marked trails. For starters, ski 1.4 miles up Jackson Creek on a snowed-under road, cross the creek, and climb east 0.8 mile to a viewpoint of Yamsay Mountain. Loop routes return either along the north rim of Jackson Creek's canyon or south through ponderosa pine woods. The area's toughest goal is Yamsay Mountain's summit, 8.7 miles from the Jackson Creek Campground and 3400 feet up.

Black bear cub.

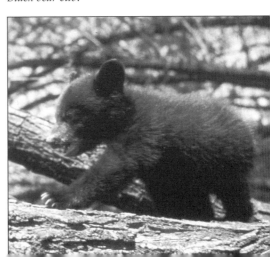

60

GEARHART MOUNTAIN

Picturesque cliffs, rock domes, and pinnacles top this long mountain. Nearby, trails climb from Campbell and Dead Horse Lakes to clifftop viewpoints above a vast pine forest.

Gearhart Mountain.

Climate

Summer days shine clear and seldom hot in this forested upland. Be prepared for possible afternoon thunderstorms

Location: 36 mi NW of Lakeview, 66 mi E of Klamath Falls

Size: 72 sq mi

Status: 35 sq mi designated wilderness (1964, 1984)

Terrain: forested ridges, cliffs, valleys

Elevation: 5700'-8364'

Management: Fremont-Winema NF

Map: Gearhart Mountain Wilderness (USFS)

and frosty nights. Snow blocks the upper portions of trails at Gearhart Mountain and Dead Horse Rim from November to mid-June. Roads and lower trails are usually clear by May. Mosquitoes are a problem at lower elevations in June, and at upper elevations in July. Winters can be extremely cold. Annual precipitation ranges from 35 inches at Gearhart Mountain to 20 inches in the lowlands.

Plants and Wildlife

Bald eagles from the Klamath Lake area to the west often visit the high lakes here in hopes of fish.

The park-like stands of ponderosa pine here survive wildfire well. Because old-growth ponderosas lack low branches, fires burn brush and grass without reaching the trees' crowns. Ponderosa bark has a jigsaw-puzzle surface that flakes off during fires to remove heat from the trunk. The bark gradually turns orange after a century or more in the sun, developing a pleasant vanilla smell.

The smaller, denser lodgepole pines burn easily in forest fires, but reseed profusely. Lodgepoles have two needles to a cluster, while ponderosas have three and other local pines five.

Mammals here include mule deer, black bear, coyotes, and porcupine. Listen for little, round-eared pikas whistling from their rockslide homes.

Geology

Both Gearhart Mountain and Dead Horse Rim began as shield-shaped vol-

Campbell Lake from Campbell Rim.

canoes built of many thin basalt layers. The older of the two, Gearhart Mountain may once have stood 10,000 feet high. Erosion uncovered the resistant lava that forms its summit cliffs, as well as The Dome and The Palisades—an area of weirdly shaped, 30-foot pinnacles. Ice Age glaciers scooped out the impressive U-shaped valleys of Gearhart Creek, Dairy Creek, and Dead Horse Creek.

Coleman Rim's cliff is the scarp of a fault block, like most cliff-edged mountains in the Great Basin.

HIKING & BACKPACKING

From the north end of the popular, well-graded Gearhart Mountain Trail an easy 2.4-mile hike reaches Blue Lake, a backpacking goal with a view of the long, low mountain. For a longer trip, either circle the lake on a 0.8-mile path or continue 4 miles up the trail to its highest point at The Notch, a spectacular 8120-foot pass directly below Gearhart Mountain's summit cliff.

From the south end of the Gearhart Mountain Trail, hikers start near Lookout Rock's tower, pass through The Palisades at the 1-mile mark, and climb another 3.7 miles to a viewpoint in a 7930-foot saddle. This makes a possible turnaround point, but it's worth continuing 1.3 easy miles through alpine meadow openings to the better view at The Notch. Off-trail explorers can find a cluster of balancing rocks on The Dome.

On a clear day, hikers atop Gearhart Mountain's summit can spot Steens Mountain, the Three Sisters, and even Mount Lassen. Take the trail from Lookout Rock 3.7 miles to the 7930-foot saddle (GPS location N42°28.927' W120°51.945'), then scramble left up to a ridgetop and follow it for an easy, nearly level mile to the summit (GPS location N42°29.761' W120°52.641'). No special gear or use of hands is required.

To drive to these trailheads from Paisley (on Highway 31 between Lakeview and Summer Lake), take Mill Street (Road 34) west from town for 19 paved miles, turn right on paved Road 28 for 2.5 miles, and turn left on paved Road 34 for 6 miles to Dairy Creek. To find the northern trailhead from this junction, turn right on gravel Road 3372 for 8 miles, and turn left on Road 015 to its end at the North Fork Trailhead. To find the southern trailhead from the Dairy Creek junction, continue straight on paved Road 34 another 4.5 miles and turn right on gravel Road 012 for 1.5 miles to its end, passing the pleasant Corral Creek Campground along the way.

The Boulder Spring Trail offers a backdoor route to Gearhart Mountain's high country. This 6-mile route gains 2600 feet from a ponderosa pine forest at Road 018 to a trail junction on the peak's shoulder, passing the meadows at Boulder Spring on the way. The first 3 miles of the trail follow an old road that was closed to improve fish habitat in Deming Creek. To reach the trailhead from Bly (between Klamath Falls and Lakeview), take Highway 140 east of town 1.4 miles, turn left on Campbell Road for 0.6 mile, turn right on paved Road 34 for 4 miles, turn left on gravel Road 335 for 1.5 miles, and turn right on Road 018 for 3 miles.

Dead Horse Rim, though nearly as tall as Gearhart Mountain, is much less craggy and more accessible. For a 4.9-mile loop in this area, start at a trailhead pullout in the midst of Campbell Lake's campground, climb 1.5 miles to a viewpoint on Campbell Rim's lip, and then keep right at junctions to return to Campbell Lake. For a slightly longer loop (7.4 miles), continue from Campbell Rim to Dead Horse Rim, and then return via Dead Horse Lake.

A larger network of faint trails, particularly popular with equestrians, extends for miles through the open, but largely viewless lodgepole pine forests beyond Dead Horse Rim. Two routes lead southeast from Dead Horse Lake about 8 miles to the ponderosa pine woods of Augur Creek at Road 34. Another two trails head northwest from Dead Horse Lake (for 3.9 miles and 6 miles) to the Lee Thomas Trailhead on Road 3411.

Cross-country hiking is easy in the area's open forests; bring a compass and topographic map. At Gearhart Mountain and Dead Horse Rim, strike off from established trails to follow ridges or find meadows in high creek basins. Old trails at Dairy Creek and to Gearhart Creek from Road 3411 provide good starts. Likewise, cross-country hikes are the way to explore Coleman Rim's interesting ridgecrests, ponderosa pine forests, and meadows. Two routes lead to Coleman Rim from the primitive Lantern Flat campsite on Road 024. Either drive 0.7 mile past Lantern Flat on Road 024 and hike east through aspen-filled meadows (known as Shepard Camp), or drive north from Lantern Flat 0.7 mile on Road 017 and hike abandoned Road 224 east to meadows along the rim.

Backpackers can hike the entire 12.1-mile Gearhart Mountain Trail or simply spend a few days in the high country

The Pinnacles.

exploring from a base camp. Firewood is scarce and fire danger often high, so bring a camp stove. Saddle stock are only allowed within 200 feet of open water in the designated wilderness for watering, loading, or travel on trails.

SNOWSHOEING & SKIING

Though none of the roads in the area is plowed in winter, cars can usually drive from Lakeview or Bly to the Corral Creek Campground (elevation 5960 feet) by early April. From there, ski or snowshoe 2 miles up to the Lookout Rock tower and another nearly level mile to The Palisades.

BOATING

Small craft do well on half-mile-long Dead Horse Lake and smaller Campbell Lake. No motors are allowed.

Blue Lake's trailhead.

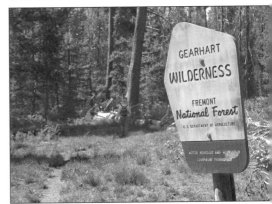

61
CRANE MOUNTAIN

Highest point in south-central Oregon, Crane Mountain lifts its sudden scarp above the sagebrush flatlands and marshes of vast Goose Lake.

Climate

Very cold winters whiten the mountain's crest by late November. The snow lingers to mid-June. Summer temperatures are pleasantly mild. Despite 40 to 60 inches of average annual precipitation, blue skies predominate.

Plants and Wildlife

May and June bring wildflower displays to the high meadows covering much of this long mountain. Expect paintbrush, aster, balsamroot, clarkia, penstemon, phacelia, yarrow, and spreading phlox. In fall, white-barked quaking aspen brighten the gulches with brilliant orange leaves. Evergreen trees range from spire-shaped subalpine fir at the highest elevations to mountain mahogany on dry slopes and tall ponderosa pine in lower forests.

Hikers may spot mule deer, jackrabbits, porcupines, and coyotes. Goose Lake's tremendously varied bird population, which peaks during spring and fall migrations, includes pelicans, herons, tundra swans, geese, and many ducks. Bald and golden eagles soar above the mountain and lake in winter.

Geology

Great Basin faulting has chopped much of southeast Oregon into broad valleys and blocky mountains. The huge fault scarp forming Crane Mountain's abrupt western cliffs continues north 40 miles to Abert Rim. Basalt lava flows that once covered this area as a level sheet have been hoisted 3700 feet to the top of Crane Mountain, exposing underlying John Day rhyolite tuff on the mountain's western flank. Rockhounds find agate nodules and thundereggs in this rhyolite layer east of Highway 395.

The optimistically named Highgrade Mining District uncovered small amounts of gold-bearing quartz in the basalt flows capping the southern end of Crane Mountain. The find still puzzles geologists, because basalt is usually a hopeless place to look for gold.

Older residents in the area recall when Goose Lake drained via the Pit River to the Sacramento. Irrigation has since lowered the lake, leaving it landlocked and increasingly saline.

Quaking aspen in winter.

Location: 5 mi E of Lakeview
Size: 60 sq mi
Status: undesignated wilderness
Terrain: forested fault block mountain, high meadows
Elevation: 5200'-8454'
Management: Fremont-Winema NF
Maps: Crane Mountain, Crane Creek (USGS)

HIKING & BACKPACKING

Start with an overview of the area from a fire lookout on Crane Mountain's crest. Dirt Road 015 leads there but is far too rough and steep for passenger cars, so park at the junction with gravel Road 4011 and walk the final 2.7 miles, gaining 1400 feet. Just before Road 015's end, the Crane Mountain Trail branches south. This scenic, 8.7-mile route, with views from Mount Shasta to Steens Mountain, parallels the rim's edge into California. Motorcycles are allowed, but rare. The highest point on Crane Mountain is a mile south along this trail and a short scramble west.

Another section of the Crane Mountain Trail heads north from Road 015. It begins 0.8 mile below the end of Road 015 and switchbacks down the ridgecrest past Red Peak for 10.5 miles to cross Road 3915 at Rogger Meadow's quaking aspen groves. For an easily accessible sample of this route, park at Road 3915 and follow the trail south a few miles to ridgetop viewpoints. Equestrians can also follow the trail north of 3915 for 3 miles and continue along backroads 6 miles north to the Walker Trailhead on Road 3615 (see area 60 map). From there, the Crane Mountain Trail continues north, mostly along abandoned roads, for 7.9 miles to the Fremont Trail at Crooked Creek.

The high meadows and open forests lend themselves to cross-country exploration. One rugged route follows a bench on the western face of Crane Mountain from Kelley Creek to Cogswell Creek.

SNOWSHOEING & SKIING

The Warner Mountain Ski Area operates one triple-chair lift and a day lodge from mid December to mid March, depending on snow conditions. The area has 25 kilometers of Nordic ski trails and serves as a base for trips south on snowed-under roads toward Crane Mountain.

62
ABERT RIM &
HART MOUNTAIN

Pronghorn antelope and bighorn sheep here roam the edges of the nation's tallest fault-scarp cliffs. Marshes at the Warner Lakes attract pelicans, cranes, and swans. In the uplands, sagebrush plains stretch to the horizon.

Pronghorn Antelope.

Climate

As upland snow melts from March to late May, dry lakes fill and mud may close some dirt roads. Wildflowers bloom in late May and June. July and August afternoons can top 100° F, although nights are cool. Fall brings mild days and frosty nights. Sub-zero snowstorms close the Plush-Frenchglen road and Highway 140 east of Adel periodically between December and March. Blue sky presides 300 days a year in this region of only 9- to 20-inch annual precipitation.

Plants and Wildlife

Graceful pronghorn antelope browse sagebrush throughout the area. North America's swiftest land animals at up to 65 mph, they flash their white rumps and release a musk when alarmed to flight. Nearly 2000 live on the Hart Mountain National Antelope Refuge, although they retreat during severe winters to Nevada. Pronghorns can easily outrun any local predator by 20 mph. They originally evolved their surprising speed to keep ahead of cheetahs, a species that died out in North America in the last Ice Age.

Overhunting and domestic sheep dis-

Location: 25 mi NE of Lakeview, 93 mi SW of Burns

Size: 718 sq mi (including Drake Peak and Fish Creek Rim)

Status: undesignated wilderness; 430 sq mi national wildlife refuge

Terrain: high desert block mountains, ephemeral lakes

Elevation: 4237'-8405'

Management: US Fish and Wildlife Service, Lakeview District BLM, Fremont-Winema NF

Maps: Lake Abert South, Little Honey Creek, Crook Peak, Drake Peak, Hart Lake, Warner Peak, Campbell Lake, Flagstaff Lake, Priday Reservoir, Adel, Guano Lake, Alger Lake, and 14 other maps (USGS)

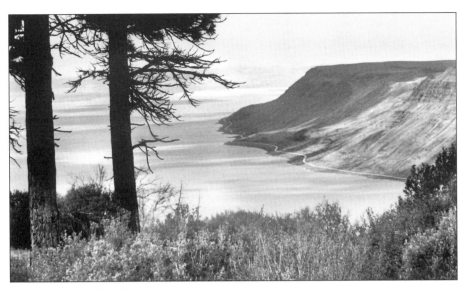

Abert Lake from Abert Rim.

eases drove bighorn sheep to extinction in Oregon by 1915. Twenty of the curly-horned sheep were reintroduced at Hart Mountain from British Columbia in 1954. They multiplied with such success that animals have since been trapped here and released at many Southeast Oregon locations. About 250 now live on rimrock ledges from Hart Mountain to Poker Jim Ridge, with smaller herds on the cliffs of Fish Creek Rim and Abert Rim.

Warner Lakes' marshes sustain elegant egrets, awkward white pelicans, eared grebes, ruddy ducks, geese, and many other birds. Visit in March or April for the spectacular spring migrations.

Bald eagles, golden eagles, and prairie falcons nest in rimrock ledges overlooking the lakes. Fish Creek Rim averages four aeries built of sticks per mile. Ask refuge employees for the best spots to watch sage grouses perform their peculiar strutting, puffing, gurgling courtship displays at the crack of dawn from mid-March to mid-May.

Twelve species of sagebrush grow here. Silver sage graces alkali playas. In rich soils, big sagebrush reaches 15 feet in height with 8-inch-diameter trunks. Near big sage, expect profuse displays of paintbrush, larkspur, buckwheat, and

Rock art at Petroglyph Lake.

Rock art at Petroglyph Lake.

sage buttercups in spring. The low sagebrush of rocky, high elevations protects different spring flowers: bitterroot, crag aster, and goldenweed. Rarest plants in the area are salty Lake Abert's endangered Columbia watercress, South Abert Rim's delicate blue-leaved penstemon, and Guano Creek's threatened Crosby's buckwheat.

In fall, quaking aspens in rim gulches turn stunning yellow and orange. Small groves of ponderosa pine—remnants of a vast Ice Age forest—survive near Hart Mountain's Blue Sky area and at Abert Rim between Colvin Lake and Juniper Creek. The snowier Warner Mountains about Drake Peak support fir forests.

Geology

Although history records no major earthquakes here, the rocks do. Very fresh-looking fault scarps at Abert Rim, Poker Jim Ridge, Hart Mountain, and Fish Creek Rim show that blocks of earth have shifted 2400 feet vertically, leaving plateaus and gaping lake valleys. The landscape here must have been mostly flat 10 million years ago, because Steens Mountain basalt lava of that age covers all these disjointed rims. Hot springs and the Crump Geyser also suggest ongoing crustal activity.

The Ice Age brought rain instead of ice to this area. Lake levels rose about 200 feet, unifying the Warner Lakes and connecting Lake Abert with Summer Lake (area 58). Beaches of these once-

The Warner Lakes from Poker Jim Ridge.

Warner Peak from upper Rock Creek near Barnhardi Basin.

huge lakes remain as gravel terraces on valley edges near Plush and along Poker Jim Ridge. Now even Lake Abert and Hart Lake run dry in lean years.

Jasper, agate, and opal have been found on Hart Mountain's western face. The wildlife refuge allows collection of 7 pounds of rocks per person. Ask in the Plush general store for directions to a designated sunstone collecting area north of that village.

History

Northern Paiute Indians sailed these lakes on rafts of bundled bulrushes to hunt ducks and to gather eggs in disposable cattail baskets. Hundreds of ancient petroglyphs remain at Hart Lake, Colvin Lake, Petroglyph Lake, and the southern tip of Fish Creek Rim. This ancient rock art can be damaged even by fingerprint oils, so touch nothing. Caves in the rimrock overlooking Guano Lake may have been occupied in the Ice Age. Arrowheads, old bottles, and all other artifacts are federally protected. Looters and collectors are prosecuted.

The Hart Mountain National Antelope Refuge was created in 1936, but cattle grazing wasn't banned until the late 1990s. The ranchers' barbed wire fences can be deadly to antelope, a species that does not leap well, and are still being removed.

HIKING & BACKPACKING

The area has few marked trails, but rim edges, creeks, and ridges offer abundant natural pathways in this open landscape.

Drive slowly along the gravel road from Plush toward the Hart Mountain refuge, watching with binoculars for birdlife in the Warner Lakes and for bighorn sheep on the eastern cliffs. A pullout at Hart Lake has a short, overgrown nature trail and a wildlife viewing blind. A more interesting roadside stop is halfway up Poker Jim Ridge, where a 0.3-mile trail loops to a viewpoint across the lakes far below. For a better view, park where the road crests Poker Jim Ridge and bushwhack north along the rim 2.2 miles to a cliff-edged knoll (GPS location N42°35.479' W119°40.999'). Rocks and matted sagebrush make for slow walking. To return on a loop, set off east across the desert a mile to Petroglyph Lake's ancient rock art (GPS location N42°34.538' W119°40.446'), and then angle southwest 1.5 miles back to your car.

At the refuge's Hot Springs Campground, relax in the hot springs' 104° F natural pool. Bring your own drinking water to this free campground (containers may be filled at the refuge headquarters), or use a filtration pump to purify water from Rock Creek.

For a nice 5.3-mile loop from the

Waterfall in DeGarmo Canyon.

campground, follow animal trails up Rock Creek 2.8 miles to a dilapidated cabin at Barnhardi Basin's broad meadow (GPS location N42°28.790′ W119°43.200′). Return along Barnhardi Road, a dirt track that is gated closed to vehicles December 1 to August 1. For a longer hike or a backpacking trip, camp near the Barnhardi Cabin and climb to DeGarmo Notch's pass (GPS location N42°29.094′ W119°43.917′). From there you can either follow a broad ridge south 2 miles to the panoramic view atop Warner Peak, the refuge's highest point (GPS location N42°27.579′ W119°44.474′), or you can hike down DeGarmo Canyon 4.7 miles to the paved road to Plush.

A nice, relatively short hike for adventurers follows a rough trail up the scenic lower portion of DeGarmo Canyon to a 35-foot waterfall. Drive paved Road 3-12 from Plush 10 miles to a "DeGarmo" Canyon pointer, back up 100 yards, and take a rough dirt road uphill 0.3 mile to a parking area at road's end (GPS location N42°29.005′ W119°47.327′). Follow the trail into the canyon's mouth for 0.7 mile to the falls. The path ends here, but if you scramble up the canyon's left slope you'll find an abandoned cattle path that leads upstream 3 miles to the canyon's upper end.

Other cross-country routes follow Rock Creek 5 miles downstream to the Refuge Headquarters, passing beaver ponds along the way. Or hike 4 miles

The Drake Lookout is not on Drake Peak, but rather on a shoulder of Light Peak nearby.

northwest onto the plateau at the head of Willow Creek to visit a bighorn sheep corral and get an impressive rim-edge view of Flagstaff Lake.

Permits are required to camp anywhere in the refuge except Hot Springs Campground. The headquarters at the refuge is often unstaffed, but a visitor information room is left unlocked, and self-issuing permits can be filled out there. The refuge bans off-road vehicle travel, hang gliders, excessive noise, and destruction of live plants. Firearms are restricted. Mountain bikes are permitted only on established roads.

Abert Rim's stark face may look unhikable, but a little-known 2-mile scramble route from Highway 395 takes hikers right to the top. Park at the watchable wildlife parking area at the southern end of Abert Lake and bushwhack up beside Juniper Creek to a breathtaking overlook of alkali-fringed Lake Abert, 1700 feet below. From the top, it's easy to follow the rim 3 miles north to a spring and ancient, rock-walled Paiute hunting blind on the rimrock above Poison Creek. For an 11-mile backpack, trek Abert Rim south from Juniper Creek to the hang gliding launch site atop Tagues Butte, a good place to leave a shuttle car.

For a break from sagebrush bushwhacking, try the trail system through fir forests and quaking aspen groves of the Drake Peak area. Three trail routes converge at the South Fork Crooked Creek Trailhead on paved Road 3615. To the west, a 6.9-mile portion of the Fremont Trail descends Crooked Creek's canyon, dropping 2100 feet to the Mill Trailhead, on a dirt spur road that joins Highway 395 near milepost 132. To the north, a fainter portion of the Fremont Trail skirts rounded Twelvemile Peak and Crook Peak through alpine sagebrush fields with far-ranging views. The trail crosses Road 3720 at the Swale Trailhead after 6.7 miles, and continues faintly 4 more miles to Vee Lake at the end of Road 3616. To the southwest of the South Fork Crooked Creek Trailhead, a third trail follows a roaded, logged rim toward Crane Mountain (see area 61).

For the best overview of the half dozen peaks surrounding the once-glaciated basins of Twelvemile and McDowell Creeks, drive to the Drake Lookout (which is not on Drake Peak). To rent the historic lookout building for overnight use, call (541) 947-3334 or check www.recreation.gov. For a hike, take spur Road 138 a mile east of the lookout, and walk cross-country along an open ridge another mile to Drake Peak's real summit.

The cliffs of little-known Fish Creek Rim rise 2400 feet above the Warner

Lakes, providing a view across 5 miles of thin air to Hart Mountain. Best routes for cross-country exploration follow the rim's edge or else descend through a break in the rimrock 3.5 miles from Cleland Spring to the Plush-Adel Highway at Crump Lake. Drive to the upper rim by taking paved Road 313 north from Highway 140 for 12 miles; turn right on a rough dirt road for 8 miles, then park and hike east.

The Fremont Trail follows Crooked Creek.

Guano Creek is a misnamed oasis. Park at the creek crossing north of Shirk Lake and hike up this green-banked stream as it meanders between low rimrock walls. From Adel, drive 21 miles east on Highway 140, and then take a dirt road 13 miles north.

On all hikes, carry plenty of water. By summer all lakes and streams are dry or undrinkable due to salinity or cattle pollution. Dirt roads shown by dashed lines on the map may be impassable for passenger cars; inquire locally.

BOATING

In wet years, the Warner Lakes feature 300 miles of canoe routes. Of particular interest are the sinuous waterways linking Campbell Lake with a primitive campsite at Turpin Lake, as well as routes linking Mugwump, Swamp, and Anderson lakes.

HANG GLIDING

Abert Rim's 2000-foot west scarp faces the west wind, and thermals off Lake Abert make 20-mile flights along the length of the rim possible. To find the launch site at Tagues Butte from Highway 140, drive 21 miles north on Road 3615, turn left at the second entrance to loop Road 032, and after 0.8 mile take a half-mile spur through a gate.

Land on the west side of the road to Simms Ranch, avoiding guarded private land along adjacent Highway 395.

The mouth of DeGarmo Canyon.

63

STEENS MOUNTAIN

Landmark for all of southeast Oregon, 50-mile-long Steens Mountain looms snowy and sudden a vertical mile above the Alvord Desert's stark alkali flats.

Huge, U-shaped gorges dissect the western flank of Steens Mountain's 9733-foot-tall plateau. Rushing western streams lead to the Donner und Blitzen River, which winds through a rimrock-lined canyon on its way to the bird-rich marshes of the Malheur National Wildlife Refuge. The vast, treeless Sheepshead Mountains stretch to the northeast, a jumble of sagebrush ridges and dry lakebeds.

Wildhorse Lake.

Climate

A sign at the foot of the Steens Mountain Loop Road notes, "Weather Advisory: The Steens Mountain area experiences frequent and sudden storms. Be prepared for sudden and extreme lightning, snow, rain and high winds." Winter snow and gates block access to the Steens' uplands from about mid-November to the first of July. However, summer on the mountain is generally cool and clear with freezing nights. Prepare for thundershowers and July mosquitoes or gnats. Avoid trees and high places during lightning storms. To check Steens weather conditions before a visit, call the BLM's Burns office at (541) 573-4400.

April, May, and June are pleasant below 6000 feet elevation, with abundant wildflowers and water. In these months, the Alvord Desert and other playas may become lakes. July and August are pleasant above 6000 feet, but these same months bring blazing heat to lower elevations, with little or no shade. Fall is cool but bone dry. December to February, fiercely cold winds rake the region.

Annual precipitation drops from 40 inches on Steens Mountain to just 7 inches in the Alvord Desert—Oregon's driest spot.

If you are ever troubled by mosquitoes at Steens Mountain, you are at the wrong elevation. Go up or down a thousand feet and all will be well.

Plants and Wildlife

Five life zones band the mountain. Above 8000 feet, expect bunchgrass, colorful rock-encrusting lichens, and a blaze of August wildflowers. Steens paintbrush, moss gentian, a dwarf blue lupine, and showy Cusick's buckwheat grow atop Steens Mountain and nowhere else in the world. In high cirques, look for bleeding heart, shooting star, bitterroot, buttercup, and wild onion. A herd of bighorn sheep also likes these cirques; watch for them from the East Rim overlook.

Quaking aspen groves dot the 6500-8000-foot zone, with flashing leaves in summer and orange foliage in fall. Look for (but do not deface) the bawdy graffiti Basque shepherds carved in the aspen's white bark near old camps in Little Blitzen Gorge and Whorehouse Meadows. Beldings ground squirrels and marmots thrive here, as do July flowers—clarkia, monkeyflower, and prairie star.

Juniper and low sagebrush dominate between 5500 and 6500 feet elevation. Listen at dawn for sage grouse strutting and puffing in courtship displays March to mid May. Wild horses and antelope run here, especially on the benchlands west of Blitzen Crossing. Jackrabbits, coyotes, and rattlesnakes are common. May brings blooms of penstemon, buckwheat, and (in the Stonehouse Creek area) rare Biddle's lupine.

Below 5500 feet, tall sagebrush rules. Watch for young burrowing owls standing about their ground holes in June. At small, multi-entranced burrows, listen for the thumping of long-tailed kangaroo rats scolding within. The kit fox, once thought extinct in Oregon, still hunts the southern Sheepshead Mountains by night. Lizards abound.

Alkaline playas such as the Alvord Desert are virtually devoid of life, but salt-tolerant species cling to their sandy fringes, including bright green greasewood bushes, leafless orange iodine bush, saltgrass, and spiny shadscale. Silver sage covers other dry lakebeds, such as Follyfarm Flat. Spadefoot toads emerge en masse from the ground after rains. Antelope ground squirrels scamper even in summer heat, shaded by their curled white tails.

Huge flocks of migrating birds begin arriving at the Malheur National Wildlife Refuge in late February: snow geese, lesser sandhill cranes, tundra swans, and pintails. The spectacle peaks from mid-March to mid-April. Greater sandhill cranes nest in April, when migrant curlews, avocets, and stilts arrive. Songbirds pass through in April and May. By June grass is so tall at the refuge that birds are more often heard than seen. Watch for muskrats in the refuge's canals, and porcupines and great horned owls in streamside willow thickets.

Because the creeks here have had no

Location: 63 mi S of Burns

Size: 1293 sq mi (including Alvord Desert and Sheepshead Mountains)

Status: 273 sq mi designated wilderness (2000)

Terrain: snow-capped fault-block mountain, glaciated canyons, desert playas, sagebrush hills

Elevation: 4025'-9733'

Management: Burns District BLM, Vale District BLM

Maps: Alvord Desert, Steens Mountain to Alvord, Steens Mountain to Page Springs, Page Springs to Diamond (Desert Trail Association); Fish Lake, Wildhorse Lake, Alvord Hot Springs, and 33 other maps (USGS); Steens Mountain (non-topographic, BLM)

outlet to the sea for millennia, unusual fish species have evolved, including redband trout and the Catlow tui chub. Wildhorse Lake, Mann Lake, and Juniper Lake have been stocked with rare Lahontan trout.

Geology

All rocks here are volcanic—a layer cake of dark basalt lava and light rhyolite ash. When this rock erupted about 15-20 million years ago, it covered most of Southeast Oregon 4000 feet deep, leveling the landscape. Nonetheless, the eruptions here were smaller than the massive Columbia River basalt floods in Northeast Oregon. The Steens basalt

Steens Mountain from Mann Lake.

looks different too, full of big feldspar crystals.

Then North America's shearing collision with the Pacific crustal plate stretched Oregon diagonally, shattering Southeast Oregon into basins and ranges. Steens Mountain rose entirely in the past 5 to 7 million years. The Sheepshead Mountains consist of smaller rims and basins. Hot springs indicate continuing fault movement.

The Ice Age brought increased rain as well as snow. A lake filled the Alvord Basin 200 feet deep all the way to Coyote Lake. When water spilled out Big Sand Gap to the Owyhee River, it lowered the lake 40 feet and sent a flood surging down the Snake and Columbia Rivers.

Ice Age glaciers on Steens Mountain gouged seven U-shaped canyons 2000 feet deep. The canyons left only narrow fingers of the original Steens plateau intact, and even these were breached by glaciers at Rooster Comb and Kiger Notch.

As the Ice Age drew to a close about 10,000 years ago, eruptions along the Brothers Fault Zone produced rugged, fresh-looking basalt flows at Diamond Craters (north of Diamond) and the Saddle Butte Lava Field.

Today, look for smooth bedrock polished by glaciers at the head of Big Indian Gorge. Along Pike Creek and Little Alvord Creek, exposed ash formations contain thundereggs, agates, and petrified wood. In desert basins, note where wind has stripped the ground to "desert pavement," fields of pebbles stained brown by "desert varnish," a crust of oxides.

History

Semi-nomadic Northern Paiute Indians lived in brush lean-tos and caves in this area, relying chiefly on jackrabbits for meat and fur. Peter Skene Ogden led beaver trappers to the area's creeks in 1825-29. Army Major Enoch Steen battled the Paiutes and named the mountain in the late 1860s, exiling Indians to reservations at Yakima and later Burns.

Pete French built a cattle empire here during 1872-97; his P Ranch near Frenchglen is now owned and maintained by the Malheur Wildlife Refuge. By 1901, Basque and Irish shepherds

Walt Riddle's early 1900s ranch house on the Little Blitzen River is open to the public.

Big Indian Creek's canyon.

were grazing over 140,000 head of sheep on Steens Mountain, obliterating once-lush grasslands. Domestic sheep were banned from public land on the mountain in 1972. Cattle were excluded from the mountain's fragile summit and canyons in 1982, and were banned from other wilderness upland areas in 2001, but, ironically, still dominate the wildlife refuge.

The Riddle Ranch preserves the ranch houses, barns, workshops, and corrals built by three bachelor brothers in the early 1900s. In summer, volunteers are on hand to answer visitors' questions. To find the ranch from the South Steens Campground, drive 0.3 west on the main road and turn right 1.3 miles to a parking area by a gate. If you have a passenger car, park here and walk the final 1.3 miles. When the gate is open (Thursday to Sunday from mid-June to October), rugged vehicles can be

driven all the way to the ranch.

HIKING & BACKPACKING

The area's most spectacular views are just a short walk from the Steens Mountain Loop Road. Start by driving the well-maintained northern portion of this gravel road east from Frenchglen. After 2.9 miles, turn right for 0.6 mile to the far end of the Page Springs Campground. Two trails begin here: a 1.4-mile interpretive nature loop that climbs to a rimrock viewpoint, and a rough scramble path that follows the Donner und Blitzen River 0.8 mile into a rimrock canyon before petering out.

Then return to the Page Springs Campground entrance, turn right on Steens Mountain Loop Road, follow it 18.9 miles uphill, and follow a pointer left 0.4 mile to the Kiger Gorge Viewpoint. A 100-yard trail leads to a cliff overlooking the colossal canyon. Adventurers can bushwhack 0.5 mile left

STEENS MOUNTAIN

0 1 2 3 4 5mi
0 2 4 6 8km
N

Follyfarm (site)

Burns 66 mi

Burnt Flat

Oriana Flat

5200' X

6330' X

Squaw Cr

Squaw L

Tencent

Renwick Canyon

Fifteen Cent L

Road

4600 Small Butte

Ryegrass

Cr

Saddle

Butte

Lava

78

Heath Lake (dry)

South

6289'

Juniper

Lake Ridge Res

Lava

Stonehouse Peak

Stonehouse Cr

Heath Cr

Sheepshead Mountains

Johnny Cr

Palomino

Cr

Palomino Hills

X 5225'

Jordan Valley 46 mi

Fields

5005' X

Sulfur Spr

Coffin Butte

Table Mtn 6060'

Bone Spr

Burns Junction

West Pk 6068'

Mickey Basin

Wildcat

4300

Bone Cr

Flat Top Mtn 4575'

Mickey Butte

6294'

Creek

Mickey Hot Springs

4100

Sand

95

5384'

Crooked Cr

Coyote Lake (dry) 4040'

X 4555'

Sand

4800

Big Sand Gap

Sand

Whitehorse Ranch 6 mi

(See Area 64 Map)

Whitehorse Ranch 8 mi

Winnemucca 101 mi

The Little Blitzen River's canyon from a riverbend above 4-Mile Camp.

along the rim to find a very steep scramble trail that descends 1400 feet to the valley floor.

Next, drive 2.7 miles farther along the Loop Road to a 4-way junction. First drive the left-hand fork 0.3 mile to the East Rim's breathtaking vista of the Alvord Desert. Then, drive the middle fork 2 miles to a parking lot at road's end, where two trails begin. For an easy 0.3-mile walk, follow a closed road up to five small radio buildings on the mountain's panoramic 9733-foot summit. For a longer hike from the parking area, take a downhill path to the right 1.2 miles into a gaping canyon to Wildhorse Lake's spectacular alpine wildflower meadows. If you're backpacking here, bring a stove because campfires are not allowed.

Passenger cars and motorhomes should return to Frenchglen as they came, but tougher vehicles can return on a longer loop. From the summit parking area, drive back to the 4-way junction and turn left—but be warned that this portion of the Steens Mountain Loop Road includes 6 miles of steep, rocky road descending the Rooster Comb's narrow ridge.

Trails follow both Big Indian Creek and the Little Blitzen River up long, glacially-carved canyons from South Steens Campground. Expect wildflowers, plenty of springs, scenic quaking aspen, and waterfalls.

From a gate in the group camp area at the far left end of the campground, hike a closed, shadeless dirt road 1.9 miles to its end at a ford of Big Indian Creek. Usually it's possible to cross dry-footed on a log downstream. A genuine trail continues up the scenic canyon (encountering two other creek crossings) for 4.6 miles before petering out at a creekside cottonwood grove—a good backpacking destination. Bushwhackers can continue through sagebrush meadows another 2 or 3 miles, but serious scrambling is required to scale the canyon's steep, 2000-foot headwall to the road on the rim.

To find the Little Blitzen Canyon trail, drive the Steens Mountain Loop Road 0.5 mile east of the South Steens Campground, and park in the marked trailhead lot on the right. Then walk up the road 100 yards to the start of the trail on the left. This path descends a mile to a bridgeless creek crossing that usually can be accomplished dry-footed. Then turn right on a fainter, brushier route another 3.1 miles to 4-Mile Camp, a backpacking destination where big cottonwoods shade a streamside meadow.

Adventurers can continue 3.8 miles up the Little Blitzen's gorge to a fork at a rimrock knoll that divides the canyon. To the left a steep, rough path climbs past a small waterfall to the Steens Mountain Loop Road. To the right the main trail continues faintly upriver 2.4 miles to a 20-foot waterfall at the lip of the valley's cirque. Climbing out of this mile-wide bowl is tricky even at the easiest spot, beside a cascade to the right.

For most of the Desert Trail's route across Steens Mountain, it is not a specific footpath, but rather a general corridor marked by cairns. Hikers must pick their own route through the open, generally treeless terrain. A topographic map and compass are essential. To see the most, plan to backpack. There is no firewood, so bring a camp stove.

A 15-mile section of the Desert Trail traverses impressive Wildhorse Canyon on the way from Frog Spring (on the Fields-Follyfarm Road) up to the Steens Loop Road. Day hikers can climb just 2 miles to a viewpoint knoll. Farther up the route, side trips explore the alpine basins of Wildhorse and Little Wildhorse Lakes.

The Donner und Blitzen River cuts a 400-foot-deep, rimrock-lined canyon through the sagebrush tablelands south of Page Springs Campground. The Desert Trail route parallels this canyon across the tableland 14 miles to the Steens Mountain Loop Road at Blitzen Crossing, Adventurers can also follow the river itself, but expect thick brush and many deep fords. Fish Creek's brushy side canyon is also explorable.

North of Page Springs, the Desert Trail follows Malheur Wildlife Refuge backroads. Camping is banned on refuge lands, as are horses, open fires, swimming, and rock collecting.

The east side of Steens Mountain also offers interesting day hikes and overnight trips. Check your gas gauge before driving the Fields-Follyfarm Road to the Alvord Desert. If the desert lakebed is dry, hike out onto the cracked, alkali surface a few miles to experience this remarkably empty playa and to admire the view of snowy Steens Mountain. Better yet, camp in the desert, continue to the greasewood-covered sand hummocks of the far shore (7 miles distant), prowl Big Sand Gap's canyon, and climb to the rimrock viewpoints nearby.

For this and other desert hikes, do not travel in midsummer heat, carry a gallon of water for each day, and bring a hat or cloth for shade. Expect roads shown by dashed lines to be passable only by four-wheel-drive vehicles.

Conclude a visit to the Alvord Desert with a relaxing soak in Alvord Hot Springs, at an easily visible tin shed 100 yards from the Fields-Follyfarm Road. The Alvord Ranch owns the springs but allows the public to use the site for a small fee. Reward this courtesy by keeping the area free of litter.

Driving north from the Alvord

Steens Mountain from Pike Creek Canyon.

Desert, choose one of Steens Mountains' steep eastern canyons to explore on a day hike. To find the trail up Pike Creek, turn off the Fields-Follyfarm road 3.7 miles south of the Alvord Ranch at a yellow cattle guard (GPS location N42°34.275' W118°31.26'), drive up a very rough road 0.6 mile to a campsite by a house-sized boulder, and hike across the creek. An old mining track leads 1.4 miles up the canyon through a rugged rock narrows with wildflowers and views of the desert playa below. Bushwhackers can continue along the canyon's right-hand slope 1.3 miles to the creek's forks.

Mickey Hot Springs features steam vents, boiling mud pots, and the 30-foot-deep, turquoise Morning Glory Pool, a dangerously scalding cauldron that has

Trekking to the summit of Steens Mountain in winter requires a three-day expedition.

claimed more than one life. The only pool that may be cool enough for humans is a bathtub-sized basin carved into the ground by frustrated bathers. Drive the Fields-Follyfarm Road 5.8 miles north of the Alvord Ranch to the second 90° corner. At a green cattle guard, turn east on a gravel road for 6.5 zigzagging miles. After cautiously exploring the hot springs area, hike to the nearby playa, or climb treeless Mickey Butte for a bird's-eye view of Steens Mountain.

The Sheepshead Mountains are the most barren and forbidding-looking hills in Oregon. And therein lies their secret charm. For even when spring fills the creeks and fires the sagebrush slopes with wildflowers, there are no crowds in this huge world of hidden canyons, cliffs, and valleys. To sample this range, hike 2 miles east from Fifteen Cent Lake (on the Fields-Follyfarm Road) through a canyon to hidden Heath Lake's playa, and scale an unnamed rim nearby for a view. To see more, backpack south from Follyfarm Flat at Highway 78, hike up Renwick Canyon, follow the high rim of the Sheepshead scarp, descend North Heath Creek's canyon, and return to Follyfarm — 23 miles in all.

Try these other utterly uncrowded scenic areas for hiking:

- The far northern end of Steens Mountain. Hike north from Stonehouse Peak's castle-shaped rock along a 7000-foot rim, or explore the lakes and aspen groves near perennial Squaw Creek.

- Catlow Rim. Walk up the canyons of Threemile Creek or Home Creek between sheer, 1300-foot walls and hike to a rim-edge overlook of Catlow Valley and distant Hart Mountain.

- Coyote Lake. Devotees of pure desert delight that this desolate playa is even more remote than its Alvord Desert twin.

Runners compete each August on Oregon's highest 10-kilometer course, the Steens Rim Run from Fish Lake to the 9730-foot East Rim. Record time is 47 minutes.

SNOWSHOEING & SKIING

Powder snow and far-ranging winter vistas are plentiful on Steens Mountain's crest, but difficult access and treacherous weather stop all but the most accomplished snow campers from skiing or snowshoeing there. Sudden whiteouts and freezing winds can occur in any month. Arrange with the Burns District BLM office (541-573-4400) to pick up a permit and gate key. Skiers and snowmobilers are issued permits for different times to avoid conflicts. In April, expect snow to block the road about 3 miles before Fish Lake.

64

PUEBLO MOUNTAINS & TROUT CREEK MOUNTAINS

South of the desolate Alvord Desert, the treeless Pueblo Mountains surprise hikers with high meadow basins nestled against snowy crags. In the Trout Creek Mountains, a dozen creeks have cut scenic, rimrock-lined canyons into a high tableland.

Borax Hot Springs.

Climate

In the Pueblos, snow blocks the Desert Trail from November to late May. Wildflowers peak in June. July and August are hot only in the lowlands. Sudden storms bring lightning and occasionally even snow in summer.

In the Trout Creek Mountains, the snowpack melts in early May and wildflowers appear in May and June. Cattle grazing July 1 to September 15 diminishes mid-summer appeal. Fall is cool and dry.

Annual precipitation, just 7 inches in the lowlands, creeps to 25 inches in the Trout Creek Mountains and 15 in the Pueblos.

Plants and Wildlife

Unusual fish have evolved here, cut off from the sea for millennia. The 90° F alkaline hot springs at Borax Lake support their own species, the 2-inch-long Borax chub. Trout Creek is named for its redband trout, while Willow and Whitehorse creeks contain Lahontan cutthroat trout, a federally listed threatened species. Many of the streams are closed to fishing. Obey signs.

Sagebrush and bunchgrass dominate, but willow, cottonwoods, and quaking aspen turn streams into linear oases. On open slopes, stubby mountain mahogany trees develop elongated crowns—a result of browsing below and shearing winds above.

Wildflowers in meadows include blue lupine, sunflower-like balsamroot, phlox, and the showy Bruneau mariposa lily. In dry areas, look for delicate penstemon and pink bitterroot. Along creeks expect tall larkspur, mint, and

Location: 105 mi S of Burns, 100 mi N of Winnemucca

Size: 641 sq mi

Status: undesignated wilderness

Terrain: fault-block mountains, creek canyons, desert flats

Elevation: 4040'-8634'

Management: Burns District BLM, Vale District BLM

Maps: Pueblo Mountains, Alvord Desert (Desert Trail Association); Chicken Spring, Little Whitehorse Creek, Doolittle Creek, Oregon Canyon Ranch, Van Horn Basin, Ladycomb Peak, and 16 other maps (USGS)

The Pueblo Mountains from cairn #14.

3-foot-tall bluebells.

At the eastern edge of the Trout Creeks, Oregon Canyon is a veritable museum of rare and endangered wildflowers—red buttercup, Lemmon's onion, two-stemmed onion, and bristle-flowered collomia. The Pueblos' Cottonwood Creek harbors one of the northernmost populations of Mormon tea, a green, leafless bush used to brew a mild stimulant. Oregon's only long-flowered snowberry bushes grow along Fifteenmile Creek.

Beavers work virtually every stream in the Trout Creek Mountains. Bighorn sheep live in the Pueblos, but mule deer are more often sighted. Partridge-like chukars by the hundreds cluck in lower canyons of the Pueblos. Listen for the California quails' three-syllable call, the western meadowlarks' territorial songs, and the omnipresent Brewers sparrows. Watch for sage grouse and prairie falcons.

Geology

Steens Basalt lava and ash buried all of Southeast Oregon 15 to 20 million years ago. Great Basin faulting then hacked the flattened landscape into block-shaped, tilted plateaus, including these two ranges. Fault scarps here have exposed the older rock beneath the basalt. Granite, greenstone, and schists along the eastern base of the Pueblos and in canyons of the western Trout Creek Mountains contain traces of gold, copper, and mercury.

Two enormous, violent volcanoes in the Trout Creek Mountains collapsed about 14 million years ago, leaving 15-mile-wide, Crater-Lake-style calderas. The lakes filled with sediment and breached their rims. Willow Creek and McDermitt Creek now drain the two basins. A long arc of cliffs between Disaster Peak and the head of Oregon Canyon marks the McDermitt caldera rim.

History

The 1860s Pueblo Mining District gave the range its name. Look for stone cabin ruins in Denio Canyon and along the Pueblos' Willow Creek. Mining continues in Denio Basin.

The Rose Valley Borax Company once shipped 400 tons of borax a year from Borax Lake to Winnemucca via 16-mule-team wagons. The Nature Conservancy bought the lake and surrounding hot springs in the late 1990s to protect the unusual ecosystem.

Whitehorse Ranch, headquarters for

John Devine's cattle empire during 1869-89, remains a showplace of the old West.

HIKING & BACKPACKING

The Desert Trail route parallels the Pueblo Mountains' crest for 22 miles from Denio to Fields. The trail's cross-country route is marked by 48 cairns, and although each rockpile is supposed to be within sight of the last, it's still easy to miss them. A topographic map and compass are essential.

Day hikers can sample the route at Denio Canyon, and from a very rough side road near Fields. To find this north-ern access, drive the paved road south of Fields 3.1 miles, turn right at a "Domingo Pass" pointer for 3.8 miles, fork right for 0.5 mile, veer left 0.2 mile to a yellow cattle guard, turn left and then keep straight on the largest road 2.1 miles to park at a cairn (GPS location N42°10.67' W118°43.25'). Hike southwest for 2 steep miles to the range's crest and follow the ridge south 1.6 miles to a viewpoint knoll at cairn #14 (GPS location N42°8.275' W118°44.20')

Other cross-country routes that climb to the Desert Trail in the Pueblos ascend

Cottonwood Creek, Colony Creek's canyon meadows, and Van Horn Creek's narrow, rugged gorge.

Perhaps the best view of all is at the 8634-foot summit of Pueblo Mountain, Southeast Oregon's second highest point. Hikers climb there by following an old road up along Arizona Creek 5.7 miles to Stergen Meadow, and then bushwhacking southeast 2 miles up a sagebrush slope.

Even named creeks are often dry in the Pueblos and Trout Creek Mountains. Always carry a gallon of water per day. Sagebrush is the only firewood.

Borax Lake's hot springs make a fascinating day-hike goal. From Fields, drive the paved road 1.3 miles north, go straight on the gravel Fields-Follyfarm Road 0.4 mile to a power substation, turn right on a dirt road along a powerline 2.1 miles to a fork, veer left for 1.8 miles, and park at a wire gate with a hot springs warning sign. Hike the road 0.9 mile to a rusting borax vat beside Borax Lake, and then follow a spur road north toward Steens Mountain 0.6 mile along a string of small, algae-colored hot spring

The Pueblo Mountains.

pools and steam vents. Be careful near these scalding, deep pools. To protect visitors and the springs' ecosystem, the Nature Conservancy bans any attempt to bathe here. If you continue 1.4 miles north, you'll reach the sandy shore of alkaline Alvord Lake.

For a desert challenge, hike the Desert Trail 25 miles across sagebrush flats from Fields to the Alvord Desert (see area 63 map). The Steens, Pueblos, and Trout Creek Mountains look deceptively near all the way. Avoid mid-summer's blazing heat. The only water source is Dixon Spring, 14 miles from Fields.

In the Trout Creek Mountains, hikers often begin excursions from base camps at Willow Creek Hot Springs, Mud Spring , or Chicken Spring.

To find Willow Creek Hot Springs, drive the paved road 8.1 miles south of Fields, and turn left on a broad gravel road for 26.2 miles to the Whitehorse Ranch entrance, where the road narrows to a single lane. Now turn around, backtrack 2.3 miles, and turn left on an unmarked dirt road 2.5 miles to a primitive campground at the swimmable, natural hot springs pool. Park here and explore upstream along Willow Creek or neighboring Little Whitehorse Creek.

If you're starting at Mud Spring instead, hike east 2 miles to an overlook of 1600-foot-deep Oregon Canyon. Many possible routes lead to the bottom. Backpackers can prowl Oregon Canyon Creek's forks and botanize. Less difficult access to this canyon requires permission to cross the Echave Ranch downstream.

Whitehorse Creek's many-branched canyon lies 1 mile west of Mud Spring. Pick one of many routes down through breaks in the rimrock and explore side canyons for beaver dams, waterfalls, and colonnades of spire-shaped rock formations.

From Chicken Spring, drive south 5 miles to McDermitt Creek and hike up the North or South Fork to high meadows amid extensive stands of quaking aspen. From there, backpackers can continue 15 miles down Little Whitehorse Creek's winding, rimrock-lined canyon.

Orevada View, this range's highest area, is a 8506-foot plateau overlooking cone-shaped Disaster Peak and four states. The 4-mile cross-country route across the plateau skirts private land at Sherman Field.

SNOWSHOEING & SKIING

Fierce winter weather limits skiing or snowshoeing in the Pueblo Mountains to experts. By late March snow level is typically at 5600 feet, but winds have sorted things into icy slopes and awkward drifts.

65
LOWER OWYHEE RIVER

Whitewater boaters on this desert river drift into a remote world of towering stone canyons, wild rapids, cliffside caves, and rock pinnacles. Hikers can follow the river canyon too, or investigate the colorfully honeycombed crags of the Leslie Gulch's many side canyons. Nearby, the Jordan Craters Lava Bed includes spatter cones and Coffeepot Crater.

Climate

Blue sky and frosty nights predominate from April to June, but even in this popular season the desert can bring surprise snow flurries or 100° F heat. July and August are too hot for travel, but autumn's coolness again allows hiking. The very cold winter brings only light snows to this region of just 11 inches annual precipitation.

Plants and Wildlife

Wild horses and bighorn sheep roam the rock gulches east of Owyhee Reservoir. In the winter they're joined by an average of 850 mule deer. Commonly sighted smaller wildlife include lizards, rattlesnakes, and white-tailed antelope ground squirrels.

The river and reservoir attract 150 species of songbirds and numerous waterfowl. Bald eagles come to hunt these birds and usually stay until the reservoir is drained for winter. Another good birding spot is Batch Lake, a cluster of marshy potholes amid the Jordan Craters lava. Look for white pelicans, sandhill cranes, and egrets.

Sagebrush dominates here, although

The Owyhee River at Hole in the Ground.

Location: 40 mi S of Ontario, 104 mi E of Burns

Size: 606 sq mi (including Jordan Craters)

Status: federal wild and scenic river, undesignated wilderness

Terrain: cliff-lined desert river, colored rock formations, lava

Elevation: 2670'-6000'

Management: Vale District BLM

Maps: Pelican Point, Rooster Comb, Diamond Butte, Jordan Craters N and S, The Hole In The Ground, Rinehart Canyon, Lambert Rocks, Owyhee Butte, and 25 other maps (USGS)

A spatter cone at Coffeepot Crater.

juniper trees survive atop the tallest peaks and gnarled hackberry trees hug some river benches. The only pine trees, at last count, were 49 ponderosas on a ridge south of Leslie Gulch. The ashy soils of this area have produced a wealth of rare wildflowers. Ertter's groundsel, Packard's blazing star, MacKenzie's phacelia, Owyhee clover, two species of milk vetch, and grimy ivesia are known chiefly from Leslie Gulch. A new penstemon was identified in the early 1980s north of Dry Creek Buttes.

Geology

Erosion carved the colored badlands and rock pinnacles here from compacted volcanic ash deposits as much as 2000 feet thick. Sandwiched throughout this immense ash layer are resistant basalt lava flows also 15 to 20 million years old. This volcanic activity may have dammed the ancestral Snake River, for the ash's stripy strata indicate lakebed deposition.

The old basalt now forms a rimrock cap at Table Mountain, Red Butte, and many other places. The partially welded ash of the Honeycombs contains weak spots that have eroded into caves, ledges, and honeycomb-like indentations. Paleontologists have unearthed horse, bear, camel and antelope fossils from ash near Red Butte. Succor Creek State

Recreation Area allows amateur collecting of thundereggs, agates, and petrified wood from ash deposits there.

Coffeepot Crater and Lava Butte vented the Jordan Craters Lava Beds within the past 9000 years. Look for lava tubes and spatter cones near these two source vents. The relatively smooth, ropy surface of these pahoehoe-style lava flows has been jumbled by pressure ridges, cracks, domes, and collapsed caves. Jordan Craters sits atop the Brothers Fault Zone, the source of a string of recent eruptions across Southeast Oregon.

History

Cave campsites, petroglyphs, and arrowheads indicate humans have lived along the Owyhee River for 12,000 years. Defacing petroglyphs or removing cultural artifacts is a federal crime. The name Owyhee—a 19th-century spelling for Hawaii—commemorates two Polynesian men hired by the Hudson's Bay Company as beaver trappers and killed here by Indians in 1819. Fish runs on the Owyhee died when the Owyhee Dam was built in the 1930s. The reservoir now teems with black crappies. The river supports sparse catfish, suckers, and carp.

HIKING & BACKPACKING

Start by visiting Leslie Gulch's narrow canyon of colorful rock crags. From Interstate 84 at Ontario, follow signs south 14 miles to Nyssa. In Nyssa, turn right at a pointer for Adrian onto Highway 201 for 20.6 miles. Then turn right on gravel Succor Creek Road for 25 miles to a sign for Leslie Gulch, and turn right down this canyon 14.5 miles to its end at the Owyhee Reservoir boat ramp. If you're driving here from Jordan Valley, take Highway 95 north 27 miles, turn left at a sign for Succor Creek for 8.4 gravel miles to a T-junction, turn left another 1.8 miles, and turn left on Leslie Gulch's road. Camping in Leslie Gulch is permitted only at Slocum Campground,

Cottonwood Cr

Freezeout Ridge

Twin Springs

Hwy 20
25 mi

Hwy 201
10 mi

Ontario
28 mi

Owyhee Dam

201

Burnt Mtn

$ Owyhee Reservoir

Creek

Dry

Owyhee Reservoir 2670

Nannys Nipple

Dry Creek Buttes ×4275

Iron Mtn

4300'

Succor Cr

$ Succor Creek

The Honeycombs

Coyote Res. #4

Page Place

Pelican Pt

Carlton Can.

Gulch

Antelope Flat

Quartz Mtn

N Table Mtn

Fingers

Long Gulch

Mud Flat Ranch

Red Butte ×4584

Badlands

Rooster Comb

Leslie Gulch

Rockville

Ontario 65 mi

Slack water (No boat launch) 2670

Hot Spring

Slocum Gulch

Cedar Mtn ×5600'

Crowley 6 mi
Hwy 78 32 mi

Mt Diamond Butte

Mahogany Mtn ×6500'

Morcum Dam Rapids

Warm Spr

Birch Cr Ranch

4100'

Jackson Hole

Ranch

Blowout Res.

Hoot Owl Spr

Iron Pt ×4364

Hole in the Ground

Montgomery Rapids

Coffeepot Crater

Table Mtn

Chalk Basin

Whistling Bird Rapids

Lambert Rocks

Crater L.

Jordan Craters Lava Bed

Cow Lakes

3600'

Bogus Ranch

Batch

95

Ryegrass

Bogus Cr

Stone Cabin

Recent Lava

4800 ×

Clarks Butte

Jordan Valley

Lava

Artillery Rapids

3200'

Lava Butte

Lava

Owyhee R

Bulls Eye Rapids

3700'

Danner (site)

Arock

Lava

Three Forks 28 mi

Crooked Cr

Walls of Rome

Rome

95

Burns 101 mi

3300'

(See Area 66 Map)

Three Forks 29 mi

Antelope Reservoir

LOWER OWYHEE RIVER

0 1 2 3 4 5 6mi
0 2 4 6 8 10km

N

a barren gravel flat 0.2 mile up from the boat ramp. Horses are not allowed in the canyon at all.

Take the time to explore a few of the five hikable side canyons of Leslie Gulch. The only official trail starts at the marked Juniper Gulch trailhead (3.6 miles up the road from Slocum Campground) and heads 0.8 mile up through a narrow wash with overhanging cliffs. An even prettier 0.6-mile route up Timber Gulch's "honeycombed" rock slot is not signed, but begins 2.35 miles up the road from the campground. The old road up scenic Dago Gulch (4.6 miles from the campground) is blocked by a gate and private land after 0.8 mile. Faint paths up Slocum Gulch (at the campground) and Upper Leslie Gulch (4.8 miles from the campground) peter out within half a mile, but adventurers can continue an extra mile or more.

Boats provide a good way to reach many hiking areas. While drifting the Owyhee north of Rome, stop at Chalk Basin to spend a day exploring the colored rock formations and delicately fluted cliffs there. Not far downstream, stop at a huge, river-level cave near Whistling Bird Rapids and hike up a sandy-bottomed gulch past rock narrows and dry waterfalls to Hoot Owl Spring. From the same base camp, another good cross-country hike climbs up 1300 feet in elevation to the canyon rim and Iron Point, practically overhanging the river.

From the shore of Owyhee Reservoir, hikable sandy washes lead to the Honeycombs, an area of gulches lined with sculpted pinnacles. The formations are most concentrated north of Carlton Canyon, but extend to Three Fingers Gulch and Leslie Gulch. Rugged passes provide routes between canyons.

Those who boat to the south end of Owyhee Reservoir can climb to viewpoints at Rooster Comb and Red Butte. Between these lies a colorful badlands of rounded hills.

To access areas along the reservoir, you can rent motorboats at the marina by the Lake Owyhee State Park campground.

Overland access to the Honeycombs is difficult, but possible, by hiking from unmarked, nearly undrivable backroads off Succor Creek Road.

Three dirt roads access the inner part of the Owyhee canyon, but they are accessible only in dry weather by high-clearance vehicles. One road heads north from Rome, coming within a 2-mile walk of scenic Chalk Basin, and within 4 miles of Iron Point.

A different, very steep road descends from the Jordan Craters Lava Bed area to the riverside Birch Creek Ranch, maintained as a museum by the BLM.

A third, unmarked driving route to the Owyhee leads to within a 4-mile hike of Jackson Hole, where Lower Owyhee Canyon is deepest and grandest. Turn off Highway 78 at Follyfarm Junction, 66 miles east of Burns. Take the gravel Crowley Road 25 miles and turn right, through a gate, onto an unmarked dirt road. After 8 very rough miles the track becomes impassable for vehicles. Continue 1 mile on foot, then hike a cattle trail down a gulch to the river.

Wear sturdy boots to explore Jordan Craters' lavaland. Coffeepot Crater is the most popular day hike goal, though Batch Lake's wildlife and Lava Butte's lava tubes are also of interest. To find Coffeepot Crater, drive Highway 95 north of Jordan Valley 8.3 miles, turn left on a gravel road 11.4 miles, fork right onto a dirt road 6.7 miles, veer left onto a rough road 5.9 miles, fork left 1.5 miles, and fork left again 1.4 miles to road's end (GPS location N43°8.77' W117°27.54').

Backpacking? Spend a few days exploring the Honeycombs, or else prowl the Owyhee's rim from Jackson Hole to Chalk Basin. From Chalk Basin it's possible to hike 24 miles south along the

The Honeycombs near Leslie Gulch are eroded ash deposits from a volcano.

trailless riverbank toward Rome. Hike up to the road before hitting private land at Crooked Creek.

On all hikes, bring plenty of water. Pure water sources are limited to infrequent springs along the Owyhee River. A U-shaped tent peg helps tap these dribbles, but by late summer many are dry.

BOATING

First floated in 1953, the 55-mile stretch of Owyhee River between Rome and the reservoir has become a popular four- to six-day trip. Intermediate-level rafters and kayakers generally portage or line through the class 4 rapids (Whistling Bird, Montgomery, and Morcum Dam). Caution is important, because losing a boat on this very remote desert river means trouble. Boaters must register at the launch site or the BLM office in Vale. Commercial boaters need special permits.

Upstream snowmelt makes the river runnable only from March to early June (kayaks sometimes run until mid-June). Bring gear for cold weather. Also carry a day's supply of drinking water, because springs are few. Motorboats are banned.

The first serious whitewater comes 11.5 miles down from the Rome launch site at class 3 Bulls Eye Rapids. Nineteen miles beyond, stop on the left to scout or portage Whistling Bird Rapids. A slab of canyon wall has tumbled into the river here on the right, forcing boaters hard left. Two miles downstream, Montgomery Rapids provides a class 4 drop at a sharp right riverbend. The last major hurdle is 7 miles farther along, where an abandoned rock dam partially blocks the river. In low water, line boats on the left. In high water, experts can also run Morcum Dam's middle.

Owyhee Reservoir's slack water at mile 55 leaves boaters 11 miles to paddle (4 hours for rafts) to the Leslie Gulch ramp. An alternative is to take boats out at the staffed campground at the historic Birch Creek Ranch, although driving there requires a high-clearance four-wheel-drive vehicle.

Canoes and sailboats can do well on the reservoir despite competing powerboats and strong winds. Shoreside campsites abound.

66

UPPER OWYHEE RIVER

Oregon's wildest whitewater river cuts a dramatic, 1000-foot-deep slot through the sagebrush tablelands where Oregon, Idaho, and Nevada meet. Drift boaters here pass cliffside caves and hot springs on their way to raging Widowmaker Rapids. Hikers either follow the branching canyon's arid rims or trace the canyon bottoms, wading when streams career between sheer cliffs.

Location: 105 mi SE of Burns

Size: 750 sq mi

Status: federal wild and scenic river, undesignated wilderness

Terrain: sheer-walled river canyons, whitewater, sagebrush tablelands

Elevation: 3300'-6500'

Management: Vale District BLM

Maps: Three Forks, Whitehorse Butte, Skull Creek, Indian Fort, Dry Creek, Scott Reservoir, Drummond Basin, No Crossing, and 23 other maps (USGS)

Climate

From March to June, when the river is high enough to be run, prepare for unpredictable weather: balmy blue sky, freezing nights, searing heat, or even snow. After a rain, dirt roads become impassably muddy—especially the final mile to Three Forks. May and June are best for hiking in the uplands. Plan canyon bottom hikes for September or October when streams are low and fordable. Avoid the freezing winds of winter or the scorching heat of July and August. Annual precipitation is just 11 inches.

Plants and Wildlife

Watch for kingfishers and water ouzels along the water's edge, fat chukars in the side gulches, and raptors nesting in the rimrock: golden eagles, bu-teos, and prairie falcons. Sage grouse, jackrabbits, and rattlesnakes are more numerous here than anywhere else in Oregon. Pronghorn antelope and mule deer are common.

Sagebrush and bunchgrass dominate this treeless terrain. Plant life in the canyons remains pristine, because cliffs restrict most cattle grazing to the uplands. Phlox and evening primrose provide delicate flowers in spring. Rabbitbrush and sunflower-like balsamroot bloom yellow in fall.

Geology

During immense volcanic eruptions 15 to 20 million years ago, rhyolite ash exploded from vents. Then basalt lava spread across this entire area. Later, as the land gradually rose, the Owyhee River cut downward, exposing the orange welded ash layers and black basalt flows in canyon walls.

HIKING & BACKPACKING

Three Forks, a remote ford near the confluence of three major Owyhee River branches, serves as a base for cross-country exploration of this trailless canyonland. Wear long pants and put on boots that can get wet.

Start by hiking up the main Owyhee River, wading across a tributary and following part of an old military wagon road. A swimmable, 96°F hot springs with a 10-foot waterfall, on the north bank 2.1 miles upriver, is on unmarked private land (GPS location N42°32.78'

W117°11.03′).

Next, put the wet boots back on and try walking up the North Fork's streambed a few miles into that river's inner gorge, where calm, wall-to-wall water reflects the towering canyon above. For a more rugged day hike, explore the Middle Fork's slot-like canyon 3 or 4 miles up from its mouth. The Middle Fork may stop flowing altogether by fall, but leaves deep, wall-to-wall pools that require chest-deep wades.

Streamside cliffs and swift water prevent hikers from following the main Owyhee riverbank downriver from Three Forks. It's possible to bushwhack atop the canyon rim for 40 miles to Rome, but a more realistic hiking goal along this rim would be the Owyhee Overlook pullout, 12 miles away.

Drive to Three Forks either via dirt Three Forks Road (which joins Highway 95 near milepost 36, 16 miles west of Jordan Valley) or on the partly paved State Line Road from Jordan Valley. Both routes are marked as the Soldier Creek Watchable Wildlife Loop. The final 1.4 miles of the spur road descending the canyon to Three Forks is so steep and rough that hikers with passenger cars should park and walk.

Antelope Creek and the West Little Owyhee River both have long, deep, scenic, and very remote canyons. Cross-country hikers following these canyon bottoms must wade (or swim!) some pools and must boulder-hop across a few rockslides, but they can discover towers, caves, columns, chutes, and colored rock walls. By mid-summer, both streams are dry in places. To access the lower ends of these canyons from Three Forks, hike up the Owyhee River 8.4 miles (to Antelope Creek) or 10.5 miles (to the West Little Owyhee).

A fairly good road accesses Anderson Crossing at the upper end of the West Little Owyhee River's canyon (also known as Louse Canyon). Drive Highway 95 south of Burns Junction 40 miles, turn left on gravel Antelope Flats Road 15 miles, and then turn right for 20 additional miles to Anderson Crossing. From here the canyon extends 35 miles downstream to the main Owyhee River. Plan on a full week for the 45.5-mile trek to Three Forks.

BOATING

The 39 miles of Owyhee River between Three Forks and Rome provide

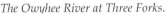

The Owyhee River at Three Forks.

one of the most challenging and scenic runs in the state. Boaters must register at the put-in or at the BLM office in Vale. Commercial boaters need special permits. The run can only be made from March to early June (kayaks sometimes run until mid-June), and only if water levels are neither too high nor too low. Possible cold weather and cold water in these months make hypothermia a danger. Wet suits or dry suits are advisable.

Just 1.5 miles below the deceptively calm waters of the Three Forks launch site, the rushing, narrow chutes of Ledge Rapids leave many a boater swimming through a rugged, quarter-mile-long rock garden. Scout this class 4+ whitewater carefully from the left side. There is no easy way out of this remote desert canyon for those who have lost their boat.

Nine miles beyond Ledge Rapids stop at a sharp right bend to scout Half-mile Rapids ahead. This class 4+ rapids begins with rocks jutting into the current on the right and continues with a full half mile of rough water. After only a 100-yard lull, boaters face Raft Flip Drop's big wave (class 3-4).

Subtle Hole (class 3+), at river mile 15 below Three Forks, is longer than Raft Flip Drop. Bomb Shelter Drop (class 3) follows immediately. Pull left in order to stop at the interesting cave below Bomb Shelter Drop. Three miles beyond, two rocks in mid stream mark the start of Shark Tooth Rapids (class 3).

Class 5+ Widowmaker Rapids, at river mile 21.5, must be portaged by all but daring experts in medium-length rafts. Part of this fall's treachery is that it's preceded by a half mile of class 3 rapids. Begin a difficult portage on the right before the river ahead disappears between huge boulders. This chute, sometimes briefly mistaken for the Widowmaker itself, is actually a class 3 drop that fills boats with water, making them unmanageable at the brink of Widowmaker's 10-foot waterfall immediately ahead.

Another, less frequented Owyhee River whitewater run begins near the town of Owyhee, Nevada, and follows the South Fork Owyhee to Three Forks.

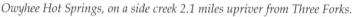

Owyhee Hot Springs, on a side creek 2.1 miles upriver from Three Forks.

UPPER OWYHEE RIVER

(See Area 65 Map)

Rome
Launch site 3300'

Burns 105 mi

Owyhee

Hwy 95 4 mi

Hwy 95 at Jordan Valley 14 mi

South Mtn 7850'

Indian Fort Cr

Widowmaker Rapids

Soldier Cr

Shark Tooth Rapids

Indian Fort Flat

Bomb Shelter Drop

Subtle Hole Rapids

Overlook 4700'

North Fork Crossing 4750'

Big Grassy Mtn 5445'

3800'

Raft Flip Drop

Halfmile Rapids

Cabin ruins

Hot Springs

N Fk Owyhee R

Squaw Cr

Ledge Rapids

Three Forks

5000'

Hot Springs

Middle

Twin Spring Gorge

5000'

Owyhee R

4000'

Owyhee River

Toppin Cr

Toppin Cr Butte 5360'

Oregon L

Oregon Hill

Spring Butte 5575'

Antelope

Cr

Fields Cr

Rawhide Spr

Pole Cr

Louse River

Canyon

Hwy 95 9 mi

Black Butte

Defeat Butte

E Fk

South Fork

Dry Canyon

Anderson Crossing

5300'

Massie Canyon

Horse Hill

Trail Cr

Jeffs Res

Owyhee

West Little

Lookout L

Idaho

Oregon

East Little Owyhee R

Hwy 95 at McDermitt 4 mi

Oregon Butte

Oregon

Nevada

UPPER OWYHEE RIVER

0 1 2 3 4 5 6mi
0 2 4 6 8 10km

N

OREGON'S TRAIL NETWORK

A network of existing and proposed long-distance trails links many of Oregon's wilderness areas. Four routes cross the entire state. Other routes follow rivers or serve as connectors between Oregon's population centers and the longer trail routes.

The Pacific Crest Trail, North Umpqua River Trail, and routes east of the Cascades are open to hikers and equestrians. Other long-distance trails west of the Cascade summit are for hikers only.

Old sign for the Pacific Crest Trail.

The Pacific Crest Trail (PCT)

The PCT follows the Sierra Nevada and Cascade Range on a 2638-mile route from Mexico to Canada. The PCT's last gap (in California) was completed in 1993. The 424-mile Oregon section was laid out in 1920 as the Oregon Skyline Trail, and was finished in 1987. The PCT was one of two trails authorized by Congress in the 1968 National Trail Systems Act. Today the well-marked route, built with a wide tread and gentle grade, has become so popular that sections near highway trailheads may be dusty by late summer. Snow closes much of this high-elevation trail from mid October to early July.

The Oregon Coast Trail (OCT)

This route utilizes the open sands of Oregon's publicly-owned beaches for much of its 360-mile route between Washington and California. Only about 70 miles of the route consist of actual trail, while 200 miles of the route follows public beaches, and about 90 miles still follows the shoulder of Highway 101 and other roads. Forested trail segments often lead hikers over headlands between beaches. Cedar posts and markers identify completed sections of this all-season route, notably the northernmost 64 miles from Fort Stevens (on the Columbia River) to Garibaldi (near Tillamook).

The Desert Trail (DT)

This route crosses Oregon's southeast corner, exploring high desert mountain ranges, rimrock canyons, and wide-open landscapes where sagebrush dominates. Rock cairns mark the trail's general route, allowing travelers to pick their own way through the open terrain. Eight maps, available for about $5 each at *www.thedeserttrail.org*, detail the completed 150-mile section between Denio on the Nevada border and Highway 20 east of Burns.

The Desert Trail Association, cooperating with the Bureau of Land Management, proposes continuing the trail as far as Mexico and Canada. The planned route south traverses Nevada to connect with an existing Southern Californian portion of the Desert Trail. The route north briefly joins the New Oregon Trail in the Blue Mountains, and then crosses Hells Canyon and Idaho to follow the Continental Divide National Scenic Trail to Canada.

The New Oregon Trail (NORT)

Only 57% complete, this route follows the crests of four mountain ranges on its 1300-mile route from Oregon's western-most point at Cape Blanco to the state's easternmost point in Hells Canyon. The NORT connects the trans-state Oregon Coast Trail and Desert Trail, and follows a portion of the Pacific Crest Trail. The route was first hiked end-to-end by William L. Sullivan in 1985.

Nearly all of the existing trail segments of the NORT are included in this book. Hikers can fill trailless gaps by following logging roads and highway shoulders, although the route is still un-marked.

The Chinook Trail

This partially completed route circles the Columbia Gorge, heading east from Vancouver through Washington, crossing the Columbia on Highway 97 at Maryhill east of The Dalles, and return-

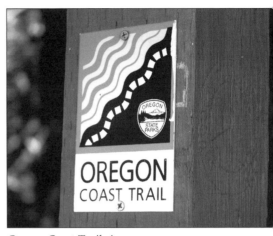

Oregon Coast Trail sign.

ing through Hood River to Portland. Only three sections are currently complete, through the Silver Star area north-east of Vancouver, across the Coyote Wall section north of Hood River, and along the Oregon side between Mosier and Bridal Veil. This latter portion includes the old Columbia River Highway and the Gorge Trail. Hikers can currently follow the Gorge Trail 25 miles from Starvation Creek (near Viento State Park) to Sheppards Dell State Park (near Bridal Veil Falls). Weather rarely closes this low-elevation route, even in winter.

The 40-Mile Loop

A 1910 study of Portland proposed linking Forest Park trails with a 40-mile route encircling Portland. Growth of the city has lengthened the mapped loop to 140 miles, but the trail's original name remains. Currently hikable throughout, the loop connects existing trails in more than 30 parks (notably the Wildwood Trail in Forest Park and the Marquam Trail at Council Crest) with a variety of sidewalk and roadside routes.

The Clackamas Trail

Eventually, this path would link the Portland area to the PCT near Mount Jefferson. The plan would utilize the abandoned Portland Traction Railroad

Old Forest Service map cover.

corridor from Gresham to Boring, as well as the existing 7.8-mile Clackamas River Trail, the 4-mile Riverside Trail, the 5-mile Rho Ridge Trail, and the 4.4-mile Red Lake Trail to the PCT at Olallie Lake.

The Corvallis To The Sea Trail

Although this 105-mile route can now be traveled, it primarily follows old logging roads. This makes it chiefly of interest to mountain bikers, but future developments are likely to increase its popularity among hikers and equestrians. The trail begins by following the Corvallis-Philomath bike path west, skirts just north of Marys Peak, and heads west to Ona Beach State Park 8 miles south of Newport. For an overview map and information, check *http://c2ctrail.googlepages.com/*.

The Eugene To PCT Trail

This 74-mile route is about 85 percent complete, and is currently hikable from Dexter at Elijah Bristow State Park to the PCT at Bobby Lake, near Waldo Lake. The completed portion follows forested ridges usually free of snow from June to November. Volunteer trail-building efforts proceed on the remaining valley-bottom route that would continue past Mount Pisgah to join the Eugene-Springfield riverside bike path.

The North Umpqua Trail

A full 79 miles of completed trail follow the wild North Umpqua River from its headwaters at Maidu Lake in the Mount Thielsen Wilderness. The completed section extends from the Pacific Crest Trail west past Steamboat down to Idleyld Park. Volunteers propose continuing construction downriver 23 miles to Roseburg.

The Rogue River Trail

One of Oregon's most popular rivers, the Rogue has three very scenic completed sections of long-distance trails. The popular Lower Rogue River Trail extends 40 miles from Grave Creek

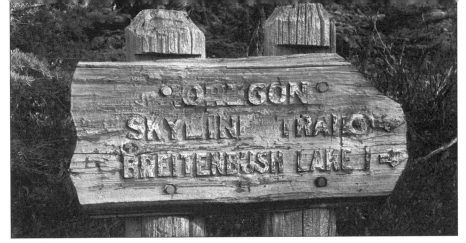

The Oregon Skyline Trail predated the Pacific Crest Trail along the Cascade Range.

to Illahe, traversing the rugged Wild Rogue Wilderness. The lesser known Upper Rogue River Trail descends 47.9 miles from the river's headwaters in the northwest corner of Crater Lake National Park down to the town of Prospect. The path then skips 4 miles of private land and continues another 18.3 miles downstream to Casey Park, just below Lost Creek Lake's dam. An ambitious proposal to extend this path 60 miles to join the Lower Rogue River Trail suggests a non-river route through Wolf Creek.

The Metolius-Windigo Trail

This completed, 45-mile path through Central Oregon's pine forests primarily attracts equestrian use and serves as a low-elevation alternative when the nearby, high-elevation PCT is blocked by snow.

The trail crosses Highway 20 at Indian Ford, 5 miles northwest of Sisters. To the north of Highway 20, the path skirts Black Butte and follows Green Ridge, overlooking the Metolius River. To the south, the trail continues as far as Three Creek Lake, near Broken Top. A Forest Service proposal would eventually extend the route south to join the Pacific Crest Trail in the Mount Thielsen Wilderness.

The Southern Oregon Intertie Trail

This route would link the Desert Trail with the PCT. This east-west route

would incorporate the Fremont Trail (147 miles currently complete, in two segments from Yamsay Mountain to the Lakeview area) and the Crane Mountain Trail (34 miles complete).

The Blue Mountain Heritage Trail

This proposed, 870-mile route would loop around Northeast Oregon, with a center of operations in Baker City. The trail is designed to offer a European-style bed-to-bed hiking/riding experience, with shuttles bringing hikers and riders back to bed and breakfast inns each night. Three initial segments of the loop are tentatively set to open in the spring of 2010, linking Baker City with Prairie City near the Strawberry Mountains, Halfway in the Wallowa Mountains, and the Anthony Lake Ski Area in the Elkhorn Range.

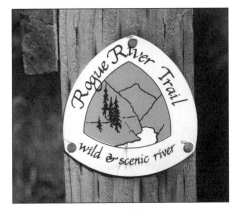

Trail sign on the Rogue River.

Managing Agencies

United States Forest Service (USFS)

Pacific Northwest Regional Office
333 SW First Ave.
Portland, OR 97204
(503) 808-2468
www.fs.fed.us/r6

Columbia Gorge National Scenic Area
902 Wasco Ave.
Hood River, OR 97301
(541) 308-1700
www.fs.fed.us/r6/columbia/

Deschutes National Forest
1001 SW Emkay Dr.
Bend, OR 97702
(541) 383-5300
www.fs.fed.us/r6/centraloregon/

Fremont-Winema National Forests
1301 South G St.
Lakeview, OR 97630
(541) 947-2151
www.fs.fed.us/r6/frewin/

Malheur National Forest
431 Patterson Bridge Rd.
John Day, OR 97845
(541) 575-3000
www.fs.fed.us/r6/malheur/

Mount Hood National Forest
16400 Champion Way
Sandy, OR 97055
(503) 668-1700
www.fs.fed.us/r6/mthood/

Ochoco National Forest
3160 NE 3rd St.
Prineville, OR 97754
(541) 416-6500
www.fs.fed.us/r6/centraloregon/

Rogue River-Siskiyou National Forest
P.O. Box 520
Medford, OR 97501
(541) 618-2200
www.fs.fed.us/r6/rogue-siskiyou/

Siuslaw National Forest
4077 SW Research Way
Corvallis, OR 97333
(541) 750-7000
www.fs.fed.us/r6/siuslaw/

Umatilla National Forest
2517 SW Hailey Ave.
Pendleton, OR 97801
(541) 278-3716
www.fs.fed.us/r6/uma/

Umpqua National Forest
2900 NW Stewart Parkway
Roseburg, OR 97471
(541) 672-6601
www.fs.fed.us/r6/umpqua/

Wallowa-Whitman National Forest
1550 Dewey St.
Baker, OR 97814
(541) 523-6391
www.fs.fed.us/r6/w-w/

Willamette National Forest
3106 Pierce Parkway, Ste. D
Springfield, OR 97477
(541) 225-6300
www.fs.fed.us/r6/willamette/

Bureau of Land Management (BLM)

Oregon State Office
333 SW First Ave.
Portland, OR 97204
(503) 808-6002
www.blm.gov/or

Burns District
28910 Highway 20 West
Hines, OR 97738
(541) 573-4400
www.blm.gov/or/districts/burns

Coos Bay District
1300 Airport Lane
North Bend, OR 97459
(541) 756-0100
www.blm.gov/or/districts/coosbay

Eugene District
2890 Chad Dr.
Eugene, OR 97401
(541) 683-6600
www.blm.gov/or/districts/eugene

Lakeview District
1301 South G St.
Lakeview, OR 97630
(541) 947-2177
www.blm.gov/or/districts/lakeview

Medford District
3040 Biddle Rd.
Medford, OR 97501
(541) 770-2200
www.blm.gov/or/districts/medford

Prineville District
3050 NE 3rd St.
Prineville, OR 97754
(541) 416-6700
www.blm.gov/or/districts/prineville

Salem District
1717 Fabry Rd.
Salem, OR 97306
(503) 399-5646
www.blm.gov/or/districts/salem

Vale District
100 Oregon St.
Vale, OR 97918
(541) 473-3144
www.blm.gov/or/districts/vale

Other Agencies

Confederated Tribes of the
Warm Springs Indian Reservation
1233 Veterans St.
Warm Springs, OR 97761
(541) 553-1161
www.warmsprings.com

Crater Lake National Park
P.O. Box 7
Crater Lake, OR 97604
(541) 594-3000
www.nps.gov/crla

Crooked River National Grassland
813 SW Highway 97
Madras, OR 97741
(541) 475-9272
www.fs.fed.us/r6/centraloregon/

Many government cabins and fire lookouts are available for rent at www.recreation.gov.

Hart Mountain Refuge / USFWS
P.O. Box 111
Lakeview, OR 97630
(541) 947-3315
www.fws.gov/sheldonhartmtn/

Hells Canyon National Recreation Area
88401 Highway 82
Enterprise, OR 97828
(541) 426-4256
www.fs.fed.us/hellscanyon

Nature Conservancy
821 SE 14th Ave.
Portland, OR 97214
(503) 802-8100
www.nature.org

Newberry Nat'l Volcanic Monument
(Fort Rock Ranger District)
1230 NE 3rd
Bend, OR 97701
(541) 383-5300
www.fs.fed.us/r6/centraloregon/newberrynvm

Oregon Caves National Monument
National Park Service
Cave Junction, OR 97523
(541) 592-2100
www.nps.gov/orca

Oregon Dept of Fish and Wildlife
3406 Cherry St.
Salem, OR 97303
(503) 947-6000
www.dfw.state.or.us

Oregon State Parks and Rec Division
725 Summer St. NE
Salem, OR 97301
(800) 551-6949
www.oregon.gov/OPRD/PARKS

INDEX

Featured areas are listed in **boldface**. Page numbers in *italics* refer to maps.

The Rogue River, in undesignated wilderness near Rainie Falls.

ALSO BY
WILLIAM L. SULLIVAN

Available in bookstores or at *www.oregonhiking.com.*

This travel guide features museums, hot springs, bed & breakfasts—and 65 best hikes.

This history of the state reads like a novel, but includes travel tips to visit historic sites.

Everything you need for a visit to Crater Lake National Park and Oregon Caves.

Learn the stories behind the floods, fires, earthquakes, and tsunamis that affect Oregon.

The Oregon "100 Hikes" Series

Continually updated, these five guidebooks cover virtually every trail in Oregon, with detailed information for hikers, backpackers, bicyclists, and equestrians. The series divides the state into five regions (*see map at left*). And yes, the author has hiked every featured trail.

These classic adventure memoirs tell of Sullivan's 1000-mile Oregon hike and the log cabin he built by hand.

Sullivan's novels are about an Einstein formula, a Viking ship, and an Oregon pioneer.